PETER ELKIND is an associate editor of *Texas Monthly*, which published his award-winning account of the Genene Jones case. For this book, he interviewed well over one hundred people—including Genene Jones herself—and reviewed thousands of pages of court and secret documents. He lives in Texas with his wife and son.

Peter Elkind

The True Story of Nurse Genene Jones and the Texas Baby Murders

The
Death
Shift

AN ONYX BOOK

ONYX
Published by the Penguin Group
Penguin Books USA Inc., 375 Hudson Street, New York,
New York 10014, U.S.A.
Penguin Books Ltd, 27 Wrights Lane, London W8 5TZ, England
Penguin Books Australia Ltd, Ringwood, Victoria, Australia
Penguin Books Canada Ltd, 2801 John Street, Markham,
Ontario, Canada L3R 1B4
Penguin Books (N.Z.) Ltd, 182-190 Wairau Road, Auckland 10, New Zealand

Penguin Books Ltd, Registered Offices: Harmondsworth, Middlesex, England

Previously published in a Viking Penguin hardcover edition

First Onyx Printing, May, 1990
10 9 8 7 6 5 4 3 2 1

Portions of this book first appeared, in somewhat different form, in *Texas Monthly*.

Grateful acknowledgment is made for permission to reprint the following works:

"Munchausen's Syndrome," by Richard Asher in *The Lancet*, February 10, 1951. By permission of the publisher.

"Munchausen Syndrome by Proxy—The Hinterland of Child Abuse" by S. R. Meadow in *The Lancet*, August 13, 1977. By permission of the publisher and the author.

"Munchausen Syndrome by Proxy" by S. R. Meadow in *Archives of Diseases in Childhood*, 1982, no. 60. By permission of the publisher and the author.

"Personal Practice: Management of Munchausen Syndrome by Proxy" by S. R. Meadow in *Archives of Diseases in Childhood*, 1985, no. 60. by permission of the publisher and the author.

"Psychotherapy for Munchausen Syndrome by Proxy" by A. R. Nichol and M. Eccles in *Archives of Diseases in Childhood*, 1985, no. 60. By permission of the publisher.

Photographs taken by Robert Latorre, copyright Robert Latorre.

For Kate

But whoso shall offend
one of these little ones
which believe in me,
it were better for him
that a millstone
were hanged about his neck,
and that he were drowned
in the depth of the sea.

MATTHEW 18:6

Contents

Preface

THERE ARE SOME people on earth who cannot bear to live an ordinary life. This quirk of personality, exceedingly rare among mankind's billions, leads certain individuals to great acts—as with the medical researcher who labors tirelessly to develop a cure for a dreaded disease. It drives others to unimaginable evil—as in the case of Genene Jones.

Genene Jones's demons—and the crimes they spurred her to commit—compose a dark and compelling tale. But this book is far more than an account of one woman's madness. Its story offers a window into the frailties of modern medicine—the petty jealousies and arrogance, the fears and ambitions, the bureaucratic paralysis—that can produce tragedy. This is a story about the criminal-justice system: of eager prosecutors, leaked secrets, and greedy lawyers. Most powerfully of all, it is an account of every parent's worst nightmare—of discovering that someone to whom he has entrusted his child has acted to harm rather than to heal.

I first wrote about these events in August 1983 for *Texas Monthly*. I am grateful to Nicholas Lemann, a gifted editor and writer, who entrusted me with that assignment—my first for a magazine—and has been a source of astute guidance ever since. I owe thanks to several others who are or have been associated with *Texas Monthly*, including Michael Levy and Gregory Curtis, who remained supportive of this project through my lengthy leave of absence from the magazine's staff; Paul Burka, who has taught me much about writing, reporting, and critical thinking; and Jan Jarboe, a candid and constant friend. Stephen Harrigan and Joseph Nocera have offered invaluable counsel, both personal and literary, over a period of years; their criticism of early drafts contributed immeasurably to this book.

I am grateful also to my skillful and patient editor at Viking Penguin, Mindy Werner, without whom this book would not exist, and to her assistant, Janine Steel. Maura Wogan has provided invaluable legal advice on this manuscript. My agents, Vicki Eisenberg and Ann Whitley, have been a steady source of ideas and support. To Adele Elkind, I offer thanks for thirty years of encouragement. But my greatest debt is to my wife, Kate, who has endured late nights, missed deadlines, and forgone vacations with grace and selflessness.

A few words about technique: Everything in this book, to the best of my knowledge, is true. It is based on reporting conducted over a period of five years, including more than a hundred interviews, as well as review of thousands of pages of confidential documents, transcripts, letters, and court records. All recounted conversations are based on the memory of at least one of the participants. While a few people requested anonymity, I have created no composite characters or fictional dialogue. Because this is a work of nonfiction, it is after much hesitation that I decided to alter the names of four characters in this story. I have used the pseudonymous first names of Edward and Crystal for Genene's two underage children, who deserve an unfettered opportunity to make more of their lives than has their mother. I have used the pseudonymous first name of Lisa for Genene's sister, who spoke frankly with me about her family, but understandably wishes to minimize her association with the events described in this book. Keith Martin is also a pseudonym, for reasons which will become obvious in the pages which follow.

I am grateful to the dozens of people who helped me compile this story. Many spoke candidly when it was particularly difficult—before Genene Jones went to trial. Special thanks to Pat Alberti, Art Brogley, John Carter, Cheryl Cipriani, Elton Cude, Chris Cuellar, Joe Davis, Vincent DiMaio, Jeff Duffield, Edwin Edwards, Karen Glenney, Gerald Goldstein, Alejandro Gonzales, Jim

Greenfield, Toni Grosshaupt, John Guest, Janet Jones,
John Mangos, Petti and Reid McClellan, Arthur McFee,
Sam Millsap, Marisol Montes, Michael Pearson, Cherlyn
Pendergraft, Jim Perdue, Ed Rademaekers, Debbie Rasch,
Annette Richardson, Nick Rothe, Jim Stinnett, Ron
Sutton, Joe Grady Tuck, and Diane Whitworth.

Any errors of interpretation within these pages are, of
course, my own.

Prologue

IT WAS JUST past noon when Petti McClellan headed for the cemetery to visit her little girl. Chelsea Ann would have been fifteen months and eleven days old that day. Petti kept track, as though there would be another birthday to celebrate, with adoring grandparents and funny hats and ice cream and, most of all, a big homemade cake, with three wax candles—one, of course, to grow on—planted firmly in a thick coat of sugary chocolate frosting. The truth was that Petti, even though she had journeyed to the cemetery daily during the week since the funeral, didn't really accept that Chelsea was gone. It had all been so sudden.

Slender and a bit frail, Petti McClellan was a girlishly pretty woman with dark hair and sad eyes. She and her husband, Reid, both twenty-seven, lived in a trailer home seventeen miles from the Garden of Memories Cemetery in Kerrville, where they had buried their only daughter. The air was dry and cool on this late-September day, despite the midday Texas sun. Situated near the geographic center of the state, Kerrville was renowned for its gentle climate. The sleepy retirement community stood in the heart of the Texas Hill Country—a dramatic highland of craggy peaks, blazing wildflowers, crisp skies, and sparkling streams. Carpeted with grass and shaded by trees, the Hill Country was a land of great beauty, a soothing relief from the parched prairie to the west, the treeless plains to the north and east, and the semitropical brush country that stretched south to the Rio Grande. But the Hill Country was also a place of hidden dangers—of thin soil and erratic rainfall, of flash floods and venomous snakes.

Petti parked her dusty Oldsmobile just inside the cemetery grounds and started on the short walk to her daughter's grave. During her first visit to this place, upon seeing the small sealed box containing the body, Petti had screamed, "You're killing my baby!" and crumpled to the ground. Family and friends had sent her to a psychiatrist to help her cope; he had placed Petti on powerful sedatives that kept her in a haze much of the day. Now it was images of Chelsea that fogged the young mother's mind: of blue eyes and tiny blond curls, and of her daughter's smile, cherubic and winsome, full of innocent delight and spoiled mischief. There was another image too: the look of terror in Chelsea's eyes when she suddenly was unable to breathe.

The sound of moaning in the distance swept away Petti's fog. Looking up, she noticed a heavyset woman kneeling at the foot of her daughter's grave. Petti McClellan knew the woman. It was Genene Jones, the nurse in the pediatrician's office where this nightmare had begun, where the world had spun out of control with the flash of a steel syringe. Genene was rocking back and forth before the mound of upturned earth that covered Chelsea. Tears streamed down her face. And she was wailing the dead child's name, over and over, in a chilling incantation: *Chelsea! Chelsea! Chelsea!*

After watching silently for several minutes, Petti crept closer and called to the nurse. *What was she doing there?* Genene struggled to her feet and stared—not at but through Petti, as though she weren't even there. Then the nurse walked off, without uttering a word. Frozen by the encounter, Petti noticed that Genene had left behind a bouquet of flowers. But she had taken something too: a bow from Chelsea's grave.

Until that moment, the McClellans had believed that Genene Jones and Kathy Holland, the doctor for whom Genene worked, had done everything they could to save their daughter's life. Now Petti began to think there was something strange about the nurse—something she didn't know or understand, something horrible and frightening.

She did not yet suspect that Chelsea had been murdered.

PART ONE

THE MAKING OF A NURSE

THE VOCATIONAL NURSE'S PLEDGE

In all sincerity and with my loyalty and fidelity, I pledge to uphold the honor of this vocation;

To assist the physician and the professional nurse in performing any service which will improve the welfare of humanity;

To safeguard any confidence entrusted in me, I will at all times apply the Golden Rule, toward friend and foe alike.

With God as my strength, it will be my privilege as well as my duty to serve the needs of my fellow man as a Vocational Nurse.

One

THOSE WHO OCCUPY the San Antonio estate where Genene
Jones grew up say that there are ghosts in the house. The
old eight-acre Jones homestead was long ago sold for
development as apartments. But the family's two-story
stucco mansion still stands, divided into efficiency apartments and a rental office, and vestiges of the past also
linger.

One spirit—he lives in the rental office—is said to be
that of a teenage boy who was killed in a terrible explo-
sion. The second apparition, who inhabits Apartment 2,
is said to be that of his father, the victim of a sad,
untimely end. No one in the house claims to have heard
voices or seen objects move through the air. But people
say they have discovered drawers open and piles of papers in places where they weren't. And according to the
apartment manager, the two rooms in question sometimes grow inexplicably cold—even in the fiery South
Texas summer.

Genene Ann Jones was similarly haunted by her past.
Growing up, she complained often that she was unwanted
and unloved. At the moment of her birth, in fact, she
was. Star-crossed from the start, Genene entered the
world on the thirteenth of July, 1950, in San Antonio,
Texas. Her parents promptly gave her up for adoption.
She became the daughter of Dick and Gladys Jones, one
of four adopted children in a family destined to suffer
more than its share of worldly misfortune.

They lived in the oldest city in a brash and youthful state. To the casual modern-day visitor, San Antonio appears the most tranquil and genteel of any Texas town, a subtropical paradise where native and tourist, Anglo and Hispanic, while away hours sipping margaritas and strolling along landscaped river walks. It seems a model of the peaceful social revolution that the Sunbelt boom has brought to America: The ninth-largest city in the nation, it was the first major city to have a Hispanic majority and the first to elect a Hispanic mayor. Civic fathers trumpet the community as a burgeoning high-tech oasis.

The picturesque image is a facade. Beneath the veneer of modern sophistication, San Antonio is one of America's poorest cities, dominated by a vast Mexican barrio, where tens of thousands live ill-clad, ill-housed, ill-fed, and ill-educated; where miles of streets lie unpaved; where infant mortality far exceeds the national average; and where more than half the people in entire neighborhoods cannot read or write in *any* language. San Antonio is a dependent city. Lacking substantial industry, it must rely economically on outsiders—on the federal payroll from a ring of military bases and on a critical trade in tourism; it is a symbol of the town's dependence that the tallest downtown building is a hotel. San Antonio is also a city that harbors a tradition of bloody deeds—of murders and lynchings and random acts of violence. The city's very history is defined by an epic massacre.

The first permanent settlement there dates back to 1718, when Spanish soldiers and missionaries established an outpost in the wilderness, two hundred miles north of Mexico, along the headwaters of a humble river. The centerpiece of their tiny colony, in what would one day become the city's downtown, was the Mission San Antonio de Valero—later known as the Alamo. Plagued by epidemics, internal squabbling, and bloody Indian raids, the settlement struggled to survive. The missions failed as religious institutions, and Spain converted them to secular military forts before the beginning of the nineteenth century. In 1821, revolution made Texas part of an independent Mexico. But the Anglos who were settling the territory felt revolutionary impulses of their own.

In quest of an independent Texas, an army of Texans and American frontiersmen captured San Antonio in December 1835. When Mexican troops arrived ten weeks later, the handful of rebels left to guard the city took refuge behind the thick stone walls of the Alamo, by then a roofless ruin. On February 23, Mexican general Santa Anna laid siege to the mission, defended by less than two hundred men, with an army of five thousand. Modern scholarship suggests that when the fortress was overrun, a handful of the famous martyrs, including Davy Crockett, actually surrendered and were executed. But by killing many times their number and holding off Santa Anna for thirteen days, the Alamo's defenders gave the rebels time to rally and inspired the quintessential Texas legend.

Through Texas's independence, statehood, and participation in the Confederacy, San Antonio grew slowly. The beginning of the great cattle drives during Reconstruction and the arrival of the railroad in 1877 attracted waves of immigrants, spawning a Wild West culture. A history of the city, written as part of a federal Work Projects Administration guide to Texas, described the late 1870s as the beginning of San Antonio's "lurid" period:

> Saloons—most of them with gaming tables—flourished. Behind their carved and polished bars flashily dressed bartenders mixed fiery drinks and dodged when bullets flew. Men whose herds ranged over ten million acres played recklessly for high stakes against cold-eyed professional gamblers and each other. Variety theaters combined the three ingredients, wine, women, and song, but the wine was hard liquor and the song was too frequently interrupted by the deadly explosion of a six-gun. A bank—now one of the city's wealthiest—originated when a merchant accommodated his customers by hiding their money in a barrel beneath his floor.

In 1898, Teddy Roosevelt filled the ranks of his Rough Riders in a San Antonio hotel bar.

Between 1870 and 1920, the population multiplied from 12,000 to 161,000. San Antonio reigned as not only the

largest city in Texas but also the most important. A base
of German-immigrant merchants made it a center of bank-
ing and commerce. An already teeming Mexican quarter
provided an abundance of cheap labor for agriculture and
manufacturing. The San Antonio River, winding through
downtown, attracted flour mills. The railroad spurred the
development of stockyards and slaughterhouses and cotton warehouses. San Antonio already had become a headquarters for the military. And a young tourism trade was
growing rapidly; the number of hotels had doubled in
five years. Cattlemen and wealthy retirees bought second
homes in the city.

Despite its new complexity and sophistication, San Antonio retained its frontier ways, catering to a catholic
assortment of tastes. In 1912, a local barkeeper hawked
a guide to San Antonio's "Sporting District," listing sa-
loons, pits for cockfights, and whorehouses; its index of
prostitutes included names, addresses, and phone numbers, and designated individual houses and women as
Class A, B, or C. Located in Bexar County, the city
justly acquired such nicknames as "The Free State of
Bexar" and "Unsainted Anthony."

Genene Jones's adoptive father was a child of "Unsainted
Anthony," and the woolly character of the city flowed
through him like blood. Born in 1911, Richard Jefferson
Jones was the consummate wheeler-dealer. At various
times during his lifetime, he owned a chain of hamburger
stands, a trailer court, a gourmet restaurant, nightclubs,
a parking garage, a billboard advertising business, a laun-
dromat, and a construction company. He came to his
willingness to roll the dice early, during a career as a
professional gambler.

Jones grew up in south San Antonio, an only child in a
working-class neighborhood where kids earned their spending money throwing newspapers. His father's premature
death had left his mother strapped. Carrie Jones lived
with her own mother and son in a tiny apartment; little
Dick slept on a bed that extended under the kitchen sink.
A clerk in a downtown ladies' clothing store, Carrie
could not even spare the change for her boy to purchase
a spot for his photo in the Brackenridge High School
yearbook.

Determined to improve his lot, Dick went into business after graduating from high school, in 1929. That year, of course, was no time to build a fortune, either on Wall Street or in San Antonio. In the decade to come, the flow of new residents into the city would slow to a trickle, allowing Houston and Dallas to surge ahead in population. A construction boom ended too; for a generation, not a single new building would join the downtown skyline. Although the federal payroll cushioned the city from devastation, the Depression initiated a decade of municipal torpor.

But Dick Jones had found an industry that knew no bad times. He operated a trio of local clubs, small bookie joints where he took bets on horses, professional baseball games, and anything else that would invite a wager. Each club worked a local market: the Express Recreation Club, in the basement of a downtown building, catered to doctors and newspapermen; the Broadway Tavern had a clientele of golfers from a nearby park; the Aviation Jockey Club, close to a military base, accommodated servicemen.

In the dreary days of the Depression, the colorful men who ran gambling houses, far from being shunned as rogues, commanded public affection. One of Jones's peers, a cigar-chewing plug named V. E. "Red" Berry, eventually won election to the state legislature, where he promptly proposed the legalization of horse racing. When conventional efforts failed in the face of opposition from Baptist northern Texas, Berry introduced a bill to split the state in two. He reasoned that if the Texas legislature wouldn't approve horse racing, the *South* Texas legislature surely would.

Dick Jones was similarly larger than life. He was a strong, hearty man—six feet tall, prematurely bald, and well over two hundred pounds—with a passion for Cadillacs and T-bone steaks. In high school, Jones had played guard on the varsity football team. When an armed robber tried to stick up one of his clubs one night, Jones lunged for the intruder as though he were a quarterback and took three slugs in the chest. Things looked bleak for a while—a priest pronounced last rites at the hospital—but Dick Jones was not the sort to succumb to anything easily. Those who knew Jones during his gambling days regarded him as equal parts honest and tough. "If there is such a thing as a clean gambler, he was one of them," said one man, a retired general in the Texas National Guard. "If you won, he'd pay you. If you lost, let me tell you, you better have your money."

In December 1933, Jones married Gladys Leola Fowler, a twenty-two-year-old native of Ohio who had moved to Texas five years earlier. In meeting Gladys at a downtown San Antonio club, Dick had discovered a partner who shared his motivation to build a better life. A tiny, bespectacled woman with a steel spine, Gladys had worked since she was a teenager, when her father's death had forced her to quit school and take a job. Although the clubs were producing a handsome living, Gladys made her new husband promise to quit gambling. She was shaken by the shooting and wanted a wholesome environment for a family; though unable to conceive their own offspring, the couple had plans to adopt. In 1937, Jones gave up the clubs and entered a business in which a man could gamble legally—oil. After drilling a dry hole, he recognized that the entertainment trade suited him best. Two years later, he opened a new club, this one large, flashy, and—almost entirely—legitimate.

Jones's place was on the edge of the city limits, on Fredricksburg Road, a major thoroughfare leading northwest out of town toward Amarillo. He christened it the Kit Kat Klub and emblazoned the name where no one could miss it, in neon letters outside the building. The Kit Kat was a bulky carnival of a place, a two-story Art Deco structure that looked like a cruise ship run aground. Jones had embellished the property with $30,000 in improvements, a staggering sum for that day. Outside, beneath giant palm trees, were a lighted terrazzo patio and a stand where Jones sold barbecue. A roomy dance floor dominated the inside. Mirrors lined the walls, and live bands performed from orchestra platforms. Dick managed the place, while Gladys kept the books and spun records on the turntable when live entertainment wasn't available. A highlight came on weekend nights, when the proprietor cut the music for hobby-horse races. Competing for a prize bottle of champagne, men and women took turns bumping ridiculously across the room.

The shadow of World War II paradoxically lifted San Antonio's doldrums. Servicemen flooded the city for training; thousands would marry there and return after the war. A WPA grant had recently beautified the downtown river with landscaped walkways and bridges. The area around the Alamo had been purchased for preservation as a park. San Antonio seemed to renew its legendary zest for public celebration. Crowds flocked there every April, when the entire city shut down for a week of parades and street fairs known as Fiesta. In this newly buoyant town, the Kit Kat became one of the hot spots, a position it would maintain for an astonishing twenty years. Walking the narrow line between dull and scandalous, Jones served up good food as well as a sassy atmosphere. He brought the first performing belly dancer to town. He hired dancing roller-skaters and magic acts and snagged big-name national bands. Celebrities—such as Bob Hope and Rosalind Russell—visited the Kit Kat when they were in San Antonio.

The owner's personality was a critical component of the formula, for Dick Jones was an inspired self-promoter. One year, he invested in prefabricated housing. To overcome customers' fear that a stiff breeze would blow the buildings apart, Jones rented a crane and deposited a truck on the roof of his model home. Jones ran his construction company by day, dressed in an open shirt, dungarees, and work boots. By night, he donned a black three-piece suit, headed down to the club, and became the dapper host, remembering names, buying drinks, telling jokes.

Jones's surviving customers say the Kit Kat Klub operated within the law, save for a few slot machines and penny-ante gambling games. These he confined to the Zebra Lounge, a private club Jones operated in one room of the Kit Kat. Ever mindful of thematic detail, Jones painted the walls with zebra stripes and covered the bar with animal skins. The members-only club designation allowed him to serve liquor by the drink. Because of strict Texas liquor laws, he could offer only setups in the main portion of the building. The private club also let

Jones isolate the less public aspect of his business. From time to time, the Bexar County sheriff conducted gambling raids. Jones avoided such unpleasantness through tips from a friendly deputy, who notified him when it was time to lock up the club's slot machines.

Though he dodged the legal entanglements of his gambling, Dick Jones would never shed its taint. In 1952, San Antonio police chief R. D. Allen publicly identified him as one of three "well-known gamblers" operating "large-stake games" in Bexar County. The chief said Jones was operating, not at the Kit Kat, but at his home. Jones was livid. Accompanied by his attorney, he marched into the city manager's office and demanded a retraction. "I'm not in the gambling business and I don't intend to get into it," he told the local papers. "I'm not ashamed for having done it, but I haven't gambled or associated with gambling for 15 years. I don't even know how to play cards." Three days later, unable to prove his claim, the police chief was forced to offer Jones an embarrassing public apology. GAMING CHARGE 'NO DICE'; ALLEN EATS CROW, read the front-page newspaper headline. Nonetheless, the Federal Bureau of Investigation pegged him too. In a postwar crime survey, the San Antonio FBI office included Jones and his club on its list of "notorious types and places of amusement."

However long the gambling continued, it became less frequent as his family grew. Dick and Gladys adopted their four children from four different families. Lisa arrived in 1943, Wiley in 1946, Genene in 1950, and Travis in 1952. They lived on Fredricksburg Road a mile north of the Kit Kat, outside the city limits in a home that was as dramatic as the family patriarch.

It was not so much the size of the residence that was memorable—although with four bedrooms, a large reception area, living room, formal dining room, family room, library, and tiled front terrace, it was gracious enough—as the setting. Two stories tall, built of white stucco and crowned with a roof of red clay tile, the house stood perched high atop a hill like a gaudy Mexican castle. It was set on eight landscaped acres, featuring a swimming pool, a private tennis court, and stalls for a pair of horses. Visitors reached the house on a formal drive marked by pillars that were decorated with the letter *J*. A wooden fence encircled the property. The Jones estate offered a stunning view of downtown, ten miles away, and a sight to those who drove past. Long after Dick Jones professed to have mended his ways, San Antonians would point and remark, "That's where the *gambler* lives."

While they were married and living alone, Dick and Gladys had enjoyed an extravagant lifestyle. They took a year off to travel around the world. They acquired pilot's licenses and went joy-riding in small airplanes. During the war, Gladys was among the few women in San Antonio who had a pair of nylon hose. But when their children arrived, they settled down—albeit in a fashion that matched their quarters. Gladys dressed the house in antiques and silver and herself in fine clothes and furs. The children all took lessons on the grand piano that dominated the living room. Dick bought the family Cadillacs with cash.

Jones shared his largesse with others. He bestowed lavish gifts on employees and was quick to pick up the tab for a tableful of friends. Friends tell many stories about Jones opening his wallet to help out a casual acquaintance in need. "He was a patsy for anyone who was down and out," said Harold Nelson, Jones's lawyer since the 1950s. Five times, the Kit Kat hosted his high school class reunion—steak dinner and drinks included—and Dick Jones footed the bill.

Despite his wealth and free-spending ways, which included generous contributions to local charities, Dick Jones remained anathema to respectable San Antonio. The least pretentious city in Texas, San Antonio was paradoxically the most exclusive. In Houston and Dallas, even the hoariest private clubs opened their doors to newcomers of sufficient wealth and power. In San Antonio, bloodlines were paramount. Powerful moneyed arrivals could go to their graves awaiting an invitation to join the San Antonio Country Club, where debutantes were introduced. Within such circles, a former gambler and his brood might as well have been lepers.

But Dick and Gladys Jones weren't interested in high society, with its stuffy pretensions and immaculate fingernails. Their home was located in what was then regarded as country, and in striking contrast to their life at the Kit Kat, they behaved in many ways like rural folk. Dick rose by 5 A.M. to plan his day, and napped for two hours in midafternoon. Gladys, stubborn and salty, rolled her own cigarettes. Like many a rural couple, they shared work as well as home, breeding the sort of mutual reliance that results from decades of daily partnership.

Their faith in the power and obligation of family was stout. However busy things were at the club, Dick headed home to preside over formal supper every night. He sat ceremoniously at the head of the table, and the entire family chanted grace. Dick employed his widowed mother at the Kit Kat—Gladys's mother lived with them—and dreamed that his eldest son, Wiley, would someday join him in business. Thanksgiving and Christmas were blockbuster family occasions, sweetened with homemade cakes and candies. Gladys spent days before each Halloween sewing extravagant costumes for the children. Every summer, Dick hooked up a trailer to the Cadillac and took everyone on long trips across the United States and into Mexico and Canada. Jones usually drove, stopping frequently at roadside parks for a hunk of watermelon, his favorite snack. Gladys served as navigator and family historian, filling albums with snapshots and little typed cards describing each destination. Everything was interesting; she kept photos with captions reading "Unusual Building," "Skyline," and "Demolished House." Born a Baptist, Gladys converted to Catholicism while her children were young, began serving fish for Friday dinner, and escorted them to St. Gregory's Church for Sunday services. They all attended Catholic schools, where nuns taught catechism classes every morning. Dick resisted formal religion, but the erstwhile gambler often went fishing with the priests.

The irony of such private moments was lost to all but the closest of family friends, for Dick Jones cultivated his public image as a carefree high roller. By the late 1950s, however, he was hard-pressed to maintain it. Nightclubs are creatures of changing taste, and after two decades, fashion had left the Kit Kat behind. Jones had squeezed a few extra years out of the place by retooling to attract a family-oriented clientele. He built a swimming pool out by the patio and started renting out the Kit Kat for fashion shows and high school proms. But that only postponed the inevitable. The place began losing money; he fell behind on tax payments for the property. To keep afloat, Jones sold off some of his land holdings and converted part of his homestead into a trailer park. Then he tried another scheme: converting the trailer park's large recreation room into a fancy restaurant. Jones tore the sprinkler system pipes out of his own lawn to use for the superstructure of a giant sign advertising the place. But the restaurant flopped too. For the first time since his childhood, Jones was under financial pressure. This was the prelude for another embarrassing episode. Much like the gambling flap with the San Antonio police chief, it would lead friends to say Dick Jones was misunderstood, and others to label him a rogue who belonged in jail.

In August 1960, a retired Sears department store executive named Charles Bramble returned late from a Saturday-night party at the Kit Kat to discover a three-hundred-pound safe missing from his home. The safe, which Bramble and his wife had kept in a bedroom closet, contained $1,500 in cash and jewels. The intruder had also ransacked several bedroom drawers and stolen three pistols. The crime became more curious when a neighbor told police detectives he had seen a man in a business suit pushing a large object down the Brambles' driveway to a late-model Cadillac. The next day, the Reverend Michael Holden, priest at St. Gregory's Church, notified police he had the Brambles' safe in his rectory. Nothing was missing, but the priest, citing his holy vows, refused to reveal who had left it. Eight days later, Dick Jones was arrested for theft and burglary.

When police told Jones they had traced paint scrapings from the safe to his Cadillac, he admitted the crime. After welcoming the Brambles to the party at his club, Jones explained, he had slipped off, entered the Bramble home through a window, hauled the safe to his car, and dropped it off at his home, then returned to the party. But the whole episode, he claimed, was nothing more than a practical joke. Jones said he was puncturing boasts by Bramble, an old friend, that no one could steal his safe. When Bramble reported the theft to police, rather than confiding in him first, Jones said, he panicked; he decided to return the safe through his priest, expecting that to be the end of things. Bramble readily accepted Jones's explanation, and police dropped the charges, but the incident filled newspaper columns for days.

The safe incident opened a decade-long run of snake eyes. In 1963, Jones sold the Kit Kat. He moved his banquet trade to the site of the failed restaurant, rechristened the Oak Hills Party House. And he began devoting his energies to a new business, Dick Jones Outdoor Advertising, which rented out giant billboards and placed ads on bus benches. Jones ran the enterprise from a shop behind the house and instructed Wiley in its ways. But it was his youngest boy, Travis, who developed a fatal attraction to the workshop.

The four children of Dick and Gladys Jones had shared childhood in pairs: Lisa with Wiley, three years her junior, Genene with Travis, two years younger. Travis had a learning disability but loved to tinker in his father's sign shop. One afternoon in November 1966, Ralph Haynes, a longtime family employee, noticed the boy, then fourteen, working there on a homemade pipe bomb. "Stop fooling with that thing before you set the place on fire," Haynes scolded. A moment later, the bomb blew up in Travis's face, shooting metal shards into his skull. Police rushed Travis to nearby Methodist Hospital in the bed of a pickup truck; he died just before midnight.

Dick Jones had been asleep in the house when the bomb exploded, and he rushed out to see his adopted son dying before his eyes. But the family member who took it hardest was sixteen-year-old Genene. The family had ordered flowers for the funeral, but Genene purchased a bouquet of her own—red gladioli and yellow carnations. When Travis's body was laid in the ground, she shrieked and collapsed. It was the first time Genene Jones crossed paths with death; it would be far from the last.

Classmates who had witnessed her reaction thought it odd to discover Genene back in school later that day. Rather than nursing her grief in private, she had returned just hours after the morning service to milk the sympathy of her peers.

In some respects, Genene was the Jones family's most promising child. Intelligent and assertive, she easily dominated conversations. She loved to tell stories. And she had the gift of magic hands: She could crochet and sew and bake, and she was captivating on the piano, with anything from classical music to ragtime.

But Genene's life was never tranquil, even in childhood, even at home. Travis's sudden death had robbed Genene of her closest friend. A natural ally was her sister, Lisa, but the two girls had always been separated by more than just seven years. Where Lisa was low-key and demure, Genene was intense and excitable. Their mother remarked that Genene was the sort of child who would burst into tears if you looked at her wrong. Genene complained often that her parents favored Lisa at her expense. She was particularly bitter one Christmas, when they bought Lisa a pair of diamond earrings and Genene a new sewing machine. The fact that her gift was more expensive did nothing to quell Genene's complaints. The slightest parental rejoinder set off her sense of being maligned. "Oh, yes, I know," she would gripe. "I'm the black sheep of the family."

By the time the younger girl entered high school, the proximate source of her resentment was gone; Lisa had married, begun having her own children, and moved out of the house. Genene's mother then became her adversary; the two strong-willed females battled often, with increasing intensity as Genene plunged into adolescence. After a fight, Genene would storm up to her room, plastered with pictures of the Beatles. Brother Wiley lived at home also, but he was quiet, attended a different high school, and traveled in a crowd of his own. Among the members of her family, Genene took solace from her father alone. She loved to spend afternoons with him, helping paint and put up billboards. He listened to her gripes and taught her to play pool. Genene would eventually embrace the most dramatic of her father's traits: the refusal to mince words, the affection for the spotlight, the gambler's comfort with risk. It was as though she acquired by *will* the paternal traits she could not possess by blood.

After attending Catholic elementary schools, Genene in 1965 had enrolled in John Marshall High. Marshall was a country school, fifteen miles from downtown and part of a suburban public school district. While some students came from the outer ring of San Antonio suburbs, many arrived from small farms and ranches well beyond the city. The faculty taught courses in agriculture, and the school had its own livestock. Among its extracurricular activities were a Pig Club, a Cattle Club, and a rodeo. Students at other schools joked that Marshall had a hitching post instead of a parking lot.

At this cowboy high school, Genene Jones was not popular. Part of the problem was her appearance: Genene was painfully plain. Her soft, doughy face was dominated by hard features—a large, bent nose and intense hazel eyes that flashed her emotions. Her mousy brown hair was blown into an inflated bouffant. And at five feet four, she was thirty pounds overweight and graceless. Genene didn't walk down a hallway; she *rushed*. Everything was frantic. "A lot of the guys would make fun of her, say she plays on the football team," recalled a classmate.

Genene's personality was even less graceful; she was often bossy and obnoxious. During study hall, she checked out books in the high school library. When others weren't working the way she thought they should, Genene told them what to do. When they refused to follow her directions, she glared at them angrily. "She thought at one point she ran the library," said Marjorie Johnson, then the head librarian. Genene was different from most of the other kids—more serious and less tolerant of teenage games. She worked an assortment of odd jobs after school, even scrubbing restaurant floors for spending money. She often showed up at Marshall smelling greasy, looking exhausted and unkempt. Sometimes she fell asleep in the library.

Members of the school staff regarded her as a minor troublemaker; when someone spiked the punch at the school Christmas party, Genene was a natural suspect. But she also elicited pity. When Genene found a sympathetic ear, she blamed circumstances for her lot: Other kids had ostracized her because of her father's reputation as a gambler; her parents favored her sister. "She was carrying a load of grudge because her life wasn't very good," said Marjorie Johnson. " She was not a very attractive girl, and that bothered her. The boys weren't asking her for dates. She wasn't getting any attention. She was desperate to be important."

It was in quest of attention that Genene first displayed a genius for the art of lying. Some of her tales were innocent adolescent fibs. She informed her best friend, Linda Rosenbush, that she was a distant cousin of Mickey Dolenz—a member of the pop music group the Monkees— and that he often phoned her to chat. Other fabrications were downright ugly. She told classmates that her parents— who had four children by choice—never loved her enough to adopt her legally. Genene always served up her stories with conviction; it took her friends a while to learn that their classmate and the truth were not always in accord. "Genene lied all the time—about anything, everything," said Linda Rosenbush. "To her, lying was just like talking."

The youth of America were soon to stage a challenge to the nation's dearest values, but the class of 1968 at John Marshall stood on the outer cusp of the rebellion. The only cause that inspired protest was the high school's strict dress code: Sideburns had to be short, shirttails had to be in, girls were not allowed to jiggle, and boys had to wear belts. The typical Marshall student dissipated his energies much as his parents had—driving, drinking, and dating.

The kids cruised a strip in northeast San Antonio called Austin Highway, where they could stop at a drive-in barbecue joint, the Bun 'N' Barrel, for a sandwich, soda, and fries. Three dollars bought an evening's entertainment; two dollars went for the gas. The rite-of-passage Saturday-night beer bust often took place in someone's vacant field. Fifteen or twenty kids would pull their pickups into a circle, crank up the radios, build themselves a bonfire, and dive into a stack of six-packs. Genene relished such events, for they provided her with an audience. Her father let her drive his blue El Camino, and Genene loved to shock the boys by daring them to drag-race. She drove fast and often won when they took up her challenge.

To teachers at Marshall, Genene Jones was an enigma. Clearly bright, she was uninspired in the classroom. She muddled through most of her courses, with a rare failure in bookkeeping. One of her top grades, a 90, came in home management—home nursing. She dabbled in extracurricular activities, such as Future Teachers of America, but seemed to have no clear ambition. She told her close friends that she just wanted a bunch of children.

As Genene began her senior year, her father was feeling poorly. In truth, Dick Jones had not been the same since Travis's death. He had lost his appetite for work, and the family had stopped taking vacations. In October 1967, he entered Scott and White Hospital in Temple for tests. Doctors informed Jones he was suffering from terminal cancer. After briefly weighing his options, he refused all medical therapy and went home. With his fate clearly in sight, Dick Jones summoned a priest and was finally baptized a Catholic.

By late November, he could no longer climb down the stairs from his bedroom. Relatives had to carry him down on a chair for a bittersweet Christmas with the family. The powerful man who had survived three bullets to the chest was withering away. Soon he could barely speak. Then he was unable to swallow food or liquid; Gladys dampened her husband's palate by placing wet rags in his mouth. She was there at the end, at 1:30 A.M. on January 3, 1968. Dick Jones was fifty-six.

The gambler's house had its second ghost.

Two

WHEN HER FATHER died, Genene Jones told a visitor many years later, "the world went dark." Yet it was only days after he was buried that Genene, then seventeen, began to talk about getting married. She was in love with a high school dropout named Jimmy DeLany, and she wanted to tie the knot on Valentine's Day—six weeks after her father's death.

Gladys Jones was horrified. The tortured deaths of her son and husband had already turned her life upside down. After thirty-four years as the supportive partner, she was suddenly in charge. Gladys delegated the daily operations of Dick Jones Outdoor Advertising to Wiley, twenty-two, who didn't really want the task. But she could not delegate Genene. Her daughter seemed oblivious of the toll the twin tragedies had taken. It was no time for a wedding.

Hoping to scotch the idea altogether, Gladys told Genene she wanted her at least to finish high school before getting married. Genene recognized that she had no choice; at her age, she required her mother's written blessing to wed. But Genene insisted on going through with the wedding later—as soon after graduation as possible. Gladys Jones had spent her entire lifetime around liquor. Caught in a vise of responsibility and grief, she began drinking heavily. Alcohol and Genene's badgering sparked mother-daughter quarrels of fresh bitterness and intensity. Genene told friends that her mother had accused her of stealing money. She declared that Gladys had never truly loved her. With her father no longer alive, marriage seemed a happy refuge.

Genene's choice for a mate was as misguided as her timing. At the tender age of nineteen, James Harvey DeLany, Jr., had all the makings of a loser. Born in San Antonio, DeLany had met Genene two years earlier at Marshall High School; he became her first serious boyfriend. DeLany's mother had died when he was young. He was raised by his father, who owned an icehouse—Texas parlance for a convenience store—where the principal commodity was cold beer.

The kinship between Genene Jones and Jimmy DeLany was built on motor oil and alienation. Homely and overweight, Jimmy had dropped out of school midway through his senior year. He traveled with a rowdy, boozing crowd. His sole passion was cars. He worked sporadically at gas stations, spent his free time tinkering with engines, and, like Genene, loved to hot-rod about town. He raced a souped-up '56 Chevy.

In the month of June 1968, presidential candidate Robert Kennedy was assassinated and James Earl Ray, the murderer of Martin Luther King, was apprehended at London's Heathrow Airport. San Antonio was abuzz with the news that Princess Grace would visit Hemisfair '68, the city's world's fair. A CBS television documentary, titled *Hunger in America,* juxtaposed scenes of bacchanalia at Hemisfair with pictures of malnourished children in San Antonio's West Side barrio. And the new Bexar County Hospital was near completion.

June represented a watershed for Genene Jones as well. Its first day marked her graduation from John Marshall High School. After finishing with an academic average of 78.61—197th in a class of 274—Genene marched into the evening ceremony to the strains of "Pomp and Circumstance." Fourteen days later, on June 15, she was married.

The wedding of Genene Jones and Jimmy DeLany took place with all the cheer and festivity that the mother of the bride could muster. In the weeks preceding, friends and relatives had feted Genene with parties and bridal showers. Lisa was the matron of honor, and Linda

Rosenbush one of the bridesmaids. The ceremony took place on a sunny Saturday, at St. Gregory's Catholic Church. Presiding was Monsignor Michael Holden, the priest who, eight years earlier, had harbored the Brambles' stolen safe. The wedding reception, held at the Oak Hills Party House on the family property, was just as Dick Jones would have had it—lavish and loud. There was champagne everywhere, and more than a hundred guests danced to an eight-piece band. But a cloud shadowed the celebration: Gladys had made it known that she considered the groom a disaster.

After honeymooning in Corpus Christi, on the Gulf Coast of Texas, the newlyweds moved into a guest cottage on the Jones estate. Despite Genene's battles with her mother, the offer of free rent was too attractive to resist. Gladys, who had bankrolled both the wedding and the honeymoon trip, gamely tried to help her new son-in-law find a clean job. Jimmy preferred to work as a mechanic. But it soon became evident that his affection for the automobile outstripped both his diligence and his ability. "Jimmy was not responsible," said Steve Seubert, an usher at the wedding. "He worked just enough to get some cash so he could ride around and drink and work on his cars." As a mechanic, he had a reputation for clumsiness. "We had a joke," recalled Seubert. "You could probably give Jimmy an anvil and he'd break it."

Genene Jones DeLany began married life as a housewife, and for a few months all went well. The DeLanys socialized with other couples from high school; they spent nights out eating barbecue, drinking beer, and playing cards—occasionally strip poker. But Jimmy's sporadic work habits soon prompted fights about money. Auto parts seemed to gobble up whatever cash he made, yet DeLany got angry when he learned that Genene was sneaking out to race his cars. Friends listened uncomfortably as the couple squabbled in their presence. Genene belittled her husband publicly, sending him into tantrums. Fearing the Vietnam War draft—and also hoping to better his life—DeLany enlisted in the navy seven months after getting married. He returned home from boot camp in San Diego to discover what others had known: His wife was fooling around.

After her husband's departure, Genene had occupied herself much as she had in high school: cruising and hanging out, usually with old friends from Marshall. While more motivated graduates attended college or found jobs, Genene spent her time at burger joints and drive-ins. It did not take her long to become bored. Genene soon told her closest female friends that she was sharing her marriage bed with other men. The revelations of the sailor's wife were not those of tortured anguish; Genene was boasting of her conquests, in the language of a men's locker room. No one knew precisely how much of Genene's talk was fiction, but at least some of it reflected fact. Friends who recalled specific liaisons said Genene was aggressive in her pursuit of men. The extramarital couplings—and her blunt talk about them afterward— seemed to bolster her self-esteem.

Genene's misguided search for affection knew no bounds of loyalty. One of her partners was Bill Myers, a married man who was buddies with Jimmy; his wife, Collene, was Genene's friend. Bill had known Jimmy since high school, and the two possessed the bond of shared misdeeds. On one occasion, they told their wives they were going hunting; they headed instead for the border town of Laredo and spent the weekend in Mexican cathouses. Myers, visiting the cottage on the Jones property one day, found himself in bed with Genene. According to Myers, she told him she was a nymphomaniac. He later described his involvement as though it were a charitable act. "She was reaching out," Myers said. "She wanted someone to know her and like her and love her."

The benevolence ended suddenly when Collene pulled up outside. In a search for her missing husband, she innocently walked through the door. With only a moment's warning, Genene threw on a bathrobe and raced out of the bedroom to greet Collene. She explained her heavy sweat by telling her friend she was sick with cramps. And no, Genene said through manufactured tears of pain, she hadn't seen Bill. Myers was hiding in the closet.

It was far from the only lie that Genene told her naive friend. She vividly recalled being stabbed during an altercation at her father's club; she even showed Collene a scar. On another occasion, Genene confided that she had been sexually traumatized by a childhood experience; she claimed to have been raped at the age of sixteen. Collene remained unaware of the lies for years. But she had other cause to feel uneasy around Genene. Collene had allowed her friend to baby-sit for her infant daughter. One day, after Collene picked up the baby, her mother discovered a photograph in the child's diaper bag. It was a snapshot of Genene in the nude.

Perhaps out of deference to his own sins, Jimmy overlooked his wife's infidelities and returned to duty with the navy. Genene remained behind, though no longer with her mother. In accordance with a plan he had devised to ensure his family's financial security, Dick Jones before his death had purchased a tract of land on Rochelle Road, in a remote neighborhood in far northwest Bexar County. Intent on privacy in her golden years, Gladys built herself a shrine to seclusion on the site: a home with no exterior windows. Set far back from the street, it was composed of one wall and three extra-large trailers forming the sides of a square. A roof covered the entire structure, creating a giant interior room as big as a dance floor. Brightened only with artificial light, the place gave visitors the sensation of stepping into a nightclub. In May 1969, after moving into the new house, Gladys sold the eight-acre Jones homestead on Fredricksburg Road, raising enough money to pay off her bills and live out her days. Wiley Jones, married now and still running the sign business, moved a trailer home onto an adjacent tract on Rochelle Road. Displaced from the family cottage, Genene took an apartment of her own.

But it did not signal independence. Genene visited her mother frequently, often to ask for money; there always seemed to be an emergency for which she desperately needed cash. Gladys implored her daughter to find a career; she was eager to see Genene self-reliant. In 1970, with her mother footing the bill, Genene enrolled in Mim's Classic Beauty College, to train as a beautician. By the time she finished, Jimmy was stationed at the U. S. Naval Air Station in Albany, Georgia. Genene left San Antonio for the first time, to join him there. DeLany's inability to hold a job carried over into uniform. He found himself in disciplinary trouble, and on September

29, 1971, after less than three years on his four-year hitch were up, the navy discharged him. Genene was happy at her husband's freedom, whatever the circumstances. She was five months pregnant.

Genene had longed for a baby even in high school. When Jimmy's seed did not find quick purchase, the DeLanys impatiently had visited a doctor, who assured them that everything was in working order. On January 29, 1972, in Albany, Genene gave birth to a son. In tribute to her dead father, she and her husband named the child Richard Edward DeLany.

The new arrival did nothing to calm the couple's tempestuous relationship. Both held jobs in Georgia, Jimmy as a mechanic and Genene as a beautician. But child care and automobiles left them perpetually short of money. While struggling to pay the utility bills, the DeLanys went into debt to buy a spanking-new Chevy Nova. Jimmy made matters worse by tearing the car apart to make "improvements"; instead of going faster, the Chevy spent weeks up on blocks. The couple's fascination with speed led them into trouble at every turn. During the spring after Edward's birth, Genene and Jimmy had joined friends for a Sunday afternoon of water skiing behind a two-hundred-horsepower racing boat. The DeLanys were passengers as the boat sped down Kinchafoonee Creek, near Albany. Approaching a bend, their craft knifed into a smaller boat going the other way. The second vessel sank, and a fifteen-year-old boy aboard it drowned. Genene escaped unharmed; Jimmy was hospitalized with a broken rib and cuts to the head.

DeLany's wounds were still healing when he returned from work one afternoon in May to find his wife and baby missing. DeLany checked the closet; a suitcase and clothes were gone. After four years of marital turmoil, Genene had taken four-month-old Edward and flown home to San Antonio. She had not left a note.

On August 10, 1972, Genene filed for divorce. In court papers, she claimed that her husband was "a man of violent and ungovernable temper and passion," who had been guilty of "unconscionable brutality and physical cruelty" and on several occasions "struck her with great force." Genene won a court order barring her husband, who had returned to San Antonio, from going near her or their son. Two months later, it wasn't necessary; the couple had reconciled, and the judge dismissed the suit. Genene later said Jimmy had promised to act more responsibly.

After spending the separation with her family, Genene moved back in with her husband, this time in their own house. She went to work at the Methodist Hospital beauty parlor; he found another job as a mechanic. But the peace did not last long. In February 1974, Jimmy blew yet another job, and Genene moved into her own apartment. She filed divorce papers a month later. The marriage came to its legal end on June 3, 1974. Jimmy got the hot Chevy Nova; Genene received the Dodge Super Bee, child support starting at $25 a week, and permission to drop "DeLany" from her name.

At the age of twenty-three, Genene was suddenly a single mother. Although DeLany had fought in court for weekly visitation rights, he displayed little interest in his son. He would promise to take Edward somewhere; the boy would await the visit eagerly, but his father would never show up. Soon DeLany stopped paying child support. Genene won a contempt citation against her ex-husband, but Jimmy simply ignored it. Genene seemed to feel guilty that her son lacked a father. She tried to compensate with discipline; when Edward misbehaved, Genene sent him to fetch a belt.

Gladys Jones pitched in to help. While Genene worked at the beauty parlor, she kept an eye on Edward. Past the age of sixty, Gladys had brought her own demon under control; she had stopped her drinking through Alcoholics Anonymous. Gladys Jones was a survivor; each misfortune just seemed to harden her, like a coat of shellac on a battered chair. But the fates were not through with the old woman—not even close to through yet. In September 1974, her son Wiley, the father of four children of his own, died of testicular cancer at the age of twenty-eight.

The deaths of her father and her brother from cancer left Genene terrified of the disease. In 1975, she developed an angry skin allergy to the chemicals used on hair. When her doctor ordered tests, she fretted that he was secretly looking for cancer. Genene would confide her fears to friends, then burst into tears. When the test results arrived, she said the allergies left her no choice but to abandon her career as a beautician. Genene described her decision in typically dramatic terms. She said her dermatologist had told her: "Get out or lose your hands."

It was during training for a new profession that Genene discovered she was pregnant. Gladys Jones was aghast at her daughter's plans to have a child out of wedlock, but Genene wanted another baby. To close friends, she confided that the father was her ex-husband, Jim DeLany—that the child had been conceived during another short-lived reconciliation. But to her mother, who despised DeLany, Genene offered another story. She told Gladys—and would one day swear under oath to others—that the child's father was Keith Martin, a beauty-supply salesman, and that he had perished in an automobile accident. Gladys Jones believed her; she knew nothing about the secrets of her daughter's life as a hairdresser.

But there were two problems with the story. The first was that Keith Martin was very much alive. The second was that he was gay.

When Jimmy DeLany's wife attended beauty school, she assumed elements of a new identity. She cut her hair short, bleached it blond, and told classmates and teachers that her name was Jojo. The young sailor's wife quickly became the star pupil at Mim's Beauty College. Her nimble fingers could bring life to the most moribund head of hair. But her greatest gift was cultivating the loyalty of those for whom she worked. When ladies sat in her beauty chair, Jojo pampered them shamelessly. She gave them massages. She brought them sodas. She used flattery to make them feel important. Jojo's customers wouldn't let anyone else do their hair. Classmates thought she was friendly but not one with whom to trifle. They found her profane vocabulary intimidating and reckoned she would make a fearsome adversary.

She spent much of her beauty career at the Methodist Hospital parlor, where everyone knew her as Genene. It was there that she met Keith Martin, about the time of her divorce, during the summer of 1974. Genene had risen to be manager of the two-employee shop; Martin called on her hawking hair spray from the beauty-supply business he had inherited from his mother. After chatting for hours on one of his sales calls, they decided to see each other after work.

Martin was a genteel man. At North Texas State University, he had majored in classical music and French literature. He rarely touched alcohol and never sullied his palate with common beer. He and Genene spent quiet evenings together, discussing cosmic matters of philosophy and taking turns on the piano. During their initial encounters, Martin thought he'd found a soulmate.

But such gentleness did not reflect the dominant side of Genene's personality. More often, she was coarse, particularly when it pertained to sex. "She'd look at a guy," recalled Martin, "and say, 'I could fuck his brains out.' " Genene paraded her lust in part out of sexual frustration; she complained that her appearance deterred men from asking her out. But it also served as a signpost of Genene's bottomless thirst for attention.

Although Genene knew Keith was homosexual, she tried to get him to have sex with her; she seemed to regard seducing him as a challenge. According to Martin, he never succumbed. But the two cultivated a strange relationship of convenience. He escorted Genene on double dates with her straight friends. She accompanied Keith to gay bars, where he picked up men. On nights when his forays failed, they often slept in the same bed. As Martin later described it, Genene became increasingly frustrated at his lack of sexual interest in her.

In late 1975, he suffered a severe bout of fever. Genene helped nurse him through it, and under the spell of confused gratitude, he consented to their engagement. Martin also saw selfish advantages to formalizing their odd alliance. He had dreams of owning a Cadillac, a large house, and a grand piano—the very things Genene had known as a child. She had told him her mother was loaded. Gladys's initial reaction to their engagement announcement had been promising. After hearing the news, she loaned them money; they had told her they were going to open a beauty parlor.

But Genene was already developing other interests. Her employment at the Methodist Hospital beauty parlor had spurred an obsession with the field of medicine. Genene had begun leafing through medical textbooks in her spare time. Her little knowledge was to prove an extraordinarily dangerous thing.

Genene fretted constantly about her own health. Her terror that her skin allergy was a sign of cancer was only an early manifestation. She soon began to offer dire interpretations of the medical problems of others. "Anytime anyone was sick, it was always extreme," recalled Genene's sister, Lisa. "Someone would lose their voice, and she'd see it as cancer of the throat. You'd have a cut, and she'd say, 'It's going to be gangrene.' One of my kids might have an earache, and she'd wonder whether it was a brain tumor." One night, Genene phoned Keith Martin at 2 A.M. from the Methodist Hospital emergency room. She said she was with her son. "I was reading about symptoms of a rare disease that causes young children to go blind," Genene explained, "and Edward fits the symptoms." After a quick examination, a doctor sent them home. "She was always trying to find something wrong with me," recalled Martin. "I have allergies. She would twist it into a medical catastrophe. She always wanted to make you feel as if you were physically ill. She would conjure up things that didn't exist."

Genene's absorption with medicine ran to sexual and mystical elements. Among the men she coveted, she reserved her hottest lust for doctors. To Genene, physicians were a turn-on, the ultimate symbol of masculinity. She encouraged Martin to go to medical school—as though it would magically alter his sexual preference. Genene occasionally turned to unearthly forces on matters of health. She liked to play with a Ouija board and appeared to place credence in its wisdom. On one occasion, she advised Martin he had a short life line and would soon be dead. On another, she asked him to join her in a séance.

In early 1976, Genene began pressing her gay fiancé to set a date for their marriage. Martin balked. Although he was hardly a man of convention, Genene's eccentricities were intimidating. Her demands for sexual favors were becoming insistent. And her mulishness knew no limits; if Keith didn't do things her way, Genene would pitch a fit. The notion of marriage—even a platonic one—to this odd, nagging woman was too much to take. By February, Genene realized that Martin would never go through with it. Bursting into his beauty-supply shop one day, she loudly vented her rage and terminated their engagement.

Genene's skin allergy had afforded an excuse to drop her beauty career as well. It was medicine that mattered to her now, medicine that was to become her life. In June 1976, after Gladys agreed to foot the bill, Genene enrolled in the San Antonio Independent School District's School of Vocational Nursing. Like most prospective licensed vocational nurses—known as practical nurses in many states—Genene had entered the one-year training program because she was eager to start work soon. Compared to those of a registered nurse, the pay, authority, and duties of an LVN were usually limited; but earning an RN degree took at least twice as long.

In LVN school, Genene Jones at last appeared to have found her niche. Most of her grades were in the nineties; in Maternal and Child Care, she achieved a 97. Genene was also popular with her classmates. Some of the women asked her to cut their hair. After moving back in with Gladys, who minded Edward, she hosted the annual Christmas party at her mother's home. But Genene also seemed less serious than her peers. She never studied during lunch hour. She peppered instructors with jokes. And she scrawled pictures of male genitalia during anatomy class.

Graduation exercises were held on May 20, 1977, at a local high school. Among the fifty-eight receiving diplomas, Genene, then seven months pregnant, was one of sixteen to earn honors. The group was serenaded with the class song, a Seals and Crofts tune called "We May Never Pass This Way Again." After a parting prayer, the graduates rose to recite the vocational nurse's pledge: *. . . to assist the physician and the professional nurse in performing any service which will improve the welfare of humanity . . . to safeguard any confidence . . . [to] apply*

*the Golden Rule, toward friend and foe alike . . . to serve
the needs of my fellow man . . .*

When Genene took her licensing exam, she scored
559—more than 200 points above the passing grade. The
transformation was complete: Jojo DeLany, beautician,
was now Genene Jones, licensed vocational nurse.

On July 17, two months after graduation, Genene gave
birth to a daughter, whom she named Crystal Jones. Like
Edward, the new baby became her grandmother's frequent ward. Gladys Jones had sold the family sign business after Wiley's death. She had paid off all her bills,
buried her husband and two of her children. At the age
of sixty-six, she had little unfinished business left on
earth—except to see her wayward adopted daughter settled. However vexing Genene might be, Gladys would do
what she could to help launch her promising new career
in nursing.

PART TWO

THE HOSPITAL

I always cry when babies die. You can almost explain away an adult death. When you look at an adult die, at least you can say they've had a full life. When a baby dies, they've been cheated. They've been cheated out of a hell of a lot.

GENENE JONES
May 5, 1983

Three

IT TOOK GENENE Jones just eight months to be fired from her first nursing job. After recovering from Crystal's birth, she had gone to work in September 1977 at an institution she knew well: Methodist Hospital in northwest San Antonio, a quarter mile from her childhood home. The premier private hospital in the city, the 487-bed Methodist had employed Genene previously as a beautician; her two brothers had been treated there before their deaths.

Genene began on a nursing shift that was to become her favorite: 3–11 P.M. Her salary was $4.02 an hour. Assigned to the cardiac intensive care unit, where patients with life-threatening heart problems received scrutiny around the clock, Genene impressed her supervisors with her enthusiasm, her energy, and her willingness to work extra shifts. A five-month performance review offered an important caveat: "Ms. Jones tends to make judgments that she has neither the experience nor authority to make."

In April 1978, she was ushered out. Genene later explained her dismissal this way: "I had a conflict with a doctor. It was a lack of feeling on the physician's part toward a patient, and I stood up for the patient, and he didn't like it. They asked me to resign." Methodist personnel records, however, show that it was complaints *by* a patient that led to her termination.

The incident began when Genene was assigned to care

for a cardiac patient whose family was visiting her in a hospital lounge. According to hospital records, Genene walked into the lounge and ordered the patient to stamp out her cigarette. She then instructed her to keep her leg elevated; when the woman did not act fast enough, Genene grabbed the leg and abruptly raised it herself, causing pain. After taking the patient's blood pressure, Genene told her: "Get back to your room and get in bed now!"

Informed the next morning that the woman had complained, Genene asked her supervisor if she could speak with the patient. The supervisor told her she could not. Arriving early for her next shift, Genene approached the woman anyway. A written hospital report described what happened next: "Ms. Jones began crying in front of patient as she was reviewing the previous evening's incident. After Ms. Jones left, patient notified 7–3 nurse, complaining of chest pain, nervousness, [and high blood pressure]. M.D. was notified of patient's complaints and upset. Narcotic and sedative ordered. Cardiac studies initiated." Genene was dismissed on April 26 for "improper or unprofessional conduct on duty."

Unceremonious failure in her first job did nothing to impede Genene's future employment. Like the nation as a whole, San Antonio was suffering from a severe nursing shortage. And the medical needs of the city were mushrooming. The once rural neighborhood surrounding Methodist Hospital—a dairy farm only two decades earlier—had grown into the mammoth South Texas Medical Center, a 683-acre complex that included six hospitals and a medical school and employed 12,000 people.

Genene moved across the medical center on May 15, to work in the obstetrics-gynecology ward at Community Hospital, a smaller private hospital. Once again, she worked the 3–11 P.M. shift. On October 16, Genene was forced to resign after undergoing abdominal surgery at a time when she had accumulated no sick leave. Although the procedure was elective, it was surgery that Genene was unwilling to postpone—a bilateral tubal ligation. At the age of twenty-eight, the woman who had grown up wanting a houseful of children had decided that two was enough.

Looking for her third nursing job in thirteen months,

Genene answered an ad for intensive care positions at Bexar County Hospital—the giant public hospital that cared for San Antonio's poor. "I originally applied to the coronary care unit, and there wasn't an opening," Genene recalled. "They asked about pediatrics, and I had questions, but I said 'yeah.' "

On October 30, 1978, Genene Jones began working in the pediatric intensive care unit at Bexar County Hospital.

For fifty years, San Antonio's charity hospital had a reputation as a butchershop. The city's unwashed were treated then at the Robert B. Green Memorial Hospital, in downtown San Antonio, near the slums where they lived. When it opened in 1917, with 208 beds, and partitions separating wards for patients of white and colored races, the Green was actually regarded as a major public improvement. Prior to that time, Bexar County had no charity hospital at all. Citizens too poor to pay had been shuffled about a series of makeshift institutions; in the early 1800s, the Alamo had housed hospital beds.

But the burden of caring for San Antonio's indigent was crushing even for the newly opened Green. The city's West Side was one of the worst slums in America—a huge, unrelenting barrio where thousands of Mexicans lived in *corrales,* tiny stalls opening on a common court, without toilets or running water. Periodic flooding flushed human waste from open sewers into the shacks. Many on the West Side shelled pecans—finger-numbing work that offered feeble pay; in 1934, the average wage for a fifty-four-hour *week* was $1.56. On San Antonio's West Side, only a few could speak English; but most in the community could not read or write in any language. Isolated from twentieth-century medicine, midwives and *curanderos*—Mexican faith healers—held sway.

Such conditions served as a hothouse for disease. San Antonio's tuberculosis rate led the nation; Mexicans died from the affliction almost three times as frequently as Anglos. Infant mortality soared. Mexican children were three times as likely to die from intestinal problems. Venereal disease was rampant. Not all the medical problems were germ-borne. The stifling conditions sparked frequent outbreaks of violence. Bar brawls, gunfights,

and knifings filled the hospital's emergency room with
the battered and bleeding. The city's far smaller black
community inhabited the East Side, in comparably squalid
conditions. Doctors at the Green spoke of their patients
as casualties of "the battle of San Antonio."

Confronting this onslaught, the Green was itself a pau-
per. Young medical residents, overworked and under-
paid, staffed the hospital, with help from private doctors
who volunteered. Operating tools were so scarce that
surgeons brought their own. Food rations were so paltry
that patients recovered from medical problems only to
succumb to poor nutrition. On several occasions, the
hospital ran out of cash entirely and had to pay its employees with scrip.

The Green was perpetually short of money because the
elected county commissioners, who provided its budget,
could take the votes of the poor for granted. San Antonio's minority groups sold their franchise to a corrupt
Anglo political machine. And there was no pressure to
act on conscience. While a few high-minded patricians
made the Green their cause, most whites wouldn't dare
set foot in the place—and didn't bother themselves about
the conditions facing those who had no choice. To the
affluent white majority, the Mexicans on the West Side
were a faceless rabble, fine as domestic help or gardeners
but lacking the need for decent medical facilities possessed by those of a higher species. This disdain was
endemic, part of what one Texas writer labeled the old
Spanish *patrón* mentality. As late as the 1960s, a San
Antonio mayor dismissed the city's Mexican-American
population as a pack of childlike manual laborers "who
just like to sing and dance and have a good time."

While World War II recharged the business community
and Anglo neighborhoods, the harshness of the barrio
was unaltered. A new wave of Mexican immigration over-
filled the West Side with unskilled laborers who worked
at the lowest wages. Conditions at the Green worsened.
In 1946, the local medical society branded the hospital "a
disgrace to Bexar County." An independent inquiry offered a disgusting bill of particulars: ants, roaches, and
fleas covered the baby beds; overflowing garbage cans sat
uncovered in the kitchen; patients with highly contagious

diseases, including typhoid and diphtheria, were left on stretchers in the hallway; few patients received baths. A local doctor publicly compared the county hospital to a charnel house. In October 1947, amid squabbling about what to do, the remaining medical residents quit and the Robert B. Green shut its doors. San Antonio became the only major city in the nation without a charity hospital.

Reopening after a year, the Green was eventually placed under the control of the newly created Bexar County Hospital District—a special taxing entity set up to fund the public hospital directly. An independent board of appointed managers governed the district, whose bylaws stipulated that it provide for the "indigent and needy sick" of Bexar County. The ultimate power of the purse— the crucial matter of setting the district's tax rate— remained in the hands of the county commissioners.

It would be the federal and state governments that would change everything—transform this Dickensian hospital for the poor, set amid the downtown squalor, into a sleek temple of modern medicine, planted in the affluent suburbs. In the years after World War II, federal dollars came to shape every aspect of American medicine. Through an array of new grant programs, Washington poured billions into health care: for construction of new hospitals and medical schools, for high-powered research, and—through Medicare and Medicaid—for treating the poor and the elderly. The opening of the federal purse produced a building boom; new hospitals and medical schools began springing up everywhere. The Robert B. Green's demise was fated with the state's decision in 1961 to award a medical school to San Antonio.

Hoping to end a persistent physician shortage, city fathers had been lobbying for a University of Texas medical branch for years. An unusual offer had brought success: a commitment to provide the medical school with a three-hundred-bed teaching hospital, free of charge to the state. In accepting the deal, the Texas legislature had added a condition that entwined the fate of the two institutions further: The hospital must be located within one mile of the medical school. This meant that the county would have to provide a hospital wherever the

state decided to put the medical school. A furious battle
ensued.

On one side stood advocates of downtown: With a
much-needed renovation, the Green, already the county's charity hospital, could serve as the teaching hospital
as well. Most teaching hospitals used sick poor people as
cannon fodder for the instruction of medical students and
inexperienced doctors; the Green obviously had plenty of
what is known in academic medicine as "clinical mate-
rial." It also made sense to continue treating the city's
indigent at an institution close to where most of them
lived. And pairing the medical school with the Green
would serve the auxiliary goal of urban renewal: The
medical school and the expanded Green would bring
hundreds of white-collar jobs to San Antonio's rotting
downtown core. Center-city merchants, the Catholic
Church, organized Hispanic groups, and the Green's
longtime patrician patrons backed downtown.

But a group of chamber of commerce leaders and real
estate speculators had an altogether different idea. They
focused not on the most obvious goals of the medical
school and hospital: to train doctors and care for the
poor. Alert to new ways of modern medicine, they looked
at the institutions and saw Economic Potential. They
envisioned the medical school and its teaching hospital, a
new teaching hospital, as anchors to a sprawling new
suburban medical complex—a rival to the famous Texas
Medical Center in Houston. A quartet of real estate
speculators already had offered a gift of one hundred
seventy acres, adjacent to the Oak Hills Country Club,
eleven miles northwest of downtown. That was enough
land to provide the medical complex with room to grow
for years. The speculators had promoted the concept by
luring Methodist Hospital to the area with a donation of
twenty-seven acres. Such benevolence was a shrewd investment, an example of what is wryly known among
land merchants as "enlightened self-interest." The speculators had snatched up more than two *thousand* acres of
surrounding land cheap; they were betting on the medical
complex to send values in the sparsely populated area
soaring.

Offered a gift of one hundred acres for the medical

school, the University of Texas board of regents opted for the suburban site. The defeated downtowners were mollified with a promise from county officials that the Green would never be abandoned. Construction of the new Bexar County Hospital and the University of Texas Medical School, situated next door, began in March 1966. By then, the seductive appeal of federal grants—Washington offered two dollars for every dollar put up locally—persuaded the county commissioners to build a far more grandiose hospital than originally planned: 564 beds instead of a mere 300.

The new Bexar County Hospital was dedicated on November 9, 1968. Amid much pomp and ceremony, Texas governor John Connally declared "South Texas Medical Center Week," and everyone marveled at what the public treasury had built. The $17 million hospital sat on twenty-nine acres, rose twelve stories tall, and contained 485,000 square feet—eleven acres of floor space. San Antonio's newspapers filled entire sections with gushing praise: THE NEW FACE OF MEDICINE IN SAN ANTONIO; NO EQUAL IN DESIGN, BEAUTY; ANY ORGAN TRANSPLANT COULD BE PERFORMED; and SERVICE AVAILABLE WILL BE WELL WORTH COST TO TAXPAYER. Even the cafeteria won acclaim: NO LONG LINES; SELDOM ANY WAITING.

A single headline captured the county's overarching ambition for the institution. It read: SUPERB CARE: NEW HOSPITAL EXPECTED TO SERVE INDIGENT AND WELL-HEELED. Since 1917, the Green had accepted only charity cases and charged nothing for medical care. Bexar County Hospital would be different; it would charge people what they could afford to pay. County officials imagined that the new hospital would draw plenty of private patients to subsidize operations. "For the first time in the history of the community," the hospital's top administrator proclaimed, "there is going to be a single kind of care—the same kind of care—for those who can pay and for those who can't."

It was wishful thinking. Despite Bexar County Hospital's location among the moneyed, despite its affiliation with the high-powered doctors at the adjacent medical school, the hospital was destined, like the Green, almost exclusively to serve the poor. No matter how much they heard about the cutting-edge care at the new institution, most well-heeled San Antonians were unwilling to rub elbows with the city's rabble.

Even before the dedication, it had become apparent that Bexar County could not afford to operate two separate hospitals. When construction on the new hospital ran $2 million over projections, administrators had cannibalized the budgets for x-ray and lab equipment to finish the building. When voters refused to raise their taxes to run the new hospital, the state legislature had to bail out the county by authorizing the tax increase anyway. A looming financial crisis prompted the resignation of the hospital administrator before the new building was a year old.

Seeking to trim expenses, county officials had begun cutting back at the Green. With the opening of the new facility, the fifty-one-year-old hospital dropped from 290 beds to 125. Most inpatient medical services moved north; along with a few emergency patients, only the maternity and newborn nursery wards remained. In December 1976, county officials announced the closing of those wards as well; they had decided to convert the old hospital exclusively for outpatient-clinic use.

Community groups organized rapidly. The past decade had seen a transformation in San Antonio's Hispanic population. Mexican-Americans now represented a majority, and after domination by Anglos since the Texas Revolution, they had learned to exercise political power. Their leaders screamed betrayal, recalling the old promises to preserve the Green. As the proposal to transform the downtown hospital wound its way through the state's regulatory labyrinth, they pushed local and federal officials to act.

In December 1978, the U.S. Justice Department and the San Antonio city government filed a federal lawsuit to block the move. Arguing that the transfer of maternity services would deprive impoverished Hispanics and blacks of proper maternity care, they branded the hospital district's plan an act of racial discrimination. The suit noted that the Green handled more than six thousand births a year, that 80 percent of the mothers were Hispanic, 7 percent were black, and that almost all of them lived much closer to the Green than to the Bexar County Hospital. The suit pronounced the new hospital in the suburbs "not only physically but also psychologically too distant from a large segment of the patient population."

The dramatic trial in federal court was a testament to the inadequacies of Bexar County's medical care for the poor. Among the parade of witnesses was a young Mexican-American councilman named Henry Cisneros, destined to become the city's mayor and a national symbol of Hispanic achievement. Cisneros testified that relocation of the maternity ward and nursery would make it difficult for Hispanic and black mothers to reach the hospital before giving birth. Most of his constituents were poor and many lacked cars, Cisneros said. Forcing them to travel to the "ridiculously located" Bexar County Hospital would jeopardize many lives.

Hospital district witnesses testified that it was the Green that endangered lives. They claimed that the old hospital was too inefficient and ill-equipped to remain in use and too decrepit to renovate properly. Echoing the words of those who had staffed the Green fifty years earlier, one doctor said conditions there resembled "a battlefield situation." After a sixteen-day trial, a federal judge agreed. ". . . Not only was no discrimination intended by the Hospital District, but none was effected," ruled the magistrate. "On the contrary, when the relocation is completed, a first-class general hospital will be provided at the Oak Hills site, without discrimination, to every qualified obstetrical patient, so that optimum health care will be made available to each indigent mother and her newborn child."

Work began promptly to transfer the maternity wards and nursery, the last vestiges of the Green's days as a full-service hospital. With the addition of new outpatient clinics, the Robert B. Green Memorial Hospital was rechristened the Brady-Green Community Health Center.

By then, the businessmen's dream for the South Texas Medical Center had become reality. With the UT medical school and Bexar County Hospital serving as magnets, the complex attracted new hospitals, office towers for private doctors, a cancer center, an institute for religion and health, and dozens of other facilities. Gifts and purchases of land enabled the special foundation set up by the chamber of commerce to expand the medical center to 683 acres—more than any comparable project in the nation and three times the size of its famous rival in Houston. Even in 1978, with construction crews toiling away on new projects, so much vacant land remained that the foundation leased out more than a hundred acres for cattle grazing.

The area around the medical center was booming too. The prairie bought by the speculators had given way to apartments, banks, restaurants, hotels, strip shopping centers, and fancy housing developments. The speculators had acquired the land during the 1950s for between $500 and $2,000 an acre; the 1961 decision to build the county hospital and medical school nearby had tripled its value overnight. As values multiplied further, the original speculators sold off some of their holdings and developed other tracts themselves. By 1978, land around the South Texas Medical Center was going for $60,000 an acre.

The new medical center shifted the care of San Antonio's poor to a vastly different kind of institution. The Green was an old-fashioned charity hospital, dirty and crowded, resigned to its miserable image, focused exclusively on patient care. Bexar County Hospital was a creature of the world of modern medicine. Its existence meant better medical care for the city's indigent: supervision by medical school doctors expert in cutting-edge technology; hands-on treatment by young residents with greater skill; and, despite the unending money woes, access to better hospital facilities and equipment. But modern medicine also was more specialized and impersonal, and the new hospital reflected those changes too. Much of the medical faculty cared more about research than about treating patients. Unlike the Green, Bexar County Hospital was striving with ambition. It cared acutely about its image and lived in fear of litigation—concerns tended obsessively by administrators in a newly burgeoning bureaucracy.

For the poor of San Antonio, who now arrived for medical treatment by shuttle bus or borrowed car, the sophisticated new hospital was a sterile, perplexing place. Still they came, day and night, bearing their children in their arms, waiting for hours in the emergency room, where patients were admitted for treatment. In a simple act of faith, they trusted the nurses and doctors and administrators who ran the hospital; they trusted them to safeguard their lives and to make them well. They trusted them because they had no choice. They had nowhere else to go.

Four

GENENE JONES SAID her first emotion on starting work in
Bexar County Hospital's pediatric intensive care unit was
"stark, raving fear." She had not treated children since
nursing school. But her doubts disappeared quickly. "The
first baby I ever took care of was a preemie with a dying
gut," she recalled. "I picked that kid up, and I knew I
was going to stay there."

Cherlyn Pendergraft, the registered nurse who gave
Genene her orientation, wasn't so sure. The infant, a
six-day-old boy with an often fatal intestinal disease called
necrotizing enterocolitis, went to surgery, returned to the
ICU, and died. Genene had cared for the child only
briefly—she'd had no time to develop an emotional
attachment—but "she just went berserk," Pendergraft
said; Genene broke into deep, racking sobs, moved a
stool into the dead baby's cubicle, and sat staring at the
body.

The pediatric ICU at Bexar County Hospital was down
a long fifth-floor corridor—past the little boys and girls
playing in the hall, past the rooms of children who had
busted a leg or lost an appendix, past the kids who would
soon leave the pediatric ward, happy and healed. At the
end of the corridor, one walked through swinging double
doors and stepped into a different world. Here the children were mostly silent and still, strapped to their beds,
hooked up to beeping monitors and a web of wires and
tubes. The pediatric ICU was where Bexar County sent

its critically ill children who could not afford a private hospital: the infant girl whose raging father had cracked open her skull, the two-year-old who had nearly drowned, the seven-year-old who was struggling to survive a congenital heart defect.

The pediatric ICU occupied a rectangular space the size of a two-car garage. During most of the time Genene Jones was there, it contained eight beds, one or two in each of six separate cubicles. The rooms had large glass windows that allowed the nurses to keep an eye on the patients and on the machines that monitored their heartbeats and breathing. In the back of the ICU was a small room where the nurses could sit and relax. It was filled with supplies and equipment for conducting simple lab tests. Near the entrance to the ICU hung a small locked cabinet where narcotics were stored; most other medications were freely available in an unlocked drug closet.

While patients in the ICU might range up to sixteen years old, many of them were infants. But the pediatric ICU did not treat newborns. Newborn children who were gravely ill went to the neonatal ICU, a floor below, where they received more specialized care and were isolated from the infection that children who had been outside the hospital might bring in. The pediatric ICU was for kids who had been out in the world. Children were brought there to recover from surgery or to be treated for a disease or an injury.

Genene Jones had been entrusted with the lives of such children after a less rigorous screening than a bank would give to an applicant for the job of teller. Facing a desperate shortage of nurses, the county hospital was in the habit of asking relatively few questions; like most busy big-city hospitals, it regarded the possession of a valid nursing license as sufficient ground for trust. On her job application, Genene had vaguely attributed her departure from Methodist Hospital to "conflict." The county hospital's personnel department routinely sent Genene's former employers a written form seeking information about her job performance and her suitability for reemployment. When Methodist returned the form with such questions unanswered, the matter went no further. Nothing in Genene's personnel file at Bexar County Hospital indicated that she had been fired from her first nursing job for abusing a patient.

Bexar County's role as a teaching hospital meant that it answered to two masters. The county hospital district maintained and equipped the building; hired and fired administrators and support personnel, including nurses; and paid the salaries of the young doctors-in-training— called residents—who staffed the hospital around the clock. But it was the UT medical school that selected the residents and supervised medical care. While the relationship was administratively unwieldy, both institutions benefited. UT provided the hospital with doctors; the hospital gave UT a place to train its medical students and residents. Because doctors learn by doing, and paying patients don't like to be practiced on, it is charity hospitals like Bexar County where most American physicians learn to practice medicine.

The pediatric ICU medical staff consisted of rotating teams of pediatric residents—most of whom had graduated from medical school no more than three years earlier— supervised by attending physicians from the UT faculty. A strict hierarchy ruled the doctors. The attendings supervised the senior residents, who had completed at least one year of residency; the senior residents guided the interns, in their first year out of medical school; interns taught the medical students. Residents learned complex medical procedures at bedside, then passed the knowledge on. An axiom summed up the process of medical education: See one. Do one. Teach one.

Residency has often been described as the hazing ritual of American medicine—a brutal rite of passage involving long hours of work under tremendous pressure, with little sleep and low pay. Internship year was the worst. In 1978, interns at Bexar County Hospital worked as much as ninety hours a week for $12,000 a year. As the survivors moved up—suicides and breakdowns were not unheard of—a new class of interns arrived fresh from medical school each July to start the process all over again. It is not myth, but statistical reality, that there are eleven better months to be a patient in a teaching hospital.

At night at Bexar County Hospital, a team of two

pediatric interns, a second-year resident, and a third-year resident took overnight call in the pediatric ICU, a shift that kept them on duty—and sometimes awake—for up to thirty hours at a stretch. During the one-month rotation, each team took call every third night and covered the sixty-bed pediatric ward as well as the ICU. While Genene Jones worked there, the doctors made rounds in the morning and drifted in and out during the day; none remained in the unit full time.

This meant that in the pediatric ICU, even more than in most hospital wards, nurses were a critical presence. A pediatric ICU nurse spent all her time on one or two patients who demanded almost constant attention—feeding, changing, drugs, and observation. These children were capable of doing nothing for themselves. Not all of them were on the brink of disaster, but many were; one out of seventeen patients who entered the pediatric ICU never left. It was a situation where the work of a single nurse could tip the scales between life and death.

The nurses who choose ICU work thrive on that kind of high-pressure challenge. They are bored with the low-key atmosphere out on the floor; they scoff at it as baby-sitting. ICU nurses pride themselves on their ability to spot problems early and intervene—to step between a medical calamity and a child like a superhero jumping in front of a speeding bullet. They pride themselves on being *aggressive*.

Genene Jones quickly came to think of herself as an ICU nurse. After spending her first three months at Bexar County Hospital working nights—11 P.M. to 7 A.M.—Genene moved once again to the 3–11 P.M. shift. Registered nurses, who have at least two years of training, often look down on LVNs, but Genene's enthusiasm, knowledge, and technical skill impressed everyone. She knew more anatomy and physiology than most LVNs. And when she didn't understand something, she would run for the medical textbooks to try to figure it out.

But Genene's most distinctive nursing skill was her extraordinary talent for putting intravenous lines into veins. Most hospital patients are given IVs to provide direct access to a vein—vital for injecting drugs, drawing blood, and giving fluids. Without IVs, nurses would have to turn patients into pincushions, sticking them a dozen times a day in a dozen different places. For a hospital nurse, starting an IV is a daily chore, but it's one that many never master. Veins move under the skin, and it is easy to miss a few times before finding the mark. The job is even trickier with an infant, whose veins offer a target only the size of a thread. But for Genene, the woman of nimble fingers, it was a breeze. There was no IV she could not start—no patient too restless, no vein too small. Her reputation spread quickly, and nurses on the pediatric floor began calling her out of the unit to start IVs for them. "She could stick an IV in a freaking fly," remarked one doctor.

Genene's natural talent dazzled her supervisors—most notably Pat Belko, the matronly head nurse of the pediatric ICU. A native of New Hampshire, Belko had earned her RN degree in 1955. Her career bridged the years when hospital nurses timidly did doctors' bidding; modern medicine advanced the notion that physicians and nurses were a team. At Bexar County Hospital, the partnership concept was practiced to a fault. While doctors called the shots on patient care, even the chief of a medical service lacked the power to fire—or even discipline—an incompetent or a dangerous nurse. A separate hierarchy of nursing bureaucrats presided over the nursing staff; they brooked no intrusion from doctors on their turf.

In a profession where annual turnover in big-city hospitals averaged about 25 percent, Pat Belko had risen to mid-level management by remaining in one place. Bexar County Hospital had particular trouble holding on to its staff. Talented young nurses went there to gain experience, then usually left after a few years for private hospitals or clinics, where the pay was better and the work softer. Married to a retired air force sergeant who became a mail carrier, Belko began at Bexar County Hospital in 1971, after taking several years off to devote to her six children. She was assigned to the pediatric ICU, where she started at the bottom: the 11 P.M. to 7 A.M. night shift. Supervisors praised Belko's solidity: They called her "reliable" and "congenial" and noted that her attendance record was virtually perfect. She rose to charge nurse on the night shift after three years, took over the day shift after four, and was appointed head nurse of the entire pediatric ICU in February 1978.

At forty-four, Belko was a cordial, moon-faced woman, pleasant enough but bland, with a fireplug build. Disinclined to offend, she quickly displayed an inclination to follow the path of least resistance, to smooth over problems rather than resolve them. Government institutions all over America were filled with people like Pat Belko; they rose to positions of authority not through brilliance or initiative but by earnestly putting in their time.

Belko's biggest headache since her promotion had been finding enough nurses to staff the ICU around the clock. Several open positions had gone unfilled for months. Genene Jones endeared herself to the boss by volunteering often for extra shifts. And unlike many of the young nurses, who openly ridiculed Pat for being stuffy and indecisive, Genene was solicitous and respectful. Uncomfortable holding the reins of leadership, insecure about how subordinates regarded her, Belko was grateful for Genene's fealty. "Ms. Jones has adapted to working with Pediatric patients well," wrote Belko, in evaluating the new LVN after three months. "She shows a great deal of enthusiasm and loyalty to the PICU. She gives priority to consideration of the patients as human beings." Genene could become an even better nurse, Belko added, if she could maintain "better control of emotionalism."

Despite the praise, Genene had already committed the first of an increasingly serious collection of nursing errors; eight were formally noted during her first year alone. She failed to obey a doctor's orders to give a child an anticonvulsant drug. She didn't notice a malfunctioning intravenous line. She set an IV solution at an improperly high rate, allowing fluids to pour into a child's body over thirty minutes instead of six hours. She miscopied drug orders, in one case transcribing 50 milligrams as 500 milligrams; before the mistake was discovered, Genene's patient received three dosages of ten times the proper amount.

Following each of her mistakes, Genene received what was known under hospital procedure as "informal guidance": She had to discuss the incident with her superiors, who placed a report of it in her personnel file. In several cases, Genene insisted she had done nothing wrong; she submitted notes for the record containing elaborate excuses for her transgressions. Genene's fourth medication error in twelve months obligated her to repeat a special class on the administration of drugs. When Genene twice failed to show up, she received another written scolding. But even during the first year, those were not her most serious offenses.

At 7 A.M. on August 11, 1979, Genene completed two consecutive shifts caring for a ten-month-old girl in the throes of terminal heart failure. Her supervisor, Cherlyn Pendergraft—the nurse who had given Genene her orientation—ordered her to go home at the end of the second shift. Genene refused. For an hour, she ignored direct orders to leave the pediatric ICU. She departed only after a higher-level nursing administrator was summoned. In a written explanation, Genene said she felt her presence was essential because she had developed a rapport with the child's parents—and because the little girl *needed* her. "I felt that seeing her through this crisis, her biggest, was very important, not only to me, but for her," Genene wrote. Under Bexar County Hospital's complicated system of personnel sanctions, Genene's action could have been classified as an act of "industrial insubordination," resulting in an automatic three-day suspension and probable firing. But Pat Belko, citing Genene's professed concern for her patient, decided to give her a warning instead. She placed her on notice that a similar failure to obey orders *would* result in suspension—and probable dismissal.

Just such an incident came less than two months later. On September 29, after completing the previous night's 3–11 shift, Genene appeared unexpectedly in the ICU at 5 A.M. Accompanied by a friend, she went to the bedside of the patient she had been treating, fetched a syringe, and started tinkering with the child's medical equipment. Smelling alcohol on Genene's breath, doctors and nurses ordered her to leave. Genene insisted she wasn't drunk, before weaving out of the room and departing the ICU.

Genene had used "very poor judgment" in returning to the ICU "apparently under the influence of alcohol,"

Pat Belko wrote in her report on the incident. Under hospital rules forbidding conduct that endangers the health of patients, the head nurse noted, Genene could have been suspended and fired for that incident alone. But she was not to miss a minute of work—previous offenses notwithstanding. Wrote Belko: "Because of Ms. Jones positive contributions to the unit, her concern for the patients and the voluntary overtime she has worked, she is notified that this is a final written warning."

The last entry in Jones's personnel file for 1979 took note not of her five medication errors during fourteen months of employment, nor of her failure to attend required classes on the use of drugs, nor of the two episodes of serious misbehavior, any one of which could easily have justified her dismissal. Instead, on December 28, 1979, Pat Belko submitted for Genene's file a written commendation for "meritorious contributions." Written by the charge nurse on Genene's shift, the letter was cosigned by Belko. "Over the last 4 months when the PICU was going through a severe staffing shortage, Ms. Jones worked in excess of 12 extra shifts to help cover the unit; these extra shifts often involved sacrificing days off. . . . Ms. Jones is to be commended for her support and dedication to the PICU."

Other nurses were amazed at Jones's ability to elude punishment. Those who had reported her for discipline became frustrated; Belko refused to deal harshly even with misconduct that endangered patients. Bitter at the head nurse's failure to back her up, Cherlyn Pendergraft— the nurse who had oriented Genene—transferred out of the ICU. Genene appeared emboldened by her apparent invulnerability. It seemed as though no one could rein her in.

Five

IN THE SPAN of twelve months, Genene Jones's presence had divided the pediatric ICU. Those who crossed her path came quickly to see her in a white or a black hat. Her most important supporter was Pat Belko—evidence of Genene's ability to appeal to people, particularly superiors, at will. But several of Genene's peers were drawn to her flame too. Foremost among them was Debbie Sultenfuss, a thirty-two-year-old woman whose devotion to Genene Jones would prove blind.

Sultenfuss met Genene after going to work on the pediatric floor in August 1979, fresh out of LVN school. Genene's fast mouth and mind quickly made a deep impression on her. In January 1980, Debbie transferred from the floor to the pediatric ICU to work the 3–11 shift with Genene. They became inseparable: Genene the clever teacher, Debbie the eager, if slow, pupil. Debbie began trying to act like Genene, even to dress like Genene. But she was a poor imitation. Debbie, a six-foot, two-hundred-pound giantess, lumbered. Her spelling, grammar, and handwriting were nearly unintelligible. On several occasions she was late to work, and supervisors regularly noted her inability to master the terminology of medicine. Debbie's infatuation with Genene prompted gossip in the ICU—never substantiated—that they were lesbians. Genene sneered at the suggestion; Debbie would later explain that they shared "a sisterly love."

Parents of the critically ill children Genene treated also

regarded her as a godsend. Genene worked them like customers in her beauty chair, and they came to see her as a comforting figure, a woman of patience and understanding. She had long private talks with them, where she confided tidbits about the hospital and listened to their complaints and fears. While faceless doctors rushed by, week after week, Genene was there, caring for their child. She called them by their first names; she became a friend. Genene took pains to cultivate even parents who were suspected of abusing their children—usually the lowest form of life in any pediatric nurse's book. While other nurses shunned such families, Genene rushed to greet them. The evidence in such cases was typically both ugly and overwhelming, but Genene would say that she believed the parents were innocent.

While Genene turned on the charm for parents, she displayed a completely different personality among colleagues. She was loud and coarse. She thought nothing of bellowing out four-letter words or telling dirty jokes in a crowd of nurses and doctors. She spoke freely of the joys of sex, boasting of past conquests and pointing out those she had in mind for the future. The ICU was no convent—unit nurses were legendarily boisterous—but Genene talked like a sailor. She had strong opinions—about doctors, other nurses, patient care, the hospital—and voiced them without hesitation.

Happiest while the center of attention, Genene told colorful stories about her life: that she had spent time in a coma after a terrible car accident; that she had shot her brother-in-law in the groin after he'd beaten her sister. Genene's peers did not know with certainty that such tales were the product of her imagination. But they sensed what friends since high school had known: that she often did not tell the truth.

In this group of medically aggressive nurses, Genene stood out as the *most* aggressive. She would spot problems in her patients before anyone else could see them— problems that the weary residents she dragged out of call-room beds often said didn't exist. Her impulse to exaggerate medical problems, harmless while Genene was a beautician, was now being exercised in an environment where it was dangerous. Exhausted doctors began to think of her as the most serious obstacle to a few hours' rest: the nurse who cried wolf. "She'd always call you for crap," said one resident who worked with Genene. "Any little thing, she'd be calling you—two, three, four times as much as anybody else. She wanted a lot of attention. After a while, you'd think she was a pain in the ass."

If one doctor rejected her advice, Genene would call another. When the intern didn't jump, she'd talk to the resident; when the resident didn't jump, she'd call the attending physician. Genene questioned medications, dosages, treatment, and diagnoses. When her recommendations for a patient were ignored, she predicted disaster. "This kid's going to die if you don't do this," she told one doctor.

Interns became special targets for Genene's tactics. Unsure of their knowledge, they were easy prey for a nurse certain of her own. Genene made it clear she believed she knew more than the interns, that she was really protecting the patients from the doctors. She was always testing, searching for an opening, seeing how much she could get away with. When an intern hesitated, she pushed: "Don't you think the baby needs this?" Strong personalities reined her in; weak ones were steamrollered.

Several residents discovered Genene drawing up drugs without bothering to wait for their orders. Dr. Debbie Rasch arrived at the scene of one child's cardiac arrest to find Jones ready to inject. "I asked her what she was pushing, and it was calcium," said Rasch. "If she had gone ahead and given the medication, it would not have been appropriate. When I got there, she had syringe in hand."

The problem wasn't that a nurse was telling a doctor what to do. The best ICU nurses could handle many calamities almost by instinct—much faster than the average resident. But the doctor must make the call. A good nurse could save him from a serious mistake; a bad nurse could get him—and his patient—in grave trouble. Genene Jones disturbed the young residents who worked in the pediatric ICU because she left many of them uncertain: In which category did she belong?

But to Genene, nothing was uncertain. It was simply a matter of fighting for her patients, of pointing out problems the residents were too green or too stupid or too lazy to spot—problems she invariably saw in life-and-death terms. "I could sit and look at a baby, and they'll smile," Genene would say. "You'll blink your eyes, and they're dead."

Jones's dramatic perspective rattled her peers. Every eight hours, when shifts changed, the nurses would meet for "report," during which those who had been on duty would detail the condition of their patients. There, Genene issued chilling pronouncements. *This baby is really bad; this baby isn't going to make it through the night!* "It wasn't like she was predicting it," recalled one young RN who began her career in the pediatric ICU. "It was like she *knew* what was going to happen. I was a new nurse. I'd come out of report shaking like a leaf."

The spring of 1980 brought to San Antonio a man who would serve first as Genene Jones's ally—and later as her nemesis. In March, Dr. James Lawrence Robotham became an associate professor at UT and medical director of the pediatric ICU. Robotham, thirty-three, wiry and bearded, was a pediatric intensivist—an expert in critical care. He belonged to big-time medicine's new breed of sophisticated subspecialists, doctors who trained specifically to transplant bone marrow or deal with fertility problems or handle trauma cases in emergency rooms—or run ICUs. He arrived from the prestigious Johns Hopkins Medical School in Baltimore, after having learned his trade at two other top programs. Robotham was a brilliant, volatile, compulsive, and demanding man, and he quickly made his mark on the pediatric ICU.

Before his arrival, the role of the ICU's medical director had been a minor one. The job was part time, and the doctors who held it were content to let the individual physicians who admitted patients to the unit manage their care. But Robotham believed that critically ill children required care from someone specially schooled to treat them; that, after all, was why he was there. He began spending much of his day in the ICU. Robotham had little formal authority to hire, fire, or set policy, but through his presence and knowledge, he shifted more and more of the burden for patients' treatment onto his

own shoulders. He told residents and nurses to call him
with any problem, at any hour. When the calls came in
the middle of the night, he didn't just tell his doctors
what to do; he showed up at the hospital.

Robotham had skills—and clout—that other doctors in
the ICU lacked, and his presence made a difference. An
LVN on the night shift saw that early one morning, when
a five-month-old boy started fading fast and Robotham
came in from home. "Blood was oozing from everywhere, and the kid was dying," she said, wincing at the
memory. "Blood was bubbling out of his mouth, blood
was bubbling out of his rectum. As fast as we could push
blood in, it came squirting out. Robotham got on the
phone: He got the chief gastro man; he got the chief
cardiologist. They pulled that baby out, and he lived. He
didn't have to come in at two o'clock in the morning
when we said, 'This kid is bleeding.' He came in because
he cared. I saw him save the kid."

Fully conscious of his own abilities, Robotham wanted
the nurses and residents to learn what he knew. At
seven-thirty each morning he led them on teaching rounds,
reviewing each patient's condition and treatment plan.
That routine goes on in every teaching hospital, but
Robotham's rounds were special. Residents accustomed
to offering shallow presentations of a patient's status
suddenly faced a barrage of pointed questions: What
were the lab results? What do they mean? Why do you
say that? Are you *sure*? When residents were caught
short, forgot a dosage or a patient history, Robotham
pressed them: *Don't you think it's important to know?* It
was painful—Robotham often wasn't satisfied until he
had humiliated a young doctor—but the residents learned.
He kept after the nurses as well. One day he walked into
the ICU and there wasn't a nurse or doctor in sight; the
nurses were meeting in the unit's back room. Robotham
stepped into a patient's room and set off the alarm on
one of the monitors. Nurses know those alarms are supposed to indicate a dire medical emergency, but no one
came out. Furious, Robotham walked into the nurses'
meeting and announced what had happened. The nurse
whose patient he had picked broke into tears. The ICU

staff quickly found a suitable nickname for the new medical director: They called him J.R.

When he arrived at Bexar County Hospital, Jim Robotham felt certain he had known many nurses like Genene Jones. You could find a few at every busy charity hospital. They populated late-night shifts, handling thankless chores during dark hours. They were unattractive and rough. Ridden with guilt about the mess they had made of their own lives, they buried themselves in their work, volunteering for extra shifts and hanging around the hospital during free hours. They had an exaggerated sense of their importance and talked big to their peers. Often they were LVNs and thus consigned forever to the lowest rung of the nursing hierarchy. But hospitals depended on them: They had savvy and experience, and they made the place run. Robotham came to think of such nurses, bruised and battle tested, as the charity hospital's staff sergeants.

Robotham had faith in their gut judgment, for it was instinct that had led him into medicine. Robotham was one of those doctors who grew up worshiping Albert Schweitzer and Tom Dooley—who knew, from early youth, that they could enter no other field. Growing up in Scituate, a tiny town on the Massachusetts coast, Robotham pored over anatomy texts, memorizing the names of bones and muscles. At seventeen, he entered a combined undergraduate–medical school program at Boston University. Robotham's middle-class parents were Presbyterian and Irish Catholic, but six years in a BU dorm, surrounded by Jewish kids from Long Island, tagged him forever with a New York accent. He graduated at twenty-three, ranked second in his medical school class.

Robotham had harbored idealistic childhood dreams of following Dr. Schweitzer's footsteps to Africa. But during his internship year in pediatrics at Boston City Hospital, which picked up the pieces from Boston's harshest slums, Robotham learned he didn't need to leave America to encounter Third-World conditions. He finished his residency at Johns Hopkins, returned to Boston City for a year as chief resident, then moved to Toronto to train at the renowned Hospital for Sick Children. There,

Robotham worked under Dr. Alan Conn, one of the fathers of pediatric intensive care. In 1976, he returned to Baltimore, where he joined the Johns Hopkins Medical School faculty and later married. In the world of academic medicine, Robotham was a hot property because he was a double threat: an expert clinician and a productive researcher. He attracted his own funding and published in prestigious medical journals. After deciding to leave Johns Hopkins, Robotham entertained several offers. The freedom to pursue his considerable ambitions lured him to San Antonio's young medical school.

Robotham arrived in Texas with a personal five-year plan. He intended to split his time evenly during the first years between the pediatric ICU and the lab. Funded by two federal research grants, Robotham was conducting experiments with baboons aimed at avoiding the lung problems that plagued premature babies placed on respirators. He planned to wean himself later from the draining ICU chores and hand over the day-to-day responsibilities to younger disciples.

Reality rewrote the plan. On inspecting the pediatric ICU, Robotham was appalled at its antiquated facilities. Even before taking over, he sent the pediatrics chairman a ten-page memo detailing $120,000 in new equipment he considered essential to raise the ICU to "an acceptable level allowing proper care of patients." Robotham ended his letter with a postscript: "I know I've forgotten something." The unit's staffing needs were just as great. Doctors had been forced to postpone several elective procedures on children because the pediatric ICU lacked the nursing staff to care for them after surgery. At times, the shortage forced Robotham to cut the ICU census from eight to four beds; when there were more than four critical patients, the hospital had to send them elsewhere.

Trying to solve problems at the county hospital was an energy-sapping nightmare. There was never enough money for anything; every purchase of basic equipment required hours of negotiation. Replacing the ICU's broken refrigerator took a special appeal to the hospital administrator. When Robotham wanted a microwave oven to reheat patient meals—which invariably arrived on the pediatric floor cold—he had to recruit a local merchant to donate the appliance. There were dozens of petty annoyances. The hospital's public areas were always dirty, and the lobby contained rudely worded messages ordering parents to mind their children. The pediatric floor had no waiting area for parents of critically ill children; when they dozed off late at night on a windowsill, hospital security guards rousted them as though they were vagrants.

Everywhere Robotham looked, administrators were holding meetings and writing memos. In addition to an executive director, Bexar County Hospital employed a senior associate executive director, three associate executive directors, an executive assistant to the executive director, an administrator, and three assistant administrators. Memoranda from the top man arrived on baby-blue paper; others used white or pink. One critical message carried the signatures of the assistant administrator for resource management, the assistant administrator for support services, the director of supply and equipment management, and the director of housekeeping; it laid out the official hospital procedure for moving things. ("Significant movements of equipment or furniture are to be accomplished . . . with the assistance of Hospital Supply.")

While some aspects of the bureaucracy were merely maddening, others threatened lives. When Robotham arrived in San Antonio, there were no beepers to contact the pediatricians on call in an emergency. Getting lab results or x-rays, particularly on weekends, often took hours. Blood samples sent for testing were frequently lost or confused. Critical pieces of equipment took weeks to replace or repair.

In this environment, Robotham toiled to impart his treatment philosophy to those who worked in the pediatric ICU. As an intensivist, he was schooled to consider the unlikeliest medical possibilities. Reviewing an ICU patient with a group of residents, he often required them to list fifteen complications the child's illness might produce—even if their statistical probability of occurring were a tenth of one percent. Day after day, he drilled his young doctors. "Look for the zebras!" he told them. After the Robothams had a child, his wife half-seriously remarked to friends: "Jim is the best person to have

around with a sick kid—and the last person you want to
have around with a healthy kid—because he thinks of
everything that could go wrong."

It was only natural that J.R. and Genene Jones would
develop a rapport. The byword of Robotham's style was
"aggressive." He taught the residents and nurses to look
for the tiny changes that marked impending disaster—the
twitch or the shift in respiration rate—then to move fast
to head off trouble. In Genene Jones, he saw a nurse
who personified that approach. "What he said was look
for the subtle signs," said Genene. *"Damn* aggressive.
He was extremely aggressive. And it was *great!"* If residents thought she overreacted, cried wolf, and woke
them up too much, Robotham thought she was often
right. When Pat Belko assigned another nurse to help
him insert a special catheter in a child, Robotham said he
wanted Genene instead. He told Belko he considered
Jones the best nurse in the ICU.

All her life, and especially since she had become a
nurse, Genene Jones had felt sure she knew the right way
to do things. Now she had two superiors—Belko and
Robotham—who felt that way about her too. After winning the medical director's confidence, Genene did not
hesitate to take full advantage of his respect. When she
got into a conflict with a resident, she would call J.R.,
knowing he would listen. "They used to call me Robotham's pet," said Genene. "To have him there was a
kind of protection for me."

Six

In NOVEMBER 1980, Genene Jones moved out of her mother's house and into an apartment of her own near Bexar County Hospital. Genene characterized the move as a personal declaration of independence. She was feeling increasingly secure about her place in the pediatric ICU; with Dr. Robotham's encouragement, she had even begun to talk about returning to school to earn her RN degree. But Genene also had a personal imperative for setting up house on her own. Gladys's relationship with Genene's son was rapidly becoming volatile.

Since beginning her career as a nurse, Genene had relied almost exclusively on her aging mother to care for Edward and Crystal. It was Gladys who was there when they came home from school, Gladys who prepared their dinner, Gladys who tucked them into bed. Genene was absent far more than the usual forty-hour week. She pulled countless extra shifts, went to work early, and often returned late. She seemed almost chronically incapable of separating herself from the hospital, as though she were the only one who could care properly for her ICU patients. She lavished less attention on her own kids.

While three-year-old Crystal was little trouble, Gladys was hard-pressed to keep up with Edward, who was nearly nine. Typical of kids raised by a grandmother, he was undisciplined. Frequently bored, he spent his free time roaming the neighborhood, where he had the habit of appearing in people's homes uninvited. When something turned up missing, neighbors would naturally think of Edward. Gladys did what she could to rein him in, but at sixty-nine, she lacked the strength to handle a rambunctious preadolescent. When Gladys yelled at him in frustration, Edward accused her of favoring Crystal. Like Genene during her own childhood, Edward was jealous of his sister.

The move to an apartment did not lighten Genene's load of personal woes. She continued to leave her kids with Gladys much of the time, and her own relations with Edward were equally poor. Genene accused him of lying to her, often about school, where he was getting into fights and stealing. Genene took Edward to a local guidance center for testing and psychological counseling. She complained that Edward never obeyed her instructions, causing her to feel inadequate and powerless, frustrated and angry. One day, Genene showed up at the ICU in tears, saying she'd just beaten up her son. At Dr. Robotham's request, Pat Belko temporarily shifted the LVN to the day shift to give her more time with her family.

Friends found Genene burdened by her work as well. She was dating Steve Seubert, a high school friend who had been an usher at her wedding. After her shift, they would meet at a bar called the Recovery Room, near the hospital. There, Seubert recalled, Genene emptied her heart. "She kept saying, 'The babies cry; they cry a lot.' She talked about the doctors making mistakes. A doctor made an assessment of one kid, and she said it wasn't right, and she talked to another doctor. She was saying she made the correct diagnosis, that she saved the babies."

Drawn compulsively to the hospital, Genene developed excuses to become a patient herself. During her first twenty-seven months of employment, Genene made thirty visits to the county's outpatient clinics or emergency rooms, where she presented an extraordinary assortment of complaints. She had diarrhea and cramps, vomiting, acute gastroenteritis, indigestion, belching, and "burning up" constipation. She felt shooting chest pains and dizziness. Her thumb was cut; her hands itched. She suffered from excessive menstrual bleeding and lack of menstrual bleeding. She had a sore throat; she experienced an allergic reaction to medication. Most of all, she experienced pain: neck pain, knee pain, abdominal pain, lower back pain.

On March 10, 1981, Genene was admitted to Bexar County Hospital with a puzzling set of symptoms, all duly noted by a doctor:

> The patient was in the usual state of health until September or October of 1980 when she noted difficulty walking up the hill from the parking lot to work. This progressed until she had to stop altogether and began parking in the handicapped parking lot. She could not manage the hill any longer and had cramping pains in the calves and thighs. . . . After several weeks of progressive difficulty . . . piano playing was prevented by cramping and weakness of all forearm muscles. The patient had difficulty blow-drying her hair. The patient also feels like she wants to sleep all the time. Has constant lack of energy. The patient denies emotional lability, early morning awakening, difficulty in falling asleep. . . . Denies chills or fever and denies weight loss or gain. [In fact, Genene had ballooned from 160 to more than 200 pounds.] Admits to sweating all the time, day and night. . . .

Assigned to the neurology service, Genene underwent a battery of tests to rule out nine different diseases. During a test cailed an EMG—a muscle study that involved insertion of an electrically charged needle in her leg—Genene became hysterical and refused to allow completion of the procedure; she returned to her room in tears. Later, she told nurses she had felt something pop in the back of her neck. On another occasion, she complained of breathing trouble. Unable to find a cause for the muscle pain and weakness that had brought her to the hospital, the neurologists sent Genene for a psychiatric consultation.

In relating her family history, Genene told the doctor that she had planned to marry the man who had fathered her daughter, but that he had died in an automobile accident. "The patient was obviously moved by this tragedy," the physician noted. "She is however able to talk about the grieving period for this loss and seems to have accepted it." The "tragedy" that "obviously moved" her— the death of Keith Martin—had, of course, never happened. The doctor concluded that Genene's personality exhibited "some hysterical features," but in general she was "more aware of her areas of psychologic conflict than most."

Unable to find any physical problem more serious than bronchitis—induced by a dozen years of smoking thirty cigarettes a day—doctors dismissed Genene after eight days of tests. She was back in the emergency room at 10 P.M. the next day, complaining of coughing spells, chills, blurred vision, and first sharp, then pounding, pains about the temples. An emergency room doctor took note of Jones's "tearful affect," diagnosed her problem as a migraine headache, and sent her home with medication.

For further study of her muscle problems, Genene was seen in the private clinic of Dr. Robert Schwartzman, chief of the hospital neurology service. After a thorough examination, Schwartzman reported his findings to Jim Robotham, who had been worried about the health problems of his ace LVN. "Careful muscle testing revealed no objective weakness," wrote Schwartzman. ". . . I am really not quite sure what the cause of her difficulty with her muscles is. I am beginning to think that it is not an objective one." Subsequent tests persuaded the neurologist that Genene Jones had fooled him. ". . . on my first two examinations, I was thoroughly convinced that she had real proximal weakness of both upper and lower extremities," Schwartzman later wrote Robotham. ". . . However after negative muscle enzymes . . . negative sed rate as well as a negative EMG and muscle biopsy, I felt that she had psychosomatic problems."

Thus was the stage set for a nightmare. A woman with a strange attraction to medicine, unable to distinguish between true illness and imagined calamity, is drawn to employment as a nurse. So powerful is her attraction that she needlessly subjects herself to invasive medical procedures. She is set loose in a hospital to care for the most helpless of human beings, where all the warning signs are ignored: her firing from Methodist Hospital, her history of telling lies, her on-the-job errors, her inability to admit mistakes, her unwillingness to follow orders, her exaggerated sense of her abilities, her need to be in control, her desperate craving for attention. For a while, Genene Jones would be satisfied to point out medical problems that didn't exist. It was only a matter of time before that would no longer be enough.

In a hospital, a medical emergency is called a code. In the pediatric ICU where Genene worked, it happened several times a month, and it was a frightening thing to watch: Someone was dying before your eyes.

A code usually began when a nurse noticed that a child's breathing or heart had stopped. The nurse would shout over to the nursing station in the center of the ICU. Whoever was closest pressed a small white emergency button, and an alarm went out across the pediatric floor, bringing doctors running. When a nurse believed there was a severe emergency, she called a code blue. An operator switched on the public-address system and announced, "Code blue to pedi ICU," throughout the hospital, summoning help from everywhere. ICU nurses rushed to the patient's bedside with the unit's "crash cart," loaded with emergency drugs and equipment. People began pouring through the ICU's double doors: doctors on the floor, nurses from the pediatric ward, respiratory therapists to handle resuscitation, pharmacists to draw up drugs, medical students. The patient's room filled with people. The doctors shouted orders; one of them would take command. Everything was happening fast.

In the middle of it all, performing CPR (cardio-pulmonary resuscitation) or injecting drugs, was the patient's nurse, the one who called the code in the first place. The code might last for several minutes, or—when a child's heart, like a sputtering motor, turned over but wouldn't quite start—it might last an hour. But in the center of the crisis, there was no consciousness of time. "You tune people out," said Genene Jones. "It's an incredible experience. Oh, shit, it's frightening. You're aware of everything, but you only tune in to two or three different people. . . . You really have to control your physical abilities, because you really get keyed up."

Most children who went through a code would die—either then or during another code later. The failed attempts to revive children, the codes that ended with a pronouncement of death, gave ICU nurses their most depressing moments. "You feel so helpless," said one RN. "It's like they just slip through your fingers. You try everything—and they just keep fading away."

When a child died in the pediatric ICU at Bexar County Hospital, his nurse had the responsibility of taking the body down to the hospital's morgue, a locked chamber in the basement known as the "cold room." Often, after a doctor pronounced the child dead, the parents wanted to hold him one last time, in which case the nurse first had to clean the body—wash off the blood and pluck out the catheters and tubes. When the parents were done, the nurse wrapped the body in a blanket or plastic shroud and summoned a security guard, who brought the key to the morgue. If the child was large, the nurse placed the body on a wheeled metal stretcher, known among staff as a "cold plate." If the patient was an infant, the nurse sometimes carried the corpse in her arms. Before the nurse left the pediatric ICU, the security guard walked down the long fifth-floor hallway, clearing the corridor and closing patients' doors so they would not witness the procession. The guard then walked with the nurse to a staff elevator that took them to the basement, and there he unlocked the morgue door. "Especially at night, it's very eerie down there," recalled one pediatric ICU nurse. "A lot of times, there would be patients who died during the day. Sometimes their bodies wouldn't be covered. You'd walk into the cold room, and you'd see blood dripping out of every possible opening. It's a creepy feeling."

The codes and trips to the cold room were the dark side of work in the pediatric ICU, the part that made a nurse, every few months, ponder whether she wanted to find a less difficult job. But Genene Jones seemed attracted to the dark side. By early 1981, she had begun asking for assignment to the sickest children. Many experienced nurses liked the challenge of a critical patient and sought it out from time to time. Genene did more. She *demanded* the sickest patients.

The charge nurse on each shift, always an RN, had responsibility for making patient assignments. Yet Genene was unwilling simply to take what she would get. If she considered a case boring, she would refuse to care for the child; she would sit in the patient's room and just rock in a chair. Often arriving early for her shift, Jones penciled in next to her name the room number of the child she wanted. Challenging Genene ran the risk of setting her off on an obscenity-spewing rampage; most preferred to let her have her way. "She pretty much made her own assignment," said one RN. "She was so strong she ran the shift like a charge nurse. She was just an LVN. She had no authority or power to do it, but she did it anyway."

Responsibility for the sickest children gave Genene patients who often had codes. But even when other nurses' patients had emergencies, Genene was involved. Anytime there was an arrest, Genene was there—in the middle and helpful. She seemed to thrive on the excitement. "If there was a crash in the unit," said a nurse who worked with Genene, "she'd climb over everyone to get there." CPR on a tiny child is vastly different from the pounding given adults during an arrest. A baby's fragile chest must be kneaded delicately, with the middle and index fingers from each hand, or it will snap like a frame of twigs. Burned in the memory of many ICU nurses was the image of Genene Jones performing compressions: her heaving, sweaty bulk hovering over a helpless infant.

When a child didn't make it, Genene broke down and cried. Nurses commonly shed tears over a longtime ICU patient, but Jones seemed deeply wounded by every death. She would ask the doctor who pronounced the child dead to wait a few moments before summoning the parents. Then she would pick up the body and rock it. Said one pediatric resident: "We all thought it was bordering on being a little pathologic."

After a death, Genene volunteered for the ghoulish task of taking the body to the cold room—even when it wasn't her patient. Other nurses wheeled all but infants down on a cold plate. But Genene would carry the corpse of a five-year-old boy in her arms. As she walked down the hospital hallway, resembling a grieving mother bear-

ing her child, the stiffened body protruded like a board
beneath its shroud.

Genene Jones had become the dominant force on the
ICU's 3–11 shift by exploiting a power vacuum. The
continuing shortage of nurses had grown dire by early
1981. To staff the ICU, Pat Belko had been forced to fill
the evening shift—which required about six nurses a
night—with newly graduated RNs and nurses from temporary agencies. The rookie nurses lacked experience,
and the skills of the agency nurses were unknown; Belko
chose not to move one of her veteran RNs from the day
shift. As a result, the 3–11 shift often lacked an experienced RN to serve as charge nurse.

While the new RNs took turns formally occupying that
role, Genene Jones took charge, telling others what to do
and claiming the sickest patients for herself. Genene
reasoned that she had no choice—that because she was
the most experienced nurse on the shift, it was her duty
to run the show. Genene saw herself as "charge nurse
incognito," and it was clear that she reveled in her de
facto authority. To experienced colleagues, she spoke
giddily of "me and my little RNs." On encountering an
older nurse in a hospital hallway, Genene sighed dramatically: "You know, it's hard being in charge all the time."

At first, the new RNs didn't mind Genene's usurpa-
tion. The pediatric ICU was an intimidating place, and
they had been thrown into the fray with little orientation.
Jones seemed solicitous and helpful, anxious to answer
their questions and teach them procedures. With their
hands full treating patients, they readily deferred to the
cocksure LVN.

Many of them even joined Genene on social occasions,
where they came to understand her reputation for saying
and doing the outrageous. For one nurse's bachelorette
party, they visited a San Antonio male-stripper bar called
La Bare. Genene announced to the group that she had
purchased each of them a man for the evening. (The
offer was declined.) On another night, they went kicker-
dancing at a country-and-western hall north of town.
Driving a load of nurses home, Genene took a scenic
detour around a lake, where she relived her drag-racing

days, burning rubber around the winding roads, barely dodging deer while her passengers held on for their lives. Spotting a man she admired, Genene would make a show of opening an extra button on her blouse. She publicly boasted of offering her sexual services to a doctor whose wife was pregnant. Despite all her heterosexual bravado, doubts about Genene's preferences lingered. During one night out with the girls, she scrawled a note on a paper napkin and slipped it privately to a friend, a female RN. It read: "My greatest fantasy is to have an affair with a woman." The nurse dodged what she interpreted as a sexual overture by telling Genene she couldn't read the message.

As they came to know Genene Jones better, the new RNs learned to depend on her less. As registered nurses, they had far more training than an LVN. When they gained the experience they needed, they stopped asking Genene questions. They were ready to claim their rightful place in charge of the evening shift.

But Genene wouldn't back off. "She was angry with us because we were not going to her for help," recalled Judy Cacciola, who started in January 1981. "If a patient came in, she wanted to assume the responsibility of making the assignment, doing what had to be done. I told her: 'We can handle this now.' She'd get angry and stalk off." Genene believed the newcomers were stabbing her in the back. Who were they to give her orders, merely because they were RNs? Hadn't she trained them? Influence and attention were slipping from her grasp. The nurses were like her son. They weren't listening to her anymore; they were making her feel ordinary and ineffectual. After all the hours that she had put in, all that she had sacrificed for the unit, she was on the verge of becoming just another LVN. She could not allow that to happen.

Seven

FOR DIANA AND Crecencio Hogeda, Jr., the sad news came by phone. It was not entirely unexpected. Their baby, Christopher James, barely a year old, had spent almost half his life in the hospital. Born with a severe heart defect, he had been admitted to the pediatric ICU with pneumonia and diarrhea in December 1980. In May, he developed hepatitis, and infection ravaged his body. The call had come from Christopher's nurse, Genene Jones, who had cared for him from the beginning, who seemed so sympathetic to their ordeal. "He's gone to play with the angels," Genene had informed them.

After gathering the clothes in which they planned to bury their son—Diana had crocheted a special blanket—the Hogedas climbed in their car and raced toward San Antonio. The Hogedas lived in the West Texas town of San Angelo, more than two hundred miles away; they had taken Chris to the big city, to Bexar County Hospital, to make sure that he received the best medical care available. Three hours later, their eyes wet with grief and fatigue, the Hogedas walked into the ICU to view baby's remains. They were stunned at what they saw: *Christopher was still alive!* He was lying quietly on his ICU bed, hooked up to the machines; everything was just as it had been for months. The Hogedas asked for Genene. The other ICU nurses told them that she had completed her shift and gone home.

Chris Hogeda was one of the children in whom Genene

Jones took a special interest. She insisted on caring for him herself, day after day, for weeks. It was during this time that Genene, never one to lavish time on her own children, stopped showing up for counseling appointments with Edward. It was as though she had transferred her maternal affections from her own children—one of whom gave her trouble—to surrogate offspring who were totally under her control. "He was *my* boy," she said later of Chris Hogeda.

On May 14, 1981, Genene left Chris's room a little after 11P.M. to report his condition to the next shift. The baby's health was so poor that no one expected him to live long; he had been experiencing unusual episodes of irregular heartbeat. But the nurses had grown weary of Genene's regular predictions of his demise. "Tonight's the night," she would announce.

As the nurses were giving report in the ICU's break room, they heard a crash. Genene rushed out and shrieked; the child with the delicate heart condition was dangling from his bed, suspended by respirator tubing and arm restraints. Genene had left Chris's bed rails down, and he had rolled out. She returned the child—apparently unhurt—to bed. Genene later recounted what had happened to nurses who were off that day with a laugh. The LVN received another written scolding for the incident, but she continued to treat the child. When Chris Hogeda died of cardiac arrest a week later, he was under Genene's care.

Summoned for good cause this time, Chris's parents asked Genene to remain with their son until they arrived. She pulled the plastic tubes out of the body and washed it, crying and talking out loud all the while. "I would bathe the children, and I would sing to them while I bathed them," Genene later explained. "If that sounds insane, tough shit. If you can't die with dignity, why live with dignity?" She paused. "We talked to them even after death. We're not God. We don't know when the spirit leaves the body." After cleaning Chris Hogeda, Genene wrapped his body in a blanket. Then she settled into a chair and held the corpse to her chest for more than an hour while she waited for his parents to arrive.

Diana and Crecencio Hogeda were unaware of some of

Genene's offenses in the treatment of their son, and forgiving of the rest. On the day Chris Hogeda was buried, Genene Jones was a welcome guest at his funeral.

The death of Christopher Hogeda marked the beginning. Over the next four months, the pediatric ICU began to experience a rash of strange events and unexpected emergencies. Kids who seemed stable suddenly stopped breathing. They had seizures. Their hearts halted—or started beating irregularly. Babies pricked with intravenous needles began oozing blood, their clotting mechanisms inexplicably gone haywire. Some of the children, like Chris Hogeda, were terribly sick and expected to die; but what befell them defied explanation.

Terry Lynn Garcia was among the victims. Admitted to the hospital at three weeks of age for diarrhea and vomiting, she entered the pediatric ICU a month later after developing fever and appearing lethargic. On the night of her transfer, Terry Lynn had three episodes of abnormally slow heartbeat, called bradycardia, before her heart stopped entirely. Doctors revived her, but she arrested again the next evening and was barely rescued with drugs, two jolts of electric shock, and ninety minutes of CPR. The next day she started bleeding, and her blood pressure plummeted. She developed breathing problems that required a respirator. After two more arrests, she died at 6:15 P.M. on August 11.

Patricia Sambrano, three months old, entered the ICU two days after Terry Lynn's death. Hospitalized after going into seizures following a routine inoculation, she arrived at 7 P.M. in the unit, where she was placed on a respirator and under Genene Jones's care. Patricia arrested that evening, but doctors revived her. Nurses on the next two shifts noted no seizures and described the girl's condition as stable. Back on duty, Genene reported seizures that were worsening at 5:30 P.M. The child soon arrested, and doctors saved her again. After a third arrest, she died at 9:36 P.M. on August 14.

Four-month-old Paul Villarreal died in late September. Taken to surgery for an elective procedure on his skull, he returned to the pediatric ICU to recover and instead went downhill fast. A day after the operation, following a seizure, doctors hooked the baby to a respirator. Blood began pouring out of a tube placed down his throat. He arrested but was revived. The next night Paul began oozing again; he arrested and died at 8:30 P.M. Lab tests showed his bleeding was caused by problems with his clotting mechanism.

Twice, doctors discovered patients' respirators improperly set. At 11 P.M. one night, two-year-old Rosemary Vega, recovering from a routine heart operation, suffered a seizure and became sluggish after being placed on a respirator. At 2:15 A.M., a surgery resident noticed that Rosemary's breathing machine was feeding her too little oxygen. ". . . Ventilator setting had been altered by unknown source . . ." one physician noted. Rosemary died at 7:52 P.M. that day. Four-month-old Placida Ybarra had entered the ICU for treatment of heart failure. At 7:20 P.M. on the day of her admission, it was discovered that her respirator was pouring out 100 percent oxygen—a dangerously rich concentration, which can throw the blood chemistry out of balance. On her fifth day in the hospital, Placida unexpectedly went limp, and her heartbeat began to race; she died at 10:25 P.M.

Too many babies were dying in the ICU—dying of problems that shouldn't have been fatal, problems that patients had been able to lick in the past. Other kids would recover—but only after experiencing unexpected problems. Doctors covering the pediatric ICU were accustomed to handling three or four resuscitations a month. There were nine CPRs in August 1981, thirteen in September. The residents wondered what was happening.

The frantic search for answers began with explanations that were benign. Was there some mysterious germ in the air? A San Antonio strain of Legionnaires' disease? Perhaps a new type of meningitis? Doctors wondered if the ICU's medical equipment had become contaminated. Or was it just a run of bad luck? As the emergencies became more frequent, a less innocent pattern emerged. The children were dying during a single nursing shift—the 3–11 evening shift. And they were dying under the care of a single nurse. *They were dying on Genene.*

One child arrested on three consecutive days—in each case on the 3–11 shift, in each case on Genene. "I'd leave a patient I thought was stable," said Toni Grosshaupt, an RN. "She'd come on, and I'd find out the patient had a bad spell—had seizures or codes. That happened consistently. It just got to the point where I hated to come back the next day."

As codes and death became more common, a job that was naturally difficult became almost unbearable. The unit was already short-staffed; everyone was working extra. Concerned about the growing pressure, Dr. Robotham had arranged for a psychiatrist to visit regularly with the staff in the ICU. Genene's predictions of medical catastrophe were becoming eerily accurate. When the LVN announced during report that a baby would die, other nurses set up emergency medications at the patient's bedside in *anticipation* of the arrest.

The burden was greatest on those who worked with Genene on the 3–11 shift, where all the emergencies were taking place. On one particularly dark night, they had two codes going at once; the doctors and nurses stabilized the first baby, moved to the second child, who died, then had to return to the first patient, who was suffering a second arrest, which would prove fatal. "It was getting too stressful," said Judy Cacciola. "I was depressed a lot of the time. It was just very frustrating to go in, work our tails off, and have all those kids dying around us. After a while, the codes almost became a joke. I had to get out of there." Cacciola quit in September, after nine months in the ICU.

Genene herself seemed devastated by the rash of deaths and near deaths. "They're going to start thinking I'm the Death Nurse because I'm always taking these babies downstairs," she told one resident. In September, another of her patients died, and Genene fell into a chair in a corner of the unit and broke into tears. A young female doctor walked over to comfort her, and Genene looked up, her eyes red and puffy. "Why do babies always die when I'm around?" she asked.

Many who worked in the pediatric ICU at Bexar County Hospital were asking the same question. Around cafeteria tables and in hallways, a growing number of people who suspected something was terribly wrong began calling Genene's hours on duty the Death Shift.

*   *   *

Pat Belko, of course, had heard the ugly whispers about Genene. She considered it vicious gossip. Belko knew that the nurses who were talking the most didn't like the LVN. Besides, their scenario was unthinkable: Nurses didn't kill babies. The notion was particularly discordant with Belko's high opinion of Genene. She seemed to care so much for the children and get along so well with their families; it just didn't fit that she would do anything to harm them. Sure, Genene was abrasive. She was even a bit odd; Pat had seen her hold a child's corpse up to a window, as if offering the body to the heavens. But Pat continued to regard Genene as an outstanding nurse. When she completed the LVN's annual performance evaluation—on September 15, when suspicions were already widespread—Pat gave her uniformly high marks. "Ms. Jones has continued to provide excellent patient care and support to families," the head nurse reported. "Her assistance in orienting new employees has been invaluable."

Pat Belko's defense of her nurse went far beyond passive skepticism. She became angry. She believed the other nurses were smearing Genene's reputation, persecuting her without cause. She knew Genene's accusers had no proof. Belko told them to document their suspicions or shut up. She threatened to discipline anyone who kept talking about Genene's harming children. The vehemence of Belko's sentiments surprised her subordinates, who had never known Pat as a woman of strong opinions. But they were unaware that their boss had personal cause to sympathize with a nurse under suspicion of killing a baby.

Her reason dated back a decade, to December of 1971, Pat's first year on the night shift in the pediatric ICU. One of the unit's patients was a sixteen-month-old baby with Down's syndrome, a collection of severe birth defects. San Juanita Ybarra came from Hondo, a hamlet thirty miles west of San Antonio. She had arrived at the hospital suffering from pneumonia and heart failure. She died at 7 A.M. on Sunday, December 5.

The physician on duty in the ICU wrote in the child's medical chart that the baby had been killed by an accidental overdose of digoxin, a powerful drug that slows the heartbeat, administered six hours earlier. A nurse had given the child .45 milligrams of the drug, ten times the amount on the doctor's written order. Hospital administrators summoned police, and the episode soon made the papers. The RN, who admitted misreading the order, was suspended pending investigation.

An impartial doctor's inquiry, completed a few days later, proved inconclusive. The physician attributed the baby's death to pneumonia, while adding that the overdose "may have contributed." Whatever the actual impact of the error, there was never any suggestion that it was anything but an honest mistake—the sort to which no nurse or doctor is immune. The RN was reinstated and went on to become head nurse in the pediatric ICU. But Pat Belko long remembered the horror of being blamed for the death of a helpless child.

Suzanna Maldonado had heard the head nurse's demands for evidence and set about meeting her challenge. A twenty-five-year-old RN, Maldonado had worked for two years on the ICU's night shift, where suspicions of Genene were high. In her early months at the hospital, Suzanna was friendly with the LVN; they had gone on a river outing together, and Maldonado had cared for Genene's daughter, Crystal, who had been hospitalized briefly for an accidental overdose of Tylenol. But soon the relationship turned to one of bitter rivalry. A slender, dark-haired woman, Suzanna had grown up on San Antonio's West Side, the sheltered and dutiful daughter of working-class Hispanics. Still unmarried, she lived with her mother. Genene considered Malonado a spoiled child—and thought herself a better nurse. Suzanna regarded Jones as an overaggressive LVN who failed to recognize her limitations.

When children started dying in unlikely numbers on the 3–11 shift, Maldonado was quick to wonder. If the kids were truly that sick, why did they always die on Genene? Why didn't they die on someone else? Suzanna began making a point of caring for Genene's patients when she came on duty at 11 P.M. She reviewed Jones's nursing notes. She began studying the ICU's patient register, the record of what had happened to children treated in the unit. She even compiled a death list—a diary of all the children who had died since January 1981, showing the time each had expired.

One morning in October, after finishing up the overnight nursing shift, Suzanna Maldonado stepped into the office of her boss. Pat Belko could not have been pleased to see her—Suzanna was not one of her favorites—and she was even less pleased when she found out what Maldonado had on her mind. Nervous but determined, Suzanna bluntly stated the suspicions that the nurses had long discussed among themselves. Belko jumped to scold; accusations like that shouldn't be made lightly. But Maldonado wasn't through. She explained that she had researched the records of patient deaths, that she knew just how many children had died on Genene's shift. "It looks bad," she told Belko.

Belko was shaken by what she heard. For the first time, one of the nurses had presented the sort of information it was impossible for her to ignore. After sending Maldonado from her office, the head nurse walked the length of the fifth-floor corridor to the pediatric ICU. She went to the nursing station, pulled out the unit's patient register, and flipped through it. Maldonado had done her homework; her numbers were correct. Dr. Robotham was in the ICU, finishing up his seven-thirty rounds. Belko asked to speak with him, and the two of them walked back to her office. She told Robotham what she had learned, and they agreed: There would have to be an investigation.

Eight

JOSE ANTONIO FLORES, six months and three days old, met a horrible end on the afternoon of October 10. His final code seemed to last an eternity. Unable to understand why Jose was dying, doctors tried for almost an hour to save him, as blood puddled beneath his body. The baby had entered Bexar County Hospital only four days earlier, suffering from a common set of pediatric problems: fever, vomiting, diarrhea, and dehydration. When he developed seizures during his third day on the pediatric ward, he was taken to the hospital basement for a brain scan, in the company of Genene Jones. He went into cardiac arrest while he was there. Doctors revived the baby and rushed him back to the pediatric ICU, where they noticed he was bleeding. Blood samples sent for tests showed Jose's clotting mechanism wasn't working. The problem cleared overnight. The next day, the child experienced more seizures and bleeding, before his heart stopped once again. He died at 5:22 P.M. On Jose Flores's death certificate, a resident blamed the bleeding for his fatal cardiac arrest. The doctor noted that the cause of the bleeding was unknown.

The events following the baby's demise were as peculiar as those that produced it. When a doctor informed Jose's family that he had died, the infant's father clutched his chest in pain. Genene led the stricken man, accompanied by a half-dozen relatives, to the emergency room—and permitted the baby's brother to carry Jose's *corpse* along too. Assigned to take the body to the morgue, Genene suddenly decided outside the ER to reclaim her dead patient. Without warning, she snatched the bundle from Jose's brother, gathered the body in her arms, and took off down a hospital corridor, with the child's relatives close behind. The bizarre chase ended when Genene lost her pursuers in the bowels of the hospital and made her way to the morgue.

There was never any question that it was Dr. Robotham who would investigate. Bexar County Hospital's nursing department certainly had no interest. After dutifully reporting Maldonado's suspicions to the medical director, Pat Belko told her boss, Judy Harris, the hospital's nursing supervisor over the area including pediatrics. The two women agreed there was nothing to worry about. The unit just seemed to be getting sicker children. Genene cared for the worst of them; it was natural that they would die in greater numbers under her care. Harris then took the problem to *her* boss: Virginia Mousseau, the hospital's assistant executive director and its top nursing administrator.

Mousseau, fifty-five, was a native of Minnesota with a degree in nursing administration. After being hired in 1979, she began convening monthly nursing management meetings, where there was much earnest talk about developing leadership skills and setting goals. Among her innovations was a requirement for new nurses to wear a tag reading: "I'm new here, please help me to learn." Mousseau was in the habit of establishing ad hoc committees to deal with problems. Said a former hospital supervisor: "Virginia could spot more problems and solve fewer than anybody I met in my life." After hearing of accusations that a nurse was killing children, Mousseau advised Harris and Belko to make sure that hospital procedures were being followed. She ordered no other action.

Jim Robotham similarly had taken the matter to his boss: Dr. Robert Franks, the acting chairman of the pediatrics department at UT. Franks had inherited the job in July, after conflicts with the faculty prompted the previous chairman to step down. At forty-seven, he was the classic caretaker. A veteran of thirteen years at the

medical school, Bob Franks was well liked by his colleagues and had no desire to keep the chair himself. Born
in Fort Worth, he spoke slowly and softly. His field of
pediatric endocrinology—the study of glands and their
secretions—possessed none of the drama of intensive care.

When Robotham brought the suspicions about the ICU
to his attention, Franks was naturally skeptical. But
Robotham wanted to investigate. The medical director
had long shared Pat Belko's high regard for Genene
Jones as a nurse. But he had sensed for several months
that something was wrong in the ICU. He had grown
concerned about Genene's personal behavior and the
conflicts among the staff. And he was puzzled by some of
the deaths. For a while, Robotham had figured that
mistakes by some of his residents and the spotty nursing
staff were to blame. But there were problems that mere
sloppiness couldn't explain. After Maldonado complained
to Belko, Robotham became determined to find out what
was going on. Franks told him to go ahead.

From the beginning, Dr. Robotham worried about heparin. Several children, like Jose Flores, had developed
bleeding problems in the ICU. Blood would leak from
old needle punctures, ooze out of suture sites, their mouths,
even their rectums, until finally their blood pressure would
drop, straining their hearts until they stopped. Doctors
had been diagnosing the bleeding as symptomatic of dis-
seminated intravascular coagulation (DIC), a relatively
rare condition often caused by severe infection, which
can set off a reaction that keeps blood from clotting. But
there seemed to be too many cases. The problem had
never cropped up with such frequency before.

There was one other possibility: heparin, an anticoagulant drug that doctors and nurses used every hour in the
ICU; a small amount kept IV and arterial lines from
clotting with blood. Was someone giving the children too
much? Or could there be a more innocent—though equally
deadly—explanation: Was it possible the drug company
had made the heparin too strong? Robotham had other
worries. Several children, like Chris Hogeda, had experienced arrhythmia, a sudden quickening or slowing of the
heartbeat, which doctors usually see only in adults. Injec-

tion of digitalis could explain it. Still other children became lethargic. Robotham wondered about Valium.

The medical director, of course, was aware of the worst suspicions about Genene. But murder was only one unlikely diagnosis on his list. As a scientist, Robotham intended to examine all the possibilities—to look for the zebras, as he advised his residents. Even a presumption of deliberate misconduct didn't necessarily point to Genene. The LVN had no shortage of enemies; as crazy as this whole business was, it was entirely plausible, figured Robotham, that someone was setting her up.

On October 15, Albert Garza, three months old, arrived in the ICU. A victim of Down's syndrome, Albert had been recuperating from dehydration, diarrhea, and a chemical imbalance called acidosis, when he had an unexplained bleeding episode during the 3–11 P.M. shift. Two residents treating the child—Larry Hooghuis and Wayne Yee—knew there were worries about heparin. When they next took overnight call, on October 17, they alternated sitting by the baby's bedside for hours, conspicuously standing guard. A skinny, strong-willed Yankee, Hooghuis was one of the residents who got along badly with Genene Jones. He knew it seemed crazy, but his patients seemed to go downhill when his relations with the LVN were at their worst. Midway through the evening, Hooghuis and Yee were called from the ICU to check out a patient on the floor. Albert's nurse, Genene Jones, summoned them back a few minutes later; the baby's blood wasn't clotting.

Yee quickly drew a sample and mixed two drops with protamine sulfate, a drug that counteracts the effect of heparin. Albert's blood clotted, suggesting that he had received too much anticoagulant. Hooghuis then noticed that Genene was preparing to clear an arterial line into the child's body with a diluted solution of heparin. Hooghuis asked her how much heparin she was using. Astonished at her answer, he told the LVN to repeat what she had said. Genene's concentration was 333 units per cubic centimeter of fluid. The proper dosage was less than *one* unit; Jones was about to give Albert a massive overdose before their eyes. When the nurse disputed his numbers, Hooghuis grabbed a piece of the baby's bed sheet and scribbled out his calculation. Genene muttered and stalked off. Albert's bleeding did not recur.

The next morning, Robotham told Pat Belko—who explained the episode as an innocent miscalculation—that he wanted heparin handled more carefully. He first reduced the concentration of the anticoagulant to be used in arterial lines. Each nurse was told that she had to have a second nurse watch whenever she drew heparin from its container. Both nurses would have to initial the bottle to show who had conducted and witnessed the procedure. Robotham also began a full-scale effort to separate true DIC cases from possible heparin overdoses. Establishing an overdose of heparin or some other drug would require extensive laboratory tests. Robotham ordered the pediatrics residents to draw and send to the lab extra blood samples whenever a child unexpectedly soured.

The nurses in the pediatric ICU weren't told why doctors were suddenly ordering an assortment of unusual lab tests. But after the first couple of times it happened, they realized there was an investigation. Many were upset; Robotham's measures placed everyone under suspicion. The ICU's lines of division hardened. Some nurses and doctors believed there was nothing wrong, that J.R. was overreacting, making much ado about nothing. Residents who had experienced no problems with Genene continued to trust her. Some were so friendly that she cut their hair in the ICU's back room.

But others openly wondered whether she was trying to preserve life or to end it. One evening, she was caring for a boy who had nearly drowned in a hot tub. When the patient arrested, Genene implored the residents running the code to give up. "Why don't we let this child die?" she demanded. "He doesn't have any brain left. Why don't we let this child die?" The patient's father asked the doctors to keep the boy on life-sustaining equipment until morning to allow the boy's mother a little more time to prepare herself for his death. One of the doctors returned to the ICU and carefully explained the family's request. Suddenly the boy went into seizures and arrested again. "She continued to badger us during the code," recalled the resident. "She gave the drugs, but she kept on badgering: 'Why are we doing this? Why are we continuing to support this child?' It was just the nagging; you wanted to go, 'Shut up and leave us alone!' "

More than one resident had caught Genene in a lie. Cheryl Cipriani's experience came when Jones issued an urgent call for the doctor to return to the bedside of one of her patients. When Cipriani arrived, Genene handed her a filled syringe. "You need to push this," she declared. The nurse said it was a sugar solution, that she had just tested the baby's blood sugar and it was dangerously low. The doctor was puzzled. There was no reason for the child to be hypoglycemic. Cipriani ran the simple sugar test herself, and it read normal.

Even those who were most suspicious handled the LVN gingerly, aware that Genene responded to confrontation by trying to prove herself right. Dr. Hooghuis's obervation had become accepted wisdom among the residents: Kids did worse in the ICU when their doctors took her on.

Genene blamed the residents. She complained often that they were slow to arrive when she summoned them. Somebody ought to investigate, somebody from outside, Jones loudly declared. In October, there were eight codes—all of them on Genene's patients. Posing as the voice of experience, the LVN offered her own explanation for the pattern of arrests. She told the younger nurses that the 3–11 shift had always been the busiest— that children just seemed to *pick* those hours to die.

As the ICU grew more chaotic, Genene's insubordination grew more brazen. When a child arrested in October, Genene directed a new male RN to handle the code. To the charge nurse's query as to why she was issuing commands, Genene said Pat Belko had ordered the arrangement to give the new RN experience. The charge nurse learned later that Belko had never issued such a directive. On another occasion, Genene clocked out of the ICU an hour early without permission. The charge nurse on her shift was unaware she had even left. "This offense could be grounds for suspension and discharge," noted Belko, in yet another incident report. But Pat merely issued Jones another "final" warning.

Even the head nurse, Genene's benefactor, experienced her insubordination. A day after directing Genene to restock the ICU's formula cabinet, Pat discovered the task was not done. "I asked why you didn't do it," Belko wrote, in her report of the incident. "You stated you hadn't heard me. At the time I made the request, you and I had been talking to each other face to face." Even for so personal an act of defiance, even after so much, Belko handled Genene as if it were her first offense. "I am concerned that you decided not to do the task as requested and want you to realize that deliberate failure to follow a supervisor's orders can be construed as industrial insubordination," Pat wrote. "You and I have previously discussed the need for an improvement in cooperation." The head nurse construed kindly; she took no disciplinary action. Genene continued to act with impunity.

During the same period, Jones's visits to the hospital and clinic for personal health complaints became more frequent. Between June and December of 1981, Genene sought medical treatment sixteen times. She was hospitalized four times. In August, she appeared in the emergency room, complaining of chest pains and dizziness, but left before being seen by a doctor. She returned two days later for stabbing pains she likened to a sharp needle in her chest. A doctor found no evidence of heart trouble and attributed her complaint to muscle spasm or depression. But Genene did not accept that conclusion; ICU nurses informed Belko that Genene was medicating herself with nitroglycerin. Three months later, she was admitted for constipation, cramping, and nausea. During four days in the hospital, she complained of several symptoms that doctors could not explain. Genene took herself off oxygen—"states she doesn't need it anymore," nurses noted—and refused to take the drugs her doctors had prescribed. She claimed she had vomited, but a ward nurse made a point of reporting that she saw no evidence. Genene spent much of her hospital stay smoking cigarettes and entertaining visitors from the ICU. Three weeks later, she was admitted again. Complaining of severe abdominal cramps and nausea—the textbook signs of a small-bowel obstruction—she went to the surgery service for observation. Genene underwent a battery of tests; she was wheeled into the x-ray room on a stretcher. When three days of studies revealed nothing, doctors discharged her, concluding that the problem had resolved itself.

During Genene's seventeen days as a patient in Bexar County Hospital, not a single child died in the pediatric ICU.

After his initial visit from Robotham, Dr. Franks had heard complaints from other faculty about unexpected deaths in the pediatric ICU. Franks asked Robotham to determine the number of children who had died in recent months. J.R. reported back that there had been eleven since midsummer—all on the 3–11 shift. Franks ordered his secretary to pull the medical charts and asked Robotham to study them closely.

Despite the extraordinary bunching of deaths on a single shift, the acting chairman remained skeptical that anything criminal was going on. In private notes he began keeping in order to maintain a factual record, Franks detailed his personal doubts. "From the outset, and to the present time, I have no evidence—circumstantial or objective—that there is a 'problem,' i.e. negligence of omission or commission. However, because the concern was expressed and the possibilities existed, I have thought it prudent to proceed with an evaluation of the possibilities." The nursing administrators had fretted that the entire stew was the product of personality conflict—that Genene Jones was being victimized by her enemies in the ICU. Franks echoed that concern, noting that he had directed Robotham to conduct his investigation "without appearance of a 'witch-hunt.' "

All the same, Franks considered the matter too hot to handle himself. This wasn't the sort of headache he had expected when he accepted the job as acting chairman. On November 10, 1981, Franks took the problem to B. H. Corum, the hospital district's new top administrator.

Lieutenant Colonel Buford Hubert Corum, Jr., USAF (ret.), was the sort of man who believed in the power of fear. A short time after his appointment as executive director of the Bexar County Hospital District, Corum slipped into the hospital's administrative suite through a back door. Discovering several employees laughing and

joking at their desks, he marched up to them, face flushed
and jaw set. "Do you know who I am?" he demanded.
They did not. "By God," Corum roared, "you're going
to find out."

Corum had taken over the $58,000-a-year post in Au-
gust, fresh from a quarter century of air force spit and
polish. He grew up in small-town Alabama, attended college at Auburn, and enlisted at twenty-one. Degrees in
pharmacy, hospital administration, and management pro-
pelled him into a career in the bureaucracy of military
hospitals. Most recently, he had served as administrator
of Wilford Hall Medical Center, a giant air force complex
in San Antonio. Corum was six feet two and a swarthy
195 pounds. He wore a small mustache and metal glasses,
and his shrinking allotment of hair stood in a tuft above
his forehead. At forty-seven, he was married, the father
of one daughter, and a deacon at his Baptist church. He
smoked short cigars.

Corum arrived at Bexar County Hospital determined
to shape the place up, and he didn't appear to mind
bullying subordinates in order to do it. He inspected his
command daily with a clipboard-carrying aide in tow, and
when he found something amiss, he chewed out employees in public. Popping in at night, he startled lounging
janitors with a sharp kick at their feet and sharper words
of warning: "I write your check, you SOB!"

A man of towering ego, Corum once arranged to be
introduced at a gathering of hospital administrators to
the musical theme from *Star Wars*. He made it known he
expected to be secretary of the U.S. Department of Health,
Education, and Welfare within a decade. Corum labored
to cut costs at the county hospital, but his efforts occasionally revealed a Queeg-like obsession with minutiae.
At one meeting, he berated a group of deputies for
failing to monitor the use of paper clips. Physicians chuck-
led at his fondness for being grandly addressed as "Doctor"—Corum had a Ph.D.—while making rounds in a
short white lab coat, the sort worn by lowly interns. But
employees bearing a grievance rarely found any humor in
what Corum told many of them: "If you don't like what
I'm doing, hit the door!"

Within the hospital Corum's hubris spawned legends.

One widely circulated story concerned a meeting he was said to have held with Sister Angela Clare, the Catholic nun who ran the downtown Santa Rosa hospital. Sister Clare had called the session to warn that the number of indigent patients falling on Santa Rosa's shoulders jeopardized the institution's survival. "Sister," Corum is said to have interrupted, "you mistake me for someone who gives a shit about Santa Rosa's survival."

Yet there were many who felt that B. H. Corum was just the man for the job, that a few swift kicks a day were precisely what the county hospital needed. The last permanent administrator had ended his eleven-year tenure in 1980, after presiding over cutbacks that set the UT doctors to revolt. So harsh were the reductions, so desperate the need for more staff and new equipment, that the medical school dean publicly branded the twelve-year-old hospital "inadequate." Hoping to calm the doctors, the hospital board filled the vacancy with a popular figure from the medical school, Dr. Charles E. Gibbs, an obstetrician-gynecologist. Filling the post on an interim basis for eighteen months, Gibbs persuaded the county commissioners to raise hospital taxes for the first time in years and raised money through better debt collection. With a slight loosening of the purse strings, Gibbs started upgrading the hospital's physical appearance and capital equipment; his mere presence boosted morale. But much remained undone. The board asked Gibbs to accept the job on a permanent basis, but he declined.

Corum was less reluctant. When the hospital announced its search for a permanent executive director, he appeared in Gibbs's office, pressing for details about the job. Gibbs urged the board to pick a doctor; after all, the hospital's basic task was patient care. But the board was unwilling to spend the extra $30,000 a physician-administrator would require. At the end of a six-month search, B. H. Corum got the nod. In his first public pronouncement, the new executive director made clear his intentions. He said he planned to run a tight ship and added: "I think I'm the man for the job."

Corum knew money was the key to ensuring the happiness of the hospital's three most sensitive constituencies: the UT doctors, hospital employees, and the Bexar County

commissioners. If he couldn't get enough public money
to run the hospital properly, he would go after private
funds—through private patients and private gifts. The
problem with that idea was that which had dogged Bexar
County Hospital since its opening: Those who could afford to do so almost always chose to go elsewhere.

Burdened by the image of his hospital as an under-
funded, overutilized public institution for the poor—in
short, burdened by reality—Corum was determined to
refashion public perceptions. Attracting private money
just required *marketing*—shedding the dismal charity-hos-
pital rap, promoting the place instead as a bustling, world-
class medical center. Corum decided to start by changing
the hospital's name; he was eager to banish the word
"county," with all its down-at-the-mouth connotations.
After pondering such possibilities as Citizens Hospital
and University Hospital, Corum in late October persuaded the board to rechristen the institution Medical
Center Hospital. Corum also laid plans to open a private
ward on the hospital's twelfth floor, where paying patients could receive care without rubbing elbows with the
unwashed. He started recruiting a special development
board, led by wealthy businessmen, to raise funds. And
he launched an aggressive public relations campaign, promoting all the changes under the slogan "New Horizons."

Thus, when Dr. Franks phoned Corum on November
10, raising the possibility that someone was killing children in his hospital, the administrator might have thought
about how such a situation—if it was true—threatened
more tiny lives every day. But B. H. Corum would likely
have thought about other considerations too: about how
calling the police or the district attorney would doubtless
make the whole matter public, about the unprecedented
scandal that would produce, and about how such a tem-
pest would jeopardize everything he wanted to accomplish.

After receiving Franks's call, Corum summoned his
young deputy, associate executive director John Guest,
and his top nursing administrator, Virginia Mousseau.
Guest wrote personal notes one day later, summarizing
the meeting: "Dr. Corum indicated a call from Dr. Bob
Franks that day. Dr. Franks concerned with # of deaths
in PICU particularly on 3–11 shift. . . . Ms. Mousseau

indicated one LVN is suspected of some involvement. Discussed concerns about Robotham getting out of hand with suspicions and emotions. Discussed control of those who know about problem. Potential need for outside investigation."

After exploring what was known about the possibility that a nurse was harming children, after hashing over the suggestion that the ICU's medical director was *over-reacting*, B. H. Corum decided that the situation required no special action on his part. If Franks wasn't sure there was a problem, why should *he* assume there was one? Corum delegated Guest to keep informed about the pediatricians' investigation. The executive director was preoccupied with other matters. His hospital had a new image to establish.

Nine

JIM ROBOTHAM WAS beginning to wonder if everyone thought he was crazy. Franks seemed to be humoring him, nursing thought he was on a witch hunt, and the hospital administration wouldn't get involved. Robotham's scrutiny of the ICU's medical charts had left him deeply unsettled. He had discovered a worrisome number of episodes where something had happened that he couldn't explain—and a nagging correlation between such events and the presence of Genene Jones.

In a confidential five-page memo to Franks, Robotham reviewed nine individual cases, documenting emergencies that were either unexpected or inconsistent with a child's illness. Several patients had experienced bleeding or other problems only under Jones's care. The special lab tests Robotham had ordered gave him more cause for alarm. A staff hematologist who tested the blood of Jose Flores— the child whose body Genene had carried on the madcap chase through the hospital—"felt the most likely diagnosis, though one which could not be confirmed to explain the bleeding, was an overdose of heparin," Robotham noted. In another case, the blood expert considered too much heparin "the most likely possibility."

Even after reading Robotham's report, Dr. Franks remained skeptical of his suspicions. "Although there are recurrent, pointed references to a particular nurse, I do not perceive a constant 'thread' which suggests misadventure," reported Franks on December 3, in another note for his private files. "I have previously discussed with Jim my concern that he has without basis prospectively identified a culprit; the report, in my view, contains conscious or subconscious expression of that view. I do not believe it substantiated by the attached." Franks informed John Guest that the chart review had turned up nothing. "This is the end of it," Franks declared.

But Robotham wouldn't give up. He had searched for other answers—and ruled them out, one by one. Could the drug company have made the heparin too strong? Robotham had sent unopened samples down to the lab; they were normal. Was there something contaminating the medical equipment? Robotham had sent intravenous bottles and tubing to be tested for bacteria; nothing was in them. Could the heparin problems result from honest nursing mistakes? Robotham knew medication errors were common in hospitals, but he had issued countless directives about the use of heparin. More mistakes seemed unlikely.

Still the awful pattern went on. Children in the pediatric ICU continued to suffer—and sometimes to die—from unexplained medical problems. Robotham's chairman and the nursing administrators—Belko, Harris, and Mousseau—were all demanding that he produce proof. They would take no action without it. *But there was no proof of anything.* Night after night, Robotham would go home to his family and lie awake in bed, wondering.

To Patricia Alberti, there was no question: Genene Jones was killing kids. A thirty-nine-year-old former army medic, Alberti was an LVN on the night shift, with seven years of experience in pediatric ICUs. Alberti had listened for weeks as the terrified young nurses on the 3–11 shift spoke of the increasing number of codes. Like Suzanna Maldonado, she had made a point of caring for Genene's patients. She had come to know the frustration of arriving for work to discover that her patient's bed was empty. "I struggled with it for eight hours, and the kid was still alive. Day shift had it for eight hours, and the kid was alive. [Genene] came in for three hours, and the kid was dead."

A native of North Carolina, Alberti was a tall, lean woman who voiced her convictions bluntly and clung to them with tenacity. Belko's threats of discipline were not about to shut her up. On two occasions, parents had informed Alberti that Genene claimed to have taken their critically ill children off a respirator—something only doctors may do. Alberti had reported the remarks to Belko, but the head nurse attributed them to misunderstandings. To the nurses, nothing they said about Genene seemed to make a difference. They felt as though they were watching a disaster unfold—and were helpless to do anything about it. While Robotham continued his search for answers, some nurses contemplated tipping off a local newspaper columnist. Pat Alberti would turn to her psychiatrist, a doctor from the UT medical school. A nurse was killing babies with drugs, she declared, and nothing was being done.

On December 8, Joshua Sawyer arrived in the pediatric ICU. Eleven months old, Joshua was suffering from severe smoke inhalation after being rescued from a fire at his family's home. He came to the ICU in a coma and covered with soot; transferred from another hospital, he had already experienced seizures and one arrest. Doctors in the ICU ordered sedative drugs—Dilantin and phenobarbital—to prevent any more seizures. Joshua's condition was critical, but a scan of his skull revealed brain activity, an encouraging sign. "Given the patient's age and early signs of brain's general recovery," a pediatric neurologist observed, "prognosis for further neurologic recovery, though guarded, probably warrants aggressive treatment."

By December 11, Joshua had started to improve. Although he remained in a coma, his seizures had stopped, and he was breathing without a respirator. Genene Jones took over his treatment at 3 P.M. that day. At 7 P.M., the baby's heart began beating too rapidly, a condition known as tachycardia. Doctors pulled him out of the emergency. Arriving for the overnight shift, Pat Alberti overheard Genene telling Joshua's parents that their son would have permanent brain damage if he survived. Their baby would have to be institutionalized, Genene declared; he would be better off dead. The next day—again under the care of Genene Jones—Joshua Sawyer died at 9:22 P.M.

The baby's sudden downward spiral had surprised his doctors. Joshua had suffered two arrests on the night of his death. His heart had begun contracting erratically at 7:55 P.M.; electrical shock and drugs had brought it back to a normal rhythm by 8:20 P.M.. Thirty minutes later, his blood pressure started to drop, and then his heart failed a final time. During the brief period between the two arrests, doctors had sent a blood sample down to the lab to check the level of Dilantin in Joshua's body. The result did not arrive before his demise, and in the chaotic aftermath—coming too late to make a difference, with parents to inform and paperwork to complete—the lab study was ignored. But it told a story that would have been difficult to attribute to mere misunderstanding, even for those who previously felt certain that nothing was wrong in the pediatric ICU.

Joshua's blood sample had gone to the hospital's third-floor pathology lab, where technician George Farinacci filled out a form identifying it as sample #3463. Farinacci took the test tube of blood and fed it into a large, complex machine called an Automated Chemical Analyzer. The normal range for Dilantin was between 10 and 20. But the number that registered was more than double that: 55.5, bumping the equipment's upper limit the way boiling water would overheat a body thermometer. To get a precise reading, Farinacci carefully diluted the sample's concentration by half, recalibrated for the dilution, and ran it through again. This time, the Automated Chemical Analyzer showed 59.6—a toxic level of Dilantin, more than enough to throw a baby's heart into cardiac arrest. Farinacci entered the result into the hospital's computer, which printed it out for Joshua's bulky medical chart, where the evidence that the child had received a massive overdose of Dilantin would go unnoticed for more than a year.

Three days after Joshua Sawyer's death, Dr. Robotham ordered nurses to immediately notify him or Dr. Victor German, the ICU's newly appointed deputy medical director, of every code on every child. But he was particularly interested in emergencies involving Genene Jones. Robotham had taken trusted nurses aside and asked them to keep an eye on the LVN. The medical director's favorite nurse had become his prime target.

Genene was well aware of Robotham's shift in attitude. J.R. had twice refused her requests for a letter of recommendation. She regarded his suspicions as an act of personal betrayal. The medical director wasn't trying to uncover what was going on; he had simply turned against her. After Robotham ordered drug tests on another of her patients, Jones phoned his medical school office with her own interpretation of the result: "Your son-of-a-bitch toxicology screen was negative."

One friendly RN counseled Genene to let tensions cool by treating less sick patients for a while. But that wasn't her style. It would be like admitting she was guilty, Genene explained. She preferred instead to take her accusers on, to remain in the center of the storm. One day she pulled Robotham aside and confronted him. "What the hell's going on?" she demanded. "Do you think I'm doing something to kids?" Robotham looked her straight in the eye. "I don't know," he told her honestly.

Another day, she issued a warning. "This unit is my life," she told Robotham and Belko. "If you try to take me away from this unit, I have my little black book with the name of every kid who's died in the unit—and the doctor who caused the death." *She was blackmailing them!* Jones had mentioned a "black book" in conversation with other nurses. Now Belko and Mousseau called Genene in to question her: Did she really have such a book? Genene backed down; she said she did not. Furious at the threat, Robotham told the nursing administrators he wanted Genene fired—or at least out of the ICU. But they saw no reason for such action; Genene was just upset. They refused to do more than briefly take her off the most critical patients.

In mid-December, the beleaguered medical director, resting at home, received another late-night call from the ICU. There was a problem with a patient; they needed him to come in. Robotham explained that his wife was visiting her family in France, and it was too late to call a baby-sitter. Could someone getting off work come to watch his infant daughter? There was a pause for a few moments, then a familiar voice came on the line: "I'll be right over." It was *Genene*.

Robotham had always told his residents to treat every patient they cared for as if the child were their own. Now his medical philosophy, so sincere in the abstract, was being put to the test. The nurse he suspected of harming patients would arrive in minutes to be alone with his little girl. Dare he trust her? Robotham figured he had no choice. After several hours at the hospital, the doctor returned to his house at 3:30 A.M. Genene was dozing on the downstairs couch. Robotham woke her up, offered thanks, and quickly ushered her out the door. Then, terror in his heart, he crept up the stairs and peered through the darkness into his baby's bedroom. The little girl was sound asleep.

The three months since Suzanna Maldonado's visit to Pat Belko had left Robotham at wit's end, brimming with fatigue and angry frustration. The unit was full, the patients critically sick, and the staff overworked and divided. Robotham had been fighting more than natural illness and injury. He was locked in a personal guerrilla war with a nurse, an adversary he was unable to entrap and powerless to remove.

By late December, Bob Franks had decided his young colleague was obsessed with Genene Jones. Since completing his chart review, Robotham had reported back to the acting chairman almost daily. Still he had no proof of criminal conduct. Belko had complained that the residents were screening for improper drugs only on Genene's patients. Franks knew the ICU wasn't operating well, but he considered Robotham's focus on Jones unjustified— and an open invitation to a lawsuit. Besides, Genene Jones was a nursing problem. There was nothing they could do.

Franks recognized that Robotham was operating under enormous pressure. For twenty-one months, as primary consultant to the ICU, he had been making rounds six or seven days a week, answering questions at all hours from home, and often returning to the hospital in the middle of the night. It was time for him to take a break—whether he liked the idea or not. The acting chairman informed Robotham that he was being temporarily relieved. He needed the time off, and besides, a fresh perspective might help dispose of this problem. Victor German would take over the unit chores during January. Franks instructed Robotham not to set foot in the pediatric ICU for a month. The medical director was relieved to have a respite but a bit sour about being exiled. "Why?" he asked Franks. "Are you concerned *I'm* doing something?"

But Robotham was in no position to quarrel. The one man who was intent on determining Genene Jones's connection to the mysterious deaths in the ICU—the only hospital official who believed there *was* a connection— would begin the New Year working with baboons in his research lab.

After the staff nurses learned that Dr. Robotham would be absent from the pediatric ICU in January, Genene Jones encouraged her peers to believe the worst. She circulated a rumor that the excitable medical director had suffered a nervous breakdown.

Even as Robotham was banished, a critical piece of the puzzle lay buried and ignored within the bureaucracy. Since early 1981, a hospital clerk named Patricia Lopez had been complaining to her superiors about the disappearance of supplies from the pediatric ICU. The young woman's duties included equipping the unit's crash cart. She checked the cart daily and showed up at codes to replace everything that was used. On about ten occasions during 1981, Lopez had found the crash cart open when no code had taken place. Each time, the cart had been opened during the 3–11 P.M. shift. Each time, Lopez discovered the same items missing: a tourniquet, a handful of gauze pads, several syringes—and a 10,000-unit bottle of heparin. Lopez reported each of the incidents, in at least one case in writing. But her supervisors worked in a different hospital department from those who knew about the problems in the ICU. They figured nurses were using the blood-thinner from the crash cart during their normal duties because it was close at hand. They told Lopez just to keep replacing the missing heparin.

December 1981 had been a special time at San Antonio's charity hospital. The first day of the month marked

Bexar County's official reincarnation as Medical Center Hospital, part of B. H. Corum's "New Horizons" campaign to boost the institution's image. The hospital district's executive director was also busy preparing organizational charts for a major administrative reshuffling; it would retitle Virginia Mousseau from assistant administrator for nursing service to associate administrator for patient care services. On December 16, the district auxiliary threw the annual employees' Christmas party in the hospital cafeteria.

But in the pediatric ICU, December 1981 had been another horrible month. After a brief calm in November, there had been ten CPRs in December, an unusually high number even for the beginning of the busy winter season. Seven children had died—six of them on the 3–11 shift, including four assigned to Genene. Two-year-old Doraelia Rios was among them.

Hospitalized several times previously for surgery on her digestive tract, Dora entered the pediatric ICU on December 21, suffering from diarrhea, dehydration, and possible inflammation of an internal membrane. At the time of her admission, Dora was listed in guarded condition. She was given fluids to deal with the dehydration and antibiotics to fight the infection, but she suffered a cardiac arrest and died at 8:12 P.M. the next day. After being present for the final code, Genene Jones finished her nursing notes with a brief message to the dead child: "A legend in her own time. Merry X-mas Dora. I love you. Jones LVN."

Ten

ROLANDO SANTOS WAS dying. Not from ravaging disease or tragic injury or even an act of God—reasons any doctor could accept—but because *someone,* someone sworn to help make him well, was trying to kill him. Why else would a baby with simple pneumonia go into seizures and cardiac arrest and begin pouring out blood? Why else would such troubles develop not once or twice or even three times, but on four separate occasions—always during the same hours? Dr. Kenneth Copeland could reach no other conclusion: They were dealing with a murderer.

As the pediatric faculty's epidemiologist, Copeland was an expert in the outbreak of disease. Thirty-three years old, he was thin and boyishly handsome, with a mop of curly blond hair. Copeland was spending January as an attending physician in the ICU, in charge of a team of pediatric residents. He was working with Dr. Victor German, who would fill Robotham's role as consultant on any sticky problems that developed. At the beginning of the month, Robotham had bluntly told the two doctors that he suspected Genene Jones was harming children. Like a baseball manager given the thumb, J.R. would be available to offer advice from the clubhouse. But it would be up to them to try to catch her.

Rolando Santos was like most of the kids who came to the pediatric ICU. His parents were Hispanic and poor. His father, Eusebio, picked crops on a farm forty-two miles southwest of San Antonio. His mother, Jesusa, made dolls and tended the couple's children. Rolando was their eleventh, born in November. On December 27, when the baby was a month old, his mother had taken him to the Brady-Green clinic in downtown San Antonio, site of the old Robert B. Green Hospital. Mrs. Santos believed Rolando had a cold. But a pediatrician there discovered pneumonia and sent the baby to the pediatric ICU at Medical Center Hospital. Placed on a respirator, Rolando improved during his first two days. His type of pneumonia was predictable; with antibiotics, most such children went home within a week. Then, during the 3–11 shift on December 29, Rolando began seizing. A brain scan revealed nothing to explain the seizure, but the baby's heart stopped two hours later. After reviving him, doctors ran more tests on his brain and heart to try to figure out what was going on. All of them came back normal.

Rolando again started to improve. By January 1, he was doing so well that doctors were ready to take him off the respirator. That afternoon, Rolando suddenly excreted a massive amount of urine, dehydrating his body. The baby's blood pressure began to drop; he showed symptoms of a seizure, then turned sluggish. Doctors poured fluids into Rolando to replace the urine and stabilized him. Copeland began to wonder if someone was giving the baby drugs. A diuretic would explain the urine output; a narcotic could made him lethargic. Searching for an answer, Copeland gave Rolando a medication that counters the effect of narcotics. But it didn't have any effect.

Rolando bounced back quickly from his crisis on New Year's Day. On the evening of January 3, nurses noticed that he was oozing a bit of blood. Doctors presumed the problem was DIC, the rare clotting abnormality caused by infection. They gave Rolando plasma, and by early the next morning, the bleeding had disappeared. On January 6, Genene Jones returned to work after three days off. As she had every day while on duty recently, the LVN assumed responsibility for Rolando Santos's care. At 7 P.M. that night, the baby began bleeding heavily. Everywhere doctors had stuck a needle in him, blood was oozing out. The hemorrhaging sapped Rolando's blood pressure, and he fell into cardiac arrest. It took electric shock and three rounds of emergency drugs to restart his heart.

Copeland sent blood samples to the lab for tests. They were inconsistent with DIC. But they were positive for excessive heparin. The next day, Copeland instructed nurses to remove the baby's arterial line. Without a line to keep clear, there would be no need for Rolando to receive any heparin. This would eliminate the remote possibility that a nurse could give him an overdose by mistake. But Copeland didn't think the previous episode was an accident. Every time Rolando got better, something terrible seemed to happen. It was as though someone was playing with him, cruelly toying with the child's health, like a cat with a crippled bird.

Jesusa and Eusebio Santos didn't understand why their baby was taking so long to get well. Lacking the money to stay in San Antonio and remain at Rolando's bedside, they phoned the hospital several times a day to check on his condition. The day nurses always told them Rolando was doing fine. But at night, they would hear that he was having problems. Genene Jones had her own explanation for why Rolando had been on a roller coaster since his arrival in the ICU. Standing near the nursing station one night, she remarked, "The doctors are fucking up."

On the afternoon of January 9, Rolando started bleeding again. Genene was the first to spot the problem, which worsened into the evening. Summoned by a resident, Copeland arrived in the ICU about 7 P.M. to find a crisis. Blood was leaking out of the baby as if he were a water balloon filled with needle holes. It trickled from old puncture sites all over his arms and his legs, his neck and his scalp. Blood oozed from the mucous membranes in his nose and mouth and eyes. Rolando's urine was red, and nurses suctioning his throat found even more blood. Working in a crimson puddle, residents were pushing plasma into the child as fast as they could. But it wasn't fast enough. His blood pressure was dropping. Then he fell into a coma; they were about to lose him.

Desperate, Copeland decided to try protamine sulfate—the drug used to reverse the effects of heparin. The doctor was gambling. Protamine could harm a child who hadn't received heparin. But there was no time to wait for lab results, no time to do anything else. At 7:30 P.M., Copeland threaded a small IV line into a vein in Rolando's scalp, drained a 100-milligram bottle of protamine into a syringe, and injected it slowly into the baby. Nothing happened. Even if his gamble was right, Copeland had no idea how much protamine he would need. He sucked another bottle into a syringe and pushed it into the IV. The bleeding continued. Copeland began to sweat; he had been pushing protamine for twenty minutes. The doctor drew up a third bottle. At 7:55, after he had injected another 30 milligrams, Rolando's bleeding suddenly stopped.

Throughout the night, the baby improved; he was awake and alert by morning. That evening, he was taken off the respirator and began breathing on his own. But Copeland believed that Rolando's life was still in danger. On January 11, when he came in for morning rounds, he ordered nurses to transfer the baby out to the pediatric floor. Rolando was really too sick to leave the ICU; he had been near death thirty-six hours earlier. But to Copeland, he was also too sick to stay. The doctor was determined to remove him from the place where uncomplicated pneumonia had almost claimed his life. Early that afternoon, Copeland returned to the ICU and discovered Rolando was still there. He was furious; the 3–11 shift would soon begin. "I want him out *now!*" he told the nurses, and they wheeled him out of the unit. Copeland secretly arranged with the head nurse on the pediatric ward to have Rolando guarded around the clock. He ordered a list kept of everyone—especially from the ICU—who went into the baby's room.

Five days later, Rolando Santos was well enough to go home.

At last, thought Jim Robotham, they had real evidence of a heparin overdose in the pediatric ICU. The medical school's blood expert put it in writing: Rolando had received too much heparin during the 3–11 shifts on January 6 and January 9. The effectiveness of the protamine sulfate—a specific antidote to heparin—had presented independent proof. Someone even offered an

explanation of how the baby might have gotten the blood-
thinner. A few days after Rolando's last bleeding episode, Robotham discovered on his desk a copy of a
nursing-journal article. Titled "You Can Inject Heparin
Subcutaneously," it detailed how the drug could be given
directly under the skin without leaving a visible bruise; a
series of accompanying photographs showed "seven steps
to trouble-free injections." Robotham's secretary could
not tell him who had placed the article on his desk.
Although no one had seen Genene Jones inject the blood-
thinner, Robotham and Copeland both felt certain she
was somehow responsible. The two men informed Bob
Franks of their belief. Finally, thought Robotham, something would be done.

But the nursing administrators had an alternative to
the doctors' ugly suggestion that one of their own would
try to harm a child. Determined to fight this smear on
their profession and on their staff, they suggested it was
all just a simple mistake. Pat Belko had complained
bitterly about Copeland's decision to move Rolando Santos out of the ICU. Now she and her superiors drew their
explanation for the baby's bleeding from the woman suspected of causing it. Genene had blamed an agency RN
working the day shift, suggesting the nurse had confused
bottles of heparin and ampicillin, an antibiotic that Rolando
was receiving through an IV. Such a mix-up was improbable. The two drugs came in bottles of different sizes that
bore labels of different colors. Rolando had bled on
3–11, not the day shift. And at the time of his final
episode, the child had no arterial line; there was no
reason for a vial of heparin even to be in his room. But
Belko, Harris, and Mousseau—without bothering to
investigate—embraced the alibi anyway, muddying waters that had briefly cleared.

Buffeted by the conflicting claims, anguished about
what to do, Franks did very little. He informed B. H.
Corum about the case of Rolando Santos. He also sought
the aid of his own boss: Dr. Marvin Dunn, dean of the
UT medical school. In a January 19 memo to the dean,
Franks detailed the history of suspicions in the ICU,
noting: "From the outset there had been innuendo that
purposeful nursing misadventure was involved." Robo-

tham's review of the patient charts "could not substanti-
ate that suspicion," Franks informed Dunn. But now
they had proof that someone had given a child too much
heparin. As a result, wrote Franks, he had "returned to a
position of not knowing whether or not there is a problem." The acting pediatrics chairman told the dean that
the nursing department—which, of course, felt nothing
was wrong—would investigate the matter further. "I have
several obvious concerns," he wrote. "One is that there
will be inappropriate comments, resulting in unjustified
publicity." Franks said he would continue to evaluate
"unexpected events" in the pediatric ICU and welcomed
Dunn's advice. The dean did not immediately offer any.

It is a fact of life in the world of medicine that considerations of turf and politics and personality can jeopardize lives as readily as an errant scalpel or a botched
diagnosis. Thus Jim Robotham's terrible suspicions about
Genene Jones could be dismissed for weeks, even months,
as the histrionics of an obsessed, hotheaded doctor. Robotham—trained as a physician, not as a criminal investigator—was left alone with the burden of trying to catch a
murderer. But one angry voice was to change that: It
belonged to the hospital's most prominent surgeon, who
believed that a child he sent to the pediatric ICU should
have recovered instead of died.

Conventional wisdom attributes a distinct bundle of
personality traits to doctors who practice in each of medicine's specialties. This lore places surgeons and pediatricians at opposite ends of the temperamental spectrum.
Pediatricians are gentle, sensitive, and kind. Surgeons
are brutish, bullheaded, and overbearing. Pediatricians
treat with drugs and fluids, and believe in letting nature
work its delicate magic. Surgeons want to cut. The eco-
nomics of modern medicine also divided the two specialties. Because of regulations governing reimbursement for
federal health insurance in the 1980s, doctors engaged in
hands-on, primary care—pediatricians, internists, family
practitioners—earned far less than specialists, such as
surgeons and radiologists, who mostly performed procedures. In 1982, pediatricians were America's lowest-paid

group of doctors, with a median income of $62,000 a year. Surgeons were among the best rewarded, at $110,000.

The pediatric ICU was a setting where the conflicting personalities and medical philosophies of pediatrics and surgery clashed. The surgeons sent children to the unit to recover after operations, and as the admitting doctors, they retained control over the treatment plan of their patients there. Infection and fluid balance—the problems children usually experienced during recovery—were actually pediatricians' area of expertise. But the surgeons thought they could handle postoperative patients better than anyone and held pediatricians as a breed in particular contempt. They regarded the baby doctors' lack of assertiveness as cause to disregard their advice. Even surgical interns learned to sneer at them as "pedi-pods." Although Robotham and his residents kept hourly watch over children in the ICU, when the surgeons rejected their counsel, the pediatricians could do nothing more than fume. The events of late 1981 had escalated the natural conflict. The surgeons were upset about several postoperative patients who had died unexpectedly in the pediatric ICU. Each death had set off feuding over who was to blame.

On January 14, the surgeons sent Patrick Zavala to the pediatric ICU to recover from open-heart surgery. Four months old, Patrick had gone under the knife for repair of a cardiac birth defect. The procedure had gone smoothly; not long after arriving in the unit, the baby was kicking his feet in his crib. By Sunday, January 17, Patrick was progressing so well that doctors were preparing to wean him from the respirator that aided his breathing. The last note from the nurse who cared for Patrick until 3 P.M. was "alert, all shift." At 4 P.M., Genene Jones recorded that the baby was "somewhat lethargic." Jones's nursing notes over the next two hours reported steadily worsening problems, even though Patrick's mother left his bedside at 6 P.M. with her child sleeping comfortably. About thirty minutes later, Genene summoned Dr. Edward Eades, the surgery intern on duty. He discovered the baby almost totally unresponsive to even painful stimulation.

Unable to tell why Patrick's condition had deteriorated, the surgeons—at Genene Jones's suggestion— decided to take him for a brain scan, despite protests from a pediatric resident who felt his condition was too unsteady. Accompanied by Genene and another nurse, the surgeons wheeled the child to the CAT-scan room in the hospital basement. As they waited for the machine to warm up, Patrick's heart suddenly stopped. Uncomfortable handling the arrest—the surgeons were uncertain what doses of emergency drugs to administer to a baby— they put out a distress call for a pediatrician. When a pediatrics resident arrived from the fourth-floor nursery to take over, he discovered that Genene Jones had already started the child on dopamine, a drug that raises blood pressure, without a doctor's order. The doctors revived Patrick, then wheeled him back to the ICU. "Very puzzling picture," one resident wrote on the child's medical chart. Not long after returning to the unit, Patrick went into seizures and arrested again. Doctors worked to save him but finally realized it was hopeless.

Just as the physician running the code officially pronounced the baby dead, Genene Jones grabbed a syringe and, like a priest sprinkling holy water, made the sign of the cross with the needle while squirting fluid on Patrick's forehead. Then Genene repeated the gesture on herself. Sobbing, she picked up the dead baby's body and clutched it to her chest.

The death of Patrick Zavala stunned other nurses who had cared for him. When she arrived for work at 11 P.M., Eva Diaz, a surgical ICU nurse who worked overtime in the pediatric unit, grilled Genene about what had happened. Jones later complained that Diaz had accused her of murdering the baby. Although Diaz denied doing so, Pat Belko barred her from working any more shifts in the pediatric ICU.

The doctors and nurses who had treated the baby were so puzzled by his death that several sat in on his autopsy the next morning. But the postmortem offered not a clue; the baby's heart was in even better shape than the surgeons had expected. On Patrick's death certificate, doctors attributed his fatal cardiac arrest to "presumed sepsis"—a medical term for infection.

J. Kent Trinkle was not satisfied with that explanation.

A beefy forty-seven-year-old midwesterner with a choir-boy face, Trinkle was the hospital's star chest surgeon—San Antonio's counterpart to Houston's legendary Michael DeBakey. Chief of the cardiothoracic surgery division, he was known throughout the hospital as a man of swagger as well as skill. Trinkle listened to country music in the operating room while he sliced through lungs and stitched veins. His worshipful surgery residents lived in fear of his temper. And despite having extracted a lung from dozens of cancer patients, Trinkle smoked a pack of cigarettes a day, as though he were immune from a disease afflicting mere mortals. At Medical Center Hospital, Kent Trinkle was a powerful figure. He performed glamorous, daring operations that brought the institution money and public attention. Everyone figured Trinkle was the man who would carry out San Antonio's first heart transplant. He was the sort of doctor whom hospital administrators worked to keep happy.

Trinkle had observed the operation on Patrick Zavala's heart, and he was furious about the child's death. There had been too many such surprises in the pediatric ICU. The surgeons had done the hard part. Why should they let another medical service botch up their cases during recovery? On January 20, Trinkle went to Howard Radwin, another surgeon, who held the post of chairman of the hospital's medical-dental staff. Something had to be done, Trinkle declared. He threatened to start sending his postoperative pediatric patients to the neonatal ICU.

Bob Franks later that day discovered that alarm about the pediatric ICU was spreading. In a memo for his files, the acting pediatrics chairman wrote of learning that Trinkle "had asked Radwin 'what the f--- is going on in the Ped ICU?' " Franks tried to calm the angry surgeon. "I discussed with him the origin of his concern re: Ped ICU," noted Franks. "He said that for 6–9 months things had 'not seemed right'—lots of friction, hostility, etc., between his people and nursing. He remarked on the difference in morale, esprit de corps, i.e. general atmosphere in that Unit vs Neonatal ICU. He commented on 'being pushed aside' by 'Jeanine Jones' following the death of a baby as she picked up and cuddled the corpse, as he was attempting to talk with the parents." By the time the conversation ended, Trinkle had agreed—for the time being—to keep using the pediatric ICU.

But the surgeons were persuaded that the pediatricians were incapable of handling the problem. Radwin was astounded to learn from Franks that pediatrics had for months been harboring suspicions that a nurse was harming children. The morning after hearing from Trinkle, Radwin dispatched a memo instructing Robotham and nursing administrator Judy Harris to investigate the surgeon's "concern over the quality of care" in the pediatric ICU and report back to a special committee on February 1. To avoid any possibility that the problem would get ignored, Radwin spread news of the ICU's crisis by circulating blind copies of his memo around the medical school. Radwin notified B. H. Corum and Marvin Dunn that he was organizing his own investigation.

Both men, of course, already knew about the ICU's problems; Corum had been informed back in early November. But Kent Trinkle's complaint spurred them to take their first independent action. Three months after the first accusation that a nurse was killing children, the top officials of the hospital and the medical school arranged to discuss the problem together for the first time.

Gathered at 10 A.M. on January 25 in the executive director's office at Medical Center Hospital was a solemn group of six: B. H. Corum, his deputy, John Guest, nursing administrator Virginia Mousseau, medical school dean Marvin Dunn, Bob Franks, and Jim Robotham. Each was destined to play a critical role in the unfolding tragedy.

Speaking from two pages of scribbled notes, Robotham briefed the group about the history of suspicion: the sudden increase in cases of bleeding and irregular heartbeat, his desperate search for an explanation, and the inevitable focus on a single nurse. Robotham detailed Genene Jones's pattern of emotional instability and burnout—her mothering of dead children, her frequent hospitalizations and family troubles, and her threat to sue them all with details from her "little black book." While nurses had pointed the finger first, senior doctors and residents had independently complained about her. The group heard about the case of Rolando Santos: about the repeated bleeding incidents that almost claimed his life, about the laboratory evidence that the baby had twice received too much heparin.

Trained as a pathologist, Dunn mused about the history of medical serial murder. Most perpetrators used a single modus operandi, he noted; children in the ICU had suffered an assortment of different problems. If this nurse was indeed using an array of drugs to cause each of the unexpected problems in the ICU—bleeding, irregular heartbeat, seizures, and limpness—she would go down in the books as one of the most sophisticated medical killers in history.

The discussion finally turned to the looming question of what to do. There was brief talk of trying to arrange surveillance: perhaps a private detective under cover as a hospital employee. Maybe even hidden television cameras. Such conversation made those sitting around Corum's office nervous. This was treacherous ground indeed—the sort of mess that led to lawsuits. It was obvious they needed help. After an hour and forty minutes, the group decided to summon the hospital's malpractice lawyer, a well-connected San Antonio attorney named Paul Green. They invited Howard Radwin to join them too.

After a break, the group reassembled at 1:30 P.M., with eight now in attendance. Robotham repeated his summary for the newcomers. Franks revealed a worrisome new nugget of information. He had recently learned that a pediatric ICU nurse had told her psychiatrist that an LVN was killing babies by putting heparin in their intravenous bottles. The unnamed nurse—in fact, it was Pat Alberti—had been voicing the suspicion since November; more recently, she had complained that no one was lifting a finger to stop the slaughter. To Franks, who had been describing the situation for months in euphemisms—"nursing misadventure" and "unexpected events"—such blunt talk was jarring. The group put the problem to the lawyer: There was trouble in the pediatric ICU, and a single nurse was in the middle of it. Could they fire her? Should they alert the medical examiner? Tip off the district attorney?

After listening intently, Green asked: Was there proof—not just that something bad was going on, but that *this* nurse was responsible? The doctors and administrators told him there was none. Green offered his advice. Without hard evidence, he informed them, firing Genene Jones or calling the district attorney could put them on shaky ground. The nurse could sue them, and she might well win. Green hinted that he might try to slip word to a friend in the DA's office informally—but any official action, he advised, would be most unwise.

Paul Green, in effect, was telling the hospital officials they couldn't do the right thing because some other lawyer might sue them. But that was merely a recommendation. The ultimate responsibility belonged to B. H. Corum; as the administrator liked to remind subordinates, he wrote the nurse's paycheck. On this occasion, however, the man who fancied himself the master of the bureaucracy lacked the will to rid his hospital of a lowly LVN. Corum made the fatal decision that the hospital could not fire her. Instead, he and the others decided to keep the whole matter quiet while launching yet another investigation.

When Dr. Alan Conn arrived in San Antonio in late January 1982, Marvin Dunn summoned him to his plush second-floor office at the medical school. Jim Robotham was already there. Conn was a fifty-seven-year-old anesthesiologist on the staff of Toronto's Hospital for Sick Children, perhaps the world's foremost pediatric institution. He was one of the pioneers of pediatric intensive care; Robotham was among the many intensivists he had trained. Now Conn had a six-month sabbatical, and he had arranged to spend it as a visiting professor in San Antonio, doing research on drowning victims in a medical school lab. At the January 25 meeting, Robotham had suggested that his old mentor would be the perfect man to investigate the pediatric ICU.

Medical school administrators often recruited outside experts to deal with their thorniest personnel problems. Often such consultants weren't expected to uncover anything new; they merely insulated timid administrators from a tough decision. The report of a consultant could give a predetermined firing an aura of objectivity, shielding the boss (it was reasoned) from bitter feelings and a lawsuit. When those attending the January 25 summit meeting agreed to seek Dr. Conn's help, Jim Robotham was pleased. He figured it would give his superiors the courage to do what he had been prodding them toward for weeks: fire Genene Jones. Robotham did not dream that he had set in motion his own undoing.

Now, in the dean's office, Dunn and Robotham detailed for the Canadian doctor all their suspicions about what was happening in the pediatric ICU. Conn agreed to investigate. The next morning, he told Dunn and Corum that he needed a team of outside doctors and nurses to conduct a proper inquiry. Corum fretted about the cost of bringing in such a committee; there was no money for it in his budget. When Dunn arranged for the medical school to foot part of the bill, Corum agreed to the plan.

The decision to retain an outside expert helped satisfy others in a position to intercede. On January 26, B. H. Corum had briefed the hospital district's board chairman, an ambitious and politically active San Antonio dentist named William Thornton. In a quick session before a board meeting, Thornton learned that there had been a documented heparin overdose but it was possible that drug bottles had been confused. As Thornton later recalled it, Corum attributed the problem to poor leadership in pediatrics and a "catfight" among nurses. Thornton asked about the ICU's mortality rate. He was told that was not a problem. The hospital board chairman saw no reason to get involved.

On February 1, Robotham and Judy Harris addressed the ad hoc committee that Howard Radwin had appointed following Kent Trinkle's tirade. Voicing faith in his old mentor, Robotham explained that Dr. Conn was assembling a team of experts to review the intensive care unit. The chairman of the surgery department asked whether a consistent pattern was evident in all the ICU deaths. No, said Robotham—taking the question literally—not in *all* cases. According to Radwin's minutes of the meeting, "the group concurred that there is no threatening situation in the PICU which would require immediate intervention."

Inside the ICU, tensions peaked, even as Dr. Conn was rounding up his team of experts. Everyone was paranoid. Rather than sleep when they had a chance, pediatric residents stood guard on their patients throughout the night. Rolando Santos's brush with death had prompted Robotham to order heparin removed from each patient's bedside and kept in the unit's drug cabinet. But many nurses had become reluctant to prepare *any* kind of drug without a witness. One RN made a practice of throwing out all medications and syringes that he hadn't drawn up himself. "It got stressful enough," the nurse remarked, "that I didn't trust anybody."

On January 23, a two-month-old baby had gone into respiratory arrest and experienced slow heartbeat shortly after Genene left his room to eat. Another nurse discovered that the alarm on the child's heart monitor had not sounded because it had been turned off. Pat Belko had defended Jones, suggesting to Dr. German that the alarm might have been switched off for days. Monitor alarms in the ICU were taped in the On position; nurses were ordered to chart at the beginning and end of every shift that all alarms were on and functioning.

Everyone knew that Genene was the prime target of suspicion. "They're out to hang me," she told a friendly RN one day. "They might as well let me go." Friends outside the hospital found her looking haggard and harassed. Genene told them that teenagers in her neighborhood kept trying to break into her apartment; she said she was going to get a shotgun to stop them.

On February 2, the hospital district announced in a press release that Dr. Alan Conn would lead an "evaluation" of the pediatric ICU. Issued to maintain the pretense that nothing was amiss, the statement characterized the inquiry as "part of the on-going review of patient care programs" illustrating "our commitment to New Horizons for the Bexar County Hospital District." But no one in the pediatric ICU believed it. They knew this Canadian doctor was conducting an *investigation*—and so

did Genene Jones. In a two-page note dated February 2,
the LVN informed Belko that she had had enough.

> . . . I will not + can not tolerate being persecuted any
> more. I'm also tired of talking to people, thinking.
> problems will be solved + having them rubbed in your
> face time + time again.
>   It's obvious to me now, after tonight . . . that my
> credi[bility] in't worth a damn.
>   As I have told you in previous conversation, I won't
> leave without a bang. I feel it is only fair that I have a
> shot a[t] persecuting people to[o].

"Call tonight a breaking point," Genene wrote; she
said she was tired of fighting a losing battle. "You people
have succeeded in doing + making me something I never
thought I'd be. A quitter. It's all yours Pat. I don't feel
that I can return to this unit today or even tomorrow. . . .
I do hope someone continues to fight for the kids. Their
worth it."

Despite the letter, Genene decided to stay. Rapidly
shifting gears, she told other nurses that she welcomed
the investigation—that she was eager to blow the whistle
on how the doctors were screwing up. It was about time
something was done, Genene Jones declared. After all,
babies were *dying*.

Eleven

ALAN CONN'S INVESTIGATORS began work at 8 A.M. sharp on Monday, February 15. The Canadian doctor had assembled a high-powered team of six specialists: the medical directors and head nurses of pediatric intensive care units at three famous big-city hospitals. Jim Robotham and Pat Belko led them through a tour of the pediatric ICU. Then they adjourned to a conference room at the medical school, a comforting distance from the turmoil, and began ushering in witnesses.

Thirty-two people had been summoned, including all the critical players in the conflict: Suzanna Maldonado, the nurse who started it all; Larry Hooghuis, the pediatrics resident who caught Genene Jones about to give a heparin overdose; Bob Franks, the anguished acting chairman of pediatrics; Kent Trinkle, the temperamental chest surgeon; Ken Copeland, the pediatrician who rescued Rolando Santos. Jim Robotham and Pat Belko were each to sit through two sessions. Genene Jones was to have thirty minutes to speak her piece.

After seeing the committee agenda, Belko fretted that the list of doctors was stacked against Genene. The head nurse mentioned her fear to a third-year resident in pediatrics who thought highly of the LVN, and Kathy Holland agreed to volunteer to make an appearance before the committee. It was but the first of many occasions when Dr. Holland was to rise in Genene Jones's defense.

The investigators conducted three days of interviews, and they got an earful. Almost everyone was angry at someone, and most were willing to speak their mind. Pat Alberti, the LVN whose complaint to her psychiatrist had rattled Dr. Franks, bluntly informed the committee, "Genene's killing off the kids." Although Dr. Robotham offered a more complex account of what was wrong, the outline he prepared for his testimony ends with a similar conclusion: "Bottom line issue centers around one nurse."

But when it came time to analyze the situation, the committee members decided to view the complaints about Genene Jones merely as a symptom of a broader malady. Privately, even before setting foot in the ICU, Alan Conn had virtually dismissed the notion that a nurse was deliberately harming children. His own hospital in Toronto was in the final throes of a remarkably similar ordeal; a cardiac ward nurse had been charged with murdering four babies with a heart drug. The whole business had destroyed careers, divided the staff, and soiled the hospital's name. To Conn's mind, nothing good had come of the matter (the scant evidence against the nurse eventually would prompt a judge to dismiss the charges). He saw no need to encourage such a debacle in San Antonio.

On the subject of the ICU's operations, however, Conn and his committee were scathing. The ICU's "growing pains," their confidential written report began, had reached "an acute stage." Staff attitudes and morale were "poor." Robotham and Belko were failing to provide "effective" leadership. The medical director had no authority to change anything. The pediatrics department offered little support. The quality of the residents was mixed, and the shortage of well-trained nurses was "critical." Nursing errors weren't being documented. Doctors and nurses at all levels had an adversary relationship, and their communication was ineffective, "even at critical times." Conn urged the extraordinary step of shutting down the unit for an overhaul—to include the replacement of both Jim Robotham and Pat Belko.

Unwilling to accept the prospect that criminal conduct was at the heart of the ICU's problems, Conn's committee embraced the more benign explanation of personality conflict and recommended the removal of combatants on both sides—without distinguishing between right and wrong. Thus the committee blamed Robotham as much as Belko, even though the medical director had done more than anyone else to try to stop Genene Jones. Looking for a graceful way to ease him out, the committee suggested a new title for Robotham: director of critical care research. After Dunn and Corum privately approved the medical director's sacking—bypassing pediatrics chairman Franks entirely—Conn summoned his former protégé to breakfast to break the news.

As he arrived for the meeting with Alan Conn, J.R. was expecting a briefing on the review panel's secret findings. Good things would result from this, Robotham was thinking. The hospital and the medical school had been ignoring his complaints about the pediatric ICU for months. The support of Conn's committee would force the bureaucrats to act, make them cough up the money and staff he needed to straighten out the ICU. Most of all, Robotham figured, it would offer the administrators the excuse they needed to fire Genene Jones.

But that wasn't what Al Conn was telling him. Speaking in fatherly tones, Conn counseled Robotham that he was suffering from burnout. This move would give him a chance to break out of the grueling ICU grind; he could concentrate on his research, spend more time with his family. But Robotham didn't buy it. Conn was telling him he was *fired*—ousted from his job in the ICU. He told friends he'd been screwed. His old mentor had betrayed him.

Genene Jones's foremost advocate was more fortunate. Dr. Franks had joined the Conn committee in urging Pat Belko's dismissal. According to the minutes of a meeting where the matter was discussed, Franks said the pediatrics department believed Belko had failed to recognize the ICU's problems and "did not have the courage or capability to deal with them." Both faculty and house staff, he concluded, gave Belko "a vote of no confidence." But Virginia Mousseau protested vigorously. Whatever the doctors thought about her performance, they couldn't fire Belko, she declared. They didn't have the *paperwork* in her personnel file to justify her removal. Belko was placed under close watch for a six-month unofficial probationary period, and when it was over, she kept her job.

The ICU's fate was resolved more quickly. Dr. Conn had urged that the unit be closed for reorganization, with its patients transferred to another ICU in the hospital, under the supervision of another medical department. The implication was clear: The pediatricians had let things get out of control, and they no longer could be trusted to run the unit themselves. B. H. Corum, suddenly alarmed after months of passivity, backed this extreme solution. The ICU's problems were so grave, he felt there was no choice. But the medical school's doctors balked. Moving the ICU's patients, they argued, would just create problems elsewhere. After a round of high-level meetings, a deal was struck to keep the unit open. A young female anesthesiologist was named to replace Robotham, and control of the unit was handed to a newly formed Pediatric ICU Committee, chaired—to the pediatricians' consternation—by a surgeon, Dr. Arthur McFee.

The thorniest problem, of course, was that of Genene Jones. On February 17, after Conn and his committee completed their interviews, they met privately with B. H. Corum and Marvin Dunn. Despite Conn's personal skepticism that anyone had harmed children deliberately, in this select group the panel acknowledged the possibility. Dunn took notes of the investigators' informal remarks: "Majority events attributable to med & nursing inadeq but not all. Response inadeq at every level; Nurses— either malignant intent or gross neglect." Genene Jones was identified as the "center of storm."

In a secret preliminary draft of its report, the committee—without explanation—urged the "immediate removal" of both Jones and Pat Alberti. Like Robotham, Alberti had been targeted for contributing to the turmoil; her primary offense was agitating loudly for Jones's removal. But the specific reference to the two LVNs was not to see the light of day. Conn deleted it from his final report, in favor of a solution that eased the administrators' fears of litigation.

Instead of firing Genene Jones outright, they would replace all the LVNs in the unit with registered nurses, employing the excuse that most big-city pediatric ICUs had all-RN nursing staffs. There were six LVNs besides Genene, and one of them had worked in the ICU since 1969. They would all have to go. "It was a case of having to use a huge stick because it was impossible to single out one," Dr. McFee, the surgeon, explained later. "If we had just gone out and fired her, we would have had a substantial suit."

At about noon on March 2, 1982, Pat Belko passed the word that Virginia Mousseau wanted to talk to the pediatric ICU nurses. The meeting was to begin at 3 P.M. Agency nurses kept an eye on the patients while the staff members from two shifts crowded into the ICU's small back room. The ICU was good, Mousseau told the nurses, but the hospital administration wanted to make it better. They were going to upgrade the unit. Following a recommendation from Dr. Conn, they were going to move to an all-RN nursing staff. The LVNs would all be offered other jobs in the hospital; their pediatric ICU positions would be eliminated as of March 22.

The room exploded in tears and shouts. It wasn't right, the nurses told Mousseau. She answered that the move was part of a trend; most ICUs had an all-RN staff. Finally, Genene spoke up. This was the sort of thing that happened in *Communist* countries. "If you want a scapegoat, take me!" she declared. "We know you just want to get rid of me. Let me go, and let the rest stay." No, Mousseau assured her, the move wasn't directed at any one person. The hospital administration planned to employ only registered nurses in all its ICUs; the pediatric unit just happened to be first. The ICU would be scaled down to four beds, she added, so it could absorb the loss of the LVNs.

Pat Alberti heard the news when she arrived for work at 10:30 P.M. The word has come down, someone told her; the LVNs have to be gone within three weeks. "This is bullshit," Alberti snapped. She walked out of the ICU and never returned.

The hospital's nursing administrators soon began individual meetings with the six remaining LVNs, who were advised that they could all have other jobs at Medical Center Hospital. Genene was informed that there were

no pediatric floor positions available, but she could apply
for a place on another ward. She submitted her resignation instead, effective March 17.

On hearing the news, Virginia Mousseau informed the
new committee overseeing the pediatric ICU that "both
LVNs regarded as most sensitive in the functioning of the
unit either have or will depart the unit and the hospital."
The doctors and administrators were pleased. Their cir-
cuitous plan had worked; they had washed their hands of
Genene Jones.

During the five months since her first complaint about
Genene Jones, a time of internal investigations and review committees and far too many sick children, Suzanna
Maldonado had continued to work nights in the pediatric
ICU, where she crossed paths daily with the woman she
believed was a baby-killer. In bedside conversations with
other nurses, Genene Jones seemed to reserve her harshest venom for Maldonado. She made it known that she
blamed Suzanna for the vile suspicions that cost her
her job—the lies that were going to take her away from the
kids she so dearly loved.

It was about 2 A.M. on March 16—during the final
week of Genene Jones's career at Medical Center Hospital—when Maldonado noticed, above her name on the
nursing assignment sheet at work, the notation "√ your
box." In her ICU mailbox, Maldonado discovered a note
scrawled in block letters on hospital scrap paper. It read:
"YOUR DEAD." Maldonado turned the note over to Pat
Belko in the morning after her shift. Belko agreed that
the handwriting on the two messages was probably that
of Genene Jones. She told Maldonado she would take
care of the matter. Then she blackened over the entry on
the nursing assignment sheet.

When Genene arrived for work that day, Belko asked
her whether she had left the note. Jones denied doing so.
Convinced that Belko was taking no further action,
Maldonado informed hospital security about the death
threat before beginning work that night. When she arrived in the ICU, she found another slip of paper in her
mailbox. It bore a single word: "SOON." This time
Maldonado turned the note over to security, whose offi-

cers interviewed Suzanna but considered the case closed after Genene Jones left the employment of Medical Center Hospital.

This sentiment—that Jones's departure closed the books on the pediatric ICU's problems—also prevailed among those who ran the hospital and the medical school. Alan Conn's committee, while making no reference to criminal behavior in its report (the final version of the document contains not a single mention of Jones's name), had heard too many horror stories to ignore the possibility entirely. In a brief appendix that served to protect it from a charge of whitewash, the committee, which had been recruited to find out why babies were mysteriously dying, urged the appointment of *another* committee to do the job. "Based upon uncertain explanation of several isolated untoward events in the care of patients, this committee recommends an immediate review by a committee of clinical care within the PICU over the past twelve months." Despite the panel's emphasis on haste, Corum and Dunn, with the troublesome LVN gone, acted with no sense of dispatch. The last internal investigation of the ICU would not begin for six more months.

That left unresolved the central question: Had Genene Jones been murdering children? But the doctors and hospital administrators felt no urgency to get to the bottom of things. Ignoring altogether the need to stop a possible baby-killer, they were content at having arranged a surgical solution to their own problem: the extraction of Jones from the ICU without scandal or litigation.

But the procedure produced complications. In the department of pediatrics, the handling of the crisis sparked impotent fuming and rebellion. After being cut out of the decision to remove Robotham from the job of medical director, Bob Franks briefly resigned his post as acting pediatrics chairman in protest. The decision to hand control of the ICU to a committee—particularly one headed by a surgeon—had also incensed the house staff. The pediatric residents contemplated going on strike. Instead, twenty-six of them signed a petition, complaining about the treatment of Robotham, the abrupt removal of the LVNs, and the absence of any explanation for the changes. The residents asked to see the Conn report—whose contents remained confidential—and demanded a meeting with Dunn and Corum. But the administrators never even responded.

Robotham himself had steamed in private for several days. Then, in two bitter letters to Dunn, he complained that his abrupt removal had damaged his reputation in the medical community. Why was he being made the scapegoat? He had been fired after struggling for months to do something about Genene Jones. Yet the nursing administrators who protected her had gone unpunished. Why, even *Jones* was still employed a month after his own removal! "The manner in which this situation has been handled," Robotham wrote, "would appear to warrant an investigation in itself."

The ousted medical director's references to his damaged reputation made the dean nervous. Dunn started to worry that Robotham might file a lawsuit—or perhaps resign. In early April, the dean met privately with the angry doctor to try to calm him. Dunn told Robotham that no one questioned his integrity or dedication; he had worked exhaustively under difficult circumstances and made great improvements in the unit. He had been replaced, Dunn explained, because the pediatric ICU needed a full-time medical director. The medical school continued to value his contributions in teaching and research.

Robotham agreed, for the moment, to stay in San Antonio. He remained worried, however, about what Genene Jones might do. Even after Rolando Santos's bleeding had placed the entire ICU on notice—indeed, virtually until the day she left the hospital—Jones's association with mysterious emergencies had continued. In late February, while the administrators were concocting their elaborate plan to get rid of the LVNs, one child had died after four arrests on three consecutive days—all of them on the 3–11 shift, all of them under Genene's care. Paul Green, the hospital's malpractice attorney, had hinted back in January that he might tip off the district attorney. Although Robotham believed the DA had been alerted—in fact, Green had decided to say nothing—there was no sign that anything had come of it. On April 26, six weeks after Jones had left, Robotham wrote Virginia Mousseau,

Medical Center Hospital's top nursing administrator, a letter that would prove prescient.

> As the cloud of dust which has surrounded the future of the PICU begins to settle, I am concerned that one serious issue has not been addressed to my knowledge. Ms. [Genene] Jones was, as you are aware, the outstanding nurse in the PICU when I first began working there two years ago. As multiple family, personal and job related difficulties mushroomed, I spoke to you on a few occasions and on multiple occasions to both Ms. Harris and Ms. Belko during the last year. I did arrange over one year ago for Ms. Jones, through Pat Holden in Psychiatry, to obtain family counseling. We spoke with regard to trying to arrange a shift change in her job to allow her more time with her children. I also referred her for a medical consultation within the University for some of her physical complaints, and quietly looked on during her numerous ER visits and inpatient admissions. The stress placed on this nurse was awesome and yet she unfortunately knowingly or unwittingly clearly contributed to the overall problem existing for both her personally and the PICU as a whole.
>
>   During the fall she twice requested that I place a written recommendation in her record, but under the circumstances at that time, I told her that as director of the Unit it would be better to wait until I could write a completely unqualified endorsement. The evolution of events did not allow that to occur. Although I have no official administrative responsibility for Ms. Jones, I do feel that there should be adequate documentation in her records of the stresses she experienced so that she will be properly protected and judiciously supervised at any future place of employment.

But Medical Center Hospital would reveal to Genene Jones's prospective employers not a hint of the sinister events that had surrounded her in the ICU. Anyone who called the hospital personnel office for a reference would be told only that Genene was eligible to reapply for employment. And

she was free to brandish a letter on hospital district statio-
nery from her former supervisor—offering not warning but
warm endorsement. Like the other LVNs, Jones had in
March been given a letter of recommendation, signed by Pat
Belko and composed with help from Virginia Mousseau.

TO WHOM IT MAY CONCERN:
   Due to the recommendation of a recent pediatric
Intensive Care Site Team Visit, the Pedi ICU Unit
is being converted to an all RN Staff composition
at Medical Center Hospital.
   Ms. Genene Jones, LVN, has been employed in
the Pedi ICU since 1978. This move in no way
reflects on her performance in the unit. She has
gained valuable knowledge and experience in pediatric intensive care nursing. During the time of
employment this employee has been loyal, depend-
able, and trustworthy.
   Ms. Genene Jones, LVN, has been an asset to
the Bexar County Hospital District, and I would
recommend continued employment.

But by the time she left Medical Center Hospital,
Genene Jones had already found her next permanent
job. She had accepted an offer from Kathleen Holland,
the third-year pediatrics resident who had testified on her
behalf before the Conn committee. Dr. Holland was
getting ready to start her own practice in the Texas Hill
Country, in the little town of Kerrville. She would open
her clinic in August 1982, and Genene had agreed to
work as her office nurse.
   With Genene Jones's departure, the rash of mysterious
emergencies that plagued the ICU suddenly stopped.
Things returned to normal. The young woman anesthesiologist, with help from Dr. Robotham, took over as
medical director; the rehabilitated Belko, despite the
pediatricians' continuing objections, remained in charge
of the nurses. As the weeks slipped by, the residents and
nurses spoke less often of the children who had died so
horribly without explanation. They spoke less often, too,
of the LVN whose hours on duty they had come to call
the Death Shift. What had taken place was becoming

history, in an inexorable process that those who ran the hospital and medical school were not about to interrupt. Their problem had been solved. There was no reason for anyone *ever* to know their terrible secret.

And there it might all have ended—but for the nurse, Genene Jones.

Several months after Genene Jones had departed Medical Center Hospital, a pediatrics resident named Marisol Montes discovered in the ICU's break room a paperback novel with Jones's name written inside. The book was titled *The Sisterhood*, and the back cover detailed its plot. Inside Boston Doctor's Hospital, patients are dying. No one knows why. No one but . . . THE SISTERHOOD. Nurses bound together in mercy. Pledged to end human suffering. Sworn to absolute secrecy. But, within the Sisterhood, evil blooms. Under the white glare of the operating room, patients survive the surgeon's knife. Then, in the dark hollow silence of the nighttime hospital, they die. Suddenly, inexplicably, horribly. No one knows why. No one but the Sisterhood.

PART THREE

THE CLINIC

I would have given my life for hers—Goodbye Chelsea. Jones LVN.

Note on Chelsea McClellan's medical chart

Twelve

GENENE JONES'S FAMILY never heard a clear explanation of why she was leaving Medical Center Hospital. She told her mother and sister she had quit because the doctors didn't know what they were doing; she said the physicians were under investigation. Gladys Jones was relieved to learn of her daughter's plans to move to Kerrville. In San Antonio, Genene was always badgering her, in the throes of one crisis after another. She'd lost her job; she was out of money; she needed Gladys to take care of the kids. Maybe in Kerrville Genene would learn to live on her own. She would have the opportunity for a fresh start.

Genene's resignation from Medical Center Hospital in March left her with five months before Dr. Holland was to open her clinic. For several weeks Genene took temporary assignments at local hospitals through a nursing agency called MedoX. In mid-June, she accepted a full-time job at Santa Rosa Medical Center in downtown San Antonio. She worked the familiar 3–11 P.M. shift in the surgical ICU. Santa Rosa administrators called Medical Center Hospital for information about Genene's job performance, but a clerk in the county hospital's personnel department said she could disclose only that Jones was eligible to reapply for employment. Genene would remain at Santa Rosa for a month—long enough for supervisors there to form their own impressions.

On July 21, a Santa Rosa charge nurse wrote an inci-

dent report on Genene: "On this date at approximately
7:30 P.M. Ms. Jones came to me almost in tears that
'they' couldn't find her child. (I don't know who 'they' is,
but just seconds before this she was on the telephone.)
She told me that she had to go home—I asked her if her
charts were up to date & time & she claimed 'no—they
were not' but that she had to leave!" In checking on the
two seriously ill patients Genene had been assigned, the
charge nurse discovered that Jones had not even opened
their medical charts. Genene had recorded one patient's
vital signs, though the patient claimed that no one had
taken her vital signs during the shift. Added the nursing
supervisor: "Since we came on shift Ms. Jones spent
most of her time (1) smoking in the nutrition room (2)
playing with the computer (3) on the phone & (4) visiting
a patient in MICU & his family. . . . Ms. Jones was not
busy and should of had plenty of time to do her work
before this last phone call." By then, Genene had submitted a resignation letter, explaining that she had "fallen"
on a better opportunity—"one in which I will be able to
use the skills I am trained for." She told her superiors
she would work through July 26. Instead, Genene announced on July 22 that she would not work another day.
She did not offer an explanation.

After leaving Santa Rosa, Genene began looking for a
place to live in Kerrville. When she had trouble finding a
landlord willing to accept pets and young children—Edward
was ten, Crystal five—Dr. Holland decided to buy a
small house as an investment and rent it to her nurse.
Genene and the doctor selected a $45,000 property: 1524
Nixon Lane, a modest three-bedroom brick house in an
isolated subdivision among the hills seven miles outside
town. Genene thought the place was perfect. In early
August, she rented a U-Haul and moved in.

To friends, Genene voiced great admiration—even deep
affection—for her new employer. Kathy Holland wasn't
like the other residents. She was honest and caring, and
unlike many of the young doctors, she didn't seem to
mind Genene's constant questions; she respected her judgment. When Genene called to warn that something was
going on with a child, Kathy Holland came running. "If
Genene says something's going to go wrong," Holland

told another resident, "then it usually does." If Kerrville would be Genene's salvation—an opportunity to escape from the distrust and persecution—Kathy Holland would be her savior.

Holland was one of the few at Medical Center Hospital who considered the LVN a victim. She viewed Genene as a strong, talented woman who was being victimized by a male-dominated hierarchy for her candor—for having the guts to speak the truth, for refusing to play political games. In coming to know Genene Jones, her rocky life and willful ways, Kathy Holland could see much that reminded her of herself.

Kathleen Mary Holland often expressed amazement that she had ever become a doctor. Early in life, her ambitions didn't reach much higher than the basement of the Albany, New York, public library, where she labored as a clerk-typist. Born in 1946, Kathy was the only child of two factory workers, one Irish, one Polish. Her parents moved several times, but never outside the confines of their blue-collar neighborhood in north Albany.

Life there was stormy. Both Kathy's parents had drinking problems, which fueled frequent arguments. Kathy possessed a stubborn streak, which her overwhelmed mother tried vainly to exorcise by whacking her with a thick ruler. When her father died at fifty-nine of pneumonia in 1963, Kathy quit school in the middle of her junior year and took a job in a pizza parlor. Forced to return to school, she rebelled, behaving so badly that the principal wouldn't let her back the next fall. She graduated instead from a predominantly black high school on Albany's south side, then assumed her position as a clerk-typist. Until she met and married a librarian named Larry Doyle, she hadn't considered going to college.

Lacking ambition and self-esteem, Kathy had given herself to an aggressive intellectual, with ambition for both of them. Larry, twelve years her senior, pushed her. She started taking science courses at a nearby community college. When Larry found work in Tucson, Kathy enrolled at the University of Arizona as a biology major. After Doyle got a job at Cornell University in New York, Kathy completed her bachelor's degree there, majoring in anatomy and physiology. Every step of the way, Larry Doyle drove his wife to perform. At his insistence, the couple lived for years without the distraction of a home phone. When Kathy scored a 97 on an exam, Larry asked why she'd missed a question. As Kathy neared completion of her undergraduate degree, Doyle drew on her affection for animals—she was perpetually taking in strays—to steer her toward a career as a veterinarian. When Cornell's vet school rejected her two years running, she was crushed. She hired an attorney and appealed the second decision to a university panel. The appeal was denied. She and Larry then moved to San Antonio, where he took a position in the public library. She managed a Taco Bell fast-food restaurant, attended graduate school part time, and started thinking about studying human medicine.

In July 1974, Kathy enrolled at the University of Texas Health Science Center, working toward both a medical degree and a Ph.D. in anatomy. Kathy had no passion for children; she had her tubes tied at age thirty. But during medical school rotations at Bexar County Hospital, she quickly decided to specialize in pediatrics. "It was just very comfortable," she recalled. "Nobody seemed to be showing each other how much they knew. Nobody was putting on airs. Nobody was arrogant." Another thing drew Kathy Holland to pediatrics: Sick children usually got well.

Kathy and Larry and three cats had settled into a frame house on two acres in a rural area north of San Antonio. After earning her medical degree, Kathy remained in school an extra year to try to complete her doctorate. But she developed a conflict with the adviser on her research project and chose to abandon the Ph.D. The decision triggered an argument with Larry that convinced Kathy she could take no more of his demanding ways. Their uncontested divorce went through on July 27, 1979.

By then, she had moved in with Charleigh Appling, a retired air force colonel who was a campus police officer at the medical school. The two made an odd match. Kathy was a sleepy-eyed woman with pale skin, a blank, moon-shaped face, and thin brown hair. She wore little makeup and dressed casually; her fondness for peasant blouses and faded blue jeans gave her the appearance of an ex-hippie. Charleigh Appling, like Larry Doyle, was Kathy's senior by a dozen years; his shiny bald head made him look like her father. Charleigh had enlisted in the air force at nineteen, trained as a jet pilot, and flown spy planes over Vietnam. He quit the military in 1974 after earning his twenty-year pension. He rode a motorcycle to work at the medical school. He and Kathy had met one night when he escorted her out to her car in the parking lot.

After rearranging her personal life, Holland began her three-year pediatric residency at Bexar County Hospital in July 1979, at age thirty-two. She quickly impressed her fellow residents as a diligent and capable doctor. But she did not mix easily with them. Older than most of her peers, she considered herself more mature and responsible. They thought her hardheaded, a bit aloof and intolerant. Holland was one of the few residents who did not sign the house-staff letter protesting Jim Robotham's removal.

But she did embrace J.R.'s aggressive treatment philosophy. Holland learned to look for the subtle signs that might signal a major problem—then move fast to intervene. She came to think of everything that might be going wrong with a child, no matter how remote the possibility. "I'm always looking for the hidden things," said Holland. "That's the challenge of medicine." It was an approach well suited to an ICU, where children were quite ill and complications were quickly fatal. It was less appropriate in private pediatric practice, where almost all medical problems are minor. Nonetheless, it was private practice that Kathy Holland had decided to enter. Midway through her residency, Holland decided that after completing her training, she would open an office of her own in Kerrville.

A community of 15,000 in the Texas Hill County, Kerrville sat along the picturesque Guadalupe River, sixty miles northwest of San Antonio. The area was a haven for retirees attracted to its clean air and rugged landscape. Each winter it swelled with fugitives from the north, who were known to locals as "snowbirds." The region had its share of trailer parks and struggling poor, but was better known for ranches and vacation homes owned by corporate executives and celebrities who loved to hunt game and play golf. Golfer Byron Nelson had a place in Kerrville; so did the chairmen of LTV and Frito-Lay. Country singer Janie Fricke was a frequent visitor. The town had been elevated to prominence by a Confederate Civil War captain named Charles A. Schreiner, a mercantile banker and rancher who amassed 600,000 acres of land by 1900. As the seat of Kerr County, Kerrville rose, squeaky clean and quiet, around a quaint courthouse square. So sleepy was the place that many year-round inhabitants dubbed it "Kerrpatch." But then, no one moved to Kerrville expecting excitement.

Kerrville drew Kathy Holland because it had a rapidly growing population of young families—and just one pediatrician. The doctors there, all of them men, encouraged her move to town. Kerrville also had the largest general hospital in the area: the 116-bed Sid Peterson Memorial. With its gaudy blue-green tile trim, the seven-story brick hospital dominated downtown Kerrville; there was no taller building in the county. Owned by a nonprofit foundation, Sid Peterson served patients from Hill Country towns a hundred miles to the north and west. Its equipment and staff could handle most illnesses and surgeries; patients who required more sophisticated facilities usually went to San Antonio. But because Kerrville had for years been a town of old people, Sid Peterson was weak in pediatrics. It had no pediatric or neonatal ICU, nor even a separate pediatric ward. It had never needed one. Weeks often went by without a single child in the hospital. As the head nurse of the hospital's general ICU put it, "A pedi patient for us is forty-five years old."

Demographics notwithstanding, Kathy Holland was appalled. New pediatricians were taught that children needed specialized care and separate facilities—that they weren't just little adults. Kerrville didn't seem to recognize that. The hospital put sick children wherever there happened to be an empty bed. No one on the nursing staff specialized in pediatrics. And the hospital lacked much of the pediatric equipment that Holland had come to consider vital. Here, thought Kathy Holland, was her challenge: to bring modern pediatric medicine to Kerrville.

Sid Peterson's lack of experience treating children made Dr. Holland determined to find a nurse with good technical skills for her private practice. "The nurses at Sid Peterson really weren't comfortable with starting pediatric IVs," she said. "They really weren't comfortable with drawing blood on kids younger than two. . . . I wanted to take a nurse with me who had those skills, who had been through codes. I wanted someone who could start IVs for me, who could draw meds for me. I was really worried about going into a whole new community where they did not have pediatric nursing skills at a level that I knew it, and not having anyone to help me."

Holland's first choice was registered nurse Pam Sturm, who worked in the pediatric ICU at Medical Center Hospital. "You can't afford me," Sturm told her; she was making $8.35 an hour. "What you need to look for is an LVN." An LVN would make about $5 an hour. Kathy Holland spoke to a handful of other prospects. Then, in the summer of 1981, she said, she brought up the subject with Genene Jones.

Genene said she turned down Dr. Holland's job offer in late 1981 because she was intent on staying at Medical Center Hospital to clear her name. Several weeks later, she changed her mind when Holland came to the ICU with floor plans for her new clinic. "The rumors were flying, and it sounded real good," recalled Genene. "It sounded peaceful and calm." They agreed to begin in Kerrville in August 1982.

Kathy Holland knew that there were suspicions about Genene Jones. One day in early 1982, Holland's best friend among the residents, a doctor named Jolene Bean, sat down with her and suggested that perhaps she should change her mind about hiring Genene. Yes, Holland told her friend, she had heard the gossip that Genene might be doing something to the children, but she had *worked* with Genene Jones. She didn't believe it. "Nothing I ever saw fit that pattern," she said later. "You show me a puppy that comes up to me and licks my hand. Somebody comes up to me and says, 'That puppy just tore up my leg,' you gotta *show* me."

Holland talked to Pat Belko, who backed Genene, warning only that she was an assertive person—"You give her an inch, she'll take a mile"—and that Holland would need to define clearly the limits of her responsibility. Wanting still more advice, Holland approached Dr. Victor German, the pediatrician who had served as deputy medical director in the ICU. "This is a new office and a new community that really needs pediatrics," she told him. "I'm not asking you to disclose any absolute evidence. Just tell me: Is it a good decision to continue, or should I reconsider? Do you think there's a possibility Genene could be doing something to hurt kids?" "No, I cannot imagine that," German responded, according to Holland.

Later, Holland ran into Robotham outside his laboratory in the medical school. He asked for a word with her, and she recalled that he said, "Hey, I hear you're taking Genene to Kerrville. You better think twice. There's a lot at stake up there." Robotham mentioned the case of Rolando Santos, the child whose repeated bleeding had been documented as a heparin overdose. Holland said she'd heard that the tests on the child's blood had been performed shortly after he had been given heparin to clear clots from an arterial line. Robotham told her he had other suspicions. She thought he seemed vague.

By June 30, 1982, the end of her residency, Holland had received several evaluations of the nurse she had hired, and most of them were favorable. The hospital had given Genene a good recommendation and offered her another job—hardly possible, Holland thought, if the administrators believed she was harming children. Robotham and some nurses had their suspicions, but their ill will toward Genene was clear. And besides, Holland *knew* Genene Jones. She would not withdraw her job offer. "How were you supposed to think this was anything but personal when all these things were coming from people that hated her anyway?" the doctor asked rhetorically many months later. "I trusted her implicitly."

Ultimately, Holland's decision had as much to do with her own personality as it did with what she was told—or not told—about Genene. Most doctors starting a practice would shun any association with a nurse who was tainted

even by gossip. But Kathy Holland had let others tell her
what to do for too long. She possessed a stubbornness
rooted in insecurity. Once she'd made a decision, she was
loath to admit it was wrong; when challenged, she got
her back up. Holland sympathized with Genene, because
she knew what it was like to be an outcast. Both women
felt maligned—by husbands, by institutions, by colleagues
who didn't like their style. And both seemed convinced
they knew more about what was wrong and right with
kids than anyone.

Grateful for Holland's decision to stand by her, Genene
Jones privately resolved to help make the new pediatric
clinic a huge success. She and Kathy would be a team.
Together, they would show Kerrville what pediatric medicine was all about.

To begin her practice, Dr. Holland had selected offices
in the Fine Medical Center, a busy one-story doctors'
complex. The renovated building, once a grocery store,
was less than a mile from downtown Kerrville and Sid
Peterson Hospital. Holland signed a five-year lease on a
1,200-square-foot suite, then spent hours selecting wood
stains for the cabinets and soothing colors for the walls.
Her clinic included a waiting area, three examination
rooms, a private office for the doctor, a business office
for her receptionist, and a little lounge area with a table
and refrigerator, where the staff could relax and eat
lunch. A table scale for weighing babies was in the hallway.

On August 18, Holland, with Genene's help, ordered a
stock of drugs from Pampell's Pharmacy in downtown
Kerrville. Included with several standard items, at a cost
of $1.25, was a small bottle of a drug not commonly
found in a pediatrician's office: succinylcholine, a powerful muscle relaxant sold in the form of clear liquid
under the trade name Anectine. Anesthesiologists routinely used the drug in the operating room to keep their
patients from gagging before insertion of a breathing
tube. But succinylcholine was rarely employed elsewhere
because it temporarily paralyzed the entire skeletal muscle system, making patients incapable of breathing on
their own. Inducing such dependence was dangerous outside the controlled environment of an operating room,

where respirators and other breathing aids were available. The drug also had a dangerous side effect: It could induce bradycardia, or slow heartbeat, which had to be countered with the drug atropine. Holland wanted succinylcholine on hand for emergencies, in case she needed to place a breathing tube down the throat of a large child whose teeth were clenched.

Dr. Holland had originally planned to open her clinic at the end of August, but the business consultant she had retained suggested that opening a week early might bring in a bit of business from preschool physicals. To signal her arrival in town, Holland placed a small, dignified advertisement in the local newspaper and had stiff buff-colored cards printed, in simple black italic type:

KATHLEEN M. HOLLAND, M.D.
announces the opening of her office
for the practice of
PEDIATRICS
Effective August 23, 1982
320 N. Waters Street
Suite F
Kerrville, Texas 78028
By Appointment from August 15, 1982

The kind of practice Kathy Holland planned promised great burdens but also offered the prospect of great rewards. Pediatrics was medicine's least lucrative specialty, and opening a new office required large loans for equipment and supplies; it was not unusual for a new doctor to go $100,000 into debt. Solo practice meant long hours and an unending stream of late-night calls from fretful parents. But a lone practitioner also enjoyed the freedom to practice medicine as she wished. And after building a busy practice, the doctor working alone need not share the fruits of her labor. In Kerrville, Kathy Holland felt sure, the harvest would be bountiful.

On April 16, shortly before completing her residency in San Antonio, Holland had married Charleigh Appling. Kathy and Charleigh had big plans for their life together. They would live outside the hamlet of Centerpoint, on a rugged sixteen-acre tract fifteen miles south of the clinic.

Charleigh had bought the land in May 1980 with the help of a loan from the state veterans' land board, and they'd been dreaming of living there ever since. They would have peace and quiet, idyllic countryside, and room for Kathy's two horses, which she was boarding at a stable. Their property would have two houses: an underground home built into the side of a hill for Kathy and Charleigh, and a second, smaller house for a couple they would hire as caretakers for the property. They would build the underground house as soon as Kathy's practice was flourishing; in the beginning, they planned to live in the smaller place. Charleigh had quit his job as a campus police officer and was building the house himself.

But as August 1982 arrived, the first house was little more than a foundation and wooden frame. Charleigh often spent nights at the site in a sleeping bag to keep an eye on things. But there was no hot water or bathroom there. Reluctant to commute daily from San Antonio, where Charleigh still owned a house, Holland arranged to stay on Nixon Lane with Genene and her children most nights during the week.

Genene's devoted friend, Debbie Sultenfuss, also had left Medical Center Hospital when the LVNs had been removed. Like Genene, Debbie had worked at the MedoX nursing agency for a time. In May 1982, with Genene's encouragement, she moved to Kerrville and began working in the Sid Peterson nine-bed intensive care unit, usually on the 3–11 shift. Debbie moved her trailer to Kerrville, but the utility company was taking its time hooking up the electricity. In her free hours during the day, Debbie helped Kathy and Genene move into the clinic. She joined them at night after work at the house on Nixon Lane.

Completing the crowd of six there was Catherine Marie Ferguson, a peculiar nineteen-year-old Genene had met in her San Antonio apartment complex. Cathy had a history of psychiatric problems and had spent part of her childhood in a Texas state mental hospital. Genene had taken her in. She persuaded the young woman to accompany her to Kerrville and serve as a live-in baby-sitter for Crystal and Edward. Once there, Genene told people Cathy was retarded and suffering from cerebral palsy.

Neither claim was true. She began introducing the young woman as her daughter.

In August, Dr. Holland hired a secretary-receptionist, Gwen Grantner, who had bounced from job to job in Kerrville. The thirty-three-year-old woman was less than five feet tall and weighed about 85 pounds—and she talked nonstop. Though Grantner was born in Chicago and had never been to England, she spoke with a strong cockney accent. Introduced by her boyfriend—a mechanic who worked on the office air-conditioning—Gwen told Holland she'd been married to a Briton, found his manner of speech appealing, and decided to affect it herself. The new doctor was intrigued. "She had this neat accent," said Holland. "She was very honest about things, and I liked honesty. She said she'd had a lot of different jobs, but that was because of disagreements." Holland asked Gwen Grantner to join her fledgling medical clinic.

The staff was complete and the office ready to open.

Thirteen

ON THE MONDAY the clinic was to open, Genene awoke early and prepared excitedly for work. There were already several appointments on the schedule; she was eager to get to the office. After donning her work clothes, Genene pinned to her chest the new brass name tag she had ordered. It read: "Genene Jones, Pediatric Clinician"— a title that customarily designated an RN with advanced training.

Genene climbed into her car and headed for the clinic. Dr. Holland met her there. Kathy had spent the weekend in San Antonio with her husband. She would bring her suitcase to begin staying in the house on Nixon Lane that night. For the opening of her office, the pediatrician sported a neat, professional look; she wore her hair in Dorothy Hamill bangs.

Gwen appeared and took up her station at the receptionist's window that looked into the waiting room. Everyone had scrambled to get things ready, but the clinic was not quite finished. The examining tables had arrived only a day or two earlier, several wall cabinets were not yet installed, and they were awaiting some supplies. To start, Holland had decided to equip fully only one of the three exam rooms—the one closest to the front of the office. Because she and Genene stored all their emergency equipment and drugs there, they called it the crash room.

During her clinic's first day, Dr. Holland would see

only one patient. But no one was worried. It was just the
beginning. Things were sure to pick up.

TUESDAY, AUGUST 24, 1982
Like many parents in and around Kerrville, Petti and
Reid McClellan were pleased when they heard that a new
pediatrician was coming to town. Here was a chance to
take their kids to a real expert, a young woman fresh
from training in the most modern medical techniques.
"Everybody was real excited about it," said Petti. "I just
had this thing about specialists."

The McClellans, both twenty-seven, lived fifteen miles
west of Kerrville, in a three-bedroom mobile home in
rural Gillespie County. Their eleven-acre tract of scrubland
lay down a dusty, rutted road appropriately named Thrill
Hill Drive. Reid repaired electric lines for Central Texas
Electric, a local utility company; Petti worked as a secretary. Although they exuded small-town geniality, the
McClellans had adopted their country ways; both had
grown up around Houston.

Petti had been raised by her mother and stepfather,
who held a minor political post in Harris County. In high
school, she was a cheerleader and member of the student
council, an earnest middle-class girl with middle-American
dreams: marriage, her own home, and a houseful of
children. After graduation, Petti's stepfather helped her
find a job at the Harris County courthouse, where she
spent two years issuing license plates and a third year
working as a secretary. In 1978, after her mother divorced
her stepfather and moved to Lake Buchanan, a vacation
community in Central Texas, Petti joined her there.

William Reid McClellan had grown up in Pasadena, a
grimy Houston suburb that bordered the city's ship channel. At age eighteen, after learning that his girlfriend was
pregnant, Reid married, then quit high school to support
his new family. He worked as a meter reader, in an oil
refinery, and in a Houston plastics plant. In 1977, he
bought the Hi-Line Fishing Lodge—eighteen cabins, a
restaurant, and a fishing dock—and moved his family to
Lake Buchanan. Less than two years later, Reid and his
wife split up. The divorce would force him to sell the
lodge and go to work as a lineman.

Petti and Reid met in the spring of 1979 in Lake Buchanan. They were introduced by her mother, who belonged to the fire company's ladies' auxiliary; Reid was a volunteer fireman. They were married on May 10, 1980, in an outdoor ceremony, and they made an attractive couple: Reid solidly built, with thick black hair and a shaggy mustache; Petti a bit slight, with a sweet face and a girlish smile. Each already had one child from a previous relationship—Reid a son named Shay and Petti a son named Cameron. Now both wanted another child, and both wanted a girl. "From the minute I found out I was pregnant, I started calling it 'she,' " said Petti. "If someone bought me a baby gift for a boy, I'd take it back."

Chelsea Ann McClellan was born at 12:01 P.M. on June 16, 1981. She was about four weeks premature, and labor was difficult; the placenta tore early, and Petti bled heavily before she arrived at Sid Peterson Hospital for an emergency cesarean section. Shortly after birth, Chelsea showed evidence of hyaline membrane disease, a respiratory problem caused by underdeveloped lungs, usually found in premature children. A helicopter ambulance rushed her to Santa Rosa Hospital in San Antonio, and she was put on a respirator in the neonatal ICU.

At Santa Rosa, Chelsea improved steadily. On July 5, after twenty-one days in the hospital, she was eating well and breathing on her own, and her weight had climbed to four pounds, six ounces. Her parents took her home to their trailer outside Kerrville, where they had moved by that time. With Chelsea safely out of the hospital, Petti went to her gynecologist and had herself sterilized by tubal ligation.

On May 6, 1982, Petti brought Chelsea back to the Santa Rosa emergency room. She was feverish and on the previous night had experienced what Petti described to hospital personnel as two "breath-holding" spells. Petti later said that Chelsea had briefly stopped breathing and turned blue after one of her brothers knocked her down. After dinner, she began vomiting and lost her breath a second time, until Petti blew air into her daughter's mouth. Then ten months old, Chelsea remained at Santa Rosa until May 11. She was treated for pneumonia, but an assortment of tests turned up no evidence of seizures or a breathing disorder. "I would just caution the parents to observe her closely," wrote Dr. Joel Rutman, a pediatric neurologist who examined Chelsea. "Her growth and development have been amazingly fine for her age, and I don't think there is any reason to suspect she is going to be slow in the future."

The McClellans brought Chelsea home and lavished attention on her. She developed a spoiled child's temper, but she was attentive and curious. She followed the large world around her closely with her blue eyes, and when someone caught her staring, she would laugh and break into a wide, coy smile. Even those who barely knew Chelsea were charmed. "She was a beautiful kid," said Genene Jones. "God, she was beautiful."

Chelsea Ann McClellan, fourteen months old, was Kathy Holland's first patient on her second day in private practice. According to Petti, she called in the morning to make an appointment and spoke to receptionist Gwen Grantner. Holland said that Gwen told her Petti was worried about Chelsea's "erratic breathing" and that when Chelsea arrived in the waiting room, she had a bluish tint around her mouth. But the McClellans said they never described any breathing problems to Holland, Genene Jones, or Gwen Grantner—then or later. "There wasn't a damn thing blue about Chelsea," said Petti, "except her eyes." She took her daughter to the doctor, she said, because Chelsea had the sniffles. On the patient information form she filled out in Dr. Holland's waiting room that day, Petti listed the reason for the visit as "bad cold."

Petti and Chelsea arrived at the clinic about 1 P.M., and Dr. Holland led mother and child to her private office in the back of the suite. As Holland began to ask Petti about Chelsea's medical history, the little girl started pulling things off Holland's desk. "Why don't you let me take Chelsea and play with her, so you can talk?" Genene suggested. She picked up the child and took her out of the office.

Five minutes later, Dr. Holland heard her nurse talking to the toddler down the hall: *"Don't go to sleep, baby. Chelsea, wake up!"* The summons came a moment later. "Dr. Holland, would you come here?" Holland excused herself, closing the door behind her, and walked back to the treatment room to find Chelsea limp on the examining table and Genene fitting an oxygen mask over her face. Genene later said that she had been playing ball with Chelsea in the receptionist's area and that the child had suddenly slumped over. But now there was no time to ask questions: Chelsea wasn't breathing. Genene began pumping oxygen into her lungs with a respiratory bag, and she and Holland started an IV in her scalp. Chelsea began seizing; Holland ordered 80 milligrams of Dilantin, an anticonvulsant drug. Gwen had left for lunch; Holland ran out of the room and told some carpenters working in the building to summon the Kerr County Emergency Medical Service.

Chelsea's mother had no idea what had happened until Holland returned to her private office to tell her. "Your daughter's just had a seizure," she said. Holland told Petti to stay put, but she followed the doctor into the hall and looked inside the treatment room as Holland went back in. Chelsea was sprawled on the examining table, Genene hovering over her. "I could see her little legs," said Petti. "She was laying there, real limp."

The EMS ambulance arrived at 1:25 P.M. Genene's assertive manner left the paramedics uncertain which of the two women treating the child was the doctor; Jones had to point out her boss. Then Genene carried Chelsea into the back of the ambulance as a paramedic followed along with an IV bottle. Holland joined them, and Petti got in with the driver. They arrived at the Sid Peterson emergency room two minutes later.

By then, Chelsea had resumed breathing on her own. She was sent to the ICU and remained at Sid Peterson for ten days, but tests showed nothing to explain the seizure and respiratory arrest. The McClellans, nonetheless, were deeply grateful. Dr. Holland and her nurse, they believed, had saved Chelsea's life. Petti went all over town, telling her friends about the terrific new pediatrician. "Take your kid to Dr. Holland," she counseled. "She's the best thing since canned beer!"

Kerrville's newest doctor also had made a favorable

first impression on the nurses at Sid Peterson Hospital. Even before opening her practice, Holland had dropped by to introduce herself. When the nurses confessed their anxieties about treating children, Holland reassured them. She carefully went over what special equipment they would need. The pediatrician seemed to regard medicine not just as a job but as a mission. To accommodate working parents, she was taking appointments Saturday mornings and on Wednesdays until 9 P.M. She had even proclaimed her intention to care for sick children whose families couldn't pay, something many doctors refused to do. "If ever a baby needs help, call me—even if they have no money," Holland advised the hospital nurses.

Debbie Sultenfuss's first months at Sid Peterson had threatened to spoil Holland's reception. Just days after beginning work in the ICU, Sultenfuss announced to the other nurses that Dr. Holland had sent her to evaluate their ability to treat children and report back what she found. She declared that Holland was going to place her in charge of pediatric nursing services at the hospital—a position that didn't exist. Debbie particularly had antagonized the registered nurses by declaring that "RNs get all the glory while LVNs do all the work." And her nursing notes angered the doctors: Debbie's spelling, grammar, and handwriting remained nearly incomprehensible.

Aware that Sultenfuss had made waves, Holland apologized profusely when she met with the nurses before opening her practice. She told them that Debbie had no business making such remarks. Debbie modeled herself after Genene Jones, the nurse who would be working in her office, explained Holland. Debbie had good instincts, the doctor added, but she lacked Genene's extraordinary pediatric skills.

When EMS radioed in that a baby who had stopped breathing was on her way from Holland's office, the Sid Peterson nurses stood by anxiously to assist the new doctor on her first emergency. Chelsea McClellan's arrival had calmed them. The little girl was obviously stable. In fact, while she seemed a bit sleepy, she didn't look sick at all. And after a few hours' rest in the ICU, she was tireless. At 9 P.M. the night of Chelsea's arrival, an RN noted on her medical chart that she was "awake, alert, playing." During the rest of her stay, she bounced about in her crib and toddled around the halls. She seemed so bright and happy; she didn't even cry. The nurses wondered: How could there have been anything wrong with Chelsea?

FRIDAY, AUGUST 27

Nelda and Gabriel Benites were worried. Brandy Lee, their one-month-old daughter, had blood in her stools and diarrhea that had persisted for two days. Brandy was their first baby, born two months premature. Nelda had given birth to her at age seventeen. She was a housewife. Gabriel, nineteen, stocked shelves at the Super S grocery store. The young couple had no telephone at their home, no medical insurance, and little money to pay a doctor.

Brandy's parents took her to the emergency room at Sid Peterson Hospital, where the staff gave them Dr. Holland's card and told them to call Kerrville's new pediatrician. They arrived at Holland's clinic late in the morning. Her nurse carried the baby back to the treatment room, while the doctor took Brandy's medical history. Dr. Holland later summarized what she was told on Brandy's medical chart: "Presents with two-day history irritability when fed formula, stopped taking formula yesterday morning, received only tea and rice water since, about 20 ounces per day. Mom noticed small amount of blood in one stool yesterday—rest of stool blackish green. Baby appears in pain with bowel movements and Mom reports stomach is distended."

Dr. Holland told Nelda and Gabriel Benites that she wanted to hospitalize Brandy for tests to determine the cause of her bleeding. Then she asked Brandy's parents to remain in the waiting room while she examined the baby. Nelda Benites soon saw the doctor's nurse rushing back and forth. Then Dr. Holland came out and told them their daughter had stopped breathing.

Holland said later that Brandy was gray and lethargic when she arrived in the office and that she left the baby alone briefly with Genene before the child stopped breathing and had a seizure. Holland's office called EMS at 11:37 A.M. After half an hour at Sid Peterson, Holland told Brandy's parents that she wanted to transfer their

daughter to Santa Rosa in San Antonio. Genene Jones
felt certain that Brandy had necrotizing enterocolitis, the
dangerous intestinal inflammation that had killed her first
pediatric patient at Bexar County Hospital. Kathy Holland listed the disease as her primary suspicion.

The ambulance set out about 3 P.M., with Genene,
paramedic Phillip Kneese, and respiratory therapist Sara
Mauldin in the back and Kathy Holland following in a
car. Holland explained to Mr. and Mrs. Benites that she
got carsick after riding in an ambulance for more than a
few minutes. As the ambulance raced toward Santa Rosa,
Genene began barking orders and pleading with the tiny
patient. "Please, baby, don't die! C'mon! C'mon!" Kneese
thought the nurse strange; she was getting out of control.
Ten minutes into the trip, Brandy's pulse suddenly grew
faint. "Stop the ambulance!" Genene hollered. The car
pulled over to the side of the road. Holland rushed in;
Genene was performing CPR, Mauldin bagging Brandy—
forcing air into her lungs with a respiratory bag. The
doctor told them to stop and placed her stethoscope on
the baby's chest; Brandy's slow heartbeat was coming
back. Holland climbed back into her own car, and the
procession went on its way again, this time with siren
whining and ambulance lights flashing. Brandy's condition was unsteady; Mauldin was still bagging her. Then
Genene started an IV in Brandy's foot. Kneese and
Mauldin didn't understand why; the baby already had an
IV going. A few minutes later, Brandy's color, already
gray from poor circulation, darkened further. Genene
lifted the child's foot and let it go. It fell like a bag of
sand; the baby was limp. "Bag like crazy!" shouted
Genene. They took turns breathing for the baby until she
arrived at the hospital.

Brandy Benites remained for six days at Santa Rosa,
where she ate well and recovered rapidly. Physicians at
Santa Rosa dismissed the possibility of necrotizing enterocolitis—it is not unusual for a child to have bleeding
with diarrhea, they explained—but they could not determine what had caused Brandy's emergency. The pediatrician who treated the baby wrote: "It is unclear as to the
etiology of her respiratory arrest."

Fourteen

IT DID NOT take long for the little brick house on Nixon Lane to become a cloister. The four women and two children who lived together in the hills outside Kerrville shared daybreak and darkness and many hours in between. Newcomers in a town that warmed to strangers slowly, they formed a tight circle of their own. Genene came to regard all those who shared the house as her family; she had a special fondness for Kathy Holland. She described the doctor as "the big sister I never really had."

Kathy Holland lived and worked in isolation from her peers. As the only woman doctor in town, she was regarded by the other physicians as a bit of a curiosity. Among a group of backslapping, good-ol'-boy Texans, Holland did not fit—and she made little effort to reach out. While she attempted to disguise her feelings, the pediatrician regarded the Kerrville medical community with contempt. Like many doctors fresh out of residency, she considered the local physicians backward, hopelessly out of touch with the fast-changing world of modern medicine. Holland's husband, her clinic, and her friends in the house on Nixon Lane became her world.

Her friendship with Genene far transcended the usual bonds of a relationship between a doctor and her nurse. Kathy and Genene shared morning coffee after getting the kids off to school. Sometimes they rode in to work together. At night, after dinner and baths, Kathy listened to Genene entertaining on the piano. When the kids were in bed, they played cards and watched television. Practicing medicine by herself, with no close friends among the other doctors, Kathy often sought Genene's advice. Doctors and nurses were struck by how much Holland depended on her nurse. At home and in the office, the two women spent hours together smoking cigarettes and talking shop, sharing confidences and dreams.

Genene spoke wistfully of the children she had treated in San Antonio. In an autobiography she later began but did not complete, she wrote of her sadness on learning she would have to leave the ICU and the kids she so dearly loved. Genene warmly invoked the names of several children who had died under her care, some of them the very patients she was suspected of harming. Among them all, Genene wrote, Chris Hogeda was "the one who taught me the most."

> He not only taught me the value of life, but the value of love. That to share your love with others, even to the point of hurting, was good and right. That when a part of you dies along with a child, an even bigger part lives because of that love. He taught everyone unselfish love. He brought that love to so many. In touching a part of Christopher's life, you felt you actually had the privilege of touching an angel. A gift from God Himself.
>
> Those gifts, no one would ever take away from me. They would always be reminders of those days when I was privileged enough to know God's true children.

In going to Kerrville, Genene wrote, "maybe I would be lucky enough to meet other angels."

Genene *had* met other angels in Kerrville; she and Kathy talked about them too. If one simply counted patients, the clinic's first week had been slow; they had seen no more than two children a day. But in terms of serious illness, it had been frenetic. Two respiratory arrests in a single week! Holland and Genene griped about the Sid Peterson staff's inexperience at handling pediatric cases. They were glad Debbie Sultenfuss worked in the ICU; she could help treat the most critical patients. The doctor agreed with her nurse that Chelsea and Brandy had been lucky to walk into their clinic at the very moment of crisis. If Kathy and Genene hadn't been around to rescue them, the two children might not have made it.

MONDAY, AUGUST 30

Mary Ann Parker, a registered nurse at a Kerrville convalescent home, brought her little boy to Dr. Holland's office at about 10 A.M. Christopher, four months old, had a condition called stridor—raspy breathing caused by constricted air passages. Genene came into the waiting room, looked Chris over, and pointed out that his feet seemed a bit blue. She took the baby back into the treatment area, while Mrs. Parker waited outside.

Then Kathy Holland came out to talk to her. "I told the mother that I felt that we should have him in the hospital so that I could evaluate his stridor and decide what the next step was," Holland said later. "And I told her that I wanted to transport him by ambulance in case something unexpected happened." Holland said the baby never stopped breathing or had a seizure in the office; summoned at 10:21 A.M., the paramedics were told he was experiencing "respiratory distress." The ambulance took Chris, accompanied by his mother and Genene Jones, to the emergency room. Genene rushed the child in and hovered over him as though expecting a disaster. The hospital nurses were puzzled; the baby had breathing problems but seemed to be stable, hardly even an emergency case. Mrs. Parker watched anxiously from close by. "I hope the baby doesn't go into arrest while we're waiting," announced Genene.

Shortly after Chris Parker arrived in the emergency room, Jimmy Pearson was brought in. Jimmy had a seizure disorder, an often fatal heart defect called tetralogy of Fallot, and a hereditary bone condition that stunted the growth of his legs and arms. At the age of seven, he was unable to walk, crawl, or speak, and weighed only twenty-one pounds. Doctors had long predicted his demise.

On this day Jimmy had gone into seizures and turned blue from lack of oxygen. His mother, Mary Ellen Pearson, had taken him to the emergency room. The nurses there called Dr. Holland over and asked her to look at

him. In addition to being blue, Jimmy was semiconscious
and frothing with phlegm. Holland consulted by phone
with the two doctors who had been treating the child in
San Antonio, then told Mrs. Pearson that they needed to
transport him to Santa Rosa Hospital. The pediatrician
called Fort Sam Houston in San Antonio and arranged
for a transfer by army helicopter ambulance, a Military
Assistance to Safety and Traffic (MAST) unit from the
507th Medical Company.

When paramedics David Maywhort and Gabriel Garcia arrived at the helipad near the city limits and were
driven to Sid Peterson, Dr. Holland asked the two army
sergeants if they could also take Chris Parker to Santa
Rosa. Chris had in the meantime been transferred to the
ICU. Maywhort went up to check on him. He looked
fine. Maywhort wondered why the baby needed to be
transferred at all, but the medics agreed to take him.
Before leaving, Holland explained that if the two children should arrest simultaneously, they should try to save
Chris first. The paramedics expected no such problem;
even Jimmy appeared relatively stable. Genene Jones,
who was to accompany them on the flight, was less sanguine. She told Garcia she thought Jimmy might go sour.

The ambulance shuttled the patients, the paramedics,
and Genene out to the helipad, about three miles from
Sid Peterson. They strapped Jimmy down on the top
litter in the helicopter, then tied the portable incubator
containing Chris Parker to the litter below. Genene hopped
in, carrying a brown paper bag of supplies. With everyone aboard, the chopper took off into a clear blue sky. It
would be a wild ride.

Everything was fine for fifteen minutes. Then Genene
got out of her seat and began looking at Jimmy Pearson.
She shouted and gestured to the paramedics; she seemed
to think Jimmy was seizing. The paramedics looked at
the boy. His condition didn't appear to have changed.
Genene took out a stethoscope and placed it on Jimmy's
chest. The paramedics looked at each other. They knew
it was impossible to hear a heartbeat over the din of the
helicopter. They yelled to her, but Genene waved back.
She was saying she could hear. *What was going on?*

The nurse began gesturing again, shouting that the

patient was going bad, that his heartbeat was irregular. Garcia checked the monitor; he saw no change. Maywhort was inches from Jimmy Pearson. He looked closely at the child; his condition seemed the same as when they'd taken off. But Genene was getting out a syringe from her paper bag. She was about to inject Jimmy with something through the IV line. Maywhort waved at her to stop, but she went ahead anyway. "Sir, mark time!" Maywhort radioed to the pilot. "She's pushing medication." Two or three minutes passed. Then the monitor started showing heartbeat irregularities. Jimmy was turning blue. The paramedics looked at his chest; he had stopped breathing. They checked for a pulse in his neck; there was none.

Genene got out a respiratory bag and began trying to pump air into the child. It wasn't doing any good; Jimmy's deformities made it impossible to seal the respiratory mask over his face. Maywhort stood over the boy's litter and began performing mouth-to-mouth resuscitation. They needed to get a tube down his throat to establish a clear airway, but there wasn't enough room to maneuver in the cramped helicopter. Maywhort ordered an emergency landing. The pilot dropped down fast into a plowed field. They opened the cabin door, moved Jimmy's litter, and tried to insert a breathing tube. The paramedics' third attempt was successful, but when they reentered the helicopter, the tube fell out.

They took off again for San Antonio, Maywhort cradling Jimmy in his arms while performing mouth-to-mouth through the boy's secretions, Garcia massaging the deformed child's heart. Genene, looking queasy and breathing heavily, sat back in a crew seat. Somehow, Jimmy clung to life. The helicopter flew at top speed, and the paramedics diverted to Methodist Hospital in northwest San Antonio. A medical team there rushed Jimmy to the emergency room and stabilized him, while the helicopter flew Chris Parker to Santa Rosa. By the time it returned, Jimmy Pearson was able to make the short trip downtown to Santa Rosa.

Genene Jones later offered a sharply different account of what happened. A short time into the flight, she said in an interview, "Jimmy turned black." Genene said

that's when she gave him an injection—of Neo-Synephrine,
a drug used to open breathing passages and dry up secretions. Jimmy's heart did not falter until ten minutes later,
she said. The army paramedics, she asserted, "are full of
shit. They didn't even want to look at Jimmy. They
couldn't stand to look at Jimmy." When they were trying
to put the breathing tube down Jimmy's throat, Genene
claimed, one of the paramedics suggested that they not
bother. "He kept telling me, 'What's the use of putting it
in? Let the kid die.'" Genene even contradicted the
paramedics on the weather. In her aborted autobiography, she claimed that the helicopter had taken off in a
"sudden downpour." The routine report the paramedics
filed after the mission describes the weather as "sunny
day—clear skies."

After the MAST helicopter took off from Kerrville,
Mary Ellen Pearson had returned home to pack before
driving to San Antonio. She reached Santa Rosa long
before her son. When Jimmy finally arrived, Genene
Jones rushed up to explain what had happened, Mrs.
Pearson later recalled. "She was very pale, she was
trembling, she had an unusual—I can't explain the look
she had in her eyes. It was something I have never seen
before. She told me that Jimmy had stopped breathing
. . . that they landed in a cow pasture. She made a joke
about the cows not producing milk for twenty years because of the helicopter."

Jimmy Pearson remained hospitalized for the next seven
weeks. He recovered enough to return to Sid Peterson,
but his condition deteriorated again. He was taken back
to Santa Rosa, where he died on October 21. Chris
Parker, who had slept through much of the flight from
Kerrville, was discharged after three days at Santa Rosa.
Doctors there found no reason to keep the baby in the
hospital.

The number of children Kathy Holland had transferred
from Kerrville to Santa Rosa—there had been three in
three days—was beginning to raise eyebrows among those
familiar with the suspicions that had surrounded her nurse
in San Antonio. Third-year pediatric resident Marisol
Montes—the doctor who discovered the copy of *The*

Sisterhood bearing Jones's name—was on a rotation in Santa Rosa's pediatric ICU when Brandy Benites arrived by ambulance. She had been surprised that a child who had arrested would be in such good condition. Montes was also on duty when Kathy Holland called to say she was transferring two more children by MAST helicopter— and alarmed to learn that Genene Jones was on her way with them.

"Kathy, did you *really* hire Genene?" Montes asked.

"Yes, she's very good," responded Holland.

"Kathy, I'm not going to accept these admissions if Genene is with them. *Please* don't send Genene with them!"

"They've already left."

Montes climbed to the hospital's rooftop landing pad to await the helicopter carrying Jimmy Pearson and Chris Parker. She soon got a call that they had made an emergency stop at Methodist. An emergency room doctor there told her Jimmy Pearson's blood tests didn't offer a clue to what had caused his arrest. When Genene Jones finally showed up, she greeted Montes. "Kathy's getting arrests and real sick babies," she told the young resident. "Never go into private practice. You don't know how awful it is."

After Monday's trauma, Kathy Holland was grateful for the next few days' routine. Business remained slow; she saw just a handful of patients a day. On Thursday, September 2, the pediatrician allowed Chelsea McClellan to leave Sid Peterson and go home. Brandy Benites and Chris Parker had already recovered and been dismissed from Santa Rosa. Things were finally settling down.

FRIDAY, SEPTEMBER 3

Misty Shayne Reichenau, twenty-one months old, was sick and fussy. She'd had mouth sores for four days, as well as fever and a cold. Misty was Kay and Larry Reichenau's second child. Kay, thirty-one, was a housewife, Larry, thirty-two, a general contractor. Their daughter had been a healthy baby, without a major medical problem since birth. Earlier in the week, they'd taken Misty to her doctor, Duan Packard, a sixty-eight-year-old family practitioner in Kerrville. Dr. Packard had prescribed an antibiotic—ampicillin—for Misty's throat and ear infections, and suggested hydrogen peroxide for her mouth. The antibiotic had cleared the infections, but the sores seemed to be getting worse. That morning, Misty had stopped eating and drinking and vomited twice. Kay Reichenau called Dr. Packard, who told her he was on his way out of town. He said there was a new pediatrician in Kerrville named Kathy Holland who could probably see Misty.

Mrs. Reichenau arrived at Dr. Holland's office about 2 P.M. with her mother and daughter and was ushered into the treatment room. Misty cried while Genene took her rectal temperature; it was 101.8 degrees. Mrs. Reichenau held Misty in her lap as Dr. Holland examined the little girl's neck, trying to bend her head down to her chest. Misty resisted, as though her neck were stiff. Holland and Genene looked at each other knowingly. "Dr. Holland said not to be excited, but it could possibly be meningitis," recalled Mrs. Reichenau. Holland wanted to admit Misty to the hospital to test for the disease with a spinal tap. But first she wanted to start an IV; Misty seemed a bit dehydrated. Dr. Holland explained that she started IVs and drew blood at the clinic on all children she was sending to the hospital. Part of the reason for this unusual policy—such procedures were customarily performed in the hospital—was that the pediatrician wanted to get the IV treatments and blood tests going immediately. The other part of the reason was that Dr. Holland didn't trust the nurses at Sid Peterson—at least not the way that she trusted Genene Jones.

Mrs. Reichenau volunteered to take Misty to the hospital herself—after all, it was less than a mile—but Dr. Holland insisted on calling EMS. While Holland left the room to summon an ambulance, Mrs. Reichenau stepped out to the waiting area to ask her mother to phone Larry. When she returned to the treatment room, Genene had prepared the IV and the fluids that were to flow through it into her daughter's bloodstream. "You might want to step out in the hall, because it's not easy on a mother to watch," Genene told her. "She's going to cry, and she's going to scream." Mrs. Reichenau said she didn't need to

leave. "I'm pretty stout; I can take it," she said. Returning to the room, Dr. Holland helped hold Misty. The
pediatrician and her nurse were struggling to start the IV.
Misty was screaming and crying. And then the IV needle
was in her arm—and she was silent. Misty stared at her
mother with a strange, far-off look.

"There's something wrong!" Mrs. Reichenau shouted.

"She's just holding her breath," said Genene. "She's
scared." The nurse ordered Mrs. Reichenau out the door.
Misty wasn't breathing.

In tears, Mrs. Reichenau stumbled out to the waiting
room, where her mother was sitting. Gwen came over to
reassure them, but her words were of little comfort. "She
said they were doing everything they could for Misty;
that they weren't going to let Misty die; that they had
saved lots of babies," Mrs. Reichenau recalled. "She said
just last week they had saved a baby that quit breathing
in her office. She said they could work miracles—that
they did it every day."

Inside the crash room, Misty was having a seizure. Dr.
Holland gave her oxygen and ordered a dose of Dilantin
to prevent more convulsions. The doctor wanted to intubate Misty—to place a breathing tube down her throat—
but the little girl's teeth were clenched. Debbie Sultenfuss
had dropped by Holland's office for lunch. Now she
appeared in the room with a bottle of the muscle relaxant
Anectine, which she said Holland had asked for to keep
Misty from struggling. Holland said later that she had
never requested the drug and that when Debbie brought
it in, she didn't know the proper dosage and didn't want
to use it. She intubated Misty without the Anectine.

The ambulance arrived at Sid Peterson at 3:07 P.M.,
and Genene carried Misty in her arms directly up to the
ICU. After a while, Holland came out and told the
Reichenaus—Larry had arrived at the hospital by then—
that she wanted to fly Misty to Medical Center Hospital
for tests and observation. Genene told the Reichenaus
they couldn't fly in the MAST helicopter. The last time
she'd flown in it, Genene explained, there had been a
crisis, and they'd been forced to make an emergency
landing in a field.

When Misty arrived in the pediatric ICU at Medical

Center Hospital, doctors found her agitated, breathing on her own, and struggling against the breathing tube, which they took out. Dr. Holland had sent Misty to San Antonio with a tentative diagnosis of "partially treated meningitis." But an assortment of tests revealed no evidence of the disease—and no explanation for the seizures. Doctors transferred Misty out of the ICU after one day and took her off the Dilantin Dr. Holland had prescribed. Misty's San Antonio physicians told the Reichenaus they could find only what had sent her to Kathy Holland's clinic in the first place: a nasty case of mouth ulcers. Misty was sent home five days after her arrival. Wrote a pediatrician in his discharge summary: "The patient's hospital course was unremarkable."

After Misty returned to Kerrville, her parents took her back to Dr. Holland for a follow-up visit. Holland asked if they wanted to use her as a pediatrician. The parents of Brandy Benites and Chelsea McClellan had kept their children under Holland's care. But the Reichenaus declined. They told Kathy Holland they already had a family doctor.

TUESDAY, SEPTEMBER 7

After seeing a couple of children Saturday morning, Kathy Holland had closed her clinic for the long Labor Day weekend. Everyone was ready for the break. Dr. Holland had left Kerrville to spend the free time with her husband. Genene tried hard to relax. She had begun taking long walks to the top of a hill behind her house, where she would sit and meditate. She had grown fond of the summer hit movie *E.T.;* she referred to her visits to the hilltop as "going to talk to E.T."

When the clinic reopened on Tuesday—four days after Misty Reichenau's first office visit—Genene told Dr. Holland that she had completed an inventory of the office's drugs and discovered a small vial of Anectine was missing. Presumably, this was the same vial that Debbie had brought to the crash room during Misty's seizure. Holland told her nurse to search the office. If you can't find it, she instructed Genene, log it as missing and order another bottle. A replacement vial was ordered from the Sid Peterson pharmacy later that day.

At night, the conversation on Nixon Lane inevitably turned to the subject of all the children arresting in the clinic. They had averaged less than three patients a day for two weeks, yet already they had sent four children to the hospital by ambulance. Holland had tried to joke about how busy they were. But one night, in exhaustion, she had broken down in tears. This was worse than residency, Holland remarked. She had never seen so many sick kids.

Still Kathy Holland failed to connect what was going on with San Antonio, or Genene Jones. It was as though her decision to hire the nurse had erased all memory of the suspicions at Medical Center Hospital, as though there were no precedent for what was happening in her clinic. Genene's exaggeration of minor symptoms was feeding Holland's overaggressive approach. The pediatrician was interpreting each of her patients' minor problems as a sign of serious illness—the sort of illness that would explain even seizures and respiratory arrest. To Kathy Holland, the one doctor in Kerrville with reason to know better, there was no pattern or common denominator. Each case was unique. The emergencies were a terrible coincidence.

Gwen Grantner offered her own contribution to the discourse. A woman of unusual ways, Gwen was an adherent of Eckankar, a religious cult that believed in reincarnation and rejected the notion that evil existed on earth. Gwen read books about mysticism. She confided to friends that she had the power to predict the future. One day at the clinic, Gwen began to scribble incomprehensibly on a piece of paper. Startled, she told Holland, "Something just made me write this." They *had* to figure out what it meant.

That night, Kathy, Genene, and Gwen met on Nixon Lane. They sent Genene's children off with Cathy Ferguson, lit candles on the counter, turned out the lights, and gathered around a Ouija board. Starting out seated at the kitchen table, they soon moved to the living room floor. Gwen asked the Ouija board: What did the message mean? Then Genene piped in: Did it have anything to do with the kids in the office? Was it *bad?* The answers weren't clear. Several days later, Debbie Sultenfuss joined them for a second session, this time with tarot cards. Gwen laid out four cards, recalled Holland. The meaning of one was uncertain. The second was "about crucifixion, about someone being unjustly accused," the doctor recalled. The third suggested the new battling the old. The fourth warned of financial ruin and bankruptcy.

Jones and Holland both said later that the mystical meetings were nothing more than fun and games, and that no individual patients were discussed. "Now they're trying to accuse us of witchcraft," complained Genene. "Shit, I don't talk to spirits. The only spirit I talk to is the Lord Himself."

Fifteen

ON SATURDAY, SEPTEMBER 11, Genene Jones returned to the emergency room at Sid Peterson Hospital—this time as a patient. She arrived shortly after 1 A.M., complaining of violent cramps in her abdomen and waves of nausea that made her vomit blood. Doctors admitted her to the sixth floor for treatment of a suspected bleeding ulcer. Lisa drove Gladys Jones up from San Antonio to visit. On their first trip to Kerrville since Genene had moved, they stopped by Nixon Lane to see Crystal and Edward, who were temporarily under the care of Debbie Sultenfuss and Cathy Ferguson. Gladys Jones was careful to hold her tongue throughout the day. She had never understood why her daughter collected such an odd assortment of friends.

Genene was to remain in the hospital until the evening of September 16. For the four workdays her nurse was gone, Dr. Holland arranged for an RN from Austin, Mary Mahoney, to fill in. The clinic had never been quieter. Only one or two patients came in each day, and none required hospitalization or emergency treatment. Mahoney busied herself filing charts and checking supplies. The nurse liked her temporary employer but was surprised when Dr. Holland told her that four children had arrested in the clinic since it opened. Mahoney had never heard of so many emergencies occurring in a doctor's office during so brief a time. When Brandy Benites came in for a checkup, appearing healthy as could be,

161

Mahoney was amazed to learn that the baby had suffered one of the arrests. Whatever caused her emergency had disappeared without a trace.

FRIDAY, SEPTEMBER 17

On the morning Genene returned to work, Petti McClellan arrived at the clinic for the first appointment of the day. Petti later said she had called Dr. Holland's office on Thursday to set it up—not for Chelsea, but for her son, Cameron, who had the flu. According to Petti, her daughter had been well since her first traumatic visit to the pediatrician, twenty-four days earlier. But when she called, said Petti, Dr. Holland asked her to bring Chelsea in for a quick checkup.

Genene Jones recalled it differently: Petti "had called in and told Gwen [that Chelsea] was having increased blue spells. She also stated she'd had two seizures that lasted three minutes each that day. She felt the blue spells were getting worse."

Chelsea and Cameron arrived with their mother at about 10:30 A.M. Gwen sent them back to the clinic's staff lounge, where Petti could talk with Dr. Holland and smoke a cigarette. Genene Jones appeared first, scooping up Chelsea to measure her height (twenty nine and one quarter inches) and weight (eighteen pounds, twelve ounces). Then Dr. Holland came in. While she and Petti spoke, Chelsea ran up and down the hallway and played. Cameron, feeling miserable, just sat. Dr. Holland briefly examined Chelsea on the carpet in the lounge, then told Petti she wanted Genene to give the little girl her inoculations. Holland ordered two: a diphtheria-tetanus injection and a measles-mumps-rubella shot. Genene suggested that Petti not watch, but Petti said she wanted to hold Chelsea to keep her from getting upset. Holland returned to her office to record her notes on Chelsea's chart, while Petti walked to the crash room with her daughter.

Genene had already filled the syringes. They were lying on a counter. Chelsea, wearing a dress and matching bonnet of red-and-white gingham and lace, sat down on Petti's lap, facing her mother and holding her hands. Genene took the first needle and pushed it into the top of Chelsea's chubby left thigh. Moments later, Chelsea began to have trouble breathing. A whimper stuck in her throat, as though she were trying to cry "Momma" but couldn't get it out.

"Stop!" shrieked Petti. "Do something! She's having another seizure!"

The nurse told Petti that Chelsea was just reacting to the pain of the injection. According to Genene, the child looked better after a few moments, so she gave her the second shot, this one in the top of Chelsea's right thigh. By the time Genene pulled the syringe out, Chelsea wasn't breathing at all. She turned blue and began having a seizure. The little girl was trying to breathe but couldn't; her body was jerking uncontrollably. Then she went limp. Petti had never seen anything so horrible.

The ambulance arrived at the office at 10:58 A.M., and Chelsea was in the Sid Peterson emergency room nine minutes later. She arrived in Genene Jones's arms, with an IV already started and a breathing tube down her throat. The emergency room staff stripped off her clothes and hooked her up to a heart monitor. Chelsea soon began struggling to pull out the breathing tube. Holland removed the tube, and Chelsea began crying. The baby was breathing on her own; the tube didn't seem necessary. But Holland explained that she was worried Chelsea would suffer another respiratory arrest. While nurses pinned her arms, the doctor replaced the first breathing tube with a larger one and ordered a dose of Valium. The drug made Chelsea sleepy. Genene taped the tube tightly in place, sealing the little girl's mouth. Doctors, nurses, and respiratory technicians hovered around the treatment table. Genene, assisting her boss at the toddler's bedside, looked up at the commotion all around her. "And they said there wouldn't be any excitement when we came to Kerrville," she remarked.

Chelsea's color had returned soon after her arrival in the ER. She was bright pink, noted Holland; she was looking very good. Nonetheless, the pediatrician wasn't willing to let Chelsea remain at Sid Peterson. *Something* had to have caused the seizures. The doctor wanted to find out what, and felt Sid Peterson wasn't the place to do that. "I didn't want her just hanging around there," Holland said. "She had already done things that were unexpected. I was wondering what was going on in her head. I felt sure something neurological was going on that we were missing."

Dr. Holland told the McClellans she wanted to transfer Chelsea to a San Antonio hospital immediately. Her plan was to fly the child to Medical Center, but the MAST helicopter was unavailable and the county hospital's ICU beds were full. She settled instead for sending Chelsea by ambulance to Santa Rosa. While Dr. Holland made the necessary arrangements, Genene and Petti recruited a hospital employee to drive them back to the clinic; Petti had left Cameron there, and Genene needed her bag of supplies for the trip. Walking out to the car, they noticed a large black hearse parked in the hospital driveway. Genene held a hand in front of Petti's eyes to block her view. "That doesn't bother me," said Petti. "Chelsea's not going to die."

The ambulance set out from Sid Peterson at 12:36 P.M. Chelsea, Genene, and paramedic Tommy James were in the back. Another paramedic, Steve Brown, was the driver. Dr. Holland followed the ambulance in her white Datsun, while Petti and Reid McClellan followed her in their own car. Chelsea was on a heart monitor and was receiving fluids through an IV. She was breathing through a tube attached to a respiratory bag. Genene and Tommy James took turns pumping oxygen into her lungs. They were cruising along at code two—a step away from a full emergency. Everything seemed stable. Eight miles down the highway, the peaks and valleys on the heart monitor fell into a flat line. *Chelsea was arresting.* The paramedic worked the respiratory bag faster. "Pull this son of a bitch over!" screamed Genene, and they skidded to a halt on the shoulder.

Holland jumped into the ambulance. "She's flat-lined!" shouted Genene, who was performing chest compressions. Holland checked Chelsea's heart with a stethoscope and heard nothing. She climbed onto the stretcher, straddled Chelsea, and took over the heart massage, while ordering Genene to draw up a round of resuscitative drugs: epinephrine, calcium gluconate, sodium bicarbonate. No response. She ordered another round. "Get me to a hospital—quick!" Holland ordered. The ambulance pulled onto the highway and took the second exit. They arrived at the Comfort Community Hospital—a tiny one-story building where the doctors' parking area is marked by a rusty sign nailed to a tree—at 1:05 P.M. and rushed Chelsea into the small emergency room. They had radioed ahead, and the hospital staff was waiting. Dr. Holland ordered up several more rounds of drugs and took turns with Genene and Steve Brown at CPR while Tommy James worked the respiratory bag. Chelsea's heart flickered on briefly, then stopped, then beat weakly again. Then stopped. After twenty minutes, Chelsea's pupils stopped responding to light, indicating severe brain damage from lack of oxygen. "That is all we can do," said Holland. Chelsea Ann McClellan, fifteen months old, was dead.

Dr. Holland left the emergency room to tell the McClellans, who were waiting outside. Sobbing, Genene removed the IV and began cleaning Chelsea up. She wrapped the body in a blanket. Then she took it out to Petti, who rocked her daughter's body and stroked it. "She's been through this before," Petti told everyone. "She's just asleep. She'll wake up in a few minutes."

The procession of cars, driving slowly this time, headed back to Sid Peterson. The staff there awaited them. Everyone in the emergency room had listened with horror as the ambulance radioed news of Chelsea's respiratory arrest, the decision to head to Comfort, and the child's death. Genene Jones had cradled Chelsea's body throughout the trip back to Kerrville; when the ambulance got back, Genene, still sobbing, carried it in her arms down to the morgue in the hospital basement.

Determined to find out why Chelsea had died, Dr. Holland asked the child's parents for permission to arrange an autopsy. Reid McClellan signed the papers. But the results from that procedure would not be complete for several weeks. When Dr. Holland filled out Chelsea's death certificate, she listed the cause of her fatal cardiac arrest as a seizure and said that the seizure had been caused by a disorder of "undetermined etiology."

Three hours after Chelsea McClellan's death, Lydia Evans arrived at Dr. Holland's office with her mother,

her father, and her five-month-old son, Jacob. Lydia,
nineteen, worked as a lawyer's secretary. She lived in
Llano, sixty miles from Kerrville, with her husband, Shane,
who was a welder. Lydia was bringing Jacob to the doctor because of his crying spells, which had been going on
for a month. She was taking her baby all the way to
Kerrville at the urging of her sister, Elizabeth Winn.

Lydia had complained to Elizabeth about Jacob's crying
during a phone conversation on Thursday. The doctor
who delivered Jacob had dismissed the problem, saying
he probably was just teething, but Lydia, a first-time
mother, fretted that something might be wrong. Elizabeth raved about the new pediatrician in Kerrville, to
whom she had already taken her own baby. She told
Lydia that Dr. Holland was smart and friendly, a physician without pretensions; she even encouraged parents to
call her Kathy. Elizabeth Winn urged her sister to give
the doctor a call.

Before she could do so—less than an hour later—Dr.
Holland's office phoned Lydia Evans. Elizabeth Winn
had notified them she would be calling, explained the
doctor's receptionist, Gwen Grantner. Jacob's crying
sounded as if it needed attention. Did she want to make
an appointment? Lydia arranged to bring Jacob in the
next morning.

Early Friday, Lydia drove with her parents, Lora and
Donald Lardie, to Kerrville. They arrived for a quick
visit at the home of Elizabeth Winn. There they learned
that Dr. Holland's receptionist had called to cancel Jacob's appointment; the doctor was transferring a patient
to San Antonio. A short time later, Gwen called again.
The doctor and her nurse would be returning because the
patient they were transferring had died. They could see
Jacob that afternoon.

Lydia Evans appeared with her parents and son at 3:30
P.M. Dr. Holland's receptionist greeted them and explained that Dr. Holland was still at the hospital but that
her nurse would begin examining Jacob. Genene Jones
introduced herself, then took Jacob, Lydia, and Mrs.
Lardie back into the clinic. Mr. Lardie, who was blind,
remained in the waiting room. The nurse chatted cheerfully with the adults as she weighed and measured the

baby and took his temperature. Lydia explained her complaint. She said that Jacob had been very irritable; at times he would start to scream and she felt there was nothing she could do to please him.

Genene placed Jacob on the examining table and began looking him over. She felt the baby's fontanel, the spot on top of his head where the skull bones meet; among infants, it is soft because the bones have not yet fused. She told Lydia it seemed larger than normal for a baby Jacob's size, that it should have closed up more. Then Genene began studying Jacob's eyes. "She said she noticed that his [right] eye did not respond to light properly, that the pupil was sluggish, and that the [left] eye seemed to be all right," recalled Lydia. "I said that I had never noticed any problem." As she examined the baby, the nurse spoke to him: "Don't have nystagmus, Jacob; that is not any fun." Lydia later learned that nystagmus is a medical term for jerky, involuntary eye movements, which often signal a serious illness.

Genene Jones left the room for several minutes, then returned to say she had spoken with Dr. Holland, who was still at Sid Peterson. The doctor wanted to transfer Jacob to the hospital, said the nurse, and had ordered her to draw some blood for tests. Genene also wanted to start an IV. "I asked her why," recalled Lydia Evans. "She said it was in case he went into a seizure while they were running tests, so they could give him medication right away. I looked at my mother and said, 'Jacob's never had any seizures.'" Genene then asked Lydia and Mrs. Lardie to wait outside. "She said, 'Now, I'm a mother, I know what it's like to see your baby crying while someone takes blood from him. Why don't you leave the room?'" Lydia recalled. A few minutes passed. Then the adults in the waiting room heard Jacob start screaming. He screamed six or seven times, then—in mid-scream—there was dead silence. Gwen burst out of the treatment room and dialed Sid Peterson. "Page Dr. Holland—*stat!*" she told the hospital operator. "Something has happened!" declared Mrs. Lardie. The baby's blind grandfather wore a look of horror. "Honey," he said sadly, "Jacob is *one*."

Mrs. Lardie jumped up and headed for the treatment

room. Gwen tried to grab her. "You can't go back there," the receptionist said. But Jacob's grandmother had reached the hallway. She could see into the treatment room, where Genene was giving Jacob mouth-to-mouth resuscitation. Lydia began crying. A doctor and a nurse from the adjacent office ran in through the front door. Lydia heard Genene Jones hollering orders: "Give me suction; he's vomiting!"

The doctor, a family practitioner named Phillip Webb, arrived in the treatment room to find a blue baby lying limp as a rag doll on the examining table. Two paramedics and Dr. Holland's nurse were already there. The doctor took charge. The baby wasn't breathing; Webb slipped a tube down Jacob's throat, then began pumping air into him with a respiratory bag. The paramedics carried Jacob out to the ambulance. As they loaded him in, Kathy Holland arrived on the scene.

Dr. Holland had remained at Sid Peterson after returning from Comfort with the body of Chelsea McClellan. Busy arranging the child's autopsy, Holland notified her office to send her next patient, Jacob Evans, directly to the hospital; she wanted to examine him there. Holland heard nothing further from her clinic until she walked down a corridor past the hospital switchboard. "Dr. Holland," called the operator. "Your office has been trying to reach you—*stat!*" Holland raced to the clinic and pulled up behind the building. An ambulance was there, with a baby in the back. When Holland appeared, the EMS driver honked his horn, and Dr. Webb jumped out. "The kid arrested," said Webb. "I had to intubate." Holland climbed in. Genene was bagging Jacob Evans. "What the hell happened?" Holland asked.

The ambulance arrived at Sid Peterson at 4:36 P.M., and Genene carried Jacob into the emergency room. By then, the baby's breathing tube had fallen out. Although Jacob's color seemed good, Holland wanted to reintubate anyway. As the pediatrician struggled to place the tube, Genene pushed her fingers over the baby's trachea to give her boss a better view of his airway. Finally, Holland gave up. But Genene kept her fingers in the airway; Jacob began to turn blue. Dr. Richard Mason, the emergency room physician on duty, pulled Jones's fingers out of the baby's throat.

After Jacob's condition had stabilized, Genene came out to speak to Lydia Evans. "She was shaking all over," said Lydia, "and she was sweating very badly. The expression in her eyes [was] like she was almost in a utopia . . . her eyes looked very excited—a happy excited. She looked like she was in her element." Lydia's husband, Shane, arrived at the hospital about 9 P.M. She introduced him to Genene, explaining, "This is the woman that saved our son's life."

After conducting her first examination of Jacob, Dr. Holland told Lydia and Shane Evans that she didn't know what had caused their son's seizure but that meningitis was a possibility. On Jacob's emergency room record, she listed "probable meningitis" as her admitting diagnosis. Holland also started Jacob on Dilantin to prevent more seizures. Jacob Evans remained at the hospital for six days, three in the ICU and three on the floor. Tests showed nothing to explain the episode in the office. After Jacob left the hospital, his parents, at Holland's suggestion, took him to a pediatric neurologist in San Antonio. The neurologist conducted more tests, which revealed no sign of any problem. He advised Jacob's parents that there was no reason to keep their baby on Dilantin.

"What the hell happened?" Kathy Holland had asked her nurse. Why hadn't Jacob been sent to the ER, as she'd ordered? Genene told her boss that the baby had arrived at the clinic with a bulging fontanel, then quickly turned blue and had a seizure. In an interview later, Genene denied examining Jacob in the office. She said she took one look at the baby in the waiting room, found him "blue and spaced out," and immediately summoned help. But Genene's own nursing notes on Jacob's visit belie her account. They describe an assortment of medical problems—most of which doctors later said didn't exist. Genene detailed a "bulging fontanel," eyes that were "large with nystagmus," a rapid heartbeat, and "tremoring" extremities. In her narrative of events in the office, Jones wrote: "Jittery, hyperactive child in good spirits. Child with obvious nystagmus and periodic neuro-stare"—a blank look—"with tremor of upper extremi-

ties. Fontanel bulging, sutures spread. R pupil sluggish to
light, L pupil brisk. MGM [maternal grandmother] states
child has had two blue spells, one lasting *20 min.*" (Mrs.
Lardie later denied ever making such a comment.) Genene
then described Jacob's seizure and respiratory arrest, including the arrival of Dr. Webb. She told Dr. Holland
that Webb had ordered her to give Jacob 180 milligrams
of Dilantin to halt his seizure, but that she had given
Jacob only 80 milligrams because she knew 180 was too
much. Dr. Webb later swore he never made any such
error. In fact, said Dr. Webb, he never instructed Genene
Jones to give Jacob Evans any Dilantin.

SATURDAY, SEPTEMBER 18

Kathy Holland had planned to spend the weekend with
her husband, Charleigh. They would stay that night on
the site of their still-unfinished new home in Centerpoint.
Charleigh had devoted himself almost full time to the
project. He and Kathy rarely saw each other during the
week; she tended to her practice, he to their future
homestead. But because Charleigh refused to hire help,
the work was going slowly; the house remained a skeleton. They would sleep together in a pup tent beneath the
stars.

Holland was eager to flee Kerrville, eager for the comfort of her husband. The events of the previous day had
left her shaken. For a month, she and Genene had been
heroes to parents, rescuing their children. Now, suddenly, their magic touch had disappeared; another child
had stopped breathing, and this one had died. Petti Mc-
Clellan's reaction had made it even more awful. She kept
saying Chelsea was just sleeping, that she would wake up
in a minute. Holland had tried to tell her that Chelsea
wasn't going to wake up—that she really was gone. But
Petti couldn't accept it. Kathy finally had to give her a
shot of Valium to make her relax. Holland, of course,
had lost patients before. But this was the first time it had
happened to her in private practice—and she hadn't a
clue why. The doctor felt helpless. *What had she missed?*

As the number of emergencies grew, Holland had tried
hard to take it all in stride, to maintain the public appearance that nothing extraordinary was going on. When

someone at Sid Peterson remarked, "You sure are having a lot of sick kids coming out of your office," the doctor had responded coolly: "We have a lot of *interesting* kids." But privately, Kathy Holland was overwhelmed and a little frightened. She felt surrounded by sick children. In residency, there had always been someone to talk to about the patients, someone to offer perspective. Here there was no one—no one except Genene. The hours they spent together, isolated in their odd little world on Nixon Lane, were reinforcing the doctor's blind faith in her nurse. *You're the town's new pediatrician, a specialist*, Genene told her. *Why should anyone be surprised that we're seeing lots of sick children?* The rash of unexplained arrests, Genene's lame explanations of what happened, even Chelsea McClellan's inscrutable death, did nothing to open Holland's eyes. She continued to embrace her naive belief with the conviction of the converted: All the kids were sick; each case was different; there was no pattern.

Elizabeth Winn had heard about the problems her sister's son, Jacob Evans, had experienced on Friday. She thought it fortunate that Jacob was in Kathy Holland's office when he stopped breathing. Elizabeth and Donald Winn had been taking their own infant, Anthony, to Dr. Holland since his birth three weeks earlier. They felt certain of her ability to provide excellent medical care. They didn't just like Kathy Holland; they believed in her.

The Winns had met Holland and Genene Jones even before their son was born. Donald had learned of the new pediatrician's arrival through the grapevine at Sid Peterson, where he worked as a data-processing manager. After an appointment with the doctor, the Winns decided immediately to have her provide their child's newborn care. When Anthony arrived on August 25, they were not disappointed; even though there were no complications, Holland remained with the baby for hours after his birth. In the next few weeks, the Winns, naturally quick to call a doctor, came to know the pediatrician and her nurse well. They were jumpy first-time parents. Kathy and Genene seemed to understand; they didn't treat the Winns as if they were crazy. Dr. Holland regularly called them to check on Anthony's progress. She and her friends even baby-sat for him at the house on Nixon Lane. In less than a month, the Winns had come to regard Kathy and Genene as close friends.

Now, on a Saturday night, Anthony seemed to be having some problems, and the Winns were worried. Although it was almost 10 P.M., Elizabeth called out to Nixon Lane for Dr. Holland, seeking a word of reassurance. Genene answered the phone. Kathy was in Centerpoint with her husband, the nurse explained. What was wrong with Anthony? The Winns told Genene that their baby was crying a lot and had mucus in his stools. Genene, sounding concerned, told them to meet her in ten minutes at the clinic.

When the Winns arrived at the Fine Medical Center, Genene explained that she'd been unable to reach Dr. Holland. She unlocked the doors, led them into the treatment room, and began examining Anthony herself. Genene told the Winns that Anthony had a staph infection and that she was going to test his blood-sugar level. The nurse pulled out a dextrose test strip—a length of chemically treated paper that provides a rough measure of blood sugar—pricked the baby's toe, and smeared a drop of his blood onto the strip. Anthony's blood sugar was dangerously low, Genene announced. If they didn't get some sugar in his system soon, he would go into a coma.

In an interview, Genene would later claim that Anthony's fontanel was sunken and he was so lethargic when she saw him that he appeared to be asleep. "I couldn't get him to wake up," she explained. The dextrose stick, Genene said, showed his blood sugar was "next to nothing." She had no choice but to move swiftly. "You get no sugar on a dex stick, that kid's going to die very quickly." The Winns were alarmed to hear that their baby's condition was so critical. He hadn't seemed that sick; everything was happening so fast. Elizabeth and Donald clutched their son as Genene started an IV in his left foot. Genene then left him with his parents and called EMS.

By then, the clinic's answering service had finally reached Dr. Holland, who had been asleep in Centerpoint, fifteen miles away. The phone there sat on a tree stump; Kathy stumbled out of the tent to answer it. "There's a call for you from your office," explained the operator. "Your nurse wants to talk to you." The pediatrician dialed her clinic.

"Anthony Winn is here," Genene announced.

"What the hell is Anthony Winn doing in the office at this hour?" demanded Holland. "Take him to the ER. Don't do anything else." The doctor jumped in her car and headed for Sid Peterson.

Genene called the emergency room and spoke to RN Marilyn Martinez-Green, the charge nurse that night. "Believe it or not, we are still here," said Genene, suggesting her boss was present. Explaining that she was coming in by ambulance with another sick child, Jones began issuing orders. She told the ER nurse that she would need an IV with several special fluid preparations; the baby was hypoglycemic, had an elevated temperature and bloody diarrhea. The ambulance carrying Anthony Winn arrived at the hospital at 10:54 P.M. The baby's terrified parents followed in their own car. Was Anthony going to live?

When the child appeared in the emergency room, Marilyn Martinez-Green was surprised to find him alert and awake. He didn't even seem hot. Genene had told the nurse the child's blood pressure was low. But when Martinez-Green took it herself, it was normal. As they waited in the emergency room, Genene paced up and down, muttering anxiously: "Come on, Dr. Holland, hurry!" Martinez-Green didn't understand what was going on. This didn't seem to be an emergency at all. Shortly after Dr. Holland showed up, Jacob had a bowel movement; there wasn't any blood in it.

Dr. Holland admitted Anthony Winn to the hospital and sent him to the ICU. The nurses there ran a blood-sugar test to check Jones's claim that the child was hypoglycemic; the test came back normal, just as it had more than a year earlier during an identical situation at Medical Center Hospital in San Antonio. The Sid Peterson nurses had caught Jones in another lie. Dr. Holland performed a spinal tap on Anthony to check for meningitis, but the test revealed no evidence of the disease. Anthony Winn left Sid Peterson after four days. There

was no evidence that anything serious had ever been
wrong with him.

After making sure Anthony was stable, Kathy Holland
had asked her nurse why she hadn't sent the Winns
directly to the emergency room when they called. Genene
told her that the Winns had phoned from a telephone
booth opposite the clinic, that she thought Anthony's
problem would be routine, and that she didn't want to
bother Holland on a rare night alone with Charleigh.
Holland scolded Jones for treating the baby herself.

"I'm not going to let some kid die because you're so
far away," Genene snapped.

MONDAY, SEPTEMBER 20

The emergencies of the previous week had made a mess
of Kathy Holland's clinic. In the morning, Genene approached Dr. Holland and told her they needed to restock the crash room with several drugs that they had
used during the codes. The nurse rattled off a list of
medications—calcium gluconate, atropine, epinephrine,
sodium bicarbonate, potassium chloride, Dilantin, heparin—and Holland authorized their purchase. An order
was placed with the pharmacy at Sid Peterson Hospital
later that day.

Dr. Holland's clinic was closed during the afternoon
for the funeral of Chelsea McClellan. Genene had marked
the event in the office appointment book:

> no appt's today
> Funeral's
> @ 2 p.m.—
> *Must go*

Petti and Reid had arranged to bury Chelsea at the
Garden of Memories Cemetery in Kerrville. Their little
girl was dressed for the occasion all in pink—dress, boo-
ties, and bow—like a fine porcelain doll. A knit blanket
covered her body. Petti and Reid had Chelsea's favorite
plaything—a foot-high yellow rubber Tweety bird—placed
in her casket and ordered a small headstone with the
words "Our Little Angel" for her grave.

The McClellans could not understand why their daughter had seemed so well and suddenly become so sick. Petti was still unable even to accept that Chelsea was gone. She walked around their trailer home carrying her daughter's toys and talking to them. When Petti saw the small sealed box containing her daughter's body at the funeral, she screamed, "You're killing my baby!" and collapsed.

Kathy Holland, Genene Jones, and Gwen Grantner all attended the ceremony, and the McClellans were grateful for their support. A few days after the burial, the McClellans took out a two-column advertisement in the *Kerrville Daily Times*. It was addressed "To All of Our Friends in Kerrville:"

> Often we live our lives without a tendency to acknowledge those friends around us. Then something will happen which causes us to become aware of others. Such was the case in the loss of our little Angel, Chelsea Ann McClellan. The response from the people of Kerrville, many of who we only knew in passing was both heartwarming and most helpful in our grief. The many beautiful flowers, cards, and letters we received made us realize the city of Kerrville has a heart.
>
> A special thanks to Dr. Kathryn Holland and Jeane Jones for extending Chelsea's stay longer by their caring in such a sensitive way. A care which extended beyond our loss and helped us more than anyone could ever know.

> Sincerely
> Reid & Petti McClellan

In her nursing notes in the office medical records, Genene Jones wrote her own tribute. She summarized the arrest, the unsuccessful attempts to revive Chelsea, and the death, then added, "I would have given my life for hers—Goodbye Chelsea."

Sixteen

THE RASH OF emergencies at the new pediatrician's office had not gone unnoticed within Kerrville's small medical community. The nurses and doctors at Sid Peterson were used to seeing adults in the hospital, not infants. But since Dr. Holland's arrival, there had been as many as three children in the ICU at a time. The number of kids getting sick prompted doctors to joke that Dr. Holland needed to change the air-conditioning in her office. Privately, they wondered what was going on.

Dr. Duan Packard, the dean of the Kerrville medical community, had been particularly suspicious ever since the incident involving his patient, Misty Reichenau. A family practitioner who earned his medical degree in 1939, Packard lacked Kathy Holland's knowledge of modern medical technique. But he possessed a wealth of wisdom leavened by decades of experience. Packard had kept a close eye on Holland ever since Misty's visit, and he was distressed by the number of arrests taking place in the pediatrician's office. "I've been in practice forty-three years and never had one," he said. "To the best of my knowledge, we've never had one in Kerrville. Something had to be wrong."

Packard speculated that the inexperienced pediatrician was being too aggressive—overreacting by cramming breathing tubes down the throats of babies who were just holding their breath because they were angry about getting shots. Packard knew most sick children get well with

176

little help from a doctor. But Holland seemed unwilling to let nature take its course. The children rushed from her office always arrived intubated and with an IV. In the hospital, Holland always performed a battery of invasive procedures, such as spinal and bladder taps. She put her patients on powerful antibiotics and sedatives before being certain of what caused their problems.

The nursing staff had also been complaining. The children brought in by Dr. Holland often didn't seem sick enough to be in the ICU. They all had experienced emergencies in her office, but in the hospital there was no sign of what had caused their crises. The newcomers, Holland and her nurse, had annoyed the emergency room and ICU nurses with their condescending attitude. Jones seemed to make a point of displaying how much more she knew about pediatrics than the nurses at the hospital. Yet when Holland and Genene arrived to handle an emergency, there was inevitably chaos. They would ask for equipment, then would toss it down angrily if handed the wrong instruments. Jones made rounds at the hospital and wrote in patients' medical records—something no office nurse in Kerrville had ever done. When nurses phoned Holland for instructions, Genene Jones sometimes answered and gave them orders, often not even saying they were on the doctor's behalf.

The incidents fueled gossip about the new doctor's personal life. Many had taken note of Holland's unusual living arrangement; they didn't understand why all those women were living together in the same house. And where was Dr. Holland's husband? Kerrville was a small, chatty town where outdated conventions were respected, but Kathy Holland made the mistake of taking few pains with appearances. She usually wore pants, used little or no makeup, and wore her hair short. For the residents of Kerrville, it was all more than enough to prompt unfounded talk that the house on Nixon Lane was a den of lesbians.

On Wednesday, September 22, Tony Hall, Sid Peterson's administrator, convened a small group in his office to discuss the problems Dr. Holland and her nurse had caused in the hospital. The group included Dr. Packard, then chief of the hospital's medical staff, two other doc-

tors, and the head ICU nurse. They went down the list of
complaints. Things would have to change, they agreed.
Hall called Dr. Holland and arranged to meet with her
shortly after noon the next day.

THURSDAY, SEPTEMBER 23

As Tony Hall prepared for his meeting with Dr. Holland
at Sid Peterson Hospital, Clarabelle Ruff brought her
five-month-old daughter, Rolinda, into Holland's clinic
for the first time. Mrs. Ruff was a secretary for a Kerrville urologist. She had called earlier to make an appointment, explaining that Rolinda had been suffering from
intermittent diarrhea for the past thirteen days.

Mrs. Ruff and Rolinda arrived about 10:15 A.M., the
same time as Mary Ann Parker and her son. Chris Parker's earlier visit to the clinic for raspy breathing had
resulted in a three-day stay at Santa Rosa Hospital. Now
suffering from diarrhea and an ear infection, he seemed
sicker than Rolinda; Mrs. Ruff suggested the doctor see
him first. But when Genene Jones came out to the waiting room, it was Rolinda she wanted.

The nurse told Mrs. Ruff she was taking her daughter
to the treatment room to check her temperature. Dr.
Holland appeared a few minutes later and invited Mrs.
Ruff into the hallway. After examining Rolinda, Holland
told Mrs. Ruff that her daughter was a little dehydrated;
she wanted to start an IV line to get some fluids into her
system, then admit her to Sid Peterson for tests and
observation. But there was no need to worry, said Holland; this wasn't an emergency.

The doctor walked back into the treatment room, where
her nurse had prepared the IV equipment. Spotting a
good vein, Holland threaded the needle into Rolinda's
left hand. Then she flushed the line clear of blood, injecting clear fluid from a syringe that Genene handed her.
Mrs. Ruff soon heard sounds from within the treatment
room—sounds of Rolinda choking and someone pleading
aloud: *"Come on, come on!"* Holland came out of the
treatment room for a moment, and Mrs. Ruff got a
glimpse of her daughter. Rolinda had an oxygen mask
over her face. Nobody in the office had even taken her
child's medical history, Mrs. Ruff said later.

At Sid Peterson Hospital, word quickly spread that there was a code blue on the way to the emergency room—a code blue from Dr. Holland's office. A crowd of doctors rushed to the ER. There was Dr. Packard, whose office was just a few steps away; Dr. Frank Bradley, an anesthesiologist, who had heard the code blue call after finishing up morning surgery; Dr. Larry Adams, Dr. Earl Merritt, and Dr. M. B. Johnston. They stood around and watched as Holland and her nurse rushed in with Rolinda Ruff.

The patient's color seemed to be returning. Her breathing was labored but growing easier. Holland wanted to insert a breathing tube. Dr. Merritt told her the child was breathing fairly well, that intubation didn't seem necessary. But Holland intubated the baby anyway. The child began fighting the tube. She was struggling to raise her right arm . . . but she couldn't quite do it. Finally, she pulled her arm up. Dr. Bradley, the anesthesiologist, was watching closely, and suddenly it clicked: *The child was coming out from under Anectine!* "It just reminded me of what I'd seen in the operating room," said Bradley later. "The child appeared to be trying to reach up, but [she] just didn't seem to be able to get [her] hand up. It was jerky, uncontrolled movements with a purpose, but an inability to accomplish that purpose." Bradley confided his revelation to Dr. Adams, who called Dr. Packard over. Packard went up to see Tony Hall. The two quickly agreed to hold an emergency meeting of the medical staff's executive committee later that afternoon.

Meanwhile, down in the ER, there was yet another emergency. As she ran out of the clinic during Rolinda's arrest, Genene Jones had told Mary Ann Parker to bring her son down to the hospital. Less than an hour later, Genene came out to the Sid Peterson waiting room for Chris Parker. She took the baby back into the emergency room and placed him on a bed being prepared for a cardiac patient coming in by ambulance. An ER nurse had to ask Genene to move Chris; after all, he was just having a routine exam. Miffed, Genene snorted, "Well, I hope to hell this baby doesn't go into cardiac arrest." After carrying Chris into another cubicle, Genene ordered some x-rays and began drawing blood for tests.

A few minutes later, she called a code, shouting that
Chris Parker had arrested.

Genene told the staff to call Dr. Holland, but the ER
physician, Dr. Mason, and two hospital nurses were first
on the scene. Chris's throat was clogged with mucus; the
nurses suctioned it out. Racing down from the ICU,
where she was tending to Rolinda, Kathy Holland ordered two different drugs to ease the baby's distress, and
the nurses injected them. Chris seemed okay. Just then,
everyone noticed a half-filled syringe on the child's bed.
Holland picked it up. It wasn't one of the needles the
nurses had just used. "What's this?" Holland asked. The
hospital nurses and Genene all looked at one another; no
one knew. "Well, let's get rid of it then," Holland said.
She squirted out the mysterious clear liquid and tossed
the syringe in a disposal box. Dr. Holland called the ICU
to ask the head nurse whether she had another bed
available. The nurse told Holland that the intensive care
unit was full. Rolinda Ruff had just been admitted; Holland decided to bump her to a ward bed to make room
for Chris Parker.

At about noon, weary from two more emergencies,
Dr. Holland showed up for her appointment with Tony
Hall. The Sid Peterson administrator was harboring a
terrifying suspicion: that, somehow, children in Dr. Holland's office were receiving succinylcholine, the powerful
muscle relaxant sold as Anectine. For the moment, however, Hall was anxious not to tip the pediatrician off. He
told Holland that her office nurse, Genene Jones, had
irritated the hospital staff by giving orders and making
notations on charts. Holland apologized. Genene might
be a bit too aggressive, she conceded; she would speak to
her.

About 2 P.M., after his afternoon rounds, Duan Packard
sat in the doctors' seventh-floor lounge, sipping coffee
and puzzling over the problem. Dr. Joe Vinas, a ruggedly
handsome young surgeon, sat down beside him and asked
what was wrong. Packard explained. Vinas was not surprised at the doctor's suspicions. "Packard's the old man
of Kerrville medicine," Vinas said later. "He smells a rat
real fast." Like the other doctors in town, Vinas believed
that the number of children who had had emergencies in

Holland's office meant that something was very wrong. "Seizure? Respiratory arrest? Cardiac arrest? *Bullshit.* That doesn't happen in Kerrville. It never has." Now, in the coffee room, Packard told Vinas he could help. Vinas had done his residency at Medical Center Hospital and would know people who had worked with Kathy Holland. "We need to find some things out," Packard told him. "You have the job of tracing her background."

The medical staff's executive committee gathered at 5:15 P.M. in a wood-paneled conference room on the hospital's second floor. The group included the chief of each of the hospital's medical specialties, but it was no bastion of power. Seats on the committee rotated annually, and the panel's usual business was mundane: granting hospital privileges and setting rules for doctors. Sid Peterson had never experienced a problem like this. Tony Hall and Dr. Packard briefed the doctors on what they knew. They related the complaints from the nursing staff and Dr. Bradley's observations concerning Rolinda Ruff. Joe Vinas was checking into Holland's background, Packard told them. They decided to see what Vinas learned, then have a talk with Dr. Holland.

Late that afternoon, after yet another frenetic day, Kathy Holland walked out of the Sid Peterson intensive care unit with her nurse. The two women stopped to contemplate a commemorative portrait hung outside the door of the ICU. "Maybe someday," said Genene Jones, "this will be the Chelsea Ann McClellan Memorial Pediatric Intensive Care Unit."

Joe Vinas, charged with investigating the two women whose arrival in Kerrville had produced so much tumult, also left for home late Thursday afternoon. About 6 P.M. he made his first call, to a surgery resident still at Medical Center Hospital. Vinas briefed his colleague on what was going on in Kerrville. The resident told him there had been problems in the pediatric ICU in San Antonio, a number of deaths no one could explain. He said there was one particular nurse who seemed to be the common denominator. But the resident couldn't remember her name. Was it Genene Jones? Vinas asked. The resident said he would check and call back. The phone rang five minutes later. "You've got a baby-killer on your hands," the resident said.

FRIDAY, SEPTEMBER 24

The executive committee met again at 1 P.M., and Vinas revealed what he had learned. *A baby-killer.* The doctors were stunned. Then Dr. Holland was brought in. She sat at the oblong table, surrounded by eleven men—one of them a psychiatrist, asked to scrutinize her behavior. The room grew quiet. A lot of children seemed to be getting sick in her office, Dr. Packard began gently. Why did she think that was happening?

Holland said she shared everyone's concern and would welcome advice, but she knew of no problem. Each of the children, she explained, was a separate medical situation. Each had displayed clear symptoms that explained what had happened. Holland began to elaborate; to the other doctors she seemed tense but self-assured and professional. She had brought index cards with her, one for each of her emergency patients, and she began flipping through them, explaining each child's symptoms and the treatment she had given. The doctors asked about the drugs she had used. Had she ever used succinylcholine, the muscle relaxant sold under the brand name Anectine? Yes, during her residency. Did she have it in her office? Yes, but she had never used it. Did she trust her nurse? Yes. Genene had taught *her* things about resuscitating children, Holland told them. Did she know the result of the investigation in San Antonio? The LVNs had been moved out to upgrade the ICU, Holland said, and all had been offered jobs elsewhere in the hospital. As the conversation continued, Packard told the pediatrician he wanted her to have another physician consult on all her hospital patients' treatment. Holland's beeper went off, and she left the room briefly, then returned. Jimmy Pearson, back at Sid Peterson, seemed about to arrest, she said. "Would one of you care to accompany me?" Holland left the room.

The doctors sat back and talked about what they had heard. The psychiatrist said Holland was bright but excessively voluble, and noted the absence of emotion in her voice; he told the group she seemed depressed. Holland had clearly offered plausible medical explanations for each individual case. But when the incidents were taken together—and Vinas's information from San Antonio was considered—there was far too much smoke. The doctors were in agreement. They would lift Dr. Holland's privileges to admit and treat patients at the hospital. The only remaining question as they left the conference room was when.

The doctors had also decided that it was time to bring others into the matter. Packard called the Texas Board of Medical Examiners to report Holland's involvement in the emergencies. Hall called the Austin office of the Texas Board of Vocational Nurse Examiners, the state agency that licenses LVNs. He spoke to the nursing board's investigator, Ferris Aldridge, who wrote a note after the conversation and placed it in Genene Jones's file. "Mr. Hall advised of drastic increases respiratory and cardiac arrests in Kerrville and suspicious deaths in San Antonio, stating that a child killer was suspected," the note reads. "Told him that this was not a matter for board investigation, but would locate the proper authority for him." Aldridge picked up the phone and called Texas Ranger Joe Davis in Kerrville. Davis said he would investigate. After more than a year of suspicions in two different counties, someone had finally notified a law-enforcement agency.

When Kathy Holland returned to the clinic from her meeting with the executive committee, Genene Jones asked what all the fuss was about. Holland told Genene that the committee had questioned her treatment philosophy and her use of drugs. The doctors had asked specifically about succinylcholine, she explained—whether she had it in her office and whether she had ever used it. The doctors had also asked her whether she trusted her nurse. Genene appeared upset. "Somebody is spreading *rumors,*" the nurse said.

By Friday afternoon, Sid Peterson was indeed buzzing with suspicion. When the pediatrician returned to the ICU that afternoon, the head nurse, on orders from a doctor, shadowed Holland every moment she was near a patient. It would not be long, however, before Holland didn't have any patients left. Hours after her daughter's arrest, Clarabelle Ruff had heeded advice from several physicians that she find another doctor for Rolinda; a Kerrville family practitioner took over her care. Mary Ann Parker, offered similar counsel, had decided to transfer Chris to a hospital in Lubbock, where a family friend practiced pediatrics. Dr. Holland fought the move, telling Mrs. Parker that her son wouldn't be stable enough to move for days. But Mrs. Parker insisted, and signed papers to transfer Chris against Holland's medical advice.

Both children would recover with no further medical problems.

SUNDAY, SEPTEMBER 26

Kathy Holland returned to 1524 Nixon Lane about noon, after having spent the weekend with her husband in Centerpoint. On Sunday evening, Genene approached her: Did she remember that bottle of succinylcholine that had turned up missing a few weeks before? *Yes.* Genene had found it, lying in a drawer of the examining table in the crash room. *Good.* There was just one problem, said Genene: The plastic safety cap had been popped. *How had the cap been removed?* Genene didn't know. But it was nothing to worry about, she added. She had gotten out the other bottle of succinylcholine—the one they'd ordered when they'd thought the first one was lost—and checked it against the bottle she'd found in the crash room. Both were completely full, said Genene. Anyone could see the missing vial had never been used; there were no syringe holes in the rubber top.

First the questions about succinylcholine from the executive committee at the hospital; now Genene's labored explanation of the fate of the missing bottle. Kathy Holland went to sleep wondering.

Seventeen

MONDAY, SEPTEMBER 27

In the morning, Kathy Holland went to see Dr. Packard in his office at the hospital. The executive committee seemed concerned that her medical approach was too aggressive, said Holland; she would be glad to bring medical faculty from San Antonio to vouch for her philosophy. Packard shook his head. Aggressive medicine was no longer the issue. "I'm concerned about your nurse," said Packard. There was going to be an investigation. "In the meantime," he said, "you'd better tell that nurse that if she cares about you, she'd better make sure your office runs as tight as a ship."

Holland returned to her clinic about 11:30 A.M. Genene and Debbie Sultenfuss were getting ready to leave for lunch. After they were gone, Holland went to her small office refrigerator to look for the succinylcholine. There were two vials in the refrigerator. One had a plastic safety cap on it; the other did not. So far, it was just as Genene had said. Holland pulled out the bottles and held them up to the light. They contained almost exactly the same amount of clear fluid. Then she looked at the tops of the vials and noticed: There were large needle holes in the rubber stopper of the uncapped bottle. "At that point," said Holland, "I damn near freaked out."

For weeks, Kathy Holland had not merely failed to suspect; it seemed as though she had *refused* to suspect. Now she had no choice. Genene returned from lunch about 1:30 P.M., carrying a bow in her hand. She had been to see Chelsea McClellan, she explained, and found the bow at the cemetery. It was on this visit that Petti McClellan had spotted Genene, sobbing and moaning on her knees at the foot of Chelsea's grave. Back in the clinic, Holland led her nurse to the refrigerator. She told her to remove the two bottles of succinylcholine and look at the top of each. "How'd the needle holes get there?" Holland asked.

"I don't know," said Genene. "There were a lot of people in the room that day."

What day?

The day of Misty Reichenau's seizure, said Genene. Didn't Holland remember? While they were having trouble getting the breathing tube down Misty's throat, Debbie had gotten the succinylcholine out of the refrigerator.

"But I didn't use any succinylcholine on Misty," said Holland. "How'd the holes get there?"

"I don't know," said Genene.

The doctor called out to Nixon Lane and summoned Debbie. When Sultenfuss arrived, Holland questioned her. Genene said she had gotten the succinylcholine out of the refrigerator and brought it into the crash room. What had Debbie done with it? Sultenfuss retraced her steps. She was ready to draw up some succinylcholine for Misty, she said, but no one could agree on the dose. So she had placed the bottle behind the cotton-ball dispenser in the crash room.

After Debbie left the office, Holland resumed her discussion with Genene. The doctor later gave the following account of the rest of the conversation.

"That still doesn't explain the holes," Holland said. "How'd the holes get there? How am I going to explain the holes in the bottle?"

"I don't think we should explain them at all," Genene told her. "We thought the bottle was lost. We should say we never found it. Just throw it away."

Holland left her office in a panic. What should she do? She had to tell someone—but who? She thought of Joe Vinas; he was young and approachable, and he had trained at Medical Center Hospital. She called his office, but he was in surgery. She left a message. In the meantime, Kathy Holland had to deal with her nurse once again; they had a patient to see in the clinic. Afterward, about 4:15 P.M., Genene approached her. "I did a stupid thing over lunch," she told Holland. "I took a bunch of doxepin." Genene had been taking the anti-anxiety drug for her ulcers, but now she was saying she had taken an overdose.

How many had she taken?

"I don't know—a handful," Genene told Holland; she had thrown the rest away.

"*How* many, Genene?"

"I don't know—not many."

Where had she left the bottle?

Genene said it was at home. Holland called the house and had the children look for it in the medicine cabinet. The bottle wasn't there. She searched Genene's purse and found it; the bottle was empty. It had originally contained thirty pills. Genene said she'd taken five before that day; that left twenty-five missing.

Genene looked woozy; she settled onto a couch in the office hallway. "I just need to lie down for a while," she said.

"You're going to the hospital, Genene," said Holland.

Frantic, Holland told Gwen to call an ambulance, then burst into Dr. Webb's office next door. "My nurse has just told me she has taken an overdose of doxepin," she announced. "Number one, I am not an adult doctor. Number two, I wash my hands of this."

Genene's overdose was a theatrical gesture. She later said she had taken four 50-milligram pills—an amount that could do her no harm—but the paramedics who arrived at Holland's office one final time reported finding her semiconscious and fed her oxygen on the way to Sid Peterson Hospital. Genene was taken to the emergency room, where doctors pumped her stomach and admitted her to the hospital. She had planned to take a lot of pills, Genene said later, but she had decided at the last minute to face her problems head-on, just as she had in San Antonio. Said Genene: "I figured if I could live the nightmare once, I could live it again."

*   *   *

Joe Vinas called back about 7 P.M., and Holland asked him to come over. "I've got something important to show you," she told him. When the surgeon arrived, Holland led him back to her private office. She showed Vinas the bottle of succinylcholine. He looked at the vial and its orange rubber top. "It's full," said Vinas. "It's full, and it's got holes in it. That doesn't make a whole lot of sense." Holland related her conversation that afternoon with Genene—the discussion of Misty Reichenau's arrest and Jones's suggestion that they throw away the tainted bottle. Vinas, anxious to find someone who knew more about succinylcholine, suggested they call an anesthesiologist, Dr. Rex Thomas, who served on the hospital executive committee. But Thomas was out of town. Vinas phoned Kerrville's other anesthesiologist, Frank Bradley. It was Bradley who had observed Rolinda Ruff in the Sid Peterson emergency room and raised the possibility that the child had received succinylcholine; Joe Vinas had made the critical discovery of the suspicions about Jones in San Antonio. Holland did not know it, but she was meeting with the two doctors who had done the most to focus suspicion on her and Genene.

Holland asked how her patients could have had seizures after receiving succinylcholine, a drug that causes paralysis. Given low doses of the muscle relaxant, Bradley explained, children might *look* as if they were experiencing seizures. There also might be twitching as the drug took effect and at the time it started to wear off. Holland showed Bradley the vials and asked what she should do with them. Bradley didn't want the responsibility, so they decided to call Tony Hall at home. The hospital administrator explained that he was in the middle of dinner with out-of-town guests. "I have found the Anectine," Holland told him. Hall said he would be right over.

Together, the four of them searched through office records for invoices documenting purchases of succinylcholine. They found three: one bottle had been purchased on August 18, when Holland ordered her initial stock of drugs from Pampell's Pharmacy; one bottle had been purchased on September 7 from the Sid Peterson Hospital pharmacy, to replace the bottle Genene had said was missing; and one had been purchased from the hospital pharmacy on September 20. But there were only two bottles in the office refrigerator, and Holland had not ordered a third. *Where was it? Who had ordered it?* They looked closely at the September 20 invoice. It was unsigned.

Searching the office for the third bottle, they found a syringe full of clear liquid in the bathroom and five uncapped vials of saline in the crash room. But there was no sign of the missing muscle relaxant. Hall placed the two bottles of succinylcholine, one capped, one uncapped, in a white envelope and sealed it. Vinas and Bradley scribbled their signatures across the flap, and Hall covered the signatures with clear tape. Hall would take it to Texas Ranger Joe Davis the next morning.

As the doctors prepared to leave, Holland noticed three paper bags in a corner of the office, stuffed with baby clothes and toys. They had belonged to Chelsea McClellan; Petti had dropped them off for Holland to give to charity. Now Holland pointed them out, as tears streamed down her face. "If that child died because of something Genene did," she said, "I'll never forgive myself."

TUESDAY, SEPTEMBER 28
When Joe Davis heard that Genene Jones had taken a drug overdose, he decided to have a talk with her. As part of the ninety-four-man Texas Ranger Force, Davis worked for the most fabled group of state lawmen in the nation. Dating back to 1835, the Rangers built their legend in the days of the Wild West, corralling cattle rustlers, bank robbers, and gunmen. The old-time Ranger tracked his prey on horseback, with a western hat on his head, cowboy boots on his feet, a silver star on his chest, and a Colt .45 on his hip. The Rangers prided themselves on embodying a slogan once uttered by one of their own: "No man in the wrong can stand up against a man in the right who keeps on a-comin'."

By the late twentieth century, some Texans had come to regard the Rangers as little more than a quaint anachronism, a vestige of rural life in a newly urban state, ill equipped to battle sophisticated modern criminals. But

most Texans still embraced the Texas Rangers; when one
candidate for governor proposed their abolition, it was
the political equivalent of committing hara-kiri. In modern Texas, urban police departments tackled the crime
that plagued Texas cities. But in rural counties and small
towns, such as Kerrville, it was the local Texas Ranger
who was called in to handle the toughest cases.

The legend of the Texas Rangers was larger than life,
but Joe Bailey Davis measured up to the myth. Based in
Kerrville, Davis was a hillock of a man, round-faced and
bull-shouldered. While modern Rangers were issued the
more powerful .357 Magnum, Davis favored the old Colt
.45 automatic. He was a crack shot, a trained hypnotist,
and a rugged gentleman who carried out his duties with
the élan of Rangers of old. After collaring a twenty-four-
year-old suspected of sexual assault in Fredricksburg, a
Hill Country town fabled for handing out long sentences,
Davis told him: "Boy, you picked the wrong town and
the wrong girl. By the time you get out of the penitentiary, girls will be the last thing on your mind."

After Davis received the September 24 phone call from
the LVN board in Austin, Tony Hall had briefed him on
the strange rash of emergencies at Dr. Holland's pediatric clinic. The clinic had been open only a month, said
Hall, and there had already been eight incidents there,
involving seven different children. When Genene Jones
was released from the hospital on the morning after her
drug overdose, Davis asked to speak with her. She readily agreed.

They sat down in the Sid Peterson conference room,
and Davis read Jones her rights. Then he asked her why
so many children had experienced seizures in Dr. Holland's office. Such episodes were quite common with
children, Genene explained; if the doctors and nurses at
Sid Peterson were concerned, it was because they didn't
know much about pediatrics. Davis questioned her about
Anectine. Genene told the lawman she had never used it.
She hadn't harmed a soul, Jones declared, and she would
take a polygraph exam to prove it, if Kathy Holland
would.

At 10 A.M., Dr. Holland was startled to see Genene
Jones walk in, dressed for work. "Genene, I hate to say

this," Holland told her, "but I think with all the things that have happened, it would be better for you and me both if you didn't work here anymore." Genene was angry. She challenged Holland to take a lie detector test; Holland said she would. "There's only one thing I'm really sorry for," Genene told her. "Someone convinced you that I'm guilty." She stormed out of the office.

A short time later, Joe Davis arrived at the clinic with Tony Hall to question Dr. Holland. While they were there, Genene called, pleading to speak with Kathy. But the doctor refused to take the call. Genene left word with Gwen that there was a letter for Holland in a drawer in the office. It was a one-page handwritten suicide note, apparently left the day before, when Genene had taken the pills:

> There isn't anyway to explain to you why things are going to change. Sometimes, as wrong as it may seem, you have to except what life dishes out.
>
> When your older, and I know your tired of hearing that, but you will be able to understand why, why I have to go away. It doesn't mean I don't love you. Please believe that. No amount of money or worldly goods could ever buy my love. It is so deep + strong, it will last for all eternity.
>
> Please explain if you can to Crystal + Edward how much I love them. It's such a strong love, I can't put it on paper. I know I'm asking alot, but I realy feel your the only one who could do it.
>
> I'm not guilty of murder, + I hope you believe that. But Daddy's way is right. It takes all the pressure off you and the seven people, whose life I have altered.
>
> No one can hurt me with my Daddy. He'll straighten this whole thing out + then we'll go home and everything will be alright. No more problems for you, no more nightmares for me.
>
> *Please* make sure Edward + Crystal are not separated. I know how my mother feels about Crystal, but I also know how she feels about Edward. If Debbie or you can't take them together, please be sure whoever does are good people. People with lots of love.
>
> Please don't be angry. I'm going with Daddy

because I miss him + I want to be with him. He'll take care of both of us.

You'll be fine. Please believe that.

> I love you,
> Genene

As with so much about Genene, the letter was both suggestive and misleading. Although Genene was vigorously protesting her innocence, the reference to "the seven people, whose life I have altered" seemed a virtual confession. Excluding Anthony Winn—whose apparent crisis was mere theater—seven children had suffered emergencies in Genene's care. And why the remark about following "Daddy's way"? Dick Jones had died a natural death from cancer. Genene characteristically spoke as the voice of experience, writing that Holland would understand better "when your older"; in fact, the doctor was Genene's senior by four years. And finally there were Genene's references to her "love" for Kathy Holland. Did it merely reflect the close friendship that had existed between the two women? Or was it calculated to smear her boss?

Kathy Holland—who had staunchly defended Jones only four days earlier—was now ruing her decision to employ the LVN. In the late afternoon, the pediatrician received a two-sentence letter notifying her that the executive committee of the Sid Peterson medical staff had suspended her privileges to treat patients in the hospital. She knew the move would cripple her medical practice. But that was the least of her problems. Holland was in the middle of a criminal investigation for murder.

That afternoon, Joe Davis took Genene to Austin for her polygraph examination. Polygraph tests are inadmissible in court, and experts debate their accuracy. Nonetheless, the Rangers liked to use the lie detector as an investigative tool. John Maxwell, a Texas Department of Public Safety polygraph operator, hooked Jones up to the machine. According to a written report of the results, "the polygraph showed that Genene Jones was not being truthful when she stated that she had not injected the drug Anectine to any child within the past two months. It also showed she was being untruthful about having mixed, contaminated, or altered any medication given to a child in the past two months. It also showed she was being untruthful when she was asked if she had administered any other medication to a child that had not previously been authorized by Dr. Holland. It also showed she was being untruthful when she was asked, 'Do you intend to answer each question about giving unauthorized or altered drugs to children at the Kerrville clinic truthfully?'" Genene later attributed the results to having taken the polygraph "on two hours of sleep and in the middle of an asthma attack. As far as I'm concerned," she added, "I told the truth."

The next day, Joe Davis and a state police sergeant drove Kathy Holland to Austin for her turn on the polygraph. John Maxwell was once again the examiner. According to a written summary of the test, the polygraph indicated Holland had answered four questions untruthfully:

"Do you intend to answer each question about giving inappropriate or altered drugs to children in Kerrville truthfully?"

"Prior to Friday did you knowingly witness anyone on your staff at Kerrville administer succinylcholine chloride to a patient?"

"Did you administer or order the administration of this drug to any patient in Kerrville?"

"Have you mixed, altered or contaminated any medication given to a patient in Kerrville that caused breathing to stop?"

After the exam, Maxwell asked Holland about the results. According to the written summary, Holland told Maxwell she had failed the test because "she was feeling a lot of guilt because she had obtained this nurse on her staff knowing that she was a prior suspect in San Antonio in similar incidents and also was feeling a lot of guilt about what had happened to her patients." Holland said she had never given succinylcholine to a patient while in Kerrville. In all her answers, insisted Holland, she had told the complete truth. Davis drove Holland back to her office in Kerrville.

By the time they arrived, Cathy Ferguson had stopped
by to drop off Holland's belongings from Nixon Lane.
The doctor was unwilling to retrieve them herself as long
as Genene was there. Holland planned to meet her husband, Charleigh, at a Kerrville hotel. She reached into an
overnight bag to get some toothpaste; there was a letter
inside—and two vials. "What's that?" asked Joe Davis.
Holland panicked. "This lady's trying to frame me!" she
said. The letter was another intimate message from
Genene, written before Holland had gone to Austin for
the polygraph.

> I have tried to convince myself that I should not
> regret the time we have spent together . . . and be-
> lieve that the talk of family and love were sincere. . . .
> All thru Bexar County Hospital accusations you were
> behind me, + now for whatever reasons, you've turned
> your back. . . .
> . . . I'm writing this after coming back from Austin.
> I flunked three questions (all concerning) sucs [succinyl-
> choline]. . . . Believe me, you'll flunk to, the way the
> questions are composed. But that probably won't mat-
> ter either. After today, nothing could change our rela-
> tionship or the damage done to it. . . . I certainly
> won't ever be as free with my feelings of love +
> sharing. . . .
> No matter what the outcome, I have never hurt a
> child, or given a child anything that might of hurt
> them. But if, as low man, I take the fall, I still don't
> think I can hate you, even @ that point. If it protects
> you, I'll do it. But believe me, I won't go down alone.
> [This remark echoed almost precisely the defiant words
> Genene had used six months earlier, while battling her
> accusers at Medical Center Hospital.]

Genene wrote that she had flunked because "nothing ever
goes by the book in medicine." Yes, she had altered medications to make them stronger or weaker. What
nurse hadn't? And she acknowledged giving benign medications without a doctor's order in both Kerrville and
San Antonio. As to whether she had administered
succinylcholine: "You know," wrote Genene, "after we

talked about Misty, I truly don't know if some was drawn up by someone and I used it . . . not knowing, anymore than you could know."

"Kathy, whatever the outcome, be a doc," Genene continued. "Your to good not to be. Fight them, and don't give up.

"As for me, I'm thru with medicine. Nothing ever changes. It's all bureaucratic bull-shit. It's all dog-eat-dog to be top dog. I'll find new dreams to think about + new goals to reach for."

Genene wrote Holland that only thoughts of her family had kept her "from going thru with suicide. . . . in my insanity Monday, I just figured my way would solve everything. I wouldn't have to fight and they could blame everything on me and you'd go on. But it can't be that easy. I have to fight for my family and myself. Thank E.T. for giving me the strength to see that in time."

Genene said she hoped that someone would understand. She ended her letter: "God + E.T. be with you girl, and I do love ya! If you need me, E.T. will find us, + make it right. Love, Genene."

Genene kept trying to speak to Kathy Holland, as though a personal conversation could undo the entire mess. But Holland wasn't about to have anything to do with her former nurse. She was afraid that Genene might try to kill her. When the doctor continued refusing her calls, Genene dispatched two more letters. The first, on a sentimental greeting card featuring a nature photo and a quotation from Wordsworth, was in an oddly familiar tone, as though nothing had come between them. It began "Dear Kathy" and ended "Love ya, Genene." The second was formal and angry. Genene insisted Holland had agreed to make the monthly house payment—"in front of witnesses, by the way"—and informed the doctor she would be "out of your house by this weekend, and out of your life."

After her dismissal by Dr. Holland, Genene had called William Chenault, a San Antonio lawyer, who had handled her divorce eight years earlier. Chenault handled civil matters: domestic disputes, wills, small lawsuits, and real estate closings. By his own admission, he knew nothing about criminal law. But Genene trusted him—and it wasn't a criminal case she was concerned about anyway. "She thought she'd been wrongfully fired," recalled Chenault. "She wanted to know whether she could file a wrongful-discharge suit or something against Dr. Holland." Chenault advised Jones not to worry about her dismissal; she was a suspect in a *murder* case. "I told her: 'The one thing you don't want to do is stay in Kerrville. Out of sight, out of mind. If you leave and go far enough, maybe it'll go away.'" Chenault advised Genene to leave Texas—or relocate to its farthest outposts, perhaps Texarkana or El Paso. Genene decided instead to move to San Angelo, a West Texas City of 84,000, less than two hundred miles from Kerrville. She had selected San Angelo in response to a longstanding invitation from the parents of Chris Hogeda, the child whose death was the first considered suspicious in San Antonio.

During the second week in October, Genene Jones moved out of the house on Nixon Lane. She left a note on the refrigerator, apologizing for leaving the place in such a mess. Debbie Sultenfuss was leaving town too. Quitting her job in the Sid Peterson intensive care unit, she submitted a letter saying that she had resigned because of the hospital's "antiquated ideals." Debbie moved her mobile home to a dusty trailer park on the southern outskirts of San Angelo. Genene, her two children, and Cathy Ferguson moved in.

Genene Jones had come to Kerrville full of hope that she would find more of the angels that she had known so well in San Antonio. She had indeed: Brandy Benites and Rolinda Ruff, the little girls who stopped breathing after coming to Dr. Holland's clinic with diarrhea; Misty Reichenau, who had mouth sores; Jacob Evans and Anthony Winn, whose parents took them to the doctor because they cried too much; Chris Parker, who suffered one emergency after showing up at Holland's office with raspy breathing, and a second, days later, after coming in for an ear infection. There was Jimmy Pearson, the sadly deformed seven-year-old whose heart stopped beating on the MAST helicopter. And there was Chelsea Ann McClellan, who stopped breathing on two visits, the last time forever. Petti and Reid McClellan would mark their daughter's grave with the words: "Our Little Angel."

On October 12, 1982—about the time Jones left town—District Attorney Ron Sutton convened a Kerr County grand jury to investigate what had befallen all the angels she had left behind.

PART FOUR

JUDICIOUS SILENCE

. . . The committee, in general, recommends judicious
silence . . .

> Minutes, Pediatric ICU Policy and
> Planning Committee, January 13, 1983

Eighteen

WHEN RON SUTTON first heard about the death of Chelsea Ann McClellan, he was busy licking the wounds from the worst humiliation of his career. As prosecutor for the 198th Judicial District, a vast Central Texas territory, Sutton had tackled the Brady triple murder case—a horrible shotgun slaying of a mother, her daughter, and a family friend. Three times, Sutton had gone to court, intent on putting a murderer behind bars. Three times, he had come up empty. Sutton's first suspect had won a mistrial, then was tried a second time and acquitted. Sutton eventually acknowledged he had prosecuted the wrong man, and he charged a second suspect with the murders. But after a grueling six-week trial, a jury returned a verdict of not guilty. Sutton had triumphed in hundreds of cases during his five years as district attorney. But for the moment, none of them mattered. He had lost the Big One.

Ronald Leon Sutton wasn't the sort of man to greet conspicuous defeat lightly. At thirty-eight, he had ambitions, dreams of statewide office. The Brady embarrassment might well have dashed them forever. But Sutton had little time to brood. His district sprawled over five rural Texas counties covering more than 5,300 square miles—an area four times the size of Rhode Island. There were dozens of cases to try, and no one else to take them to court; the 198th Judicial District had only one full-time prosecutor on its payroll. Sutton returned home and set himself to work.

Home was Junction, Texas, population 2,593, the seat of Kimble County. Sixty miles west of Kerrville, twice that distance from San Antonio, Junction was typical of the little towns that dotted the Texas Hill Country. Most of its residents were ranchers, who raised sheep and goats and ran a few cattle. Many grew pecans and leased sections of their property during hunting season to city slickers who liked to shoot game. The only child of Baptist parents, Sutton had grown up in Junction. His father had owned a pecan and fur warehouse on the downtown square. Sutton's law office was across the street.

The DA carried his heritage into the courtroom, where he cultivated the image of a simple country lawyer. At the beginning of every jury trial, he introduced himself as Ronnie, then spoke for several minutes about his small-town roots. The prosecutor's appearance buttressed the impression. Sutton was a burly man, with a round, ruddy face, short neck, and big gut. Shuffling about a court-room, he looked ill at ease in his rumpled suit; he was quick to ask judges for permission to shed his jacket and yank loose his tie. Jurors could easily imagine the prose-cutor more at home in blue jeans on his back porch, shooting the breeze with a few buddies and downing six-packs. In truth, there was much of the good ol' boy in Ronnie Sutton. But there was also an undeniable ele-ment of calculation in the image. When Sutton appeared before a jury, there was no sign of the flashy diamond-rimmed Rolex that he usually wore on his left wrist. For trial, he carried his father's gold pocket watch. Defense lawyers learned fast that Ron Sutton was no rube. The DA had a razor-sharp eye for detail, a gift for florid rhetoric, and fire in his belly for courtroom warfare.

Sutton's passion for legal drama took root early. As a child, his favorite television show was Perry Mason. His favorite theater was the Kimble County courthouse. Be-cause the courthouse in Junction had no air-conditioning, trials often were held at night. Little Ronnie showed up regularly, joining standing-room-only crowds who turned out for the community's liveliest evening entertainment. During high school, Sutton revealed his attraction to center stage. He worked as a disc jockey at the local radio station and played guitar in a hillbilly band.

After graduating from college in 1966, Sutton enrolled at St. Mary's Law School in San Antonio. Previously an uninspired student, Sutton flourished in law school, winning several academic prizes and graduating with high honors. The big Texas law firms began to court him, but Sutton put them off in favor of a one-year appointment as a briefing attorney for the Texas Supreme Court. Afterward, he joined a small law firm in San Antonio. By then, Sutton was married, with a toddler at home and a second child on the way. He was defending claims for giant insurance companies, working in the big city, on the fast track. His future and fortune seemed assured— until he abruptly reversed direction. After a year, Sutton quit his job, moved back to Junction, and hung out a shingle across the street from the Kimble County courthouse.

Sutton was happier in a small pond, but he wanted to be a big fish. He won a seat on the county hospital board. He joined the Junction Rotary Club, the Junction Jaycees, and the Junction Chamber of Commerce. He won election as county attorney, a job that involved prosecuting misdemeanor crimes and giving legal advice to county officials. He served as chairman of the Junction Rodeo Association and president of the Hill Country Fair. The public activities offered a relief from the boredom of rural legal practice. A small-town lawyer accepts any job he can get, no matter how insignificant; he can't afford to specialize. Ron Sutton's private practice included the work older local lawyers didn't want: divorces and child custody cases, workmen's compensation and personal injury work. Politics was more fun—and top elected positions paid more than most Hill Country attorneys could make from the practice of law.

In 1976, at the tender age of thirty-two, Sutton reached for the top elected position in sight—a state district judgeship. He won the Democratic party nomination, but a Republican from Kerrville, the district's biggest town, beat him in the general election. Opportunity knocked just one year later, when the sitting district attorney resigned to accept another judgeship. Prodded by a state legislator friendly to the Junction lawyer, the governor named Sutton to the vacancy in September 1977.

The DA's weekly routine in the 198th Judicial District was far from glamorous. There were hearings, grand juries, and trials to attend in five different counties. Sutton spent much of his time driving from courthouse to courthouse in his battered station wagon. The vast majority of cases he handled were small stuff: vandalism, bad checks, burglaries, and thefts. Every now and then, a drunk Mexican or drifter would stab someone in a bar. And unlike his big-city counterparts, who had dozens of investigators and lawyers to aid them, Sutton had to do almost all his own legwork. His staff included only a secretary, a legal assistant, and one part-time lawyer.

The job exacted a price. Sutton's marriage broke up just a year after he became DA. And when a convicted felon threatened his life, he began making a habit of stashing a 9-millimeter pistol in his car. But he won far more cases than he lost—even sending one man to Death Row—and voters seemed to like him; in two elections, no serious opponent took him on. After four years in the job, Sutton began to think about the old Texas tradition of electing small-town boys to statewide office. Until the Brady triple murder case, that is. Then he began to worry about someone running against him for DA.

Beaten and battered, Sutton was far from excited when Texas Ranger Joe Davis called with the story of a baby-killing nurse in Kerrville. He figured it was just angry parents looking to blame somebody for their daughter's natural death. But when Davis relayed details of his nascent investigation, Ron Sutton realized this was a case that could dwarf anything he had ever touched.

On October 12, Sutton drove sixty miles east on the interstate to Kerrville, where he convened a Kerr County grand jury to investigate the death of Chelsea McClellan. As Sutton began to gather information, he was struck by the complexity of the case. Eight different children had experienced apparent emergencies under the care of the pediatrician or her nurse. While most of the episodes had taken place in Holland's clinic, children had also developed problems in the Sid Peterson ER, in ambulances en route to San Antonio, and on a MAST helicopter. There were dozens of people to interview. This case was a giant jigsaw puzzle, and Sutton wasn't even sure he knew where to find the pieces.

The state police crime lab offered a start. Its chemists had analyzed the bottle of succinylcholine with the needle marks in the top. While the vial was almost full, the lab reported that its contents were only one sixth the normal concentration. Whoever had withdrawn the drug had replaced its volume with saline solution. Accustomed to dealing with death by handgun, shotgun, or switchblade, Sutton soon realized a syringe filled with succinylcholine made an equally lethal weapon.

Succinylcholine chloride was a man-made compound that resembled the jungle drug curare, which South American Indians used to tip poisonous darts. Known among doctors as "sux," it worked as a neuromuscular blocking agent, intercepting the transmission of nerve impulses to the muscles. Doctors began using succinylcholine regularly during the 1950s, chiefly to paralyze patients receiving breathing tubes in the operating room. Because the drug was so powerful, it was administered almost exclusively by anesthesiologists.

A dose of succinylcholine could produce an unimaginably horrible death. It left a person completely paralyzed yet conscious, unable to breathe yet totally alert. As the drug first took effect, a person's hands would often twitch and his eyelids would flutter. An adult might gasp for help; a toddler unable to speak would take on a look of helpless panic. When completely under the drug, a person would be unable to cough or even to blink. So nightmarish were these sensations that doctors in the operating room first administered an anesthetic to dull their patients' consciousness of the experience. Anyone who did not receive help breathing under succinylcholine would soon turn blue from lack of oxygen. A short time later, the victim's heart would sputter and stop.

Sutton felt certain that Chelsea McClellan had met such a fate. Holland's patients had been given the drug, Sutton theorized, to induce arrests that would require rescue; the new pediatrician and her nurse would then appear to everyone as heroes. But in Chelsea McClellan's case, something had gone awry; Chelsea had arrested a second time in the ambulance, and the rescue attempt had failed. Sutton wasn't sure just whom to blame for the toddler's death. Jones was the primary suspect, but how could the doctor not have known that something was going on?

As he struggled to assemble a theory of the case, Sutton had yet to speak with either of the principal suspects. In early October, Dr. Holland had retained a lawyer and abruptly ceased cooperating. Genene Jones was less reticent. A few days after moving to San Angelo, Genene had phoned Texas Ranger Joe Davis to alert him to her new address and telephone number in Debbie Sultenfuss's mobile home at the South Concho Trailer Park. She would be happy to answer any questions, anytime, Genene cheerfully announced. But Ron Sutton wasn't ready to talk to Genene Jones. There was still too much he didn't know.

In early November, Sutton received the results of the autopsy on Chelsea McClellan. Because there had been no immediate suspicion of foul play, the autopsy arranged by Dr. Holland had been conducted not by a county medical examiner but by a private San Antonio pathologists' group called Severance & Associates. On the day after Chelsea's death, Severance had dispatched a junior physician, Dr. James Fletes, to Kerrville. Fletes had performed the autopsy in a back room at the Kerrville Funeral Home, and on opening Chelsea's body, he had discovered nothing unusual. But the on-site examination was only the first part of the procedure. Fletes took samples from Chelsea's major organs, removing some of them entirely, for further study back in the lab. On examining the tissues under a microscope, Fletes and his boss, Dr. James Galbreath, still could find nothing to explain the little girl's death. They decided to send Chelsea's brain to a neuropathologist, an expert in studying such tissue. Dr. Kathleen Kagen-Hallet, a faculty member at the UT medical school, was the only such civilian subspecialist in town. Her microscopic examination uncovered signs of gliosis—scarring—in Chelsea's brain stem. Kagen-Hallet reported back that her findings were "subtle." But the scarring provided the basis for her conclusion: Chelsea had died of SIDS, sudden infant death syndrome. With no other explanation at hand, Dr.

Galbreath embraced Kagen-Hallet's finding. In his final written report, he identified the cause of Chelsea's death as an atypical form of SIDS.

The autopsy presented Sutton with yet another thorny problem. How could he convict someone for murder when an autopsy of the victim attributed the death to natural causes? Sutton took stock of his prospects for successful prosecution. He had one dead baby and several more who had suffered. He had witnesses who described the chidren's symptoms as consistent with the effects of succinylcholine. He even had a bottle of the drug that had been tampered with, and a second that remained missing. The evidence was chilling—but circumstantial. Sutton lacked an irrefutable link between the drug and the victims, someone who could swear she saw the children receive what she *knew* to be succinylcholine. Holland and Jones were the only possibilities. But such a statement from either one would amount to self-incrimination.

Physical evidence was the only alternative. Sutton needed a laboratory test that could prove succinylcholine was in Chelsea's body. But that prospect seemed impossible. Succinylcholine was chemically unstable; it broke down rapidly into substances found naturally in the human body. Medical wisdom held that the muscle relaxant was impossible to trace. This characteristic had earned it notoriety as the drug of choice for doctors who wanted to commit murder; it was the presumed instrument of death in the sensational 1967 trial of Florida anesthesiologist Carl Coppolino, convicted of murdering his wife. After the trial, Coppolino's defense attorney, the renowned F. Lee Bailey, called succinylcholine "an ideal murder weapon."

A defense lawyer's "ideal murder weapon" was a prosecutor's nightmare. Now Sutton had a doctor who wouldn't talk, victims who couldn't, a murder drug he was unable to trace, and an autopsy that concluded the victim wasn't murdered at all. He began to wonder if he was dealing with an unwinnable criminal case.

Nineteen

ALTHOUGH IT WAS unfolding behind closed doors, Ron Sutton's grand jury investigation was producing considerable consternation sixty miles away in San Antonio. In sending Genene Jones off, the doctors and administrators at Medical Center Hospital had expected never to hear from her again. They had granted the nurse a full reprieve for whatever mischief she had committed in the pediatric ICU. Any rational person would be grateful and live out her life in anonymity. The possibility that she would start up *again* simply wasn't part of their calculation.

The distressing news had filtered down from Kerrville even before the formal investigation began. In checking on Jones's background in September, Joe Vinas had spoken to Dr. Arthur McFee, the surgeon at the UT medical school who had been appointed to chair the new committee supervising the pediatric ICU. Even though his area of expertise was far from lofty—McFee specialized in gastro-intestinal surgery—he was the medical school's resident aristocrat. A short, balding man of forty-nine, McFee collected fine wines, frequented the local symphony, and exuded erudition. Proud of his Harvard pedigree, he kept a captain's chair with the Crimson seal in his office. McFee had been recruited to the medical school at its inception, after two years in the navy. In the fifteen years since, he had become one of the most influential members of the faculty. Impressed with McFee's work overseeing the surgical ICU, the Conn committee had recommended that he preside over the reorganization of its troubled pediatric counterpart.

On October 21—nine days after the Kerr County grand jury began its investigation—McFee convened a meeting of his Pediatric ICU Policy and Planning Committee. Deputy hospital district administrator John Guest, nursing administrator Virginia Mousseau, pediatric ICU head nurse Pat Belko, and the new pediatrics chairman, Dr. John Mangos, were among those present. Hospital district executive director B. H. Corum and medical school dean Marvin Dunn received the meeting's minutes. "Considerable discussion was given to PICU concerns transcending the Hospital District and with specific reference to a current situation arising in Kerrville involving individuals hitherto employed at MCH," according to the committee minutes, compiled by McFee. "Dr. Corum has expressed to the chairman that the view of the committee will be the official view of the hospital district. The committee feels that the hospital should cooperate in every way possible when asked to do so in the course of a legitimate investigation." This cooperation, however, was to have limits. The minutes state: "The committee does not feel that the hospital district should volunteer any information regarding prior employees under any circumstances at all." Officials of two public institutions—the county hospital and the UT medical school—possessed information that was surely relevant to a criminal investigation of murder. Yet they were setting out a policy of saying nothing unless asked.

The two institutions' top officials would cling to this strategy, even as they received new evidence linking Genene Jones to suspicious deaths. In January 1983, they received the report of the most detailed internal investigation of the strange deaths in the ICU. This was the study recommended by the Conn committee, which in March 1982 had urged an "immediate" review of "several isolated untoward events." But the inquiry had not begun for six months, until September 17—coincidentally, the date of Chelsea McClellan's death. The responsibility had fallen to a three-member panel led by the new pedi-

atrics chairman, John Mangos, who had relieved Dr.
Franks of his interim duties. Its other members were
John Guest and Jean Foster, a mid-level nursing admin-
istrator.

The Mangos committee's report focuses on the cases of
thirteen children treated in the ICU during 1981 and
early 1982 who experienced "sudden and unexplained
problems"—arrests, seizures, or bleeding episodes. Ten
of the thirteen died. In all ten cases, Genene Jones was
present at the child's bedside during what the report
gently terms "the final events." There are three possible
explanations for Genene Jones's presence "during events
leading to the death of children and infants in the PICU,"
the study says. "This presence could be: 1) coincidental;
2) Because Nurse G. Jones volunteered the care of very
sick infants and children; 3) Due to negligence or wrongful doings by Nurse G. Jones resulting in the sudden
deterioration and death of patients." The report con-
cludes: "This association of Nurse Jones with the deaths
of the ten children could be coincidental. However, negligence or wrongdoing cannot be excluded."

After four months of study, Mangos's committee had
documented the extraordinary pattern that Jim Robotham,
Suzanna Maldonado, and Pat Alberti, among others, had
flagged more than a year earlier. But instead of being
alarmed at the prospect that they had harbored a murderer, the doctors and administrators took solace in the
report's failure to uncover proof of wrongdoing. On January 13, the Pediatric ICU Committee convened in a
hospital meeting room over lunch. At the end of the
session, the discussion again turned to Kerrville. "In
general, the apprehension of the committee is that an
investigation is proceeding in Kerrville under the aus-
pices of the grand jury," note McFee's minutes. ". . . A
review of charts of all patients seen in the PICU in
December, 1981, and January and February of 1982, has
revealed absolutely nothing for which the hospital district
could be held liable in the opinion of Dr. Mangos. . . .
The committee, in general, recommends judicious silence
on the issue."

Kathy Holland believed she was a victim of judicious

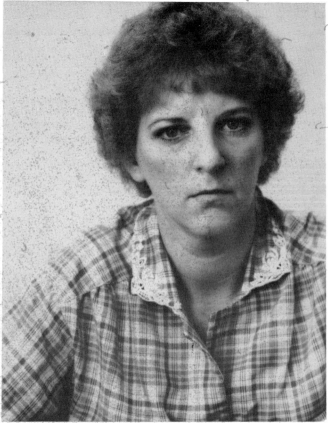

Robert Latorre

Genene Jones, 1983

Right: Genene Jones, senior class photo, Marshall High School yearbook —

Dick Jones, ca. 1959

Mrs. James Harvey DeLany Jr., 1968

Dr. James Robotham

B. H. Corum

Dr. Marvin Dunn

Pat Belko

Robert Latorre

Dr. Kathleen Holland

Robert Latorre

Petti and Reid McClellan

Robert Latorre

Chelsea Ann McClellan, aged fourteen months

Robert Latorre

San Antonio Light/Byron Samford

The prosecutors:
Kerr County D A Ron Sutton
(above); Bexar County D A
Sam Millsap *(left)*

Genene Jones in custody

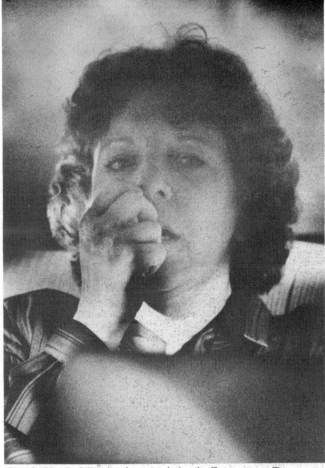

Genene Jones, following her conviction in Georgetown, Texas

silence. After discovering the opened bottle of succinylcholine, she had turned to members of the medical school faculty for aid and counsel. Eight of them wrote letters on her behalf to Dr. Packard in Kerrville, in support of Holland's campaign to win restoration of her privileges to practice at Sid Peterson Hospital. But as Holland's predicament deepened, she grew bitter at her former teachers for failing to save her from herself. In a visit to Dr. Mangos a few weeks after the grand jury investigation began, she explained how her dreams of a thriving practice had collapsed. Holland knew Mangos was investigating what had happened in San Antonio. Why hadn't someone done more to stop her from hiring Genene?

The fifty-year-old Mangos, lured to San Antonio from the University of Florida medical school, was an eminent academic physician, nationally known for his research into cystic fibrosis. But now, speaking to Kathy Holland, he donned a different hat—that of an ordained Greek Orthodox priest, a title that prompted the pediatric residents to dub him "Father John." Mangos told Holland that he realized she was going through a tough time but assured the former resident that the pediatrics faculty was behind her; everyone knew she was a caring person and a good doctor. Mangos advised Holland that his review of the ICU records had revealed absolutely nothing that suggested she was guilty of wrongdoing in San Antonio. Sensing her anger at the medical school, Mangos told Holland that he, too, had been victimized by the errors and omissions of others. He could have sued—but he had decided not to do so, Mangos explained, because he knew litigation would just disrupt more lives. Mangos urged Holland to follow his example. It was best not to harbor vengeance, he counseled; the Lord would take care of things.

Kathy Holland was inclined to give providence some direction. In the first days after her discovery of the tainted bottle of succinylcholine, the doctor had spoken freely to Texas Ranger Joe Davis. On October 1, she retained a hard-nosed San Antonio criminal lawyer named Jack Paul Leon, who promptly phoned Ron Sutton to ask if his new client was a target of the DA's criminal investigation. When Sutton told Leon she was, Leon instructed the doctor to say nothing more to the authorities.

When Holland first contacted Leon, she wanted to sue the Sid Peterson executive committee for its refusal to restore her hospital privileges. Why couldn't the other doctors see that she had done nothing wrong? By refusing to let her treat patients in the hospital, they were ruining any chance she had of rebuilding her practice. Leon cautioned Holland to slow down; they first needed to make sure she didn't go to prison. An intense man with an impressive record of defending against charges of white-collar crime, Leon contemplated the worst-case scenario. Sutton was convinced that Genene Jones had harmed children. And he appeared to believe that Holland had known what was going on—or at least that she should have. If Holland was charged with the death of Chelsea McClellan, was there any danger of conviction? Leon concluded there was not. In turning over the opened bottle of succinylcholine, Holland had provided the prosecution with its most important piece of evidence—unlikely behavior for a co-conspirator to murder. Besides, what motive could Holland have to deliberately harm her patients? She had a bright career ahead of her, everything to lose.

While Leon felt certain he could win at trial, he knew a criminal indictment would shadow Holland for the rest of her life. Grand juries were notorious for following a prosecutor's inclinations. If Sutton wanted to go after Holland, reasoned Leon, he could surely indict her for something. Leon turned his attention to avoiding the doctor's indictment in the first place. That meant just one thing: convincing the DA that Kathy Holland was innocent.

Sutton had already moved to turn up the heat on the beleaguered pediatrician. On October 12, on Leon's advice, Holland had appeared before the grand jury and refused to testify, citing her Fifth Amendment rights against self-incrimination. When the doctor also refused to comply with a grand jury subpoena for her office medical records, Sutton asked a district judge to hold her in contempt of court. At the contempt hearing on November 5, Leon agreed to hand over Holland's records.

But the far more critical issue was the lady doctor's testimony. At an informal session with the prosecutor after the hearing, the defense attorney made his pitch. As long as she faced criminal indictment, Leon stated, his client would continue to take the Fifth. Leon knew Sutton had a tough circumstantial case. If you go after Holland, he told the DA, you won't convict anybody. There's no case against Holland, he argued, and an indictment against the doctor would keep her from testifying against the real culprit, Genene Jones. You *need* Holland's testimony, insisted Leon. And Sutton could have it—if only he would pledge not to seek the doctor's prosecution. "My client should be on *your* team," Leon argued, "and you should be on hers."

Sutton listened quietly. Leon was a sharp lawyer—a fellow alumnus of St. Mary's Law School—and correct in his assessment of the difficulty of Sutton's case. But the DA from Junction was far from ready to abort his investigation of Dr. Holland, unwilling to accept that she had known nothing about the unlikely events unfolding literally under her nose. Sutton would consider what Leon said, but he was not yet ready to make a deal.

Shortly after moving to San Angelo, Genene Jones had phoned her mother to explain that there might be trouble. Gladys Jones did not doubt it; Genene was *always* in some kind of pickle. After their hurried relocation, Genene and Debbie Sultenfuss had both found nursing work at the state school for mentally retarded adults. Edward and Crystal enrolled in the local public school system. Cathy Ferguson, who had discovered during her stay in Kerrville that she was pregnant, watched Genene's children when the other adults were away. The manager of the South Concho Trailer Park was surprised to see so many people living in the fourteen-by-sixty mobile home. But she thought Genene Jones and her crowd were friendly— just normal, everyday folks. The manager did not notice the law-enforcement officers who cruised by Debbie's trailer from time to time, following Ron Sutton's instructions to keep an eye on its occupants.

On December 15, intent on removing an obstacle to

punishing anyone for Chelsea McClellan's murder, Ron
Sutton drove to San Antonio with Ranger Joe Davis.
Sutton had arranged a meeting with Dr. Kagen-Hallet,
the medical school neuropatholgist who had ruled that
Chelsea died of SIDS. Kagen-Hallet worked in a cramped,
third-floor office at the Veterans Administration Hospital, connected by a walkway to Medical Center Hospital.
Pathologists as a group were a macabre lot, brimming
with anecdotes about some flesh-mangling injury or especially ravaging disease. When the two burly lawmen located Kagen-Hallet's office, they discovered a pale,
thin-faced woman of forty, who wore her graying hair in
a tight bun behind her head. Plastic jars filled the doctor's bookshelves. Each contained a human brain, float-
ing in fixative. In discussing individual cases, Kagen-Hallet
occasionally gestured toward one of the jars, remarking
enthusiastically, "I've got his brain over there," as though
speaking of a prize coin she'd placed on display.

Sutton spoke to the pathologist about Chelsea McClellan. A doctor and her nurse were under investigation in
the child's death, the DA explained. He had reason to
believe the toddler had received a shot of succinylcholine.
Would the knowledge of such an injection alter her certainty that Chelsea had died of SIDS? Kagen-Hallet said
it would. The brain-stem scarring she found in Chelsea
might have damaged the baby's normal breathing-regulatory
mechanism. Such a child whose breathing was interrupted—by a shot of succinylcholine, for example—might
have trouble resuming respiration. Kagen-Hallet agreed
to research the subject and write an addendum to her
findings—an addendum that would acknowledge the possibility that succinylcholine had caused Chelsea's death.

The DA's visit did not represent Kagen-Hallet's first
encounter with Genene Jones. In addition to examining
brain tissue, Kagen-Hallet handled most of the autopsies
performed on children who had died at Medical Center
Hospital. While a nurse in the pediatric ICU, Jones had
shown up for several of them. Kagen-Hallet had no trouble remembering her; she had stuck out because she
asked so many good questions. Kagen-Hallet recalled
something else about that period: a couple of pediatric
ICU autopsies that had drawn unusually large and tearful

crowds. Perplexed by the sudden death of their patients, nurses, pediatricians, and surgeons had sat in on the postmortems.

After Ron Sutton's visit, Kagen-Hallet could not resist the temptation to make a few discreet inquiries about Genene Jones. A friendly pediatrics resident told her that the LVN had a reputation for being strange—that she told dirty jokes at inappropriate times. The resident added that everyone was relieved when Jones quit.

For a month, Kagen-Hallet went quietly about her duties. On January 11, she left work early to attend the monthly afternoon meeting of the San Antonio Society of Pathologists. Held in a medical school auditorium, the session drew a crowd of fifty or sixty doctors for a slide presentation by the Bexar County chief medical examiner, Dr. Vincent DiMaio. Afterward, Kagen-Hallet chatted with a professional acquaintance, Dr. Corrie May, a deputy medical examiner. While she and May cleaned up the darkened auditorium, unplugging coffeepots and gathering slides, Kagen-Hallet related what she knew about the death of Chelsea McClellan.

Kagen-Hallet revealed that the DA in Kerrville suspected murder. She mentioned Ron Sutton's inquiries about succinylcholine, and the two pathologists discussed the difficulty of tracing the drug. Kagen-Hallet told May that the targets of the investigation were Kathy Holland and Genene Jones, a doctor and nurse who had both worked at Medical Center Hospital, and that Jones had a reputation for being odd. May recalled that Dr. Holland had phoned when Chelsea died, asking if the medical examiner's office would perform the autopsy; May had told Holland that because there was no suspicion of wrongdoing, it was not a medical examiner's case.

According to Kagen-Hallet, the conversation ended there, and both women went home. But according to Dr. Corrie May, Kagen-Hallet went on to make a startling revelation: There also had been suspicious baby deaths in San Antonio—a number of babies had died mysteriously at Medical Center Hospital.

When she arrived at work the following morning, May passed this news on to her boss, Dr. DiMaio. Bexar County's forty-one-year-old chief coroner was a famous pathologist, known nationally in medical circles for his expertise on gunshot wounds. He had recently been summoned to participate in the celebrated exhumation of the body of presidential assassin Lee Harvey Oswald. At the moment, however, DiMaio was in the midst of a feud close to home. Several months earlier, the UT medical school had failed to renew the employment contract of his wife, also a pathologist; DiMaio had responded by resigning his own part-time faculty appointment. DiMaio had also been complaining that doctors at Medical Center Hospital were ignoring state laws requiring them to report all questionable deaths to his office. Corrie May's information was thus grease on a burning fire.

Several hours after speaking with his deputy, DiMaio dictated a memo for his files detailing the information she had provided:

> At 9:15 this morning Dr. Corrie May informed me of a conversation she had with a Dr. Kagen-Hallet of the University of Texas Health Science Center at San Antonio. This latter physician informed Dr. May that she was currently involved in a case in Kerrville involving the suspected murder of two children. The suspects in this case are a physician and a nurse. During this conversation Dr. Kagen-Hallet informed Dr. May that these two individuals have formerly worked at the Bexar County Hospital. During the time they were at the hospital, there were approximately eight suspicious deaths of infants. Because of these deaths the hospital ordered an investigation. Subsequently the nurse and doctor were given an opportunity to resign. From what she could gather from the conversation, the investigation of these deaths were conducted by members of the University staff and possibly some outside physicians.

As in a children's game of telephone, the relayed information—from Sutton to Kagen-Hallet to May to DiMaio—had strayed on two important points of fact. The Kerrville investigation involved only one suspicious death. And Kathy Holland had never been suspected of wrongdoing while working in San Antonio; she had completed her residency to everyone's satisfaction. But the information spurred DiMaio to do what doctors and administrators at Medical Center Hospital fervently hoped would never happen. Two hours after speaking to Corrie May, DiMaio drove from his office on the edge of downtown San Antonio to the Bexar County courthouse. There, he rode up to the third floor, entered the district attorney's office, and revealed everything he knew.

Twenty

WHEN SAM D. MILLSAP Jr., learned of suspicions that babies had been murdered at Medical Center Hospital, he had served as district attorney for Bexar County for only twelve days. Yet he had already revealed a hearty appetite for conflict and a lust for the public stage. The youngest DA in Texas, Millsap, thirty-five, had won office in a bitter campaign against an incumbent. Unwilling to let his vanquished opponent remain in power any longer than necessary, Millsap declared that he would heave him out the window if he found him in the DA's office a single minute after his term expired. The incumbent vacated the premises. Millsap and his chief deputies were sworn in at 12:01 A.M. New Year's Day, before a covey of television cameras and a crowd of four hundred.

Sam Millsap grew up in San Antonio, the eldest child in a family of scrappers. His father, legally blind since childhood, had begun in business running a snack bar in a refrigeration plant, while his family lived in public housing. By the time Sam junior entered college, his parents owned a comfortable home in the suburbs and operated a chain of office cafeterias. The younger Millsap was consumed with politics. At the University of Texas in Austin, where the state's future leaders learned to wheel and deal, Millsap was the master strategist of a potent campus political machine. Based in a men's social club, Millsap's organization fielded slates of short-haired moderates who seized control of student government in the mid-1960s, postponing the inevitable rise of antiwar radicals. Millsap remained at UT three more years for law school. Then, gravitating naturally toward power, he joined Texas's preeminent corporate law firm, Baker & Botts in Houston. Finding the atmosphere stultifying, he returned after a year to San Antonio, where he worked as an aide to a Democratic congressman between stints in civil law practice. Millsap began to specialize in defending claims against railroads. But his passion remained politics. In 1978, Millsap organized the Bexar County campaign of the Democratic candidate for governor, a job that honed his reputation as a skillful back-room operative. But by then he was already planning his own campaign for public office.

Bored with private practice, Millsap had decided that the job of district attorney was the one he had been "born and bred for." Opponents would later note that Millsap had never tried a criminal case. But the young attorney didn't envision his role as that of courtroom prosecutor. While most DAs limited their public comment to cases before their office, Millsap viewed the job as a bully pulpit—a platform to create issues by speaking out. Millsap had opinions he wanted to voice, on everything from crime and sentencing to the performance of judges and the county sheriff. He wanted to be one of the people defining the public debate.

Ever the political strategist, Millsap was also drawn to the job because its occupant was an inviting target. The incumbent was Bill White, a lumbering former football player who was part of the old Democratic courthouse crowd in Bexar County. A Romanesque red sandstone building in downtown San Antonio, the Bexar County courthouse had a long reputation as a place where those with connections could get a sweet deal. Judges, prosecutors, and certain defense attorneys had close relationships. Plea bargaining was endemic; even serious felonies like rape were being downgraded to misdemeanors. To Millsap, White was a hack who was part of the problem. Planning to campaign as a reformer, he felt confident he could beat the DA in a head-to-head race.

But there was another attorney mulling over the same idea: Courand Nicholas Rothe, Jr. Part of an eminent

San Antonio family, Nick Rothe was one of the savviest criminal lawyers in town. When Millsap heard reports that Rothe was thinking of jumping into the race, he invited him to lunch at the exclusive San Antonio Club. The two potential adversaries worked in different worlds. As a corporate lawyer, Millsap hobnobbed with executives and wore Brooks Brothers clothes. Rothe, two years Millsap's senior, dealt with less ambiguous rogues; he drew his clients from the ranks of murderers and thieves. Rothe was a dapper, round-faced man with silver hair and a neat mustache, but his contact with the lawless had worn a few rugged edges. Rothe could be both eloquent and gruff, a dichotomy reflected in his wardrobe; he often showed up in court wearing a Bill Blass suit and black cowboy boots.

Sam Millsap was familiar with one other element of Rothe's background: The criminal attorney had no experience in politics. Although the two men seated for lunch were little better than acquaintances, Millsap wasted no time laying his cards on the linen-draped table. "I understand you're thinking of running for DA," he told Rothe. "There are two major differences between me and you. The first is that you're competent to be DA and I'm not. The second is that I can win and you can't."

"I was a railroad lawyer," Millsap later explained. "I had a lot of ideas about how the DA's office should be structured—and they were good ideas. But I didn't know anything about criminal law." Millsap and Rothe reached an accommodation. Rothe promised not to run and agreed to serve as Millsap's secret campaign adviser. Millsap committed, if elected, to instituting the kind of reforms Rothe felt the DA's office needed.

The road was clear for a *mano a mano* battle royal, but Millsap transformed the May 1982 Democratic primary campaign into nothing short of a mugging. Knowing White was more accustomed to argument in the courthouse than in the media, Millsap shrewdly went on the attack. He produced statistics suggesting that White was letting violent criminals and drunk drivers off easy, and he pledged to cut back sharply on plea bargaining. In 1978, when two of the DA's investigators drew guns on a pair of kids they suspected of tearing down his campaign posters, White had backed up his men's actions. In 1982, Millsap used the incident to dub his opponent "Shoot-to-Kill Bill." "My goal was to keep jabbing at him to the point that he would take a swing at me in public," said Millsap. That didn't happen, but White did stage a last-minute round of massage-parlor raids that made him look foolish and desperate. Attracting a peculiar coalition of reformers and hard-line conservatives, Millsap took 61 percent of the primary vote and faced no Republican opposition in the general election.

Early in the DA's term, a local magazine profile of Millsap used the word "mean" thirteen times. But mean was not a word that came to mind when one met him. Blond-haired, with a boyish face and a toothy grin, Millsap looked more like an overgrown Eagle Scout than the sort to inspire terror. His views toward criminal justice, however, were anything but gentle. No soft-headed talk about rehabilitation from this DA; Sam Millsap didn't believe it worked. He wanted to lock criminals up and throw away the key. "People who commit crimes of violence and people who commit economic crimes and are repeat offenders need to be sentenced to long periods of time in the penitentiary. Period." As for nonviolent criminals: "The typical burglar or auto thief is a bum; the overwhelming majority are strung out on some sort of dope." If Millsap seemed inclined to tough talk and confrontation, it was because such tactics were central to his strategy. The DA had run for office embracing the philosophy of "political jujitsu"—a phrase coined in *Playing to Win*, a 1980 book by national political analyst Jeff Greenfield. The practitioner of political jujitsu would do and say the unthinkable, wrote Greenfield; by keeping opponents constantly off balance, a politician could make others respond to his agenda. "I read that, and said, 'This is me,'" recalled Millsap. The young attorney relished the prospect of being *feared*, like a rocket-armed pitcher willing to throw at the head of an opposing batter. "The other guy thinks you're nuts—but he doesn't want to fuck with you."

When medical examiner Vincent DiMaio arrived at the Bexar County courthouse on January 12, 1983, he first visited Sam Millsap's newly appointed chief deputy for felony cases: Nick Rothe. Stepping into Rothe's tiny, windowless office, DiMaio asked if he might shut the door.

"Sure," said Rothe.

"Can I lock it?" asked DiMaio.

After the medical examiner laid out his story, Rothe took him to repeat the tale to Millsap. When DiMaio had left, Millsap summoned a handful of his top subordinates, and threw the questions at hand to the group: Could this really be true? If so, where did they start? Unlike Ron Sutton, the district attorney of Bexar County had vast resources at his command: seventy-one attorneys, nineteen investigators, a support staff of fifty-five, and an annual budget of $3.5 million. Nonetheless, Millsap—uncharacteristically—decided to proceed slowly. If true, the baby-deaths story was dynamite. But at this point, he had only scuttlebutt.

Millsap also knew that he was playing with fire. DiMaio's tip involved not only Medical Center Hospital but the UT medical school as well. The DA did not want to erode public trust in the county hospital needlessly. And to an ambitious young politician, the prospect of taking on UT could not be regarded lightly. The University of Texas System, which included eight universities and four medical schools, had a combined annual budget of $1.6 *billion*. It controlled an endowment portfolio worth another $2 billion—including 2.1 million acres of land. UT institutions enrolled more than 100,000 students and conferred almost 20,000 degrees annually. In Texas, its loyal graduates—doctors, lawyers, politicians, an executives—were everywhere. A seat on the nine-member board of regents, which ruled over the entire empire, was the most coveted political appointment in Texas. There was no greater amalgamation of wealth, connections, and power in the state.

One of Millsap's lieutenants began by phoning Ron Sutton to see what the Kerrville DA knew. Sutton relayed the information that had emanated from Kerrville doctor Joe Vinas—that a surgeon in San Antonio had identified Genene Jones as a baby-killer. Sutton also buttressed DiMaio's belief that someone at Medical Center Hospital had conducted an in-house investigation. Investigations, Millsap knew, usually led to reports. The DA decided to try to get his hands on such a document.

Millsap was nervous that informal inquiries at the hospital and the medical school might prompt destruction of important evidence. He wanted to swoop down with subpoenas and physically seize everything he needed before anybody knew what was going on. Uncertain where to begin, the DA decided to go fishing. On February 3, he hauled before a grand jury six officials he *suspected* would know if an investigative report existed. In response to a subpoena, medical school dean Marvin Dunn appeared at 9:45 A.M. With special crimes deputy DA Luis Vallejo conducting the questioning, Millsap's strategy struck pay dirt:

VALLEJO: My name is Luis Vallejo, and as I told you, I work for the district attorney's office, and you do understand that this is an official meeting of the Grand Jury of Bexar County, Texas?

DUNN: Yes, sir.

VALLEJO: I will get straight to the point so we don't waste your time and we can hopefully expedite the matter. We are interested in specific information that we have received concerning a possible investigation by a team of doctors, either from out of state or out of the country, into an unusually large number or inordinate amount of deaths in the pediatric ICU, and we understand that there was an investigation done and there was a report made. Are you familiar with this report?

DUNN: Yes, sir.

VALLEJO: Are you familiar with the investigation?

DUNN: Yes, sir.

VALLEJO: Could you please tell us what prompted the investigation?

DUNN: I will be glad to.

During the remainder of the morning, Dunn revealed that there had been not one, but *two* formal investigations of the ICU—the first by Dr. Conn, the second by Dr. Mangos—each resulting in a written report. Millsap dispatched an investigator to seize both of them later

that day; Mangos's report was still in second-draft
form.

Millsap now knew: The scuttlebutt was for real. The
Mangos report confirmed the suspicion of Genene Jones—
and even detailed the unexpected deaths of individual
children. Dunn also had made it clear that top officials at
the medical school and the hospital had harbored fears
about the LVN for more than a year—an astonishingly
long time, thought Millsap. There were not merely vague
suspicions; there had been blunt accusations.

DUNN: . . . There had been comments made about one or
    two of the LVNs as being individuals who might have
    done something wrong. We couldn't get any hard evi-
    dence that anyone really could point their finger.
VALLEJO: Could you elaborate on that, sir, that there might
    have been instances?
DUNN: Yes. We heard from one nurse that one of the LVNs
    was killing babies, okay.

While the dean asserted that there was insufficient evidence "to say that somebody had done something wrong,"
the LVNs had been removed, he testified, because "one
should not take a chance." Dunn acknowledged that the
departure of Genene Jones and the other LVNS had
brought an end to the "unexplained and untoward events."
Yet even then, no one had notified law-enforcement
authorities. How many babies might have been murdered? The Mangos report discussed ten unexplained
deaths. Dunn estimated a dozen. Clearly, the answer to
that question remained to be found.

Millsap now knew they were about to investigate the
unthinkable: that someone at the county hospital had
been killing babies—and that those who ran the place
had covered it up. Millsap assigned Vallejo to begin the
inquiry and detached a pair of staff investigators to work
with him. The DA ordered everyone working on the case
to take extreme precautions to keep the investigation
secret; they were forbidden to discuss their work even
with colleagues in the office.

As he stood at the beginning of what was certain to be
an extraordinary inquiry, Millsap felt a little bit over-

whelmed—and a little bit thrilled as well. "This could be the biggest thing *any* DA has to tangle with," he told Rothe. "This could be the biggest thing that's ever happened in this community."

Twenty-One

ON WEDNESDAY, FEBRUARY 16, viewers of the 6 P.M. broadcast of *Eyewitness News*, San Antonio's top-rated local news show, received a jolt. As the snappy music introducing the program faded, a sober-faced anchorman announced: "One of the most incredible stories in the history of Texas medicine is unfolding right now in our community." The camera then cut to a pale, reedy reporter named Ted Dracos, dressed in a dark suit and horn-rimmed glasses, and seated theatrically at a desk behind a typewriter.

"Eyewitness News has learned that two grand juries are investigating suspicious deaths of at least twelve infants in Kerr and Bexar counties," intoned Dracos, as the words EYEWITNESS NEWS EXCLUSIVE flashed on the screen. "Right now they're trying to determine whether those deaths are accidental, through negligence, or through the intentional administration of drugs." The camera cut to film of sick infants in hospital beds. "According to a variety of highly reliable sources," Dracos continued, "investigations are being focused on the pediatric intensive care unit of the Bexar County Hospital District. It is believed that as many as twelve children died there under suspicious circumstances during portions of 1981 and 1982. All the deaths were unexplained. All died from sudden cardiac arrest. Since then, the hospital has made major personnel changes and launched an internal investigation. Officials at the hospital district would not comment to Eyewitness News."

Hospital public relations man Jeff Duffield appeared on camera, standing expressionless in a hospital hallway: "Ted, at this point in time, we have nothing to be ashamed of, and we're very proud of our intensive care unit, but we, under advice of attorneys, are not making any comment."

Dracos: "When will you be able to make comment on an investigation that's ongoing?"

Duffield: "That would be difficult to say when we might be able to make a comment."

Dracos: "Is there an investigation ongoing, Jeff?"

Duffield: "I cannot comment on that."

"Our attempts to review death certificates were denied," Dracos went on. "District Attorney Sam Millsap is just as terse."

Millsap appeared onscreen. "At this time," he said, "I can't confirm or deny anything regarding any matter that may be pending before the grand jury."

Dracos resumed his narration. "An investigation is also ongoing in Kerrville." Film of the city appeared. "A grand jury has been convened in this Hill Country community. During a one-month period, sources told Eyewitness News, seven to eight infants had mysterious respiratory arrests. Investigators are looking into the possibility that an anesthetic drug may have been administered to the children. Ted Dracos, Channel 5, Eyewitness News."

In the next several days, Dracos offered revelation after revelation about the secret investigation that Millsap had ordered his subordinates to protect. On February 17, Dracos reported that a Toronto doctor had led the hospital's internal inquiry. On February 21, he spotlighted the suspicions of Vincent DiMaio, firing his questions at the medical examiner with pinpoint precision.

DRACOS: Did the hospital district report to you suspicious deaths, a group of suspicious deaths, in 1981 and 1982?
DIMAIO: No, sir, they did not.
DRACOS: Have they since reported those suspicious deaths to you?
DIMAIO: No, sir, they have not.

DRACOS: Do you know if there were any suspicious deaths over there?

DIMAIO: Yes, sir, there were. But I'm afraid I cannot comment any further than that.

On the 10 P.M. news that evening, Dracos struck again. The reporter identified succinylcholine as a suspected murder weapon, and even detailed the problems the drug presented investigators. "It's called the doctor's poison because it acts quickly and it's extremely hard to trace once it's entered the body," explained Dracos. ". . . Whether or not there are any criminal indictments in this case may depend on whether any traces of this drug can be found in the victims."

Those on the DA's staff who had labored to keep their probe confidential were astonished at how much the TV reporter knew. For a week, Sam Millsap declined all public comment. Then, on February 23, the DA called a press conference to confirm that he was investigating the possibility of "multiple infant homicides" at Medical Center Hospital.

Instantly, the case became a major national media event. While a baby murder is big news in any city, the prospect that a *dozen* or more babies had been murdered—in a hospital, of all places—was a sensation, fodder for the TV networks, and the front page of *The New York Times*. I was assigned to write about the case for *Texas Monthly*. The man who had broken the story basked in the glory of his scoop. In an interview for a local newspaper feature, Dracos attributed his success to old-fashioned sweat and worn shoe leather. It had begun back in October with a tip from Kerrville, he explained.

It was about 4 P.M., Dracos recalled, when the woman called. The mood in the Eyewitness Newsroom was frantic—the hectic pace that precedes deadline.

"They're killing babies up here," she shrieked.

"But it was 4 P.M. on deadline, and there was no way to check it out," he said. "So I stashed it in the back of my memory."

A week later, he received a note from co-reporter and 5 P.M. Eyewitness News anchorwoman Kelly

Chapman. The note was from another Kerrville woman and said infants were suffering from respiratory problems.

"She felt something was going on with a specific nurse," he said. "She didn't have a name, and I stashed it away."

"Kelly thought it was a good story, but it got caught in the rush of things. You know how that is."

Then two and a half weeks ago, an attorney friend of Dracos called him about "problems at the hospital."

In the past, the friend had provided Dracos with reliable information, and the reporter was convinced "there would be something there."

Dracos began checking his sources, relying on information from three people from the medical community and two from the criminal justice system and interviewing a variety of individuals, between 60 and 100, for two weeks.

Each new lead got more bizarre. Dracos developed an insatiable appetite for the assignment, working weekends and after his normal shift. "I had never gone to this length before," he said.

Publicly, Sam Millsap called the early revelation of his investigation "unfortunate." Secretly, he was delighted— and for good reason. It was Millsap who had leaked the story in the first place.

"I was Dracos's source," Sam Millsap privately confided to his deputy Nick Rothe. "I told him everything."

Public officials leak stories not because they are fond of reporters but because they want things to go their way. Such was the case with the new Bexar County district attorney. Less than a month into his investigation, Millsap had come to regard the county hospital and UT medical school as fortresslike institutions, populated by doctors and administrators who were protecting a terrible secret. As an outsider, the DA could seek to extract the truth by calling reluctant witnesses, one by one, before a grand jury. But that was already proving painstaking; the doctors and administrators he had summoned weren't exactly rushing to cooperate. Millsap felt certain there were many more people who knew something—people whose names his investigators didn't even know. By making the investigation public, Millsap reasoned, he could not only apply pressure to the institutions but encourage those with valuable information to come forward. The DA told a skeptical Rothe of his plans. "We need to have the tree shook," Millsap explained. "If we're sitting here and thinking something horrible is happening, and there are dozens of people who have pieces of the puzzle, how do we get those people to talk to us? It seems to me one way to do it is through the press."

Millsap, who had ordered his subordinates to keep the existence of the investigation secret, had decided to leak it himself. Now he had to pick an accomplice, a vehicle for his disclosure. Ever the pragmatist, he selected the star reporter for the TV broadcast with the largest audience in town. Ted Dracos was the classic local television investigative reporter—smart, confrontational, self-righteous, and vain. He would later submit to painful hair transplants to recarpet his balding scalp. Dracos had grabbed Millsap's attention just days into his four-year term, with a report on the DA's decision to lock the front doors to his office. The reporter had made the move sound like a body blow against democracy.

"Locked doors and escorts to some reporters are like waving a red flag in front of a bull," railed Dracos in his report. "But that's just what's greeting all the media at DA Sam Millsap's office. . . . If you need information or an interview in the DA's office, you cool your heels until somebody gets time to come and escort you." Dracos embarrassed the DA, catching him off balance with a classic how-long-are-you-going-to-keep-beating-your-wife question.

DRACOS: How long is there going to be a closed-door policy—a *locked* door?

MILLSAP: We, we, we, the policy will exist for as long as it's felt to be needed. Uh, you know, that may, it may well be that we'll sit down in a group, in, in the next day or two and decide that we're comfortable enough with the circumstances that exist, that we know what we need to know about the evidence vault, for example, and how it's secured, to be comfortable having people in the office.

Dracos ended his report by rattling the locked door. "So where do things stand?" he asked rhetorically. "Well, right now they stand with the doors still locked. [Rattle, rattle.] Sam Millsap hasn't said when—or *if*—the doors to the DA's office will be unlocked."

"Part of it was that I wanted to get him off my ass," Millsap said later, explaining his selection of Dracos. "The main reason was that he was the guy people paid attention to back then." The DA called the TV reporter and invited him to stop by for a chat. The two men ended up spending the entire evening at Dracos's apartment; Millsap not only fed Dracos the story but dictated how he could use it. Reporter and public official thus consummated a classic symbiotic transaction: Dracos had the biggest story of his life; Millsap had enlisted a powerful ally for the prosecution.

With Millsap's information to guide him, Dracos conducted some quick and aggressive reporting in both San Antonio and Kerrville. He stopped by Kathy Holland's office, but the pediatrician—mortified by the visit—refused to grant Dracos an interview. A few days later, he called Medical Center Hospital and asked for B. H. Corum. John Guest took the call; Corum was out of town, Guest explained, but he would be glad to answer any questions.

"I don't want to talk on the phone," said Dracos. "It's better if we're not seen anywhere around the hospital."

Guest agreed to stop by Dracos's TV station, less than a mile from the medical center. When he arrived, the reporter sat him down in a conference room and shut the door. It was time to play hardball, Dracos decided. Jones was still at large; lives might still be at stake.

"We've got the goods," Dracos declared, striding back and forth across the room. "We know it *all*. I know about the number of deaths. I know about heparin. I know about succinylcholine. Heads are going to *roll*. Lives are going to be *ruined*. It's time for you to come clean. If you stonewall this, your credibility and the hospital's credibility are blown. If your family can bear to watch your integrity getting annihilated, I wish you luck."

Guest sat stolidly during Dracos's speech. Then he smiled and politely declined to comment.

Dracos's TV reports began airing a few days later— about two weeks after his night-long meeting with Millsap.

The DA took pains to avoid being fingered as Dracos's source. To keep his own staff guessing, he made a point of having Dr. DiMaio present at several sessions where the case was discussed. The medical examiner was his cover. He involved DiMaio in meetings to create one other person who could have leaked to the press. When Dracos began airing his stories, courthouse reporters suspected the DA because Dracos's information was so good. Millsap needed something to throw the other newshounds off the trail. "The reporters are after me because they think I'm your source," Millsap told Dracos. "You're going to have to make a horrible mistake—immediately. *Or I'm not going to tell you anything else.*" Millsap had raised his media manipulation to an unprecedented level. He was no longer merely leaking secret information; he was urging a journalist, a man paid to report facts, to deliberately present *wrong* information. Would any reporter go that far?

On February 23, Dracos profiled Genene Jones, the "central figure" under investigation in the case of the mysterious baby deaths. To illustrate his report, Dracos showed film of a heavyset nurse shielding her face as she rushed from the office of her San Antonio attorney.

"Genene, could you tell us if your kids are having problems in school because of this whole situation?" Dracos shouted.

"No comment," responded the woman.

Dracos went on to reveal that Jones had worked in the pediatric ICU between 1978 and 1982, had two children, and was divorced. There was just one problem with his report: The woman on film was not Genene Jones but her friend Debbie Sultenfuss.

Dracos refused to comment on Millsap's admission that he leaked the story, saying only that he had "a multiplicity of sources" for his reports. But he recalls no demand for a mistake from Millsap, and insists that he would never accede to such a request. The misidentification was a simple, egregious goof, says Dracos; he had only a general description of Jones, had been informed that she was inside the attorney's office, and simply assumed that it was Jones who was leaving. "It's impossible for me to make that mistake on purpose. It's too pregnant with litigious circumstances. Here I am, libeling this woman, saying she's a suspected baby-killer? That's beyond the realm of possible. I would never take that kind of risk."

Sam Millsap never spoke to Ted Dracos about what had happened. The DA was satisfied that he had the mistake he needed.

While the story of the mysterious baby deaths made front pages across the country, in San Antonio the investigation became a civic obsession. The tale Millsap had leaked fed a peculiar Alamo City appetite for municipal hysteria. Part of it was demographics: the product of a huge population of predominantly Mexican-American poor, much of it illiterate and ill-educated, susceptible to demagoguery and superstition. But the appetite for civic turmoil ran deeper than lack of schooling; even many of the educated comfortable possessed a cranky, hidebound outlook, a raging paranoia that someone—usually someone associated with government—was conspiring to screw them. Civic improvements quietly accepted elsewhere met rejection in San Antonio. This was a town that refused to put fluoride in its water for fear it would damage the gene pool.

San Antonio's media both reflected and fed this fear-and-loathing mentality. The local TV stations crammed their news broadcasts with carnage, usually opening with film of a sheet-draped corpse or a mangled automobile. "If it bleeds, it leads," was the unspoken slogan. The city's top radio talk-show host was a reactionary old coot who painted himself a populist heading a little people's call to arms; mostly, he led the charge against anything that resembled progress. Yet when out-of-towners shook their heads about the San Antonio media, they were usually talking about the newspapers.

Outside of New York, San Antonio was the only American city with three major dailies. Australian press baron Rupert Murdoch owned two, the morning *Express* and the evening *News*, which published joint editions on weekends. The third paper, the *Light*, belonged to the heirs of William Randolph Hearst. The *Light* had for years ranked as the most sensationalist daily in Texas, but Murdoch's 1973 purchase of the *Express* and *News* immediately lowered the standards. The two sides joined in a sewer fight for readers and advertising. Their weapons were screaming headlines, preposterous stories, self-promotion, and cash giveaway games with improbable names like Wingo. The national press labeled the combat the "sleazepaper war."

The shrillest voice belonged to Murdoch's *News*, whose red ink and glut of apocalyptic nonsense made it resemble a supermarket tabloid. Day after day, the *News* greeted its readers with headlines like ARMIES OF INSECTS MARCHING ON S.A. and UNCLE TORTURES TOT WITH HOT FORK. Its sister paper, the *Express*, was a bit calmer, though given to similar foolishness, as in a 1983 headline, TRUE LOVE CONQUERS 30 TONS OF GARBAGE. By then the *Light* seemed almost respectable—as much by comparison with the competition as by virtue of a new editor's first improvements. But local violence, political squabbling, and giant headlines still dominated the paper.

The baby-deaths story was precisely the kind of horror that San Antonio's newspapers loved. Loath to credit the competition, the papers rushed to outdo Dracos. GRAND JURIES PROBE TOT DEATHS, LVN'S ROLE, announced the jointly published editions of the Saturday, February 19, *Express-News*. The paper's medical writer reported that the Bexar County grand jury was investigating the death "of at least a dozen babies"—about the number that Dracos had cited. But by the following Wednesday, the purported death toll had multiplied. GRAND JURY PROBING DEATHS OF 42 INFANTS, screamed the double banner headline in the *Express*. "The Bexar County grand jury is investigating the sudden deaths of as many as 42 infants at Medical Center Hospital," its story began. "The babies are believed to have died by injection of drugs which brought on cardiac arrest, sources said." The afternoon

News shrieked in agreement: TOT DEATH PROBE SHAKES HOSPITAL. An overline added: 42 DEATHS INVESTIGATED BY JURY. The *Light* came up with its own number, attributing to an anonymous source the report that the grand jury was "looking at as many as 35 infant deaths."

The numbers game became a theme of the early coverage: How many murdered babies were there? Even the best papers couldn't decide. On one day (February 24), the *New York Times*'s front-page headline read: TEXAS INQUIRY ON 47 BABY DEATHS. On the next, the paper reported: INVESTIGATION IN TEXAS FOCUSES ON 12 CHILD DEATHS. The second *Times* article made a distinction that the San Antonio papers obscured: Every death under investigation was not necessarily the result of hospital homicide. In fact, during the period under closest scrutiny—Jones's last fifteen months in the ICU—a *total* of forty-three children had died. Horrifying as the details of this case were, no one in the DA's office believed that *all* of them had been murdered.

Although she had been charged with no wrongdoing, the media spotlight fell harshly on Genene Jones. By January, before the story broke, both Genene and Debbie Sultenfuss had left their jobs at the state school and gone to work at the Park Plaza Nursing Home in San Angelo. Genene trained nurses' aides. On February 2, she and Kathy Holland had become defendants in a wrongful-death lawsuit filed by the parents of Chelsea McClellan. On being served with the legal papers in San Angelo, Genene flew into an angry funk. She called the Houston office of the McClellans' attorney to scream that the malpractice claim was an outrage. When Dracos broke the story, the lawsuit, as a public document, gave newspapers an excuse to publish the names of Jones and Holland. With a little encouragement from the DA's office, reporters soon began identifying Jones as the "central figure" in the case.

Sam Millsap and Ron Sutton had signed a mutual-assistance pact to coordinate their separate investigations, which were proceeding in different counties. In February, they decided to summon their chief suspect before the Bexar County grand jury in San Antonio. Genene's attorney, Bill Chenault, had complained of the media's decision to publish her name but insisted his client had nothing to hide. And indeed, when subpoenaed, Genene seemed eager to appear for questioning. On February 24, a pack of national and local reporters staked out the third floor of the Bexar County courthouse for their first peek at the suspected baby-killer.

Burly investigators from the DA's office led Genene and Debbie Sultenfuss—suggestively identified the next day as Jones's "roommate"—through the mob of reporters and cameramen in the hallway. "I have no comment, gentlemen," shouted Jones, as she made her way to the witness room. Inside the closed grand jury chamber, however, Genene had plenty to say. Disregarding her attorney's advice to take the Fifth and remain silent, she wove a tale of medical malpractice, caused not by nursing errors or misdeeds but by incompetent doctors who would lie to stay out of trouble. While there might have been five or six questionable deaths in San Antonio, Genene herself had done nothing wrong. During three hours of questioning, Ron Sutton asked the nurse about what had happened in Kerrville. Jones said she had just followed Dr. Holland's orders; she had no idea who had used the opened bottle of succinylcholine.

Eight days later, Genene Jones held a press conference in her attorney's office to repeat her story to the public. "I didn't kill any children," she insisted to a pair of Texas newspaper reporters and a camera crew from NBC News. Genene attributed her problems to her abrasiveness, complaining that she had been singled out because "doctors don't like to be told when they've done something wrong." Complaining of media implications that she was a lesbian— and thus making the subject suitable for publication— Genene volunteered, "I am not a homosexual. . . . I like men." She complained that media sensationalism had destroyed her career and prompted threats against her life, and added—oblivious of the contradiction—that she was speaking out to clear her name. But as she spoke, Genene Jones did not appear besieged and beset. She seemed cool and collected, even cocky and a little jocular, as though she were enjoying the attention. And if she had truly hoped that a press conference would dim the spotlight in which she was cast, she would discover the next morning that it had precisely the opposite effect. The banner headline in the San Antonio *Light* was the biggest one yet. "I DIDN'T KILL THEM," it read.

Genene Jones was not the only one protesting her innocence. Following the public disclosure of the investigation, those in charge at Medical Center Hospital professed ignorance. "We have not had any evidence of wrongdoing in this institution," declared William Thornton, the dentist who served as chairman of the hospital district's board of managers. Informed that the DA was investigating multiple deaths at the hospital, Thornton told a reporter: "I'm totally shocked and stunned." In fact, the hospital board chairman had been told about allegations of wrongdoing more than a year earlier. On January 26, 1982—the day after the summit meeting that had prompted the Conn investigation—B. H. Corum, executive director of the hospital district, had briefed Thornton on the ICU's problems. Yet in an interview with a local paper, Thornton actually waxed indignant, attacking medical examiner DiMaio for asserting that there had been suspicious deaths. "What is motivating him to go public with such serious accusations and then not provide the details or documentation?" Thornton asked. "If he had known all along about some questionable deaths, why in heaven's name hadn't he told us at the hospital district?"

B. H. Corum was equally disingenuous. At a February 22 hospital board meeting, Corum was asked about reports that the hospital had conducted an internal investigation of unexplained deaths in the pediatric ICU. Corum responded that he knew nothing about it. "I do not believe personally that there was any wrongdoing," he told reporters. ". . . We hope whatever the truth is, it comes out." Corum, in fact, had not merely known about the Mangos report but authorized it. And it was with the knowledge of the executive director, the very man who proclaimed his interest in getting out the truth, that the Pediatric ICU Committee had set hospital policy toward the unfolding investigation in Kerrville—the policy of "judicious silence."

On March 16, Dr. Mangos sent Corum and Marvin Dunn an addendum to his committee's report on care in the pediatric ICU. The document included a breakdown of deaths by nursing shift. Of thirty-five children who had expired during 1981 in the ICU, twenty-five had died during the 3-11 shift. The next day, Dr. McFee convened another meeting of the Pediatric ICU Committee. In the absence of the anesthesiology department chairman, Dr. Malcolm Orr was sitting in. For almost an hour over lunch, the group discussed fund-raising to finance new equipment and recruitment of pediatric faculty. McFee reported on plans to restore the unit back to an eight-bed capacity by June. The committee ended its meeting by turning to the messy events under criminal investigation, with talk not of remorse but of revenge. "Dr. Orr raised a final issue regarding the possibility of redress for the hospital district regarding the appalling publicity that has been circulated as a result of the grand jury investigation," McFee's minutes state. "In general, it was the view of the committee that redress should be sought, but not until after the investigations of the grand jury are terminated."

For the presumed target of such redress, the "appalling publicity" was having precisely the desired effect. Within days after the story broke, Sam Millsap's office began receiving a flood of unsolicited calls. Many were from crackpots, but others came from residents, nurses, and parents who had known Genene Jones. And the flow didn't let up; each new leak produced a fresh stack of phone messages. To Millsap, the response had vindicated his strategy of leaning on the medical school and hospital through leaks to the press. It had also given the DA pleasure. The baby-deaths case had made Millsap the talk of the Texas legal community. Crowds of reporters were appearing in his office for press conferences every day. People were responding to his pronouncements, even thousands of miles away; Millsap's disclosure of the investigation had prompted Moody's, the Wall Street firm, to suspend the hospital district's bond rating. Those under the DA's scrutiny didn't merely respect him; they *feared* him. It was political jujitsu at its best—the very definition of power, the ambitious officeholder's dream.

The hospital district and the medical school had pledged total cooperation, but Millsap sensed a need to maintain the heat. When doctors and administrators seemed to be holding back or dragging their feet, Millsap lobbed a media grenade in the direction of the medical center. "I want to impress how absolutely essential it is that we have the full cooperation of the Bexar County Hospital District," Millsap would tell reporters. "In some cases, we have been disappointed and that is a source of real concern."

Assembling a criminal case in San Antonio required sifting through dozens of incidents and scrutinizing thousands of pages of documents. As the stacks of subpoenaed records and lists of witnesses to interview began to multiply, it became clear to the DA that uncovering the truth would take months. In early March, Millsap placed his top gun, Nick Rothe, in charge of the investigation. Rothe felt familiar with the territory. His father, a doctor, was director of the San Antonio Metropolitan Health District. Rothe's great-grandfather had once chaired the county hospital's board; his portrait hung at Medical Center Hospital. After securing $30,000 extra funding from the county commissioners, Millsap expanded the baby-deaths task force: Rothe's team would include a second full-time attorney, Joe Galenski; a pair of staff investigators; and as much extra legal and secretarial help as he required. Needing extra room, tight security, and an out-of-the-way place to interview witnesses, the group moved from the courthouse into the old Bexar County jail. The drafty stone building had been vacant for years; to the best of oldtimers' knowledge, no one had ever broken *in*.

Fifty-one-year-old investigator Art Brogley quickly emerged as the probe's most valuable asset. Brogley was a veteran of twenty-one years in the army, the father of six children, and one-hundred-percent business. He had served a tour in Korea and two more in Vietnam, where his duties included investigating atrocities against civil-

ians. Six foot four and balding, perpetually troubled by
an ulcer, the potato-faced Brogley had the hard-bitten
manner of a Mickey Spillane gumshoe. Pretty girls were
"dollies" and "dames"; bad guys were "scumbags." He
hung out at Dunkin' Donuts and ate in coffee shops and
cafeterias where the waitresses knew his name. Brogley
was suspicious of money and power in all its forms, but
his heart bled at every dumb slob's misfortune. His dogged compulsiveness suited him perfectly for an investigation that would rest on a foundation of detail. Millsap
had assigned Brogley to the case after asking his chief
investigator for a man who would lie awake in bed at
night, worrying about what remained undone.

A few weeks after starting on the case, Brogley returned a call from Cathy Ferguson, who had taken up
residence at the Buckner Baptist Maternity Home for
unwed mothers in San Antonio. The investigator knew
nothing about the woman who had baby-sat for Genene's
children. When Ferguson informed Brogley she had much
to tell him about Genene Jones, Brogley arranged to
meet her at a Dairy Queen near the home. Arriving with
a fellow investigator, Brogley found a young woman in a
ripe stage of pregnancy—and eager to talk. As she
munched on french fries, Cathy explained that she had
met Genene in San Antonio, lived with her at the house
on Nixon Lane in Kerrville, and accompanied her to San
Angelo. Around Christmas, Cathy had decided to leave;
she explained that she wanted to give birth to her baby in
San Antonio. Ferguson was so big, Brogley worried that
might happen at any moment.

Cathy then startled the investigators. She said she had
been in the crash room of Dr. Holland's clinic on about
five occasions when Genene had taken a bottle of clear
liquid from a drawer in the examining table, drawn some
of its contents into a syringe, and injected children with
the liquid. In each case, said Ferguson, the child began
seizing a few moments later. The exam-room table drawer
was where Genene had told Dr. Holland she had found
the missing bottle of succinylcholine. Ferguson was offering an eyewitness account of unauthorized injections—
precisely the link needed for prosecution of Jones in
Kerrville. As Cathy gobbled down more french fries,

Brogley began writing out a statement of her comments in longhand. The young woman's tale was vivid and detailed, but the investigator immediately wondered about her credibility. Tall and fresh-scrubbed, Ferguson had no apparent ax to grind. But she also possessed a curiously benign affect. Brogley had a rule: He never believed anyone the first time around. Besides, how could you buy the story of someone you'd met in a Dairy Queen? After three hours of conversation, Brogley, with his fellow investigator, drove Ferguson back to the Baptist Home. He had struck up an easy rapport with this curious young woman. As he escorted Cathy to her dormitory, Brogley offered a word of fatherly advice: He told the expectant mother to lay off the greasy food.

In the days that followed, much about the meeting troubled the investigator. Why had Cathy Ferguson suddenly turned on Genene Jones, spinning a tale that could send her longtime benefactor to prison? In her grand jury appearance, Genene had said that Cathy was mentally retarded. Brogley did not believe that; troubled seemed more like it. But Brogley soon learned that Cathy had spent time in a state mental hospital. It was not the sort of background that inspired faith in a witness. He would need to speak with Cathy again. Time would tell if she would stick by her story.

But less than two weeks later, Cathy Ferguson disappeared. A caseworker at the Baptist Home reported that Ferguson had met Genene Jones on March 3 at a local supermarket and returned with the happy news that Genene had asked Cathy to rejoin her. Cathy resurfaced in San Angelo on March 6, when she gave birth to a healthy baby boy at Angelo Community Hospital. When released from the hospital, Ferguson took her infant back to the South Concho Trailer Park and resumed living with Genene—the woman whose willful efforts to harm children she had recently detailed for investigators. Ferguson's behavior was as inexplicable as it was irrational; she seemed to have fallen back under Jones's spell. Cathy even named her son Travis, making him a living memorial to Genene's beloved baby brother, who had blown himself up with a bomb sixteen years earlier.

Travis Ferguson was to suffer a brush with a similar

fate. On March 13, the newborn was rushed from the mobile home to a local hospital. Genene Jones, identifying herself as Travis's grandmother, took the baby to the emergency room. She explained that the child had suffered a sudden episode of breathing problems.

Twenty-Two

IT WAS IMPOSSIBLE for Petti McClellan not to feel guilt over her daughter's death. Day after day, she replayed the horrible events in her mind, torturing herself with thoughts of how she might have interrupted the unfolding nightmare. Why hadn't she suspected something after Chelsea's first arrest in Dr. Holland's office? Why had she brought Chelsea back and handed her to Genene Jones? Why, as the nurse prepared to stick the deadly needles into her daughter's thighs, why hadn't she grabbed Chelsea and run, taken her someplace far away, someplace where her baby would still be alive? Petti rolled the nightmare back even further. Why had she brought Chelsea to a doctor she didn't even know?

For a month after Chelsea's death, Petti had stumbled about the family trailer home in a fog, unable to accept that her daughter was gone. Every few days, she changed the sheets on Chelsea's bed, as if her little girl were still sleeping in it every night. When Petti stumbled across one of Chelsea's socks while cleaning the house, she sat and stared at it mindlessly, tears streaming down her cheeks. Reid had sent his wife to a psychiatrist, who had prescribed powerful sedatives and antidepressants, which seemed only to thicken Petti's daze. Shay and Cameron, nine and four, were bewildered by their mother's behavior; she screamed at them every time they ran out of her sight. One night, Reid grabbed Petti and shook her until her teeth rattled. "Either you accept what's going on, or

243

I will go someplace else!" he shouted. "Look what you're doing to the boys. Look what you're doing to me. You're either going to face it, or I'm *out* of here!" They cried together for hours. The next morning, Petti threw away the pills she'd been taking; she soon reclaimed her grip on reality.

The McClellans read books about coping with the loss of a child and waited for their passions to fade. But there was no outlet for their guilt and anger, and everywhere there were reminders of what had happened. People gawked at them at the grocery store. "Those are the *parents,*" folks would whisper. In January, Petti had run into Gwen Grantner at the Kerrville K mart, and Dr. Holland's receptionist had lit into her, telling her she had no right to be angry at Holland, that the doctor had done everything she could to save Chelsea—even that the McClellans ought to take Cameron back to her for his medical care. An assistant store manager had been forced to separate the two women. When Shay developed tonsillitis, his little brother was terrified. "Is he going to the same hospital where Chelsea went?" asked Cameron. Petti and Reid said that he was. "Shay's going to die!" screamed the four-year-old. No, Petti and Reid explained, Shay was going to be fine. Cameron shook his head. "That's what you said with Chelsea." A month after her daughter's death, anxious to fill the void, Petti had visited her gynecologist to ask if it was possible to reverse her tubal ligation. They could try, but the procedure was tricky, the doctor told her; the odds were only fair that she would ever conceive another child. Petti and Reid decided she should not attempt the operation.

After learning from Ron Sutton that their daughter's death might have resulted from murder, the McClellans had retained Jim Perdue, a prominent Houston attorney who specialized in medical malpractice cases. Perdue filed a wrongful-death suit against Holland and Jones in Kerr County. When news of the baby-deaths case broke a few days later, reporters began appearing in the McClellans' front yard and calling their house at all hours of the day and night. Petti and Reid described their lawsuit as a search for answers, a chance to find out who was ultimately responsible for what had happened to Chelsea.

They felt certain that Dr. Holland either knew Genene was harming children or should have known. And as they learned that similar events had taken place in San Antonio, they wondered why Medical Center Hospital hadn't warned anyone about Jones. Petti and Reid wanted answers. But they also sought a measure of simple human revenge—a salve for their fury at the doctor and the nurse whom they had trusted with Chelsea's life. "I want them to suffer for a long period of time," Reid told me one day. "I want them to suffer like they caused my daughter to suffer."

Kathy Holland felt she had suffered enough.

On an afternoon in April, she slumped into the last chair left in her pediatric clinic, looked around the vacant office, and cried. Not long ago, the Fine Medical Center in Kerrville had seemed such a wonderful place to begin her career. Now, at the age of thirty-six, she was moving out, a step ahead of the sheriff and a few steps short of bankruptcy. The patients had stopped coming when the publicity hit, but the bills hadn't, and there just wasn't enough money to pay the landlord. Even now, he was hovering outside, watching the doctor and a handful of friends pack up her things.

In addition to the McClellans, Holland faced lawsuits from the parents of two other children, Misty Reichenau and Jacob Evans, who had stopped breathing in her office. Although she continued to live with Charleigh Appling, she and her husband had divorced on December 30. The threat of indictment still hung over Holland's head. And the doctors at Sid Peterson—despite the letters from the medical school faculty—refused to restore her hospital privileges. "I'm tired, I'm so *tired* of all this," said Holland, as she folded herself into Charleigh's arms. The doctor's eyes reddened and the tears began to flow again. "Now you see what she's been reduced to," Appling, the former air force pilot, told me, shaking his head. "She's determined. She'd make a great prisoner of war." Kathy and Charleigh had recently discovered a door to the clinic ajar. They instantly suspected that their tormentor, Ron Sutton, had hidden a listening device inside. "I don't care what they say," Charleigh went on.

"They don't deserve her." Appling stared suspiciously up at the ceiling tile. "Hear that, Ronnie baby?"

The news that Holland had taken the Fifth Amendment before the Kerr County grand jury had led many in town to conclude that the pediatrician had plenty to hide. One day, Holland paid a visit to Joe Vinas and asked the surgeon what she could do to get back on the Sid Peterson staff. "I'm not going to vote for you," Vinas told her bluntly. To clear her name in the community, he said, she would need to stop taking the Fifth—to tell all to the grand jury and let the chips fall where they may. Added Vinas: "When you say, 'I refuse to answer that question,' every doctor on the staff is going to say, 'The bitch is guilty.'"

But Holland stood by the counsel of her attorney, Jack Leon. In February, Sam Millsap's office had called the doctor to testify before the Bexar County grand jury. Leon advised Millsap's deputies, as he had advised Ron Sutton, that Holland would say nothing without immunity from prosecution. Millsap had refused to make the deal, then briefed the press, producing a fresh run of damning headlines—KERRVILLE DOCTOR WILL PLEAD "FIFTH," and PHYSICIAN SILENT IN INFANT DEATHS.

In the face of such a storm, a handful of families had stuck by Holland. The parents of Brandy Benites and Chris Parker brought their children back to the pediatrician, despite the emergencies the babies had suffered in her office. They believed that if something was done to their children, Dr. Holland had nothing to do with it. Another Kerrville mother wrote a letter to the editor published in the San Antonio *Light,* vouching for Holland's skill as a physician as well as her personal integrity. But such people were the exception. In the little town of Kerrville, the lady doctor became a pariah.

Forced out of her clinic, Holland set up a makeshift office at the house on Nixon Lane where she had lived with Genene Jones. There, she struggled to keep her practice alive, seeing a patient or two a day. Without a receptionist—Gwen Grantner had quit in January—Holland spent much of her time dodging a barrage of bothersome phone calls, half from reporters, half from creditors. "Dr. Holland's office," the pediatrician said in a falsetto, after picking up her office phone one day while I was visiting. It was a woman demanding money, insistent on speaking to the doctor. Holland held her hand over the phone for forty-five seconds, then spoke into the receiver in a deeper, professional tone: "This is Dr. Holland." Recognizing the deception, the caller became abusive. "No, I did *not* answer the phone," insisted Holland. "I happen to have a secretary who *sounds* very much like me." After more angry words, the doctor hung up the phone. "I have a right to do this," Holland said defensively.

It was a pathetic sight, this hounded woman reduced to lying to strangers. Nine months earlier, Kerrville had been the setting of her dreams; now it had become her prison. Many wondered why Holland didn't just pack up and leave town. But the doctor was stubbornly determined to ride this thing out—as determined as she had once been to give a San Antonio nurse another chance. *That* was her mistake, Holland told her friends. She had been naive to trust Genene—naive and stupid. Now she was paying the price.

Ron Sutton's grand jury had spent much time debating whether stupidity and naïveté were Kathy Holland's only crimes. After all, Chelsea McClellan was not the only child who had suffered in Holland's office. There had been nine separate incidents, involving eight different children—in a span of thirty-one days! And according to several Kerrville doctors who had testified before the grand jury, Holland had staunchly defended her nurse until the end. Even now—although Sutton did not know it—Holland was expressing doubt that Genene Jones had done anything to harm her patients. "To this day, I don't know," Holland told me, as the DA pondered her fate. "I don't know in the way that God would know. They were eight different cases medically. There was not anything in any way resembling a pattern." Would Holland be a criminal defendant or a prosecution witness? Ron Sutton still wasn't sure.

The DA had no such doubts about Kathy Holland's former nurse. Even without the pediatrician's testimony, he felt ready to indict Genene Jones by March. Sutton had held back at the urging of Sam Millsap, who wanted more time to build a criminal case of his own. But he wasn't happy about waiting. For six months, he had been parading witnesses before the grand jury: doctors and nurses, hospital administrators and technicians, paramedics and parents. Although his evidence against the nurse remained circumstantial, Sutton figured it was as good as it would get. This was a case, reasoned the DA, where the smoke would convince a jury that there had to have been a fire. Even if he hadn't been able to catch Genene holding the matches, the nurse was the only one who had been at the scene of every blaze. Sutton knew it was a risky strategy; a skillful defense attorney could poke holes in that kind of evidence. But Sutton also knew he had the critical factor of emotion on his side. It would take more than a few doubts to prompt twelve upstanding citizens to turn a baby-killer loose. Sutton was itching to go to trial, to do battle with this evil woman before the world. Genene Jones's conviction would represent his greatest triumph—a victory that would make everyone forget the unavenged Brady triple murder.

Sutton had reconciled himself to the limitations of his evidence, when he learned about the revelations of Cathy Ferguson. Her statement to Millsap's investigators was astonishing; it represented an eyewitness account of unauthorized injections in Holland's office—the critical missing link between Genene Jones and the deadly drug. So why was Art Brogley, Millsap's gumshoe, so unenthusiastic? Sutton dispatched a Texas Ranger to San Angelo to subpoena the young woman to appear before his grand jury.

On March 30, Brogley and his boss, Nick Rothe, drove up from San Antonio. Amid an air of much expectation, Ferguson began her testimony by *defending* Genene Jones; she portrayed the burly nurse as a benevolent surrogate mother. Sutton's heart sank with every word. He reminded Ferguson of her written statement to Brogley, filled with detailed allegations that Jones had deliberately harmed children. Was she saying all that wasn't true? Pressed by the DA, Cathy reaffirmed her original remarks. Yet she incongruously saw no problem entrusting Jones with the care of her own baby—even after Travis's recent unexplained emergency in San Angelo. For five hours, Cathy Ferguson offered such maddeningly problematic testimony. One moment, she would swear by tantalizing new information, such as her account of unauthorized injections. The next moment, she would present details of a child's emergency that were discernibly untrue. Ferguson claimed she had seen Genene committing horrible acts, but Cathy's observations seemed to have had no effect on her personal opinion of the nurse. Hoping to drive a wedge between the two women, Rothe informed Ferguson that Genene had testified she was retarded. Sutton offered to move Ferguson to Kerrville, to find her a job and a place to live. But Cathy just wasn't interested. When the grand jury session ended, she returned to the trailer home in San Angelo and resumed living with Genene Jones. Ferguson, concluded Sutton, would not make an acceptable witness.

That left only physical evidence to tie Genene Jones to the drug. Two days before Cathy Ferguson's testimony, Sutton had learned of a new test that might do what he had believed impossible—find succinylcholine in embalmed body tissue. The test had been developed around the globe by an eminent Swedish physician named Bo Holmstedt; he claimed to have developed a procedure to detect even minute quantities of the drug in embalmed human tissue. Sutton and Joe Davis flew to Philadelphia, where they met with Dr. Fredric Rieders, who had worked with Dr. Holmstedt. Rieders and Holmstedt agreed to run the tests, which would cost more than $10,000. But to conduct their evaluation, they would need samples of the victim's tissue from the sites where she had been injected. The test would require the exhumation of the body of Chelsea McClellan.

They began digging at 8 A.M. on Saturday, May 7, at the Garden of Memories Cemetery. Chelsea's grave lay in space 20, lot 2, in the Babyland section. Ron Sutton, hoping to keep it all quiet, had waited until after business hours Friday to have a judge sign the papers authorizing the exhumation. The McClellans had given their approval but didn't want to know when it was taking place. Somehow the reporters had found out anyway. They were already there, hovering about the fringes of the ceme-

tery; Sutton had obtained a court order to keep anyone
from coming closer. A three-sided tent shielded the
gravesite. Thirteen men stood inside the canvas, Ron
Sutton, Joe Davis, and Nick Rothe among them. A Kerrville police detective snapped pictures of the proceedings
for later use as evidence. Vincent DiMaio, the chief
medical examiner from San Antonio, would take the
tissue samples from Chelsea's remains. Dr. Rieders, who
had arrived two days earlier from Philadelphia, would
carry them to Dr. Holmstedt's laboratory in Stockholm.

Chelsea's coffin lay only three feet underground. The
workers unearthed it at 8:35 A.M. They set the tiny white
fiberglass casket on the grass beside her grave, then
broke its seal and lifted the top. The corpse lay beneath a
knit blanket of pink, yellow, and green. The blanket was
removed, and Dr. DiMaio got his first look at the body.
Chelsea wore a pink dress, white socks, white panties,
and a disposable diaper. A pink ribbon was in her hair,
and a tiny star-shaped earring in each lobe. Around her
neck was a metal chain with a heart-shaped pendant
hanging from it. Remarkably well preserved after eight
months in the ground, looking like a fragile china doll,
the child's body rested beside her favorite toy, a yellow
rubber duck.

During fifteen years as a coroner, Vincent DiMaio had
performed almost four thousand autopsies, witnessing
every grisly permutation of man's inhumanity to man.
But the sight of Chelsea McClellan in her coffin left him
shaken. This wasn't some sleazeball who had gotten it in
the local beer hall; this was a child, an innocent, snuffed
out before her time.

The corpse was removed from the casket and placed
on an oblong table set up nearby. DiMaio had arrived for
the exhumation dressed in a tie, a vest, and suit pants.
Donning a long green smock and pink rubber gloves, he
sliced open Chelsea's clothes with a steel scalpel, expos-
ing the Y-shaped chest incision made at the time of her
autopsy. DiMaio opened the abdominal cavity and cut
samples from the kidneys, liver, gallbladder, and urinary
bladder. After removing each piece of tissue, he handed
it to Dr. Rieders, who placed the sample in a plastic jar
and labeled it carefully. DiMaio next inspected Chelsea's

thighs—the site of the injections that had preceded her death—for needle tracks. None were visible, but DiMaio wasn't surprised; modern needles were so fine that it was often impossible to find marks. DiMaio cut into the front of each of Chelsea's thighs, handing sections of muscle to Rieders. After marking the samples, the Philadelphia doctor placed them in a Styrofoam cooler filled with dry ice. The outside of the cooler read: "Welcome to Miller Time." DiMaio was finished. Employees of the Kerrville Funeral Home re-dressed Chelsa's remains, then placed them in a fresh casket with her blanket and rubber duck. They sealed the coffin, placed it in Chelsea's grave, and buried it. Everything was done by 9:45 A.M.

In addition to the jars he had filled during the exhumation, Rieders had taken samples from the tissues at Severance & Associates, the San Antonio pathology firm that had performed the autopsy on Chelsea. Now he picked up his beer cooler filled with body parts for the ride back to the San Antonio airport. Arriving in Philadelphia at 10 P.M., the toxicologist drove to his laboratory in suburban Willow Grove and placed his specimens in a locked freezer. In another week, Rieders would take the tissues to Dr. Holmstedt's laboratory in Stockholm, so very far from Kerrville, Texas. Soon they would all know whether it was succinylcholine that had sent little Chelsea to her grave.

Twenty-Three

CHERYL CIPRIANI WAS frightened. The newspapers were full of horrible stories about Genene Jones, and the young pediatrician had known the nurse well. Cipriani thought back to when they had met, early in her residency at Medical Center Hospital. Cheryl, a short, soft-spoken woman, had liked Genene at first; unlike some of the nurses, she seemed to care a lot about her work. Then Cipriani had caught Jones telling lies about her patients.

On one occasion, the nurse had insisted that a child's blood sugar was dangerously low; she handed the doctor a filled syringe and told her to push it. Wary, Cipriani had run a sugar test on the patient herself; the child's blood sugar was normal. On another night, Cipriani had raced to the ICU after Genene sounded the alarm in the residents' call room. When the doctor arrived, Genene explained that her patient was having trouble breathing. But Cipriani had checked, and the child was fine. Early the next morning, a new shift of nurses had found the baby's heart beating too quickly. Cheryl discovered his respirator pushing air into his lungs dangerously fast, even though it had been set properly before Genene came on duty.

Cipriani, of course, had informed Dr. Robotham about the incidents—and about several others as they occurred. Robotham told her that they suspected Genene was giving children drugs to make them arrest. He advised her to double-check what Genene did and to order drug tests when a child began to bleed or crash for no apparent reason. Cipriani exploded. In addition to taking care of these sick children, they were supposed to play policeman? *Why was this nurse still there?* Robotham calmed the resident down, told her that nursing wouldn't move Genene out, that they were trying to come up with evidence to get her fired. So Cheryl had continued working with Genene, as the hospital investigations dragged on. One day, they were in a room together, taping down a patient's IV line, when Jones turned on Cipriani, her eyes burning with malevolence. "Dr. Robotham thinks he's going to get me," Genene muttered darkly. "But he's not going to get me. Nobody can. I'm keeping records on you all. I've got a little black book. Nobody can *touch* me." It had seemed that way, thought Cheryl. All the LVNs had been ousted, though everyone knew it was just Genene who was the problem. Remaining at the medical school after residency for a fellowship in the care of newborns, Cipriani had always retained a measure of doubt about what had happened in the ICU. When she heard about Kerrville, she instantly felt certain: Genene had tried to murder children.

After the story hit the papers, Cheryl went to the pediatrics chairman, Dr. Mangos, to ask what she should say about what she knew. Mangos sent her to an attorney: Thomas H. Sharp, Jr., a partner at the downtown San Antonio law firm of Groce, Locke & Hebdon. The medical school had retained Sharp to defend against lawsuits resulting from events in the ICU. A specialist in such work, Sharp was smart, aggressive, and tough; he had a wide reputation as the best man in town to have on your side if you were a doctor and had screwed up.

It is an exalted axiom of the legal profession that an attorney serves not only his client but the truth—that he is not merely a hired hand but an officer of the court. In reality, most lawyers do not act in accordance with this principle. A lawyer paid to fend off civil claims will reason that his cause is strengthened by a criminal investigation that ends without indictments. Thus he is unlikely to encourage the volunteering of damaging infor-

mation—even concerning a suspicion of murder. Such
was the case with Paul Green, the private attorney for
Medical Center Hospital, who told B. H. Corum in January 1982 that the hospital district should not contact the
DA because Genene Jones might file suit. Such was also
the case with Tom Sharp.

When Cipriani sat down with the lawyer, sat down and
told him all the terrible things that had happened, Sharp
grew cold.

"What you need in an investigation is proof," he informed the doctor. "Did you ever *see* her inject anything
bad?"

Cipriani said she had not.

"You don't have any proof, then, do you?" said Sharp.
There was no reason for her to tell the DA anything.

Cipriani had good reason to heed the lawyer's advice.
As a neonatology fellow, she was an employee of the UT
medical school, dependent on good recommendations from
the faculty with whom she worked. Provoking their ill
will would jeopardize her future. But this lawyer had
made her angry, with his insulting insistence that she had
seen nothing wrong. The county hospital officials had
angered her too, with their statements in the local papers
that they were ignorant of any internal investigation of
the pediatric ICU. When she received a call in early
March from Sam Millsap's office, Cipriani readily agreed
to testify.

The doctor appeared before the grand jury late one
afternoon, after the testimony of a nurse who had worked
in the ICU. Terrified, Cheryl sobbed continuously as she
told her story. When it was over, several female jurors
embraced her. Grateful for Cipriani's candor—particularly
helpful at this early stage of their investigation—Millsap
and Rothe pledged to defend the shaken doctor against
retribution. Now she had to escape.

In what had become a weekly ritual, a pack of reporters and cameramen loitered outside, in hope of catching
a glimpse of the grand jury's latest witnesses. Like a
quarterback directing his offense, Millsap laid a plan to
keep Cipriani from having to face the press. He handed
the pediatrician a bundle of papers and medical charts so

she would look like a legal clerk. Then the grand jurors bunched around her like blockers, and Millsap led them out. While Millsap distracted the media by convening an impromptu press conference in the hallway, the grand jurors took Cipriani to a side door, where she raced down a fire escape and climbed into Nick Rothe's waiting car.

The local headlines the next morning read: INFANT DEATH WITNESSES HIDE and DOCTOR, NURSE SMUGGLED IN TO TESTIFY. That day, Dr. Mangos summoned all the pediatrics residents to a special meeting at noon. When the two dozen or so doctors had gathered, Mangos introduced a pair of attorneys, one from the medical school, the other from the UT System headquarters in Austin. They were there to issue a warning. The lawyers told the pediatricians to be careful about what they said to the DA's investigators and the grand jury. Irresponsible remarks could lead to lawsuits, they declared, and *you* could end up as a defendant. In fact, the lawsuits concerning the ICU would name not a single hospital resident; it was the hospital district and the medical school that had the most to fear. But the residents didn't know that, and many were frightened by the admonition. They had all heard horror stories about groundless malpractice suits plaguing doctors for years; no one wanted that kind of problem at the outset of a career. If summoned by the DA, most of the residents concluded, they would probably have to talk. But anyone who volunteered information was issuing an invitation to trouble.

Marisol Montes didn't agree. Months after the LVNs had been removed, it was Montes who had discovered the novel called *The Sisterhood* with Jones's name on the inside. Now in her third and final year of residency, Montes saw no reason for any of the residents to fear a lawsuit; *they* hadn't done anything wrong. Marisol remembered well her final month in the unit with Genene. It seemed as if babies were crashing all around her. If the LVN had deliberately harmed them, Montes wanted to see her punished. Only hours after listening to the lecture about the dangers of injudicious talk, Montes drove to a San Antonio coffee shop to meet with Sam Millsap and tell him what she knew.

*   *   *

For the DA and his men, the task of assembling a criminal case in San Antonio was proving even more difficult than they had feared. The patients in the pediatric ICU had been desperately ill; this made it tough to isolate what had killed them. Even if investigators could amass evidence that a child had been murdered, they faced the equally arduous assignment of proving to a jury that Jones had done it. Millsap's men had to locate such an offense among an untold number of emergencies suffered by dozens of different children.

To bring order to the chaos, Millsap enlisted help from high-powered medical experts with the federal Centers for Disease Control in Atlanta. More accustomed to tracing outbreaks of meningitis and influenza, the CDC investigators would scrutinize hospital medical records, searching for statistical patterns in the suspected epidemic of murder. The CDC work would provide the big picture, an outline of what had happened and a correlation of individuals with deaths. But all that would merely provide a background for prosecution. To bring Genene Jones to trial, they still needed evidence in a specific case.

The job of finding it fell to the DA's investigators, who were interviewing everyone who knew anything about the problems in the ICU. The prosecutors dreamed of finding an eyewitness—a person who had *seen* Genene inject a patient with a drug that had clearly caused the child's death. They called their quest for such an account "the search for the smoking syringe."

The hospital's administrators had provided the DA with a private office in the building's basement. Art Brogley often operated from there, studying Medical Center Hospital as he would any other crime scene. Day after day, Brogley prowled the hallways, sucking information from doctors, nurses, clerks, and secretaries. In the process, he tapped into the secrets of the institution. He learned which doctors were having affairs, about hacks hired because of connections, about mistresses placed on the payroll. He especially came to know the large cast of characters who had played out the tragedy in the pediat-

ric ICU. He interviewed those who had opposed Genene
Jones and fought to have something done, such as Suzanna
Maldonado and Pat Alberti. He met those who had backed
her, such as Pat Belko and Virginia Mousseau. Despite
the events in Kerrville, the nursing administrators stood
by Genene even now. Mousseau openly lamented that
Jones had been singled out for such abuse.

Brogley also met Jim Robotham, by then a deeply
bitter man. Robotham saw himself as a modern-day
Cassandra, damned for his warnings and damned when
they came true. He recalled his April 1982 letter to
Mousseau, urging that Jones's problems be documented
in her record so that she would be "judiciously supervised at any future place of employment." Mousseau, of
course, had ignored him—just as Kathy Holland had
ignored his advice against hiring the LVN. Now a child
was dead in Kerrville. The hospital had refused to fire
Jones for fear that she might file a lawsuit. Now they
were indeed facing litigation, but instead of wrongful
termination, the claim would be wrongful death.

Robotham had arrived in San Antonio riding the fast
track. His rude firing from the ICU had already tarnished
his image; the scandal that was unfolding threatened to
derail his career. Only two years earlier, Johns Hopkins
had eagerly recruited Robotham to rejoin its faculty. His
recent inquiry about doing so had gone unanswered for
months. Most of Robotham's colleagues viewed the DA
as the enemy. To Robotham, those who ran the medical
school and the hospital constituted a far greater threat.
They had ousted him, yet allowed those who protected
Genene Jones to remain. Now they were blaming everything on poor management of the ICU. Certain that the
potentates would continue to make him the scapegoat,
Robotham retained attorneys and began making noises
about filing a lawsuit of his own. For a time, he contemplated leaving medicine entirely. Finally, an offer from
Johns Hopkins came through. Robotham resigned his
post as associate professor of pediatrics and laid plans to
head east in July. After hearing that their former medical
director had decided to leave, the nurses in the pediatric
ICU presented J.R. with a farewell plaque. "To Dr. James

Robotham," it read. "With sincere gratitude for your guidance and inspiration from the pediatric ICU nurses of Medical Center Hospital."

When Brogley had been assigned to work the baby-deaths case, he told his boss the investigation would take a year, maybe two. As the winter gave way to spring, the DA came to believe him. After four months of investigation, Brogley and the others were convinced that Genene Jones was a murderer. But they had nothing approaching proof; they had discovered no smoking syringe. This meant that they would have to piece together a case the hard way—snippet by snippet, with circumstantial evidence.

The track record of such prosecutions was not encouraging. At the Toronto hospital where Dr. Conn worked, a nurse had been indicted on circumstantial evidence in a similar case; the charges had been dismissed before they ever reached a jury. Millsap's investigators had taken dozens of written statements and paraded countless witnesses before the grand jury. They had gathered more than a ton of subpoenaed documents. Yet even now, many months of work remained. The investigators had only recently begun to target the most promising cases for prosecution.

In the early weeks of the investigation, the DA's frequent comments on the case had fed an atmosphere of public expectation. "It's like a snowball rolling downhill," Millsap had declared on the last day of February in 1983. "Every time it tumbles over, it's bigger than it was before." The DA reveled in the excitement he had generated. As the case dragged on, he came to realize that it was a double-edged sword. When a deputy DA publicly compared the baby-deaths investigation to the serial child murders in Atlanta, county commissioners attacked Millsap's staff for trying the case in the press. Oblivious of its own role in spreading hysteria, the San Antonio *News* joined in the carping. DA SHOULD CURB DAMAGING TALK, an editorial was headlined. "Medical Center Hospital is a referral center for critical cases," the paper intoned. "It is irresponsible for officials to frighten those in need of its life-supporting services by spreading vague talk of mass murders." Only a few weeks later, the same paper reported that Millsap was considering exhumations of children who had died in the ICU. At that point, in fact, the DA was contemplating no such thing. But the *News*'s lurid front-page headline raised the specter of unearthing entire cemeteries:

Tissue drug tests ordered for 122
TOT PROBE MAY DIG UP DEAD BABIES

Certain city fathers thought Millsap had unearthed enough. A few months into his probe, a pair of prominent San Antonio businessmen paid a visit to the DA's office. One man was a banker who served on an important city board, the other a high-profile developer. Millsap numbered both among his most important campaign supporters; they had made sizable contributions to his election and raised more money from their friends. It soon became apparent that they constituted a delegation from the city's business community. Their message: Back off. "Nothing you do is going to bring these babies back," Millsap's visitors told him. Pursuing the case, they warned, would exact both a civic and a personal price. The scandal was tarnishing the medical school and the county hospital and jeopardizing the future development of the entire South Texas Medical Center. It could cost the city thousands of jobs. Moreover, it was certain to make plenty of powerful people mad. If you don't end this soon, they warned Millsap, you'll wreck your political career. The DA politely thanked his visitors for their advice. "I'm glad it's you who came to me," he said, "because you're my friends and would never suggest I do anything improper."

After weeks of quietly taking their lumps, Medical Center Hospital and the UT medical school had also begun firing back. Now when reporters phoned for comment, spokesman Jeff Duffield didn't just pledge that the hospital would cooperate with the DA; he declared that the charges under investigation would prove groundless. Speaking off the record to reporters, the hospital spokesman added that the inquiry was a waste of time.

The outcome of the internal inquiries by Conn and Mangos was fueling a sense of contempt. Those who had presided over the probes felt certain: If they could not find proof, neither would the DA. Each week without indictments emboldened their public statements. From Toronto, Dr. Conn told a reporter that the pediatric ICU had experienced nothing more than "growing pains." In April, a Philadelphia paper quoted a "top hospital official" as saying that nothing would come of Millsap's investigation. "There never will be an indictment," the unnamed source declared. "The evidence simply does not bear it out." In early May, Dr. McFee expressed skepticism that any child had died as a result of Jones's actions. "If they're sick enough to be in the pediatric ICU," McFee told me, "they're fucking sick enough to die."

In the midst of the storm swirling about Medical Center Hospital, the man at the top remained silent. Jeff Duffield had implored B. H. Corum to speak freely—to let the public know the hospital felt it had nothing to hide. But Corum's initial encounter with reporters had been a fiasco. Confronted after the story broke, Corum had denied the existence of any internal investigation. Duffield had been left to correct his boss's statements. A newspaper story noting the duplicity had sent Corum into a rage. Since then, he had refused to say anything to the press.

Always moody, Corum under fire had become almost inaccessible. He had delegated his deputy, Guest, to deal with the DA's investigators, just as he had delegated Guest to monitor the ICU's problems back in November 1981. Absorbed in his dream of boosting the hospital's image, Corum had been flying high before all this happened. He had orchestrated the hospital's name change, launched the "New Horizons" PR campaign, and spent much of his time hobnobbing with the rich and powerful, campaigning for their support. The ugly headlines had burst the bubble. A man accused of presiding over baby murders was hardly fit company on the social circuit. Now the administrator spent most of his day holed up in his office, looking wounded.

Many at the hospital and the medical school had come

to regard Kerrville as the cause of all their problems. If Jones had not continued her shenanigans up there, they reasoned, no one would ever have *cared* about San Antonio. From Kerrville as well, they believed, would come their salvation. The newspapers said Jones was supposed to have used succinylcholine. Everyone knew the drug was untraceable. The Kerrville DA soon would realize he could never convict anyone. Then Millsap would have no choice but to reach the same conclusion. It was just a matter of time. This whole business would blow over.

Twenty-Four

I FIRST MET Genene Jones on May 5, 1983, while she inhabited the purgatory of an unindicted criminal suspect. We talked in San Angelo, in the two-bedroom mobile home she shared with three adults, three children, two cats, and a cocker spaniel named Sprout. Debbie Sultenfuss's trailer had once housed a pair of finches as well, but their bamboo bird cage now sat empty. One of Genene's cats had eaten them.

Genene greeted me with a smile and took her place at one end of a Herculon-upholstered sofa in the living room. She sat like a female Buddha, with each foot tucked under a thigh. Opposite Genene, a small sign atop a cabinet read:

ALWAYS TELL THE TRUTH
NO MATTER WHO IT HURTS

She said she lived by that wisdom. "I'm not a good liar," she explained. "You tell one lie, and you've got to tell ten more to get out of it."

Genene Jones was thirty-three years old. At five feet four, she carried about twenty or thirty pounds more than she needed, even after losing weight since becoming front-page news. Her short, red-brown hair was neat that day, her makeup modest and careful. She wore purple slacks and a flowered blouse, with a gold chain around her neck. She had dressed for our meeting as though for a Saturday-night date.

In the middle of the couch, clutching Genene's hand, was the newest inhabitant of the trailer: Garron Ray Turk, a pale, doughy, blond-haired nurse's aide. Garron was a nineteen-year-old high school senior and Genene's new husband. They had married on April 24 in San Angelo, six weeks after meeting at the Park Plaza Nursing Home, where Genene had trained him. Garron, who spoke in a whine, had little to say during the evening. He sat beside Genene, pecked her on the lips from time to time, and fetched more iced tea and cigarettes. At the far end of the sofa was Debbie Sultenfuss. In her press conference in San Antonio, Genene had gone to the trouble of publicly denying that she and Debbie were lesbians. This evening, she pounced on that subject with an angry wave at her new spouse. "Ask my *husband* if I'm a les," she said. "It's nothing but trash."

Until late into the evening, Genene led me through her story—about her life, about her patients, and about the terrible suspicions that swirled around her. She sucked on a chain of low-tar cigarettes and gulped down several mugs of iced tea while we talked. "I'm sick and tired of being crucified alive and having people think I'm a baby-killer," said Genene, explaining why she was ignoring her lawyer's instructions not to talk about her case. "I haven't killed a damn soul." She said all the publicity had forced her to quit her job at the local nursing home; she was being made a scapegoat because she was abrasive. "My mouth got me into this," Genene said with a grin. "And my mouth's going to get me out of it."

In six hours of conversation, Genene Jones was alternately friendly and defiant, sincere and threatening. She had an answer for every question, a response for every charge. When she heard that others had contradicted her account of the past few years, she leapt to the attack: They were liars, "full of shit," politically motivated, "a real turd"; she was right, they were wrong. She was quick to slip nasty tidbits about her accusers into the conversation—the RN who had an affair with a married doctor, the parents who made love in a hospital room as nurses walked in and out.

Genene spoke about the sick children she had treated, many of them now dead. She confessed that she sometimes got too close to her patients—as though they were members of her family, like her own two young children. "I'm a very feeling person. You can't help but fall in love with those kids." That was why this was all so incredible. She was *devoted* to the kids; nothing upset her more than the death of a child. "I always cry when babies die," said Genene. "You can almost explain away an adult death. When you look at an adult die, at least you can say they've had a full life. When a baby dies, they've been cheated. They've been cheated out of a hell of a lot."

During a brief sojourn from the couch, Genene scooped up a sleepy infant from his crib: tiny Travis Ferguson. Travis had bounced back without complication from his sudden episode of breathing problems. "This is my grandson," Genene announced cheerily, while cradling the baby in her arms. I asked why she identified herself as Cathy Ferguson's mother. As far as she was concerned, Genene responded, she *was* Cathy's mother. Jones complained that Ron Sutton had tried to manipulate the young mother. "He offered to set her up in a very comfortable apartment, pay all her bills, and take care of her and that baby, if she would sign a statement that she saw us or heard us talking about giving medications to kids that would hurt them." Ferguson, in fact, had signed such a statement—before even meeting the Kerr County DA.

Ron Sutton's disclosure that he had found a scientific test for succinylcholine was much on Genene's mind; Chelsea McClellan's exhumation was to take place two days later. "You can get any idiot for $10,000 to say the [drug is] in there," she said. "Ron Sutton sits on his ass and spends all this money just so he can crucify me—just so he can become governor."

"Somebody needs to investigate Mr. Sutton," Debbie piped in. "And I mean down-*dirty* investigation."

"He's going to put my ass in jail," predicted Genene. "He wants nothing but publicity—dragging the baby-killer to jail." But it wouldn't happen like that, she insisted.

"I've got it all prearranged." The nurse had a vision of her own arrest, choreographed as carefully as a scene from a play. When the time came, no one would lead *her* to prison in handcuffs. She would instead turn herself in—confronting her fate like a martyr, not a murderer. Then it would be only days before a magistrate set her free. "If the judge doesn't laugh it out of court," said Genene, "he needs to have his head examined."

Three days later, Cathy Ferguson was rushed by ambulance from the mobile home to a San Angelo hospital. She had gone into seizures shortly after starting to eat dinner with Genene. Cathy recovered quickly. But doctors were unable to determine what had caused her problem. Ron Sutton, who was receiving regular intelligence reports from San Angelo, suspected that Jones had poisoned Cathy's food in an effort to keep the young woman from testifying against her. Sutton also knew that his chief suspect had begun identifying herself as Genene Jones Turk. The DA regarded the nurse's marriage to the effeminate teenager as a sham, a clumsy attempt to disguise her identity.

On May 9, after one hour of work, Garron Turk quit his job at the Park Plaza Nursing Home. He told his boss that he needed to leave town for personal reasons. Garron and Genene then drove with Genene's daughter, Crystal, to San Antonio, where they stayed with Gladys Jones. Genene's son, Edward, remained behind with Debbie Sultenfuss. On May 13 in San Antonio, Genene gave a deposition in the civil suit filed by Chelsea McClellan's parents, who were now requesting $7 million in damages. It was during this interrogation that Genene declared that Keith Martin was Crystal's father—and that he was dead. Genene also told the attorneys questioning her that through the time when she worked in Kathy Holland's clinic, she knew nothing about the use of succinylcholine.

A few days later, Ron Sutton received a letter from Genene's attorney, Bill Chenault, who was offering his services "to avoid unnecessary efforts by your office." Chenault informed the DA that he had retained doctors to review Chelsea McClellan's medical records. They had not only found "absolutely no indication of wrongdoing" but concluded that the deceased child had received excellent medical care. Chenault volunteered to arrange similar reviews in the cases of other children. He would happily discuss sharing such information with the DA, with the "expectation of receiving favorable action or at least no unfavorable action" against his client by the grand jury.

On May 18, the call from Stockholm finally came: Dr. Holmstedt and Dr. Rieders had confirmed the presence of succinylcholine in the body of Chelsea McClellan. Sutton moved quickly. Kathy Holland's attorney, Jack Leon, had continued lobbying the DA on behalf of his client, even sending Sutton the results of a private polygraph he had commissioned; this time Holland had passed. After months of equivocation, Sutton notified Leon that he was satisfied the doctor bore no criminal responsibility for what had happened; he was ready to deal. The DA gave his commitment that he would not seek Holland's indictment; Leon agreed to have his client testify freely, doing whatever she could to put Genene Jones behind bars. Once Jones's staunchest ally, Holland had agreed to serve as her chief accuser.

On Wednesday, May 25, Sutton convened his grand jury in Kerrville. After signing a routine waiver for Leon, who preferred that his clients never appear before a grand jury, Holland testified for more than three hours; Debbie Sultenfuss and Gwen Grantner also appeared. After eleven hours, the grand jury issued eight criminal indictments, all against Genene Jones. She stood charged with murder in the September 17 death of Chelsea McClellan. And she was charged with injury to a child in the nonfatal episodes experienced by Chelsea McClellan, Brandy Benites, Chris Parker, Jimmy Pearson, Misty Reichenau, Jacob Evans, and Rolinda Ruff. All eight indictments alleged that the nurse had "intentionally and knowingly" injured the children by injecting them with succinylcholine or some other drug. Each charge carried a maximum sentence of ninety-nine years.

More than a week before the grand jury session, Ron

Sutton had also issued a subpoena for Genene Jones to testify. At this performance, however, Jones was the missing star. She had dropped out of sight after her deposition, and the subpoena had never been served. Chenault had written the grand jury foreman that his client did not know she had been subpoenaed. Genene had decided to take several weeks off to rest, Chenault explained, "in an attempt to get away from this whole matter as much as possible." Chenault asked the grand jury to notify him if it still needed his client. Such notice would allow Chenault to orchestrate Jones's voluntary surrender—the sort of dignified scene that the nurse had wished to arrange. But Sutton had no intention of *requesting* Jones's appearance. The nurse was now under criminal indictment; that made her a fugitive. Sutton gave orders for the Texas Rangers to track her down.

A bulletin was dispatched immediately to law-enforcement agencies all over the state. They were advised to look for a late-model pickup truck, a 1983 silver-and-blue Ford Ranger. Advised that Garron Turk's mother and stepfather lived in the West Texas oil town of Odessa, a pair of Rangers based in nearby Midland went to check out the address that evening. They soon learned that Jones and Turk, accompanied by Genene's eleven-year-old son, Edward, were staying with other relatives in Odessa and planned to skip town the next morning.

When the Rangers arrived at 10:30 P.M. at the house on Beechwood Lane, they discovered the Ford pickup in the garage, loaded with a bed and several boxes of belongings. The two men knocked on the front door. A young woman answered. The Rangers identified themselves, then asked if Genene Jones was inside. "Yes," the woman told them. "There is more tension in this house than you can imagine." Just hours after the indictments, the Rangers entered the house and arrested Genene Jones for murder.

The TV news the next day showed Jones in handcuffs, tears streaming down her face as she was hauled off to jail. It was precisely the scene that the nurse had been so confident she would avoid—one way or another. And it was precisely the kind of scene that Ron Sutton had sought. After eight months of investigation, his waiting was over.

Two days after her arrest, Genene Jones was arraigned in Junction, where she pleaded not guilty to all eight charges against her. The nurse declared that she was indigent, and District Judge V. Murray Jordan appointed Bill Chenault to represent her at taxpayer expense. Sheriff's deputies then took Jones back to Kerrville, where she was locked up in the Kerr County Jail, adjacent to the courthouse. On her second night there, Genene complained of severe stomach pains while in her cell. She was rushed across the street for treatment at Sid Peterson Memorial Hospital—to the distress of those who worked there. Jones remained for two days, then was returned to jail.

The circumstances of Jones's arrest had peeved her attorney. The Texas Rangers had found Genene while Chenault was attending a real estate seminar in Houston; he'd had to leave two days early and rush back to San Antonio. Chenault had long ago informed Sutton that he would surrender his client voluntarily; yet the DA hadn't made even the slightest effort to contact him. Chenault wondered if it was because of the comments that he'd been making to the press. He had ridiculed the succinylcholine test and called Sutton a "country DA" who hadn't done his "homework." Now Chenault had to figure out a way to spring Genene from jail. Her bond had been set at the lofty sum of $225,000—$50,000 for the murder charge, $25,000 for each of the seven other charges.

The problem was that Chenault knew little about criminal law. When Jones had testified before the Bexar County grand jury, for example, Chenault had been unaware that such hearings were closed to witnesses' attorneys. Now, after studying a handful of newly purchased criminal-law books, Chenault began filing all the motions he could dream up; he'd have preferred handling a real estate case. Recognizing Chenault's limitations, Judge Jordan appointed Joe Grady Tuck, a former Kerr County DA who now practiced in Kerrville, to aid Jones's defense.

At a pretrial hearing on June 16, the judge provided the defense lawyers with $4,000 for investigative expenses. Jordan also granted their request for a gag order prohibiting everyone involved with the case from discussing it with the press. Dressed in a pink polyester smock and white slacks, Genene sat expressionless as the hearing dragged on. Also in the courtroom were Petti and Reid McClellan. When interviewed by reporters, Petti noted that were Chelsea alive, she would be two years old that day. "We have to go out to the cemetery to wish her happy birthday," Petti said.

Jones's bid for release came at a second hearing, twelve days later. Her lawyers wanted her bond cut to $45,000, an amount they said her family could produce. The purpose of a criminal bond is to ensure that a defendant shows up for trial. Failure to do so results in forfeiture of the money. A high bond also serves to keep someone considered dangerous in jail. So to persuade the judge to reduce Genene's bond, the defense lawyers needed to convince the judge that she wouldn't run—and that she wouldn't harm anyone while she was free.

Tuck began his pitch by calling the accused murderer to the stand. An experienced criminal-trial lawyer, Tuck knew that Sutton would make much of Genene's disappearance during the week prior to her arrest. Tuck led his client through an explanation of where she had been. Jones testified that she had spent much of the week with Garron in the Hill Country town of Brady, living with her new husband's grandmother and fixing up a house where they planned to live. She had then gone to Odessa, she explained, to attend Garron's high school graduation. Until shortly before her arrest, she had no idea that anyone was trying to find her; after learning of the indictments, she had planned to turn herself in.

Ron Sutton was licking his chops. The DA relished the courtroom clash of wills, and he despised this woman as much as she despised him. Sutton also was armed with a shocking piece of information; he would spring it on the nurse at a suitable time. The defense lawyers had called their client Genene Jones; intent on highlighting the defendant's unusual marriage, Sutton opened his cross-examination by pointedly addressing her as "Mrs. Turk."

"Mrs. Turk, you forgot to tell us about going to Colorado, didn't you? About your whereabouts?"

"We went on a honeymoon for—"

"Went on a *honeymoon?*" Sutton interrupted. "Did you take Debbie Sultenfuss with you on that honeymoon?"

"Sure did," said Genene.

Sutton suggested that after learning the DA had discovered a test for succinylcholine—no longer the perfect murder weapon—Genene had laid plans to flee the state. "Now, isn't it a fact, Mrs. Jones *Turk,* that you married Garron Turk so that you could seek some kind of anonymity—so that you could disappear into Colorado under the name of Turk and nobody would know where you are?"

Genene denied it, saying she was only considering moving to Colorado in "the far future."

Sutton asked how long Genene had gone without dating anyone before suddenly marrying Garron, who was sitting in the courtroom. Tuck objected, calling the question irrelevant.

"Your Honor," responded Sutton, "this goes right to the heart of it that she married this *boy*"—Sutton spat out the word—"just to seek anonymity and get to Colorado."

Sutton asked Jones why the Rangers in Odessa had found her with a pickup truck filled with belongings. Genene said she was taking them to the house in Brady.

"If you were released on some kind of bond, what would you do?" Sutton asked.

"I would get ready to fight you in court," Genene responded.

"You wouldn't take on any type of employment?"

"I probably couldn't, thanks to the publicity."

"So you would just take a full-time job on me, is that right?" demanded Sutton.

"That's right," said Genene.

A few minutes later, Sutton decided the time had come. The DA asked Jones whether she had ever met a friend of Cathy Ferguson whose name he announced in court. When Genene acknowledged that the man had visited the trailer in San Angelo, the prosecutor dropped his bombshell.

"You made a statement a while ago that you wanted to get out of jail so you could fight me," he began. "Isn't it a fact, Mrs. Turk, that you are aware of arrangements to be made with [this man] to *kill* me as a result of this prosecution?"

"No, sir," said Genene, looking stunned. "You are unbelievable."

Tuck jumped to his feet. "I think it's obvious to the court that this is an attempt to make some kind of an inflammatory courtroom dramatic statement," he objected. The judge cut Sutton off, but it was too late. The DA had painted Jones as a woman with a continuing propensity for violence. From that point on, nothing the defense tried seemed to work.

Tuck called Chenault to the stand to buttress Genene's claim that she had planned to turn herself in. But Chenault acknowledged that he and Jones had at least contemplated an alternative. "We had had prior discussions some time back," testified Chenault. "It was our feeling— myself and several of the lawyers in the office—that probably they [the authorities] would be coming after her at some point anyway, so we discussed the percentage of trying to run . . . we felt it was a much more forthright proposition to go on and appear just like you should and fight it that way versus trying to run."

Tuck called Jones back to the stand to rebut Sutton's insinuation of a murder plot. "Do you have any idea what he's talking about other than an attempt to sensationalize this already sensational case?"

"No, sir," said Genene.

With another crack at Jones, Sutton asked her once again about Garron Ray Turk. "You had your husband out running around over in Brady interviewing people, trying to dig up something on me, that you were going to get me one way or the other, isn't that right?"

"No, sir, he was looking up information that would benefit my case," said Genene.

"The best way to benefit it would be to get me out of it?"

"No, sir."

Sutton took advantage of the opportunity to put Garron on display. "As a matter of fact, the husband we're talking about"—you could practically hear Sutton snicker, as he turned toward the back of the courtroom—"is this him right here in the light blue suit, [the] blond-headed *boy?*"

Genene allowed as how it was.

After brief arguments by both sides, the judge decided to leave Jones's bond at $225,000.

When the hearing was over, reporters rushed to question Sutton. But the prosecutor declined to elaborate on the death plot, citing the judge's gag order. In fact, Ron Sutton knew virtually nothing more than he had said in court. The information was unsubstantiated, and it had come from Cathy Ferguson.

Since early June, the befuddling young woman had engaged in a fresh round of conversations with Art Brogley. Ferguson had left San Angelo by bus shortly after Genene's arrest, then taken up residence with her parents in San Antonio. From there, she called the DA's investigator almost daily with fresh revelations, each more sensational than the last. Yet she told Brogley that she was afraid to take the stand.

In fact, both Sutton and Millsap doubted that they would ever call Ferguson as a witness. Cathy's mother had given Brogley an account of her daughter's troubled past—her history as a runaway, her placement in foster homes, her stints in private and state psychiatric hospitals. Cathy, she said, had a tendency to fantasize. Brogley knew Ferguson probably was useless as a witness, but he was reluctant to dismiss everything she said; too much of it had the ring of truth. One day, Cathy told him that while she was living in San Angelo, Genene had instructed her to have her friend locate someone who would be willing to "bury" Ron Sutton. Brogley had passed the information on to the DA, who had received a similar report from a state social worker who also had spoken to Ferguson. Sutton had revealed the information in open court before the investigator could check it out.

The purported hit man turned out to be a retired San Antonio resident who had once worked at a facility where

Ferguson had lived. There was neither evidence of violence in his past nor any indication that he was plotting Sutton's demise. A few days after Brogley told Sutton of the purported bid to do him in, Cathy was committed to the San Antonio State Hospital for the mentally ill.

Despite its dubious foundation, the murder-plot story had served the useful purpose of helping keep Genene behind bars. Or so Ron Sutton thought. Just hours after the bond hearing was over, the DA received a call from the Kerr County jail. Genene Jones's family had posted the $225,000 bond she said she could not afford. The Death Nurse had been set free.

Twenty-Five

IT WAS GENENE Jones's mother who had come to her rescue. At the time she fled Kerrville, Genene had warned Gladys that there might be trouble. But nothing could prepare her for *this*. At seventy-two, Gladys Jones was in failing health, stooped from a hard life, and wheezy from bad lungs. Breathing problems had forced her into the hospital only a few months earlier. Now she required intermittent mist treatments to ward off bronchial spasms; the medication she was taking had left her face moon-shaped and puffy.

Gladys was bewildered and heartsick about her daughter's predicament. She just wanted to be left alone, to live out her days quietly with a small circle of friends and family. Now she had reporters badgering her, trespassing on her property and phoning the house for comment. Prosecutors had even subpoenaed her telephone records. The newspapers made Genene sound like a baby-killer—an accusation no mother could bring herself to believe. But Gladys also knew from bitter experience that she couldn't trust her daughter. Genene had filled her mother's golden years with disappointment; even as she accepted help, she was never grateful. Yet Gladys had always stood by her because she was *family*. Now, in the worst scrape of her life, Genene was demanding that her mother save her again.

Terrified that this latest disaster would deplete her life's savings, leaving her penniless, Gladys had allowed her daughter to languish in jail for thirty-six days. She hoped that the judge would reduce the bond. In a series of anguished letters, Genene begged her mother to free her immediately. She cared only about being with her family, Genene wrote; she couldn't survive in jail. In one letter, she sent Gladys a two-page suicide note, to be saved "for the right time." "It's the only way out I have," she wrote. Genene pleaded with Gladys to pour any inheritance she was to receive into the cash payment a bonding company would require to bail her out. "Isn't my life worth $25,000 to you?" she demanded.

When the judge refused to lower the bond, Gladys relented, with the help of an unusual arrangement. Most bonding companies required security and at least 10 percent in cash—in Genene's case, $22,500. Dale Moreau and Edd Hodges of the newly formed Hill Country Bonding Service in Kerrville agreed to write Genene's bond in exchange for the posting of property and a nonrefundable payment of $10,000. Gladys did not ask why; it was soon to become apparent that the two men were eager for publicity. When the sheriff asked for additional security, Gladys placed a $50,000 certificate of deposit in a Kerrville bank, subject to seizure by the county if Genene failed to appear in court.

At the time of her release, Genene's attorney, Bill Chenault, instructed her to stay in one place and maintain a low public profile. The other half of the defense team was equally nervous about how Genene would make use of her freedom. There was much about Genene Jones that disturbed Joe Grady Tuck.

More than a few people still regarded Joe Tuck as the best criminal lawyer in Kerr County. A prematurely balding man with a graying red beard, Tuck, at thirty-seven, already had a career as a political wunderkind behind him. Once the youngest DA in the country, he had been elected at the age of twenty-six in a district that adjoined Ron Sutton's territory. Having retired to private practice after a couple of terms, he was not the least bit eager to represent Genene Jones; defending an accused baby-killer wouldn't win him many clients in Kerrville. But Murray

Jordan's request had left Tuck little choice. Jordan was a longtime friend; besides, a small-town lawyer knew better than to refuse a judge's call.

When Tuck paid his first visit to Genene Jones, then still in jail, he was struck by the simpleminded nature of her apparent belief in her innocence. The nurse had a rapid-fire answer for every question he could ask. Genene had got him going. As he listened to her, he could not help thinking: "This poor woman's getting railroaded." Tuck left with the thought that Jones might make a good witness. The trick was to have her appear softer and more demure; careful coaching, a little makeup, and new clothes could do it. But as Tuck studied the details of the case, he came to a different judgment. Out of Genene's bewitching presence, Tuck concluded that his client was guilty.

Like many criminal-defense attorneys, Tuck usually tried to avoid reaching such a conclusion. He never asked a client if he had committed the crime with which he had been charged. Instead, he simply asked each to tell his story. If that account wasn't likely to produce a happy result, Tuck would suggest an alternative—or perhaps a plea bargain. But in Genene Jones's case, Tuck found a conclusion of guilt inescapable. In looking at the facts, he couldn't think of any other explanation. Genene was the common link in all the children's arrests; she *had* to have done it.

The belief that he was working to free a woman who had committed horrible crimes was not, in isolation, what bothered the lawyer; most of the people he represented were guilty. What really disturbed Tuck was that Jones was unlike any criminal defendant he had known. He had defended people who falsely professed innocence; they lacked Genene's extraordinary conviction. He had also represented individuals who were truly innocent; they regarded their situation with outrage and fear. But Genene seemed to revel in her plight. She was actually eager to battle Sutton. It's almost like megalomania, Tuck thought. "She was above all this. She had nothing but contempt for everyone against her, and never doubted for a minute that she could beat them."

Tuck decided that Genene Jones was insane. That was why the nurse acted so certain of her innocence; she didn't *know* she was guilty. The lawyer began to plot strategy for a psychiatric defense. Tuck would admit that Jones had committed the crimes with which she was charged, but plead that a mental disability absolved her of any responsibility for them. Before a jury of self-reliant Texans, an insanity plea was a high-risk defense, a lawyer's last resort. But Tuck could think of no other approach that would work. If everything went right, Genene might walk free after a few years of confinement in a state mental hospital.

The biggest obstacle to such a plan was Genene Jones herself. Tuck had hinted at the approach, and the nurse was having none of it. To the defense lawyer, that merely reinforced his theory. But Tuck needed Jones's cooperation to execute his strategy; he decided to try to persuade Genene that she was insane. Tuck contacted Dr. Franklin Redmond, a prominent psychiatrist in San Antonio, and made arrangements for him to examine Genene Jones. Tuck wanted the doctor to furnish evidence that Jones was crazy—to provide him with ammunition to confront Genene with her guilt. Tuck and Chenault told their client a psychiatric exam would aid her defense. But Genene did not know the nature of the help that they sought. She believed she was seeing Redmond to prove her sanity. In fact, she was there to prove her *in*sanity. In arranging the appointment, Tuck frankly confided to the doctor his own theory: His client was "some kind of homicidal maniac" and didn't know it.

Redmond interviewed Genene Jones only once, in a three-hour session on July 15. The psychiatrist entered the meeting with little information about Genene's background. He had no knowledge of her history of lying, which dated back to childhood. He was unaware of her frequent hospitalizations and countless visits to emergency rooms, the vast majority of which had revealed nothing wrong. He knew nothing about the false reports of emergencies she had made while a nurse at Medical Center Hospital, or of similar incidents in Kerrville. He was not informed of Genene's untruthful stories about the identity of her daughter's father and Cathy Ferguson's medical history. And he knew nothing of the many witnesses—doctors, nurses, paramedics, parents, and others—who contradicted Jones's account of what had happened to the children under her care. Thus Dr. Redmond relied entirely on his single session with Genene Jones—a woman who had fooled many others before.

After completing his interview with Genene Jones, the psychiatrist phoned the attorneys for the defense to inform them of his findings. Several weeks later, he sent a written summary of his conclusions to Bill Chenault.

> Her mental status during the evaluation revealed that she was a 33-year-old woman who was casually dressed, who was friendly and cooperative to the interview. She established and maintained good eye contact throughout the interview. She showed no hesitancy in answering the questions that were put to her. She seemed relatively comfortable, with no overt signs of anxiety. Her mood seemed neither depressed nor elated. Her affect was appropriate. She was oriented to person, place and time. She was of average to above average intelligence. Her recent and remote memory seemed intact. Her thoughts were goal directed. There was no evidence of hallucinations, delusions, loose associations, blocking, ideas of reference or other evidence of thought disorder.
>
> I asked many probing questions along some of the lines that we had previously discussed, specifically about her relationships with Dr. Holland, [Debbie] Sultenfuss, [Cathy] Ferguson, Petti McClellan, Gwen Grantner and Garron Turk. I asked her specific and probing questions about her sexual orientation, about her previous relationships, about her interpersonal interactions on all of her jobs, including the Bexar County Hospital experience. I explored the issue of her reaction to stress and emergency type situations.
>
> Throughout the interview, I found no evidence which would make me think that Ms. Jones in any way is suffering from a major psychiatric disorder, such as schizophrenia. I found no evidence for psychosis such

as hallucinations or delusions. I found no evidence
that she might have done things alleged in the indictment as part of a delusion or a psychosis and be
unaware of them. She reports no amnesia for the
events surrounding the incidents with the children included in the indictment. She has explanations which
are coherently put together and make sense. She further denies any of the specific actions such as injecting
any kind of medication into the children that was not
specifically ordered. Further, she seems to be clearly
aware of her current situation in terms of her indictment and the impending trial and has the capacity to
cooperate in her defense.

Ms. Jones does seem to have personality character-
istics which by her history may have caused her diffi-
culties in the past. She appears to be a very outspoken
person and it seems that there have been incidents in
her past where this outspokenness has caused friction
with her supervisors and/or co-workers.

Based on the data available for me to evaluate, I
feel that this summary, with the expressed opinions as
stated, exhausts the relevant contributions of clinical
psychiatry to the legal aspects of this case.

Redmond's findings torpedoed Tuck's plan for an insanity defense. The psychiatrist had not only concluded that
Genene was sane but also appeared convinced that she
was innocent. It was the only psychiatric examination
that Genene Jones would undergo.

After gaining her freedom on June 29, Genene had
moved her children and her new husband to Gladys
Jones's house in northwest San Antonio. Gladys was less
than delighted to host the circus that surrounded her
daughter. Genene's presence meant a fresh wave of visits
from nosy reporters. Gladys was also sickened by Genene's
marriage—in her letters from jail, she had called Garron
the love of her life—and puzzled by her evident excitement about her plight. Genene pored over the stories
about her case that Gladys had clipped like an author
reading rave reviews. Keith Martin, Genene's old friend
from her beauty-parlor days, visited the house. He found

Genene plotting strategy and Gladys Jones depressed. Martin mentioned to Gladys that Genene, in her deposition, had testified that he was dead. "Keith, you know what Genene's all about," said Gladys. "She's a pathological liar. I've had it with her." After less than a week in San Antonio, Genene and Garron moved to the home of Turk's grandmother in Brady. The woman who had written of her desperation to be with her family left her two children in San Antonio with their grandmother.

For about one month, Genene followed her lawyers' instructions and kept a low profile. Then, as if to stare down the community that accused her of murder, she and Garron moved back to Kerrville. Their new residence was a stone cottage just west of town. It was the home of Edd Hodges, Genene's bail bondsman, who eagerly assumed the role of the nurse's protector and public spokesman. Explaining the odd arrangement, Genene told Tuck she had moved in with Hodges for safety; she said she had received a death threat in Brady. Genene brandished the note excitedly, explaining that she had found it on her typewriter. It read: "YOUR DEAD." The note—even down to the misspelled contraction—was identical to one sent in March 1982 to another nurse in another city. The city was San Antonio, and the nurse was Suzanna Maldonado—the RN who had complained that too many children were dying on Genene in the pediatric ICU.

Genene's car had been repossessed after her indictment. The nurse also owed money from her treatment the previous fall at Sid Peterson Hospital. But in moving to Kerrville, she had selected the one town where she was certain to find no work. She did not make much effort to find any; Genene was preoccupied with her case. She lived off borrowed money from her mother and with the help of free housing; bail bondsman Hodges was charging Genene's entourage no rent. After a few weeks, Garron took a minimum-wage job at a Kerrville Pizza Hut to help pay for the groceries.

Despite Genene's apparent poverty, the Kerr County Attorney, noting her ability to arrange a $225,000 bond, petitioned Judge Jordan to free the county from paying her legal bills. Hoping to prove that the defendant was not indigent, the county attorney subpoenaed Gladys to appear in Kerrville for questioning about the family assets. Genene's sickly mother greeted the summons with disgust. "Why am I being bothered with this thing?" she asked. When she failed to show up on the scheduled date because she was ill, the county attorney moved to have the seventy-two-year-old woman cited for contempt of court. Instead, Gladys testified at a second hearing, where in a barely audible voice she made it clear that she intended to offer no more financial help to her daughter. "It was understood that if I went [on] her bond and got her out of jail, that would be all I could possibly do for her," Gladys testified. The judge agreed that Genene was entitled to her indigency status; the contempt motion against Gladys was withdrawn.

By then, Edward had again proved too much for his grandmother to handle. Gladys told her daughter to reclaim the children. Still living at the home of her bondsman, Genene began sending Crystal and Edward to school in Ingram, near Kerrville, where their schoolmates included the two sons of Petti and Reid McClellan. Provoked by the presence of the woman he believed had murdered his daughter, Reid McClellan kept a close eye on the house where Genene was staying. Several times, he cruised by in his old pickup in the middle of the night. Reid knew his truck backfired when he shut down the engine; he would park it in front of the cottage, then turn off the key. Ka-*boom!* The noise would bring Hodges running out of the house, shotgun in hand. Hodges called the county sheriffs, who told Reid to knock it off.

Genene was first to face the charge of murdering Chelsea McClellan. In August, Judge Jordan had granted a motion to move the case to Georgetown, the seat of Williamson County, located a hundred miles northeast of Kerrville and twenty-eight miles north of Austin. Genene's lawyers had sought the change of venue, arguing that the glut of pretrial publicity made it impossible for her to receive a fair trial in Kerrville. Much of the recent press, however, had come from the defendant.

One day after the trial was moved, Genene told the

San Antonio *Light* that someone was trying to kill her. "I'm frightened," Genene declared. "I fear for my life." Jones's vivid account of death threats produced a banner front-page headline: VANDALS TERRIFY NURSE JONES. Ignoring the gag order issued at her request, Genene said she was granting the interview to counter the bad publicity she had received in the past. "I want people to know I'm human too," she said. Later that day, Genene also gave interviews to radio and television reporters.

Jones and Hodges reported no fewer than four break-ins at his house. In the first incident, the word "DEAD" had been written in shaving cream across the front door; inside the house, Genene's purse had been dumped out, and a sheet had been cut up in the shape of a woman's body. Then on a single day, they complained of two break-ins. They said medical records Genene was studying for her defense had been taken, a shower curtain torn, and the word "BITCH" scrawled on a bathroom mirror. In the last episode, reported to have taken place while Jones and Hodges were at a court hearing, the word "DEAD" had appeared once again in shaving cream, this time in the bathroom. In each case, Edd Hodges had called the office of the Kerr County sheriff. In each case, the sheriff's deputies could find no clue to the identity of the perpetrators. When Hodges reported the fourth incident, chief deputy sheriff Ed Slater investigated the complaint personally. The deputy interviewed neighbors and inspected the hole in the window screen that was the supposed point of entry; the screen appeared to have been cut from the inside. Slater concluded the break-in reports were a hoax.

On Saturday night, August 13, a familiar face appeared in the emergency room at Sid Peterson Hospital. It was Genene Jones, complaining of stomach pain; she was worried it was an intestinal obstruction. A doctor concluded that Genene's problem was not serious. After treating her in the ER, the physician sent her home. At 6 P.M. the next day, Genene returned, this time with her husband and Edd Hodges, who was complaining of numbness from a back problem. When Genene tried to enter the emergency room cubicle where Hodges was being treated, the Sid Peterson staff ordered her to leave the hospital. Apparently puzzled by the staff's reluctance to let her near patients, Genene complained to reporters, asking, "Why did they want me to desert Edd when he needed me?"

Two days later, Hodges informed reporters that Genene was negotiating with a prominent Dallas lawyer, Douglas Mulder, to defend her. Mulder was Ron Sutton's nemesis, the attorney who had acquitted the capital murder defendant in the DA's final bid for a conviction in the Brady triple murder case. The negotiations with Mulder never progressed beyond a preliminary stage; Gladys Jones refused her daughter's pleas to pay the attorney's hefty retainer. Tuck and Chenault were disappointed; Genene's court-appointed lawyers were both eager to be replaced.

Joe Grady Tuck had never had a more exasperating client. Shortly after being assigned to the case, the defense lawyer met Genene's new husband. Shocked at his youth and effeminate appearance—"it made her look like a lunatic," the attorney said later—Tuck instructed Jones to keep Garron under wraps. "The presence of your husband is going to hurt," Tuck delicately told Genene. She ignored the advice; Garron had showed up for the bond-reduction hearing, allowing Sutton the opportunity to point him out in court. Tuck cautioned Jones not to argue with the DA on the witness stand; Genene had tried to put him down anyway. And when Jones made bail, she became even more troublesome. She was constantly calling or stopping by Tuck's office unannounced; when she walked in the door, she seemed to expect all other business to cease. Most of all, Genene refused to obey her attorneys' orders to stop talking to the press. "I have a right to do it," she told her lawyers. "What you have a right to do and what it's smart to do are two different things," they responded. "She thrived on crisis like a vampire," Tuck said later.

In September, the ABC television news program *20/20* began preparing a report on her case. Genene told the Kerrville paper that she wanted a court order to bar the *20/20* crew from coming near her. Just days later, she let the network fly her to New York City, where she granted

an extensive filmed interview. Accommodating the TV
cameras further, Genene fetched her children, who were
visiting their grandmother, to stage a family stroll through
the Kerrville countryside.

On September 15, Tuck took advantage of the change
of venue to ask Judge Jordan to replace him with an
attorney from Georgetown. Genene had frustrated Tuck
at every turn. If he could not even stop her from chattering to reporters, how could he control what she said on
the witness stand? The judge granted Tuck's request.
The defense lawyer felt like a newly freed man.

On the morning of October 17, Dale Moreau appeared
in the office of Kerr County chief deputy sheriff Ed
Slater. Leonard Dale Moreau, thirty-one, was the owner
of Hill Country Bonding Service, which had written the
bond that freed Genene from jail. He was Edd Hodges's
boss. Although the deputy sheriff did not know it, Moreau was also a felon and a con man; in 1979, he had
received five years' probation after pleading guilty to
bank fraud. Moreau and Hodges had begun their Kerrville bond firm in early 1983. When Genene was arrested, they had attached themselves to her in the correct
expectation that it would garner publicity for them. Now
Moreau claimed that Hodges had misappropriated the
$10,000 premium Genene's mother had paid. He informed
Slater that Hodges no longer worked for his firm. Explaining that he could not guarantee Jones's appearance,
Moreau announced that he wanted to revoke her bond.

The Texas Rangers arrested Genene later that afternoon and returned her to the Kerr County jail. Although
it was the squabble between the bondsmen that had cost
Genene her freedom, Moreau filed court papers stating
that he was unaware of Jones's whereabouts. Bill Chenault
saw more than a little irony in the claim; he had been
trying to persuade his client to be *more* difficult to find.
"Every reporter in the state knew where Genene was,"
noted Chenault.

With Genene's rearrest, Gladys Jones worried about
her grandchildren, abruptly left in Garron's care. She
asked a state social services caseworker to check on them.

Livid about the inquiry, Genene wrote to accuse her sickly mother of scheming to claim custody of Crystal. Gone was the sweet talk of family she had offered when begging Gladys to post her bond; now Genene was issuing threats.

Mother,

I should of known that you'd pull some under-handed trick to get my daughter.

Maybe you think of me as a wimp but when it comes to my children your sadly mistaken.

If you in any way try to take my daughter away from me or Garron, if you continue to interfere in my life, I will make sure that your entire sordid, drunken past is spread from coast to coast. I'll get T.V. interviews from San Antonio to New York. Don't push me lady. I'm dead serious. I'll make sure you can never hold your head up in public again.

As far as I'm concerned, my mother is dead. Don't try to dig her up. You'll regret it. . . .

Mr. Hodges will be in touch with you if your assistance is required in obtaining a new bond. You will do so. I don't think you'd enjoy being [in] the headlines.

Genene Turk

Frightened by the letter, Gladys Jones gave a copy to her attorney. A few weeks later, she visited the lawyer again to cut Genene out of her will.

Now estranged even from her mother, Genene would remain in jail until her murder trial, scheduled for January. The change of venue meant that both the prisoner and all future legal proceedings would move to Georgetown.

Genene's final court appearance in Kerrville took place one week after her rearrest. Explaining that he could not afford the time required for Genene's defense, Bill Chenault won permission to withdraw from the case; he was replaced by a second Williamson County lawyer.

But the news that day was once again generated by the defendant. In a telephone interview from jail with a

Light reporter, Genene announced that she was pregnant. Garron Turk—who would soon voluntarily return Crystal and Edward to Gladys—told the paper that he was "pleased deep down inside." Genene's attorneys diplomatically expressed their surprise. Ron Sutton labeled the story "bullshit." In 1978, the DA noted, Genene had undergone a tubal ligation, a procedure that rendered her incapable of bearing children.

Twenty-Six

GENENE JONES'S ARREST had sparked fresh life into the investigation in San Antonio. For months, Sam Millsap had been taking it on the chin from those who proclaimed that his long and costly probe would come up with nothing. But the charges in Kerrville—against the nurse who was Millsap's prime suspect—made the allegations in San Antonio impossible to dismiss.

Bill Thornton, the hospital district board chairman, continued to insist that his institution's internal investigations had uncovered nothing more than leadership and morale problems—and that the probes were merely part of an effort to better the ICU. "There was never anything suggesting criminal activity," Thornton told a Dallas newspaper. But media leaks were offering a different impression.

GRAND JURY PROBE FOCUSES
ON BABY DEATHS COVER-UP

Some at Bexar Hospital
"did nothing," source says

Quoting anonymous officials—including "one high-level source close to the probe"—the San Antonio *Light* revealed that the DA's office was investigating "the possibility of a cover-up by hospital administrators and staff." Four days later, Ron Sutton joined the attack. The Kerr

County prosecutor complained—correctly—that doctors at Medical Center Hospital knew about his grand jury investigation of Genene Jones but never attempted to notify him of their own suspicions about her. "It's a pretty poor way to run a railroad," snapped Sutton. Asked why hospital officials did nothing, he responded: "I think it's obvious. They didn't want anybody to know they had an investigation going."

The question now being raised openly—what did the hospital know and when did it know it?—flushed out a new account of what had happened. In a written statement to the press, the hospital attorney, Paul Green, acknowledged that "allegations of criminal conduct" had indeed been raised—during a meeting between top hospital and medical school officials on January 25, 1982. Green was referring to the critical summit session that had led to the decision to bring in Dr. Conn. "I advised officials of the administrative and medical staff of Bexar County Hospital District that there was insufficient evidence indicating any specific wrongdoing in the pediatric intensive care unit," stated Green. The attorney added a perhaps unintentionally revealing explanation of why he had counseled against saying anything to law-enforcement authorities. "Unfounded allegations of criminal conduct are serious business and could well result in a suit for substantial damages." The counterpoint to such reasoning was inescapable: Criminal conduct was also a serious business; it could well result in death.

Fresh headlines notwithstanding, Millsap's investigators had been exploring the culpability of the hospital district and the medical school for months. The DA's criminal probe had split onto two tracks. The first involved building individual cases against Genene Jones. The second focused on the question of a cover-up; Millsap was contemplating charges against those who had failed to stop her. The officials under scrutiny, having at last acknowledged publicly their early discussion of criminal conduct, pointed to the Conn and Mangos investigations as evidence of their determination to probe the ICU's problems. In the failure of their own inquiries to find proof of wrongdoing, they saw justification for their decision to keep their suspicions to themselves.

Millsap considered that reasoning irresponsible. The hospital's internal detective work had been scattershot and sloppy. Dr. Mangos's committee had conducted the most intensive chart review. That panel had divided up the patient records for initial screening, and two of its three members were not even doctors. Millsap's staff and medical consultants were finding countless suspicious episodes that had eluded their scrutiny. (The remarks on Joshua Sawyer, for example, made no mention of the lab test showing a toxic level of Dilantin in his blood.) Throughout the entire debacle, residents and nurses had made specific allegations of wrongdoing that hospital supervisors had failed to pursue. And in deciding for fear of litigation that Jones could not be fired, administrators had not even bothered to look at the record of misconduct—everything from drunkenness to rank insubordination—that was documented in her personnel file. "We have our roles," said Millsap. "My criminal investigators, hopefully, would have the good sense not to practice medicine. By the same token, I hope members of the medical community would have the good sense not to conduct criminal investigations."

But Dr. Alan Conn believed the hospital's failure to find evidence was proof that there was none. During a telephone interview in July with a reporter from the San Antonio *Express*—TOT DEATH EXPERT SLAMS NEW PROBE, the headline read—Conn branded the entire investigation "a waste of taxpayers' money." "You'll never disprove or prove anything," Conn said. "If there's any reasonable chance of finding such a thing, they would have found it by now." Saying once again that he had discovered nothing worse than "growing pains," Conn described his committee's inquiry as merely a routine quality-control review. Before he began his investigation, Conn insisted, allegations of possible infant homicides "were not broached."

By publicly declaring that San Antonio administrators had kept him in the dark, Conn was enhancing the impression that his internal investigation had been a whitewash. Marvin Dunn, the medical school dean, was not pleased. "I have been concerned at the report in the press that Dr. Alan Conn was unaware of the background problems in the Medical Center Hospital Pediatric Intensive Care Unit before the review team first met," wrote Dunn, in an August letter to a medical school attorney. "I do not know if these press reports are accurate. . . . However, Dr. Conn did indeed know of the background problems of the PICU." Dunn detailed how he informed Conn of "essentially everything I had heard at the meetings on January 25," how Conn had insisted on a full committee of doctors and nurses because of "the seriousness and complexity" of the allegations, and how Conn had asked for a meeting room at the medical school because "he felt psychologically people would feel more freedom to speak frankly and openly outside the hospital, away from the PICU. . . . If one who did not know these facts views the actions by Dr. Conn, I believe it would be difficult to explain them assuming that he felt this was some kind of a casual routine review." Dunn added: "As you well know this has angered me to no end, and except for your strong advice to the contrary I would have called Dr. Conn and told him so."

Sam Millsap was less interested in what Dunn had told Conn than he was in the question of what Conn had told Dunn. In March 1983, at the outset of the DA's investigation, the grand jury had issued a subpoena to Dunn for "all files, notes, memos, and documents" concerning the pediatric ICU. Among the materials Dunn had surrendered was his copy of the final Conn committee report, which recommended the removal of all LVNs from the ICU. In late October, hospital administrator B. H. Corum informed one of the DA's investigators that Dr. Conn's committee had submitted a *preliminary* report—a report the DA's office knew nothing about. Furious that the document had not been turned over eight months earlier, Millsap hauled Dunn before the grand jury on October 31 to demand an explanation. The dean showed up with not only the preliminary Conn report but also a set of handwritten notes that he had taken during the exit interview he and Corum had conducted with Conn and his committee.

The preliminary Conn report contained a single important recommendation that was deleted from the final document: It urged the "immediate removal" from the pediatric ICU of nurses Genene Jones and Pat Alberti.

Dunn's handwritten notes described the most sensitive problems Conn and his committee had identified. They included the comment: "Nurses—either malignant intent or gross neglect." To Millsap, the documents proved that Dunn and Corum harbored potent suspicions about Jones in early 1982. (The DA regarded Alberti's suggested removal as an attempt to oust a capable nurse for complaining vigorously about Jones.) By October 1983, that information was not news to Millsap. But in March— when the documents should have been turned over—the records would have advanced the investigators' knowledge greatly.

Dunn told the grand jury that the preliminary Conn report had been misfiled. As for the handwritten notes of the exit interview, Dunn testified that he had given them to UT attorneys in 1982 because they contained references to Dr. Robotham, then making noises about filing suit over his removal from the ICU. Nick Rothe asked the dean why he had not turned over his notes in response to the March summons. Dunn said the UT lawyers had advised him that notes in their possession were not subject to the subpoena.

The dean was nonplussed at being in the middle of such a mess. After all, *he* was not responsible for what happened in the pediatric ICU. In a letter to two of his attorneys, the dean said he had acted merely as "a volunteer firefighter in a conflagration that rightfully belongs to the Hospital District." Nonetheless, during a break in Dunn's testimony, the grand jury unanimously decided to cite him for contempt. In filing the necessary legal papers later that week, Millsap acknowledged that Dunn's documents provided little new information, but said that he suspected other records were still being withheld. "How many other caches of documents are there that have not been surrendered to us?" asked the DA. To those who might have such materials, said Millsap, the contempt charge would serve as a warning. A district judge eventually found Dunn—the top administrator of the state medical school—guilty of contempt for withholding the documents. "It is my feeling that Dr. Dunn's conduct, whether it is based on the advice of his attorneys, correctly or incorrectly, is still such an act that it puts the grand jury in such a position where the investigation could not continue," the judge said, in announcing his ruling. Dunn was fined $100.

The flurry of activity came as speculation was growing that Millsap might file charges against the hospital district and the medical school. The DA had recently filed a brief with a Texas appeals court supporting the legal theory that corporations and governmental entities could be held responsible for crimes such as murder. Millsap said he believed that governments could be charged if prosecutors proved that a ranking official "recklessly tolerated a dangerous situation to continue." Millsap was also exploring the possibility of charging individual administrators for their failure to intervene. But to pursue either course, the DA first had to prove that "a dangerous situation" had existed.

On November 9, 1983, in northwest San Antonio, Medical Center Hospital celebrated its fifteenth anniversary. At a gathering of dignitaries outside the building, William Thornton, chairman of the hospital district board, spoke eloquently about how the institution would continue to serve the health needs of Bexar County. That same day, in downtown San Antonio, chief deputy DA Nick Rothe summoned the members of his investigative task force and several trusted senior attorneys from the DA's staff. There they decided, after ten months of investigation, to proceed with their first criminal charge—to allege that a nurse at the county hospital, an institution committed to saving lives, had pushed a child to the brink of death.

On November 21, the special Bexar County grand jury investigating the pediatric ICU charged Genene Jones with injury to a child in the case of Rolando Santos. Santos was the infant whose repeated bleeding problems in January 1982 had been diagnosed as a heparin overdose; only Dr. Copeland's daring decision to administer protamine had saved the baby's life. One week later, the grand jury held its final meeting. The jurors engaged in a long discussion about indicting the Bexar County Hospital District. In the end, the jurors accepted Nick Rothe's advice that they could not yet make such a charge stick.

It was agreed that the DA's office, on its own, would continue to investigate additional charges against Jones, as well as indictments against the hospital, the medical school, and the officials who ran them.

Sam Millsap told reporters that he was not concerned that after ten months, his special task force had produced but one indictment—and that only for injury to a child. The DA noted that additional indictments could be issued by a regular grand jury; he pledged that his baby-deaths investigation would plug on. But privately, Millsap was skeptical that he would ever file more charges—at least against Genene Jones. He knew the best chance to convict the nurse of murder lay not in San Antonio but in Georgetown, where she was soon to go on trial for the death of Chelsea McClellan.

PART FIVE

JUDGMENT

. . . provide out of all the people able men, such as fear God, men of truth, hating covetousness;

And place such over them, to be rulers of thousands, and rulers of hundreds, rulers of fifties, and rulers of tens:

And let them judge the people at all seasons . . .

If thou shalt do this thing, and God command thee so, then thou shalt be able to endure, and all this people shall also go to their place in peace.

Exodus 18: 21–23

Twenty-Seven

WILLIAMSON COUNTY, TEXAS, had a long reputation for harsh justice. Stretching east of the Hill Country, to where the earth flattened into rich blackland, it was settled by stern European immigrants—Germans, Swedes, and Czechs—who grew cotton and worked cattle. Theirs was a world of thrift and backbreaking labor, where those who went astray could not pay too high a price. Back in the 1930s, the lawyer for a freshly convicted murder defendant in South Texas railed wildly that his client's twenty-year sentence was unfair. Angry at the barrister's behavior, the judge granted the defendant a new trial—in Williamson County, where after convicting the murderer again, a jury assessed the death penalty. A half century later, the county was swelling with new immigrants, as the Austin suburbs spilled north. But the modern arrivals were no less certain of the value of a stiff sentence. Many had moved to the county's affluent subdivisions to flee the filth and crime of the big city. They were not disposed kindly toward those who intruded on their paradise.

Jim Bob Brookshire, one of Genene Jones's two new court-appointed lawyers, was well acquainted with the temperament of Williamson County. His ancestors had moved there in 1860, and his great-great-grandfather had served as county sheriff. Brookshire, forty-two, was a short, dapper man with curly white hair, silver temples, and a well-trimmed mustache. He practiced law by himself

in Georgetown from a storefront office across the street
from the courthouse. The son of a contractor and a
schoolteacher, Brookshire had grown up in the tiny town
of Granger, in the fertile eastern half of the county.
After law school, he enlisted in the Marine Corps and
went to Vietnam, where he tried military crimes as a
judge advocate general. After stints in private practice
and with the federal government, Brookshire married
and hung out his own shingle back in Georgetown. His
personality retained a slice of small-town redneck, and
his wartime encounters with the gruesome inclined him
toward gallows humor. In his first murder trial, just weeks
before Jones's court date, Brookshire defended a man
accused of dousing his wife with gasoline, then setting
her on fire with a disposable lighter. In conversations
with friends, he referred to his client as "Zippo." Brookshire had a nickname for Genene Jones as well. Noting
her penchant for wielding needles, he called her "Spike."

Working with Brookshire was Burt Carnes, from the
nearby town of Taylor. A tall, lanky thirty-four-year-old
man with straight black hair, a mustache, and glasses,
Carnes looked like the gawky, overgrown center on a
high school basketball team. He was the son of an FBI
agent and had three years' trial experience as a criminal
prosecutor in Dallas and Austin. Where Brookshire enjoyed burying himself in the case's complex medical evidence, Carnes was eager for the give-and-take of the
courtroom. The Mutt-and-Jeff defense team had voluntary help from Laura Little, a tiny, blond-haired young
woman who had spent her three years since law school
researching cases for the Texas Court of Criminal Appeals. Little, who had never participated in a criminal
trial, was in the throes of a personal crisis. Her mother
had recently died, and she was contemplating leaving law
to become a doctor. She thought that this case—with its
glimpse into both professions—might help determine her
future.

To the defense team, the forces arrayed against them
seemed overwhelming. Ron Sutton had supplemented his
own limited resources by tapping state criminal-justice
grants; he had $50,000 available for travel and medical
experts alone. Sutton also had important help from his

Bexar County counterpart. Eager to aid—and share the credit for—the murder conviction of Genene Jones, Sam Millsap had given freely. His ace investigator, Art Brogley, had spent weeks assisting Sutton; Nick Rothe would join the Kerr County DA at the prosecution table. Sutton had enjoyed fifteen months to assemble his case; his list of potential witnesses contained more than seventy names. The defense lawyers, by contrast, had $10,000 for expenses. Brookshire had worked on the case just four months, Carnes only two. And like Chenault and Tuck, whom they had replaced, the new defense team had the handicap of its own nettlesome client.

Brookshire's first rude surprise from Genene Jones came when a reporter called him for comment about the nurse's insistence that she was pregnant. One day in November, less than two weeks after her transfer to the Williamson County jail, Genene had begun screaming that she was having a miscarriage. She was rushed to the Georgetown Community Hospital, where doctors found no serious problem and sent her back to jail the next day. Playing out the fiction, Genene appeared for pretrial court hearings in loose-fitting clothes. Finally, Brookshire advised reporters that his client was not pregnant after all; somehow, she had been mistaken. While publicly critical of the circumstances that produced the cancellation of Genene's bond, the defense lawyer was secretly delighted. Jones's reimprisonment provided an opportunity to rein her in. Brookshire ordered jailers to allow Genene no media visitors and strictly limit her phone calls. At last, he thought, he had found a way to keep his client out of the headlines. But on December 20, Brookshire awoke to a new story in the San Antonio papers. Bill Thornton, the chairman of the Bexar County Hospital District board, had received a Christmas card from the murder defendant. "I feel compelled to write to you and wish you all the best," Genene had written. "I feel we are comrades in this tragedy since we both know the real truth. I do want to ease your mind and doubts by telling you that under no uncertain terms have I injured or killed anyone."

A small consolation for the defense was that Garron Ray Turk had dropped out of sight. After Genene's indictment in Bexar County, Garron had sued for divorce in San Angelo, bizarrely filing court papers with fake names. Instead of Garron Ray Turk and Genene Ann Jones Turk, the documents sought the divorce of "Ray G. Tucker" and "Ann G. Tucker." Genene stopped signing her name "Genene Jones Turk" and spoke of Garron no more. It was as though her teenaged second husband had never existed.

But Genene—always eager to manipulate those who infuenced her fate—sought other affections, even in jail. On several occasions, she called deputy sheriff Jim Stinnett back to her cell, where he discovered her wearing nothing but an unbuttoned housecoat, which she made no effort to close. Others were more receptive to her charms. Ronnie Rudd, a thirty-three-year-old convicted auto thief and trusty, given the run of the jail, met Jones while delivering meals to the female prisoners. After the two developed a romantic relationship, Rudd was dispatched to a state prison to serve out his sentence.

Despite being handled with kid gloves, Genene complained bitterly to the sheriff about her treatment. She demanded special favors and threw herself into tearful, screaming tantrums when she did not get them. The nurse was particularly enraged about the attention accorded another notorious jail resident—a one-eyed drifter named Henry Lee Lucas, who claimed to have killed more than a hundred women, including his mother. Lawmen were spending hours with Lucas because their chats seemed to prompt fresh rounds of confession. Genene thought he was disgusting. Why should she share the spotlight with *him?*

Brookshire became so fed up with his client that he could barely stand to be in her presence. He left personal dealings with Genene to his legal secretary, Patty Jones, and to the young attorney Laura Little. Even to the eve of the trial, Jones tried to dictate the strategy of her defense. Smoking cigarettes, stalking back and forth in the visiting room, Genene acted as though in command. She patted her lawyers on the back like a football coach, voicing her certainty that they would win her acquittal.

But Genene's lawyers were deeply skeptical about the prospects for such an outcome. To begin with, Brook-

shire and Carnes—like Joe Grady Tuck before them—
doubted their client's innocence. In private strategy sessions, they spoke as though it were a foregone conclusion
that Jones was guilty. But their personal beliefs were not
the issue; their job was to defend Genene Jones, innocent or guilty. Brookshire and Carnes decided to employ
a classic legal strategy—the "inconsistent defense."

It is cynical wisdom that if you tell a criminal lawyer
his dog has just bitten you, the barrister would first say
he didn't have a dog, then claim his dog didn't bite, and
finally insist that his dog didn't bite *you*. Unable to
contest that Chelsea McClellan was dead, Brookshire
and Carnes planned first to challenge the prosecution's
claim that the child had died of succinylcholine; they
would try to block admission of the Swedish doctor's test
as evidence. Failing that, they would battle to bar testimony about the incidents involving other children, known
in legal language as "extraneous offenses." Finally, they
would suggest that if Chelsea indeed died of succinylcholine, Genene Jones had not done it—or at least had
not done it alone. They would imply that someone else
was involved, who wasn't even on trial. That person was
Kathy Holland. They would go after the prosecution's
star witness, in hope of muddying the waters.

None of the defense lawyers believed that this approach would sway twelve Williamson County citizens.
Their hope was to instill a reasonable doubt in the mind
of a stray juror or two—enough to produce a hung jury.
Then maybe Kerr County, which was footing the antici-
pated $100,000 bill for staging the trial, would decide
against trying Jones again. Their prospects for success
would rest equally on judge and jury. It would require
the jurors to focus sharply on the seams in Sutton's
circumstantial case. And it would be up to the judge to
decide whether the jurors would hear the most damning
evidence in the first place.

The change of venue to Georgetown had placed Genene
Jones's fate in the hands of the Honorable John Rice
Carter, a relative newcomer to the bench. Carter, forty-
two, had grown up in the Houston suburb of Bellaire.
After moving to Williamson County, he had become

active in Republican politics and run unsuccessfully for the state legislature in 1980. When Williamson County's population boom forced the creation of a second district court, Texas's Republican governor appointed Carter to the judgeship in 1981. He won election on his own the followng year. Carter was a swarthy man, with a three-hundred-pound frame and a close-cropped thatch of salt-and-pepper hair. Charming and voluble off the bench, he affected a no-nonsense demeanor inside the courtroom. Local attorneys liked him. Carter was tough, but he worked hard and didn't play favorites. The judge also shared a rural Texas tradition: He dipped snuff, even while presiding in court. Carter camouflaged his habit by keeping two Styrofoam cups on the bench, which he lifted alternately to his lips. From one he sipped coffee; into the other he spat.

The Genene Jones murder case was Carter's first big trial, and the judge was determined to keep it from becoming a circus. Press interest was so great that a local university had set up a special media center with sixteen phone lines. On Sunday, January 15, 1984, the day before jury selection was to begin, Carter met with reporters and cameramen to dictate rules for their behavior. The judge explained that he was issuing a gag order barring witnesses, attorneys, jurors, defendant—and anyone else connected with the case—from making statements to the press. As a second step, Carter barred cameras and recording devices not only from his second-floor courtroom, but also—with specified exceptions—from the entire courthouse. Cameras were to be permitted in the first-floor lobby for three forty-five-minute intervals, just long enough to film the comings and goings of the principals for the evening TV news. And even then, rather than being free to chase their suspects, cameramen were required to remain within an eight-foot square in the center of the lobby. The box was marked with white tape. The confined cameramen quickly dubbed it "Carter's Corral."

The murder trial of Genene Jones was to take place on a worthy stage. The Williamson County courthouse, which dated back to 1911, was a hulking four-story fortress. Built of beige brick with limestone trim, the Greek Revival building boasted a triple-arched stone entryway, with a set of two-story Ionic columns above, on each of its four sides. Crowning the building was a giant copper dome with a large clock face on each side. And atop the dome stood the figure of Liberty, bearing her sword in one hand and the scales of justice in the other. Easily the tallest structure in town, the courthouse stood visible for more than a mile in every direction. In the early 1920s, it had hosted a famous series of trials that helped whip the Texas Ku Klux Klan and launch the political career of a future governor.

Georgetown did not appear to have changed very much from those days. The city was named for George Washington Glasscock, builder of a local water mill, who had donated ten acres to establish the community in 1848. Bestriding the Balcones Fault, which divided the rich farmland to the east from the Hill Country to the west, Georgetown grew up as an agricultural center. The nearby junction of two rivers made it a stop on the Chisholm Trail, along which Texas cattlemen drove their giant herds north to Kansas. Now the vital byway was Interstate 35, a ribbon of concrete that sliced from the Mexican border in Laredo, through San Antonio and Austin, up through Dallas and Fort Worth. I-35 had carried the émigrés from Austin, many of them employees of new high-tech plants, who settled in the southern half of Williamson County. But the population boom in the early 1970s stopped short of Georgetown. In 1930, 3,583 people lived in Georgetown. A half century later, its population was still less than 10,000. Although Main Street had been gussied up for tourists and there were plans for a fancy new subdivision just outside the city limits, Georgetown remained a simple place. The busiest restaurant in town was the L&M Café, where the specialty of the house was chicken-fried steak with white cream gravy.

Jury selection began on Monday, January 16, with the summons of 329 Williamson County citizens—about three times the usual number for a murder trial. Both sides were worried that the widespread publicity might make it difficult to locate twelve unbiased jurors. To avoid any possibility of taint, the defense also wanted the jurors sequestered for the duration of the trial. Carter decided

it wasn't necessary; he promised to warn them to avoid
media reports and discussions of the case outside the
courtroom. The first day cut the pool of prospective
jurors to 111. It also brought the first flare-up between
the press and the testy judge.

As the routine of jury selection droned on into the
afternoon, Carter asked his bailiff to open a window. The
judge gazed outside and spotted a TV cameraman in a
second-floor window across the street, zeroing in on the
proceedings through the open courtroom window. "Deputy!" barked Carter. "Go across the street and arrest
that son of a bitch!" Dragged before the judge, the
cameraman insisted that he was merely filming the exterior of the courthouse for his Austin station. Carter was
not amused. He advised the cameraman that he would
make a point of watching his station's broadcast that
night. He warned he would throw the man in jail if a
second of film of the courtroom was shown.

Launching three days of jury selection, Ron Sutton
had opened his remarks by making a production of loosening his tie, saying he never liked the darned things
anyway. Then the DA began spooning out legal formali-
ties with dollops of hayseed charm. Describing himself as
a country lawyer, Sutton explained that his great-grandfather was buried in Williamson County, next to the
grave of a famous outlaw. And he joked about the courthouse in Concho County, part of his district, where the
only ventilation came from a sheep feedlot down the
road. Sutton apologized for the time occupied with for-
malities. "But, you know," he went on, "anything important in life . . . takes a little bit of time; whether you are
out preparing your fields in plowing or whether some of
you ladies are making a real nice cake or preparing a
Sunday dinner, it takes some time. Just think how much
more important it is to do *justice.*"

When the defense turn came, Brookshire told the prospective jurors he was "nervous as a cat"—and he was.
Most of his experience was as a civil attorney, where
pushing paper and out-of-court negotiations were more
important than courtroom eloquence. The defense attorney reminded the jurors that his client merely stood
accused, "that as she sits here today, she is innocent, just

like you. . . . So I am not going to refer to her as 'the
defendant' or as 'the accused,' because simply because
someone says she did something does not take away her
humanity. She is a human like the rest of us. And I ask
that you look upon her as a human and not as a thing or
title." As Brookshire spoke, his client shuffled from chair
to chair at the defense table, tears streaming down her
cheeks.

On the first day, a media throng had gathered outside
the courtroom, awaiting the defendant's arrival from jail.
Genene stepped out of the sheriff's car like a movie star
emerging from a limousine to greet a crowd of paparazzi
on her way into a glitzy Hollywood premiere. For trial,
the nurse had undergone a dramatic physical transformation. Gone were her baggy maternity clothes and scraggly
hair. Thinner after weeks in jail, Genene wore a neat tan
outfit with a gold medallion around her neck, blow-dried
hair, eye makeup, and bright nail polish. It was the work
of Brookshire's legal assistant, Patty Jones, who had
purchased her five new outfits, a slip, and panty hose.
Patty had given Genene a permanent and would dress
her carefully each morning before court.

After thirty-two jurors passed the preliminary screening, each side had the right to strike ten more at will. In
making their decisions, the lawyers would rely on the
prospects' responses to individual questioning, on their
body language, and on instinct. The jurors had also filled
out a three-page questionnaire probing their education,
family background, contacts with the legal system, and
tastes in music, religion, politics, film, television, and
literature. Among the twenty-nine questions: "Have you
ever had unpleasant experiences involving medical or
hospital personnel?" Sutton put great stock in such information. From last names and religion, he made judg-
ments of political philosophy. Italians, Latins, and Jews
tended to be liberal, Germans, Scandinavians, and Lu-
therans conservative. Prosecutors loved crime victims;
defense lawyers invariably struck them. A prospect married for many years tended to be a compromiser, unlikely
to become a holdout on a jury. Military service was a
plus. Sutton liked men who belonged to the National
Rifle Association, women who read *Better Homes and*

Gardens, and anyone whose favorite book was the Bible. He automatically cut candidates who belonged to the American Civil Liberties Union.

With questionnaires in hand, the defense and prosecution teams retired to separate rooms to hash over their selections. Defense attorneys usually sought unsophisticated jurors with liberal political leanings; they reasoned such a background would prompt suspicion of the state and sympathy for the accused. Jones's lawyers had a different strategy. Recognizing that an accused baby-killer was unlikely to receive much sympathy, they wanted a panel that was both intelligent and dispassionate—a group of nitpickers who would seize upon flaws in the prosecution's technical evidence. Carnes described his ideal jury for this case as "twelve cold-blooded accountants." Fulfilling that ideal was, of course, impossible. There weren't many cold-blooded nitpickers in Williamson County. So the defense hoped to throw in a few jurors with discordant personalities. Conflicts within the group would boost their prospects for a hung jury.

The defense's acceptance of educated jurors played right into Sutton's hands. Seeking the opposite result, the DA felt he needed an intelligent jury. Sutton planned to present an extraordinarily complex case. He needed to educate the jurors—to school them in the effects of drugs, to make them believe in scientific tests, to persuade them of the wisdom of the medical experts he would call to the stand. Sutton believed it would take a bright group to digest such a case. He reasoned that a strong jury would be not skeptical of his evidence but impressed. Time would tell which side was correct.

Judge Carter, meanwhile, was amusing himself in his chambers by picking his own jury for the defense. Carter decided Genene's ideal jury would contain only dummies; educated members of the panel would help others understand the evidence. So the first name he struck was that of the most attractive woman in the courtroom—a thirty-year-old microbiologist by the name of Ann Bradley.

The challenges by the two sides seated a panel of seven women and five men. Believing in their unusual jury strategy, the defense attorneys felt relatively pleased. But Ron Sutton was delighted. Eleven of the twelve jurors had reached high school, six had attended college, and one had a master's degree. There was an electrical engineer, a production manager, a salesman, a store manager, an official with the state veterans' commission, the business manager for a steelworkers union, two secretaries, and three housewives. And one microbiologist: Ann Bradley. All the jurors were married, most for many years. Happily for Sutton, prosecuting the death of a child, all but one were parents; they had thirty-four kids among them. The jurors' ages ranged from thirty to sixty-six; only three were younger than fifty. Eleven of them listed religious affiliations. One taught Bible school, a second listed the Bible as the last book she had read, and a third was married to a minister. Ten jurors had served in the military or were married to veterans; the five men included a former air force colonel, a former marine major, and a former army intelligence captain. All who listed their political leanings described them as moderate or conservative. All the jurors were white.

As the dozen members of the panel settled into the jury box, a grizzled *New York Times* reporter named Wayne King surveyed the group from a wooden bench in the courtroom. King leaned over to Michael Pearson, a much younger reporter covering the trial for Harte-Hanks newspapers. "You know, Mike," he said, "that's the best jury I've seen since I left Mississippi."

Twenty-Eight

ON THE FIRST day of testimony, Ron Sutton rose in the darkness, at 5 A.M. The prosecution team had set up a command post at the Georgetown Inn, a one-story motel next to the interstate, with shag carpet and cheap paneling. Sutton had rented an entire bank of rooms for his entourage: his legal assistant, Nick Rothe, Joe Davis, Art Brogley, a Kerr County deputy sheriff, and assorted witnesses. They worked out of a large improvised conference room adjacent to Sutton's quarters, where the beds had been replaced with a portable refrigerator, a giant coffeepot, work tables, and a typewriter. A half-dozen members of Petti McClellan's family were bunking at the Georgetown Inn as well; her sisters, mother, and grandmother had all come up for the trial. Part of another wing of the building had been reserved for reporters and defense witnesses. The fifty-nine-room Georgetown Inn was the only major motel in town.

Dressed in an undershirt and Jockey shorts, Sutton went over his notes alone one more time. At 6 A.M., he woke up Rothe. The two men showered and donned suits, then rehearsed testimony with their first witnesses. Sutton felt both passion and pressure to put Genene Jones behind bars. With everyone around him focused on the trial, it seemed as though the whole world was watching; everything had to be right. When the time to head for the courthouse neared, Sutton stepped into his motel bathroom and threw up.

Inside the seventy-three-year-old courthouse, the scene
was chaotic. Judge Carter's chamber had seats for only
seventy-two; with standing room, he could squeeze in
perhaps one hundred ten. But far more than that number
had lined up before the courtroom doors were unlocked.
When the bailiff opened up, people scrambled for seats
like cattle rushing through a squeeze chute; the overflow
would have to wait outside for someone to leave. Carter
had reserved one row for attorneys' staff and a second
for members of the principals' families, but he refused to
make any special arrangements for the press. The media
soon learned to come early and wait in line. Ron Sutton
was pleased when he arrived at the courthouse and saw
the crush of spectators inside. He liked performing before a crowd.

Sutton plotted his case to open as dramatically as a TV
movie. Things were going to get complicated; he needed
to hook the jury fast. The prosecutor also believed his
tale was too bizarre to feed the jury all at once. Eschew-
ing the traditional opening argument, with its summary
of what was to come, the DA instead spoke briefly,
tantalizing the jurors. "I want you to see this story, this
tragic story of the life and death of Chelsea McClellan,
unfold before your own eyes and for your own ears," he
said. "Now, you are going to be wondering: Why? Why,
why would something like this happen? *Why, why, why?*"
Sutton noted that there was no legal requirement for the
prosecution to prove a motive. "But I think we are going
to be able to do so as these chapters of the sequence of
events in the months of August and September 1982
unfold before you. And as the testimony begins to draw
to a close, not only do I feel that you will be absolutely
convinced that the state has proven these elements, but it
will become inescapably clear as to the reason why, without me even having to tell you."

The DA had carefully plotted his drama's opening
scene. He called it "Code Blue." It began with a little
girl unable to breathe, rushed by ambulance to the Sid
Peterson emergency room on September 17, 1982. The
child was Chelsea Ann McClellan, and she had come
from Kathy Holland's clinic.

Sutton's first witness was Sharon Keith, the head nurse

in the ER. Keith told the jury she had treated the toddler
during a remarkably similar emergency that had struck
twenty-four days earlier, also at Holland's office. This
time, Keith spotted two needle marks on Chelsea's legs.
Jones told her that the little girl had reacted badly to
baby shots. Keith testified that she had never seen inoculations cause a child to stop breathing. Dr. Richard Mason then described his observations of Chelsea's treatment
in the emergency room. Mason saw Chelsea struggling
clumsily to pull out her breathing tube, as though unable
to coordinate her arms. Mason testified that the child's
behavior resembled that of patients emerging from the
effects of succinylcholine. On cross-examination, the doctor acknowledged that other medical problems could produce such symptoms. But Sutton didn't mind. He had
planted the seed.

The district attorney called Steve Brown, the young
ambulance driver, to take the jurors along on the transfer
to San Antonio, Chelsea McClellan's last ride. Brown,
who was from Junction, Sutton's hometown, had worked
as a paramedic since high school. "I was driving along
and everything seemed to be going real good, and I
established that there was a lot of movement going on in
the back. There was a lot of—well, you know, you heard
things pushed, like boxes hit something, or something.
And Genene Jones, I got eye contact in the rearview
mirror, and she says, 'Pull this son of a bitch over!' So I
immediately pulled over to the right-hand side of the
road." Brown recounted the roadside rescue effort, the
frantic, hopeless trip to the tiny hospital in Comfort, and
the final scene in the emergency room.

Trixie Anthony, the 3–11 P.M. nursing supervisor at Sid
Peterson, recalled Chelsea's uneventful stay there after
her first arrest, as well as the next occasion when she saw
the child—in the hospital's basement morgue. Anthony
had the chore of identifying the body before its release to
the Kerrville Funeral Home. Sutton handed the nurse a
studio photograph of Chelsea dressed in a frilly eggshell-
blue dress and matching bonnet; he asked her to identify
the picture. Sutton offered the heartbreaking photo as
evidence and passed it around the jury. Then Anthony
described what she saw in the hospital basement. "She

was in the morgue wrapped up in the blanket, and I took the blanket off her face and looked at her. And, of course, her eye were closed, and I saw her ringlets and her little gold earrings and her eyelashes, and it was the same child I had seen in the hospital. It was Chelsea."

In the first day of testimony, Sutton had imprinted the haunting image of Chelsea's death on the minds of the jurors, raised the specter of succinylcholine as its instrument, and placed Genene Jones close to the crime. Now came the second act in the DA's drama. He had to follow the little girl's body, to recount the gruesome indignities—embalming, burial, and exhumation—that ended with pieces of her tissue in a scientist's laboratory in Sweden. The testimony was so graphic it would rout members of the McClellan family from the courtroom. It also sparked the first round of sparring over the cause of Chelsea's demise.

Brookshire, who had settled down after his early jitters, was intent on proving that the child had died of natural causes. The private pathologists who conducted the autopsy had even put it in writing: Noting the subtle scarring in her brain stem, which governs the natural breathing mechanism, they had attributed her death to SIDS. *Here* was the true explanation of Chelsea's death, Brookshire suggested to the jury on cross-examination. He pressed the private pathologist from Severance & Associates, Dr. Galbreath, to stand by his finding. But the doctor wriggled out of the trap. Galbreath said his SIDS finding was little more than a guess, a straw grasped in the absence of any other evidence, based on Dr. Kagen-Hallet's discovery of brain scarring. Galbreath added that concealment of facts about Chelsea's medical history—such as an injection of succinylcholine—could have produced an incorrect finding. Dr. DiMaio, the Bexar County medical examiner, called to testify about the exhumation, dismissed the SIDS explanation altogether. The coroner called SIDS a "wastepaper-basket diagnosis," misused to explain deaths from many different causes. Virtually all true SIDS deaths occurred during the first six months of life, DiMaio said. Chelsea McClellan had been fifteen months old.

Kathleen Kagen-Hallet, the brain expert, would close

the circle with a new hypothesis on Chelsea's death. The subtle scarring she discovered on the child's brain stem would have made her sensitive to respiratory insult, Kagen-Hallet would later testify. If Chelsea's breathing was interrupted—as by a shot of succinylcholine—it might never resume.

"May it please the court," announced Ron Sutton, as the second week of the trial opened, "the State calls Petti McClellan." Sutton's summons was a surprise. Prosecutors usually saved their most emotional testimony for the end, so it would still be simmering in the minds of jurors when they retired for deliberations. But in this case, Sutton had a vast amount of technical evidence yet to present. He wanted the jurors, before they sat through it, to understand the pain caused by this crime.

The timing of Petti's appearance had been a surprise to the McClellans as well. Sutton had told Petti to show up in Georgetown the night before. There was no reason to bring Reid, he said; he just wanted to prepare her to testify at week's end. But when Petti arrived, the DA told her he was putting her on the stand the next morning. Sutton had misled the McClellans because he figured giving Petti less time to worry about testifying would be easiest on her nerves. And he wanted to keep Reid out of the courtroom. Reid was so filled with loathing toward Jones—he talked about wanting to kill her—that he made Petti more upset. Sutton was also afraid of what Reid might do in Genene's presence; an outburst could produce a mistrial. So Reid McClellan, who had wanted to be present, remained unaware of what was happening as his wife took the stand on Monday morning.

Months of living with a nightmare had taken their toll. Petti looked weary as Sutton led her through Chelsea's fifteen months of life. Frightened and tearful from the start, Petti spoke so softly Sutton had to ask her repeatedly to speak up. Finally, they came to the final visit to Holland's clinic, to the moment when Petti clutched her daughter in the crash room after Genene gave Chelsea the first injection.

"What did you notice about her eyes, Mrs. McClellan?" asked the district attorney.

"They were just looking at me," said Petti. "They were funny."

"Just looking at you?"

". . . She was whimpering . . ."

"Whimpering?"

"Yes, like she was trying to say 'Momma!' . . ."

"Trying to say 'Momma'?"

". . . And she couldn't get it out."

"Couldn't get it out?"

"And her eyes—like, 'Help me!' And I didn't know what to do. I told Genene that something was wrong, to *do* something."

Sutton asked about Genene's response.

"She said she was mad because she had to have a shot," recalled Petti.

"What did Genene do after she said that?"

"Gave her another shot."

And then?

"She went limp like a rag doll," said the mother. "She was just like a rag doll."

Sutton went on, to Chelsea's final moments at the hospital in Comfort, after the emergency stop on the highway. Petti and Reid had followed the ambulance in their own car.

"Did you go in the hospital?" Sutton asked.

"When they took her out of the ambulance—" Petti began to break down.

"I am sorry, Mrs. McClellan," said Sutton.

". . . she was just laying there, just blue, and she was just laying there."

Petti said she waited across the hall from the emergency room. Finally, her husband returned after speaking with the ambulance driver, Steve Brown.

"I guess Steve must have told him, because he kept saying, he kept saying that I had to get, you know, just in case, just prepare, just in case, because I didn't know what was happening. I got real mad at him. I was so mad at him." Petti's eyes filled with tears. "I told him there was no way that Chelsea could die. There was no way. She wasn't sick. She wasn't *sick!*"

Sutton approached the child's mother, now sobbing freely on the witness stand in the hushed courtroom.

"Petti," he said gently, "I would give anything if I didn't have to do this." Sutton showed her the color photograph. "Is this Chelsea?"

"*Yes!*" Petti shrieked.

A defense lawyer challenges such a witness at the peril of his own client. Despite the buffer of legal procedure and endless directives to stick to facts, it is emotion that governs most murder trials. And there is no surer way to alienate a jury than by treating a victim harshly. But the defense needed to prove that Chelsea's death did not strike like a bolt from the blue. The child had a history of medical problems, dating back to her premature birth; Genene's lawyers thought they could force Petti to acknowledge them. Treading gently, Burt Carnes reviewed her reports to doctors about her daughter's various ailments. But Petti gave no ground. She explained each episode surely and insisted that Chelsea's health had been excellent before her death. After several minutes of probing, Carnes gave up.

Before Judge John Carter now came his first pivotal decision: whether to permit the jury to hear from Bo Holmstedt, waiting at the Georgetown Inn—or to send the eminent doctor back to Stockholm without the opportunity to utter a word. The stakes were great. Rejecting Holmstedt's testimony would rob the prosecution of its only solid evidence that Genene Jones's syringe contained not baby inoculations but deadly succinylcholine. That would leave Sutton and Rothe with a baldly circumstantial case—and vastly boost the prospect that Jones would walk free. Both sides had submitted written briefs on the question, but Carter knew the legal ground was uncertain. The national standard for determining admissibility of scientific evidence dated back sixty-one years, to a case called *Frye* v. *United States,* which ruled such evidence acceptable where it enjoyed "general acceptance" in its field. Did Holmstedt's succinylcholine test meet this standard?

At sixty-four, the Swedish doctor boasted impeccable credentials. Recently retired as a professor at the world-famous Karolinska Institute, he belonged to the Royal

Academy of Sciences—which selected recipients of the
Nobel Prize—and served as president of the International
Union of Toxicology. Holmstedt had published more than
two hundred scholarly articles. Using extraordinarily sensitive computerized equipment, he had developed his test
for succinylcholine over the previous three years, through
studies on the embalmed tissue of rats. The amounts he
was tracing were almost unimaginable, measured in
billionths of a gram. While refining his technique,
Holmstedt had had himself injected with succinylcholine
during a routine surgical procedure. His test had been
the subject of two articles in major toxicology journals
and four papers at scholarly conferences.

Yet Holmstedt had published nothing on testing human
tissue, and only his own collaborators had replicated his
results. In a hearing outside the jurors' presence, which
consumed an afternoon, Brookshire ripped into Holmstedt,
branding the distinguished Swedish doctor a "salesman"
for his procedure. Arguing that the technique flunked the
"general acceptance" standard, Brookshire said it had
"emerged from a twilight zone of scientific theory." Why,
the test had been developed on *rats!* Rising from his seat,
Nick Rothe noted wryly that there were not many oppor-
tunities to test for succinylcholine in the embalmed body
tissue of humans. How much testing was enough? Rothe
demanded. "How many people have to die . . . how
many exhumed bodies and embalmed bodies of individuals who have been murdered by the use of succinylcholine have to go into the ground . . . before a court
sitting in a county in Texas can admit the testimony?" By
day's end, the judge had decided: He would permit the
jury to hear the evidence.

Ron Sutton was worried that Holmstedt's testimony
would confuse the jurors. They were about to enter a
world of molecular weights, gas chromatography, ion-
pair extraction, and nanograms. Sutton feared the Swedish doctor might even alienate the jurors by speaking
over their heads. But when Holmstedt took the stand,
the DA relaxed. Holmstedt was a balding, white-haired
man who spoke in thickly accented English. He instructed
the jury about his craft as gently as a grandfather teaching an eight-year-old arithmetic. On cross, Brookshire

challenged the doctor's methods, but Holmstedt was un-
assailable; he brushed off the attack with wit and gentle-
manly charm. Holmstedt focused on the history and
technique of his test. Dr. Rieders, the Philadelphia toxicologist who carried the frozen tissue from Texas to
Stockholm, disclosed the results. While arcane details
were quickly forgotten, the damning message of the two
experts stuck: There were traces of succinylcholine in the
body of Chelsea McClellan.

By the second week of testimony, the crowds seeking
admission to the courtroom had started to get surly.
When the doors opened every morning, spectators shoved
and elbowed one another for seats. During a brief recess
one day, three elderly women accosted a bailiff for being
unable to find them a place. At lunchtime each day,
Carter ordered his staff to clear and lock the courtroom
to protect evidence. Regular trial-watchers, many of them
elderly women, assured themselves a seat for the afternoon session by bringing sack lunches in brown paper
bags and camping out on the floor outside the courtroom. The judge had made matters worse by setting
aside two rows for local high school students whose teachers thought the Jones trial would make an excellent les-
son in civics. "Hey, these people are *taxpayers*," Carter
told complaining reporters. Finally, the judge relented
and reserved a handful of seats for the press.

Ron Sutton's relations with the media were more cordial. Each day after trial, he held an impromptu press
conference outside the courtroom, where he commented
on the proceedings, in casual defiance of the judge's gag
order. Then the DA and his colleagues retired to the
Georgetown Inn to unwind. Gathering in their large conference room, they popped a few cold ones from the
refrigerator, held court with reporters, and waited to see
how their day's work played on the six o'clock news.
After dinner, Sutton stayed up late, hashing over the day
and preparing for the next.

Sutton's legal assistant had noticed that amid the crush
of spectators, the courtroom seats reserved for Genene's
family and friends were almost always empty. Not even
her children made an appearance. Crystal was with Gladys

Jones, who lacked the strength or inclination to travel regularly to her daughter's trial. The Texas Department of Human Services had assumed legal custody of Edward.

In addition to losing her children, Genene faced the permanent loss of her career. The Texas Board of Vocational Nurse Examiners was considering suspension of her license. Worst of all, she stood to lose her freedom. Yet Genene was oddly blasé toward her plight. During jury selection, she had cried briefly while Brookshire made opening remarks, and once bolted from the courtroom, complaining of a stomach ailment. Returning with a filled carafe of milk, she had begun sipping it at the defense table, explaining that it would soothe her ulcer. But since testimony began, Genene had remained impassive, appearing bored with the proceedings. She doodled on pads and wrote letters and gobbled candy while court was in session. One day, she wanted to bring a book into the courtroom. And not just any book, but a copy of *Pet Sematary,* a best-selling horror tale by Stephen King. Genene was persuaded that courtroom reading would be unwise. But her lawyers couldn't get her to behave in a manner that showed she realized this was serious. "She acts like she's on trial for jaywalking," said Laura Little.

Genene insisted that her casual manner was merely evidence of a positive attitude, that she was dead certain she would win acquittal. Her lawyers saw it as proof that their client was living in a realm of her own, a world apart from reality. Nothing about the trial seemed to capture Genene's attention—until Kathy Holland took the witness stand.

Twenty-Nine

RON SUTTON had wanted to keep the timing of Kathy Holland's testimony a surprise. He subscribed to one of the rules of courtroom warfare: Never alert the enemy. But word had leaked out after Holland wrote a prescription for a member of the prosecution staff who had the flu. From a local drugstore, the rumor that the *doctor* was going to take the stand spread through Georgetown like a brushfire. After several days of numbing medical evidence, Kathy Holland's appearance promised the trial's most dramatic moments—unless, of course, the *nurse* testified, and whether that would happen was anyone's guess. On Thursday, January 26, it was standing room only once again.

No one was looking forward to Holland's testimony with greater anticipation than the defendant. The doctor was a prosecution witness, but Genene *knew* Kathy wouldn't say anything to harm her. They had shared not just a house and a workplace but a life together in Kerrville. They had spoken of loyalty and of friendship, of family and of love. A lot had come between them since. But the nurse still felt certain: Kathy was going to vindicate her. With Valentine's Day three weeks off, Genene had acquired a package of candy hearts with little messages stamped on them. She showed her lawyers the one she wanted to put on the witness stand for Kathy. It read: "Be True."

Since the trouble broke in Kerrville, Kathy Holland

had experienced a hellish fifteen months. She had suffered financial devastation, public scandal, and the breakup of her second marriage. Charleigh had finally gone his own way, after standing by Kathy for several months after their divorce. Holland had been forced to moonlight at Santa Rosa Hospital to try to pay her bills. She had struggled to rebuild her practice in Kerrville, but the unending publicity had thwarted her efforts. It didn't help that the Sid Peterson medical staff still refused to restore her privileges. Desperate for a place to see patients after hours, Holland had finally applied for privileges at the tiny hospital in Comfort, where Chelsea McClellan had died. Her application was tabled indefinitely; Holland would later claim in legal documents that the Sid Peterson chief of staff had told his Comfort counterpart she was a lesbian.

Holland hoped her testimony in Genene's trial would erase all the black marks against her. Since receiving the assurance that she would not be prosecuted, she had spent hours helping investigators in both Kerrville and San Antonio. Sutton and Rothe had worked on Holland's testimony in the San Antonio office of her lawyer; Jack Leon had even helped them coach her. The problem was that the pediatrician recounted events with a detached, clinical effect; it made her seem cold and abrasive. "She would be a better witness," observed Leon, "if she spoke as a *woman* rather than as a doctor." The lawyers urged Holland to loosen up and express emotion, maybe even shed a few tears on the stand. For trial, they told her to dress feminine, as part of the effort to soften her appearance; it also would repudiate the unsubstantiated rumors that she was a dyke who had consorted with Genene. In Kerrville, the doctor usually wore slacks and little makeup or jewelry. Holland showed up in Georgetown wearing a dress, earrings, stockings, and a visible coat of makeup.

Genene was at rapt attention and chipper as her former boss climbed the witness stand. Here, seated before her in this den of snakes, was a friend. Genene believed that this woman she loved would help her win her freedom. Holland was there, of course, to do just the opposite.

Avoiding Genene's gaze, the pediatrician quickly served

up a string of damaging revelations. Sutton led Holland
through Chelsea's first respiratory arrest on August 24.
The doctor testified that the child had suffered a period
of slow heartbeat, or bradycardia. The jury had already
heard testimony that bradycardia was a side effect of
succinylcholine. The DA moved on to the day of Chelsea's death. Holland said she had ordered routine immunizations after Genene had told her that the child's
temperature was a flat 100 degrees; pediatricians considered up to 100.4 degrees within the range of normal. But
when she later checked Chelsea's medical chart, the doctor testified, she discovered that Genene had recorded
Chelsea's temperature as 100.6 degrees.

"If you would have known that Chelsea McClellan had
100.6 temperature," asked Sutton, "would you have directed Genene Jones to give immunization shots?"

"No," said Holland.

"Why, Doctor?"

"I don't give immunizations to a child with a temperature that is clearly within the febrile area, the fever
zone."

Holland said Genene came to her on September 20,
the day of Chelsea's funeral, asking for permission to
restock several medications used in the clinic's emergencies. Sutton handed Holland a pharmacy invoice showing
the purchase of a vial of succinylcholine on that date. He
asked the doctor if she had authorized the purchase.
Holland said she had not. She testified that her nurse had
also ordered a vial of atropine without permission. Atropine was a drug often given with succinylcholine to coun-
teract bradycardia. The jury would soon hear that one
bottle of each substance turned up missing and had never
been found. The implication was clear: Jones had obtained a private stash of drugs to work her mischief.

Then there was the matter of another bottle of succinylcholine—the one Genene claimed had been lost, then
rediscovered. Holland had ordered that vial before she
opened her clinic. Jones informed her it was missing on
September 7. On September 11, complaining of a bleeding ulcer, Genene had entered Sid Peterson Hospital for
six days. Chelsea died on the day she returned to work.
Holland informed Jones of the hospital committee's in-

quiries about succinylcholine on Friday, September 24. Before the weekend was out, the nurse told her boss that she had located the missing bottle.

But Holland suggested that Genene had told two important lies. Jones reported that she had discovered the bottle in a drawer of the examining table in the clinic's crash room. Mary Mahoney—the nurse who filled in while Genene was hospitalized—had already testified that she had gone through the drawers and discovered no medications. Genene also claimed that the rubber seal on the bottle of succinylcholine remained inviolate; Holland had discovered needle holes in the top. The doctor then described confronting Genene to demand an explanation for the holes. She ended her day on the stand by testifying that Genene had suggested they just throw the bottle away.

"She's lying! She's lying!" hissed Genene to her attorneys, as tears streamed down her face. *Why was Kathy betraying her?* The lawyers told her to shut up and wait; they'd have a crack at Holland on cross-examination. But Genene wanted to speak to Kathy *herself.* If only they could talk, maybe everything would be all right. Brookshire wouldn't allow it. When the doctor finished her testimony and left the courtroom, Genene broke down. For the first time, she was reluctant to run the gauntlet of press outside the courthouse. As she was led in handcuffs to a sheriff's cruiser for the trip back to jail, Genene hid her teary face from the cameras. Brookshire's legal assistant, Patty Jones, visited the nurse in her cell that night. She found her looking broken. "I can't believe Kathy did that to me," Genene moaned.

For the defendant, it would get worse. The next day, Holland described Genene's halfhearted suicide attempt, the events that prompted the nurse's firing, and her discovery of Jones's suicide note, with its semiconfessional reference to "the seven people, whose life I have altered." Holland had turned the opened bottle of succinylcholine over to authorities. State police chemists would inform the jurors that most of its contents were missing and had been replaced with salt water.

Sutton worked hard to end each day's testimony with a

bang—to feed the jurors a damning chunk of evidence to chew on overnight. On this Friday, as the close of testimony neared, he asked Holland to read Genene's final notes in Chelsea McClellan's medical chart: "Fifteen minutes into transport child noted to be mottled with eyes deviated upward. No response to pain. Cardiac monitor shows asystole. CPR begun. Dr. Holland in EMS unit. Five milliquivalents bicarb IV push; .8 cc's epinephrine IV push and 2.5 cc's calcium gluconate IV push without response. Meds repeated without response. Code eight to Comfort to Comfort Hospital. CPR continued. Meds repeated times six at Comfort Hospital without response. Pupils fixed. CPR discontinued. Parents informed of death by Dr. Holland. Post consent obtained. Baby transported from Comfort to Sid Peterson Memorial Hospital by EMS and myself and taken to morgue. I would have given my life for hers. Goodbye, Chelsea. Jones LVN."

Ron Sutton remained in Georgetown over the weekend to review medical records with his star witness. He was pleased with the way things were going. Holland hadn't taken all their coaching to heart; she was still too detached and methodical. But the doctor had answered his questions with confidence, and there was still plenty of opportunity for her to show the jurors some emotion.

Genene spent the weekend quietly licking her wounds in jail. She received a visit from her friends at the New Life Ministries, a group of born-again Christians who did missionary work with prisoners. Genene had been studying the Bible with them and had pledged her commitment to Jesus Christ as her savior; proclaiming Jones's innocence, they had appeared in court regularly to offer the accused baby-killer support. On Monday, Genene finished a letter to her old San Antonio friend Keith Martin.

Addressing her note "Hi Babe," Genene wrote that it had been "quite painful to hear people I thought of as friends + family lie so blatantly. It seems I'm crying a lot these days." Genene expressed optimism about her acquittal, telling Martin that he would have to treat her to dinner when the trial was over. She noted that she was "again free of the marital bonds," and said her children were receiving counseling. Genene added: "Guess I'll need it when this is over."

It was not until Kathy Holland's third day on the witness stand that the defense had a chance to cross-examine her before the jury. Holland's testimony was clearly damaging, but the defense attorneys felt they could make the jury doubt her credibility. Kathy Holland was walking a tightrope. She faced a $7 million civil suit filed by the McClellans, which asserted her negligence. In her sworn deposition for the lawsuit, she flatly declared she saw nothing to indicate that any of her patients had been given succinylcholine. But now Holland and the McClellans were on the same side. To buttress the prosecution, the doctor was suddenly recalling symptoms *consistent* with succinylcholine—symptoms that weren't documented anywhere. She was trying to have it both ways; the attorneys for the defense didn't intend to let her get away with it.

Burt Carnes shuffled to his feet to handle the interrogation. After Chelsea's first arrest, he pointed out, Holland had diagnosed the problem as a seizure disorder and placed the child on Dilantin, an anticonvulsant. How could she now attribute the problems to succinylcholine, a *paralyzing* drug?

Holland said her diagnosis had originated with Genene's initial statement that Chelsea had suffered a seizure. In the days that followed, Holland testified, Genene's report prompted her to interpret behaviors that she would otherwise consider normal as subtle signs of seizures.

Carnes worked to remind the jury that it was the doctor, not the nurse, who bore the ultimate responsibility for patient care. He drummed the message home. "You were the doctor, *you* were there," he told Holland. If the jurors would blame the pediatrician, they might not blame his client.

"To what degree did you rely on your LVN to make your diagnosis of seizure activity?" Carnes asked.

"I didn't rely on Genene to make the diagnosis of seizure activity, but every doctor relies on a nurse to report what they see as having happened, and uses that information appropriately."

Carnes read Holland excerpts of her medical records,

where she had described *personally* observing signs of
seizures by Chelsea—both in the clinic and in the hospital. For September 17, too, Holland's own notes reflected that Chelsea had suffered "tonic-clonic" seizures—
characterized by rhythmic jerking of the arms and legs—
during her clinic arrest.

"Would you say that was a tonic-clonic seizure activity
that you observed?" asked Carnes.

"That was my impression at the time," said Holland.

"What is your impression today, Doctor?"

"My impression is that there could be other things that
could have been happening."

"What is that, Doctor?"

"Based on what I now know about the possibility of
succinylcholine having been used, it is possible that that
could have been the result of succinylcholine being
administered."

"And you are going to tell this jury that what you
observed was momentary limpness, followed by . . . tonic-
clonic seizure movement. You are saying *that* was succinylcholine?"

"Mr. Carnes, I am saying that in retrospect now, the
movements that I saw and the sequence of events that I
observed are consistent with an administration of succinylcholine. Looking at them at the time, in the context of
the moment of their happening, my initial impression was
that these were seizure-like movements."

Carnes pressed his point. "You understand the experts
have come in here and testified that if you are under the
effects of succinylcholine, [you are] absolutely, totally
limp like a rag doll. You understand that?"

"I understand that," said Holland.

"You observed and reported in both instances tonic-
clonic seizure movement. You administered [Dilantin],
an anticonvulsant drug. . . . Is that right?"

Holland acknowledged that it was.

"And you were the doctor there. You were the one
observing whatever those movements were."

"That is correct."

"*Now*," said Carnes, his voice dripping with disbelief,
"you want to back off and say, 'well, it could have been
succinylcholine.' "

"That is correct," said Holland.

Burt Carnes ended the day content with what he had accomplished. Holland had testified previously that the seizure-like movements Chelsea displayed during the clinic arrests might have been caused by a low dose of succinyl-choline, or the child's emergence from the effects of the drug. But Carnes thought he had delivered his message to the jury—that Holland was rewriting medical history to aid the prosecution.

Ron Sutton recognized that Carnes was scoring some points. Holland sounded much worse under attack; she was retreating into a defensive shell. Hoping to minimize the damage, the DA was doing everything he could to distract the jurors during cross-examination. He shuffled papers and fiddled with lawbooks. He took out his gold pocket watch, dismantled it on the prosecution table, and then put it back together. On another occasion, as the defense lawyers preached that Genene was innocent, Sutton pulled out a handful of syringes he'd brought as evidence and lined them up in front of him, where they remained in the jurors' sight.

Midway through the trial's third week, Judge Carter confronted his second pivotal decision. The issue was whether to treat the jury to testimony from a new realm of incriminating evidence: the "extraneous offenses"—the cases of other children who had experienced emergencies in Genene's presence. The prosecutors were eager to open that door. The defense might raise questions about the case of Chelsea McClellan, but the wholesale pattern was overwhelming. It had the power to snuff jurors' doubts like a bucket of sand on a burning match.

Genene's lawyers were similarly determined to slam the door and turn the key. In a hearing where samples of the testimony were heard outside the jury, Laura Little called the extraneous offenses prejudicial and inflammatory. The issue was what happened to Chelsea McClellan, not the other children; their emergencies were irrelevant.

Nick Rothe countered that the extraneous incidents were "strikingly similar" to the case on trial. Genene Jones, noted Rothe, pointing his finger at the defendant,

was "the common denominator at all times." This made
Chelsea's death not an isolated event but part of an
ongoing scheme. The jury *had* to hear about the cases;
only when all of them were examined did the horrible
pattern become apparent.

The judge had spent the previous night mulling over
the law; he fell asleep on the couch in his chambers amid
a pile of briefs and legal books. Now, after a break,
Carter returned to announce his decision: He would allow the testimony on the other children. The judge had
dealt Genene's defense another powerful blow.

Wave after wave of damaging evidence now spilled out
before the jury. The army paramedics who had treated
Jimmy Pearson appeared, dressed in uniform and wearing medals, to describe their wild helicopter ride with
Genene. The jury heard about Misty Reichenau, who
had stopped breathing after showing up in Holland's
clinic for mouth ulcers. The civilian paramedics who had
transported Brandy Benites recounted how the baby went
limp after Genene started a second IV in her foot. Dr.
Webb recalled that he had been summoned to Holland's
clinic when Jacob Evans had arrested while the pediatrician was away. Webb told the jury he had ordered no
medication for the baby, even though Genene had reported on medical charts that he ordered her to give
Dilantin. And there was the story of Rolinda Ruff, brought
in for diarrhea, the last of the babies who mysteriously
had stopped breathing.

The nightmarish testimony draggd on, even as the horrible events had gone on, one after the other, until Genene
Jones left Kerrville. Sutton summoned five mothers to
the stand. Each told a tearful story of how one encounter
with the LVN had pushed her child to the brink of death.
The DA illustrated the pattern by marking each of the
arrests in red ink on giant calendars placed before the
jury. Several witnesses described Genene Jones's appearance following the emergencies—her sweating, heaving
body, her white face, and the strange, terrible look of
excitement in her eyes.

For the defense, fighting the prosecution onslaught had
become like sticking fingers in a bursting dike. And Sut-

ton and Rothe were shrewdly foreclosing almost every
path of counterattack. One opening was Genene's explanation that she knew nothing about succinylcholine. How
could she employ the drug as a weapon if she had no
knowledge of how to use it? Sutton summoned Dr. Sheila
Schwartzman, an anesthesiologist at the UT medical school
in San Antonio, to answer that question. Schwartzman
testified that in November 1980, she had given the nurses
in the pediatric ICU an hour-long lecture on pediatric
anesthesia drugs. Schwartzman still had the outline from
her talk, which included a discussion of succinylcholine.
It had spelled out appropriate doses for children, and it
had noted that the drug's tendency to cause bradycardia
could be avoided through the use of atropine. Schwartzman
was certain that Jones was present; the LVN had asked
her to give the talk.

The defense lawyers thought they could exploit an
inconsistency with the timing of Chelsea's death. Everyone agreed that the child, after the injections and arrest
in Holland's clinic, had recovered almost completely in
the emergency room. By the time Chelsea was readied
for transport to San Antonio, the effects of succinylcholine—if indeed she had received the drug in the first
place—clearly had worn off. How, then, could the prosecution blame Jones for Chelsea's fatal arrest in the ambulance, more than an hour after the injections in the
clinic? Sutton called DeAnna Armour, a woman whose
mother baby-sat for Chelsea. Armour said she had accompanied her mother to Sid Peterson on September 17
after hearing of Chelsea's arrest. She had seen Chelsea
just before she was loaded into the ambulance. Armour
testified that she also spotted Genene Jones near the
child—and that she saw her give Chelsea *another* injection in the upper thigh. Genene explained that the child
was getting Valium, Armour said. But Sharon Keith, the
ER nurse, had told the jurors previously that she had
already administered Valium, on Holland's orders. The
defense lawyers thought the story nonsense—a blatant
fabrication to cover a gaping hole in the prosecution
case. But there was no way they could rebut it. Sutton
had his explanation: Genene had stuck Chelsea before

the ambulance trip, sending the child into terminal arrest on the interstate to San Antonio.

To tie his case together, Ron Sutton turned once again to Kathy Holland. Led carefully by the prosecutor, the pediatrician shaped the suffering of her patients into a coherent pattern. Holland testified that it was Genene who prepared the injections and IVs that preceded the office emergencies. In each of the cases, she said, Jones had done it out of her presence. Sutton asked the doctor to consider the patients she had treated on the days when Genen was present. He focused on the children who were two years old or younger—and thus unable to talk. Wasn't it true, asked Sutton, that every time Genene prepared an IV for a nontalking patient, the child "went down"? Yes, said Holland. The only patient older than two who had suffered an emergency was seven-year-old Jimmy Pearson, who was unable to talk. Sutton displayed this trend for the jury on a giant chart in the courtroom. Carnes rose to object. "This is no statistical analysis," he complained. "This is something the State has put together in a motel room!" But Carter ruled for the prosecution once again.

First the judge had admitted the drug test, then he allowed the extraneous offenses. Now Holland was painting the events in her clinic as an obvious example of a nurse run amok. If it was all so clear, why hadn't Holland *done* something—stepped in before a kid was dead and a half-dozen others had suffered? Carnes was determined to show the jury that the pattern was far from certain.

He challenged the doctor's account that she had left Genene alone with each of the children. As he pressed her for detail, Holland's memory began to falter. She hedged many of her answers and on more than one hundred occasions responded that she couldn't recall the answer to a defense question.

Growing testy at the doctor's memory lapses, Carnes questioned her claim that Brandy Benites had gone limp. He pointed out that Holland's emergency room note on the incident—and even her civil deposition in the McClellan lawsuit—made no mention of limpness.

"I don't always use the term 'limp,' Mr. Carnes, because I don't always describe every single sequence of what the children do," responded Holland. "I generally characterize the event."

Carnes opened a copy of Holland's deposition, adding his own emphasis to the reading. "In discussing Brandy Benites, the question was, 'Was it evidenced to you at *any* time *any* symptoms which you felt looked like withdrawal from the effects of succinylcholine?' And your answer was, 'no.' Not 'maybe,' not 'I don't recall,' not 'perhaps.' An unequivocal no."

"And that would still be my answer," responded Holland. ". . . My interpretation of that question was that he was asking me for what I was feeling and thinking at the time of the occurrence of the events."

Carnes didn't understand how the doctor could have interpreted the question that way, but he pressed on. "Doctor, you have testified that you are a highly trained medical doctor with seven years of training, trained to make clinical observations of people whenever they are having a problem. In every single one of these cases, there is no indication in any record made at or near the time of the event, or in the deposition you gave in May of 1983, that any one of those additional children went limp for any period of time, is there?"

That might be true, said Holland, "but that doesn't necessarily eliminate the existence of that."

"Now, Doctor, in retrospect, here today in the courtroom, all of a sudden in every single one of these cases you have come forward and said there is this period of limpness. But you can't remember how long it lasted, you can't remember when it started or when it stopped, and it was always followed by what you, in your clinical observations, referred to as some seizure activity."

"Uh-huh."

"What is that based on, Doctor?"

Holland said she was relying now on a "retrospective view" of events. She said she had never been asked specifically whether children went limp "at any time."

"Come on, Doctor," snapped Carnes. "You knew what they were looking for in this two-day deposition. They were trying to find out whether there was evidence of succinylcholine having been used. Right?"

"All I know is that they were trying to find out the facts, and that is what I was trying to give them."

"And they asked you every way possible whether, in your clinical opinion, succinylcholine was involved on any of these other children. You said *no.*"

"I did not have the back-up information at that May deposition that I now have." Holland said she had become convinced by Dr. Holmstedt's succinylcholine test on Chelsea. "At the time of that deposition, I didn't have that information and was not about to speculate on a suspicion."

Holland remained on the stand for parts of eight days— more than eighteen grueling hours in all. By the third day, she looked tired. On the sixth day, she cried while again describing her confrontation with Genene about the bottle of succinylcholine; Ron Sutton was pleased. By the seventh day, Holland had come down with flu and had to interrupt her testimony several times to ask for water. After she'd been through five hours of cross-examination, Sutton persuaded the judge that the doctor was too sick to continue. She finished her testimony the next morning.

Burt Carnes believed he had totally discredited the prosecution's star witness. She had been forced to resort to memory lapses and semantic excuses. Carnes felt certain the jurors would not trust their grandchildren to the pediatrician's care. But would they transfer enough blame to Holland to get Genene off the hook?

On the morning of February 7, the trial's nineteenth day, Ron Sutton rose, as usual, at 5 A.M., to prepare the last of his evidence. Through the testimony of forty-three witnesses, Sutton had chronicled the life and death of Chelsea McClellan, the drug test that showed succinylcholine was in her body, and the emergencies that had stricken other children under the care of Genene Jones. There was only one thing left. He had promised the jury a motive.

Throughout the prosecution case, the DA had sprinkled hints. Witnesses had mentioned the nurse's complaints about the inadequacy of pediatric care at Sid Peterson Hospital. Holland had recalled the day when

Genene, walking out of the hospital's ICU, had spoken wistfully of her hope that it might someday be named in memory of Chelsea. And Jacob Evans's grandmother had told the jurors of Genene's insistence that children required an ICU just for them.

Sutton had teased reporters with the remark that the prosecution's case wouldn't be over "until the fat lady sings." Now, as his forty-fourth and final witness, Sutton called Mary Virginia Morris, a heavyset LVN who worked at Sid Peterson Hospital. Morris told the jury that she and Genene had gone to nursing school together in San Antonio. She had lost contact with her classmate—until 2 A.M. on September 11, 1982, when Jones was admitted to Sid Peterson for a complaint of bleeding ulcers, while Morris was working the night shift.

Morris had dropped by Genene's room for a friendly chat later that morning. The nurse said she asked what Genene was doing in Kerrville. "She said that she was up there to help Dr. Holland run her clinic," Morris recalled, "and that she was up there to help start a pediatric intensive care unit."

"Did she discuss how it would be staffed or anything?" asked Sutton.

"She said that it was going to be run by all LVNs, which struck me as odd." Morris voiced her skepticism to Genene—registered nurses customarily supervised ICUs—but she said Jones was "very adamant."

"Did you discuss a need with her for a pediatric intensive care unit?" asked Sutton.

"Well, that was the next thing we talked about. I said, 'And the other thing is, I don't—we have sick children, but I don't think there is enough sick children [in Kerrville] to constitute a pediatric ICU.'"

"And when you told her that you didn't think there were enough sick children there to justify a pediatric intensive care unit, did she respond to that?" asked Sutton.

"Yes, sir," Morris told the jurors. "She said, 'Oh, they are out there. All you have to do is go and find them.'"

The state rested its case.

Thirty

FOR THE COUNSELORS to the accused baby-killer, there was only one significant decision to make: whether to put Genene Jones on the witness stand. Jim Brookshire, Burt Carnes, and Laura Little had been wrestling with that question since accepting the case. After the prosecution rested, Judge Carter adjourned the proceedings for a day. It offered Genene's lawyers a chance to ponder their strategy.

Three considerations weighed in favor of placing the nurse before those who sat in her judgment. The first was that Genene could be magically persuasive; each of the lawyers had felt the tug of Genene's perfect belief in her innocence. They also needed to consider the impact of Genene's *failure* to testify. Juries were instructed to conclude nothing from a defendant's refusal to take the stand, but it was human nature to believe that those following such a course had something to hide. Finally, there was the distinct possibility that the defense had nothing left to lose. Genene's attorneys had tried to block admission of the succinylcholine test—and failed. They had fought to bar testimony about the extraneous offenses—and failed. They had chipped away at the credibility of the prosecution witnesses, particularly Kathy Holland—but with uncertain results. The accumulated weight of prosecution evidence now stood revealed as overwhelming. Perhaps Genene Jones's force would prove as beguiling to one or two jurors as it had to Kathy Holland.

There were also powerful reasons to shield the nurse

from scrutiny. For Genene to help herself on the witness stand, she would need to project a transformation that far transcended new clothes and fingernail polish. Painted by prosecution witnesses as an egomaniacal, cold-blooded killer, Genene would have to come across as truthful, compassionate, and—most of all—benign. While her lawyers held the stage, they could try to build such an image. Through carefully rehearsed questioning, they would portray Genene as a dedicated mother, summon up her determination to fight for her "little angels," and evoke her grief at Chelsea's death. Genene would play the part of the humble nurse, just an LVN following orders, who enjoyed little power to affect the health of her patients, for better *or* for worse. If all went well, at the moment the performance was over, the jurors would doubt such a woman could ever harm the fragile children entrusted to her care.

But then Ron Sutton would rise, and Genene would stand exposed to a brutal cross-examination. A defendant who remained calm and steadfast in the face of such an onslaught might actually bolster her case further. But with this defendant, that seemed unlikely. Genene's blood seemed to boil at the mere mention of Sutton's name. And the district attorney would come to the interrogation with precisely the fuel to turn up the heat. The problem was that Genene had already talked far too much. She had told her story to a Texas Ranger, to two grand juries, in a civil deposition, and to reporters from television, radio, magazines, and newspapers. Already the prosecution testimony had revealed a score of conflicts with the single version of events that Genene had given her own lawyers. From the untold number of occasions when Genene had gabbed away to others, Sutton had surely uncovered dozens more inconsistencies. Worst of all, the defense attorneys didn't have a clue what they were. Putting Genene on the stand would be like walking across a minefield; any move they made might blow up in their faces.

Sutton, in fact, was plotting precisely the strategy the defense feared. He had already composed his first question for cross-examination. "Miss Jones," the DA intended to ask, "is it not a fact that you're a *liar?*" To the nurse's legal team, the scenario was vivid: Sutton would ravage Genene's credibility, and, equally important, he would prod her into a fury. The defense lawyers had seen how Genene looked when she lost her temper. Her mouth twisted into a sneer, and her eyes lit up with hate. She had already shown flashes of this behavior in court when listening to unfriendly testimony. More than any single fact or witness, such a reaction would persuade the jurors that Jones was indeed capable of murder. The defense attorneys could gamble: They could work on Genene, make her promise to keep cool, and hold their collective breath as they turned her over to Sutton. But the nurse had rarely followed her lawyers' advice. Besides, putting her on the stand would represent a wholesale departure from their conservative strategy of trying to hang the jury. In the end, their decision was governed by a simple truth: Genene Jones's lawyers could not trust their client. They did not want her to testify.

Genene, of course, was eager to slug it out with Sutton. This would be High Noon, the ultimate showdown with the man who had ruined her life. The press was already brimming with speculation about whether Genene would take the stand. Under Texas law, a defendant who wanted to testify was always free to do so—even if that meant rejecting her lawyers' advice. Genene's attorneys would have to persuade the nurse that it would be a mistake for her to testify. Sutton would goad her, they told Genene bluntly, and he would surely get her goat. For once the nurse accepted their recommendation.

With the drama's climactic scene suddenly excised from the script, Genene Jones's murder trial moved rapidly toward its conclusion. The defense devoted its energies to buttressing the notion that Chelsea had died of natural causes. Debbie Sultenfuss took the stand to tell the jurors that she had never seen her friend administer succinylcholine. But under cross-examination, Sultenfuss admitted that she and Genene had conducted their own research on the drug after seeing it used at Medical Center Hospital. Sultenfuss also acknowledged that she and Jones had discussed opening a pediatric ICU at Sid Peterson. But she insisted the idea had originated with Dr. Holland, not Genene.

The defense put forth a parade of medical experts—a nurse, two toxicologists, and a pediatric neurologist—to challenge those who had testified for the prosecution. Angela Clark, a University of Texas nursing professor, went through a painstaking review of Chelsea's medical history. Brookshire wanted to show that Chelsea's history of hospitalizations proved she was seriously ill even before her death. But when Sutton read aloud notes from doctors that described Chelsea's recovery, the nursing professor looked surprised. "That sounds like a much healthier description than the notes that I was reviewing," she said. Under Sutton's prodding, Clark admitted that she had searched Chelsea's records for symptoms of illness but not signs of recovery.

To question the succinylcholine test, Brookshire called toxicologist Joseph Balkon. An associate professor at St. John's University, Balkon had phoned Brookshire after hearing news reports about the trial after it was already under way; Balkon informed the lawyer that he had developed his own technique for detecting succinylcholine. After confirming that Balkon was not a quack—the defense had received dozens of crank calls—Brookshire had invited Balkon to testify, at a consulting fee of $150 an hour. The toxicologist told the jurors about his rival technique, but he was unable to pronounce Holmstedt's approach invalid; he merely interpreted the prosecution results as inconclusive, remarking, "We would have to say, you know, no cigar in terms of confirmation." Such flip responses helped make Balkon a flawed witness. Juries liked experts to have gray hair and a regal bearing. This toxicologist was young and abrasive, sprinkled wisecracks into his testimony, and often wandered off into extended digressions. He also spoke in a distinct New York accent. A pale challenge indeed, thought Sutton, to the distinguished Dr. Holmstedt.

"Did you happen to bring the results of your testing procedures or test results on tissue of Chelsea McClellan?" the DA asked the toxicologist on cross-examination.

When Balkon admitted that he had not personally analyzed the child's tissue, Sutton lifted his eyebrows in mock surprise. "Don't you think it would be important," he demanded, his voice dripping with sarcasm, "if you are such an international expert in this, having published in an international journal, that you would run your own tests, rather than come in here and criticize Dr. Rieders' or Holmstedt's testing procedures?"

Balkon said he had lacked the time to test Chelsea's tissue, but the answer sounded lame. The DA swarmed all over the defense expert. Balkon acknowledged that his own laboratory lacked the equipment to conduct a succinylcholine test and that he had never attempted the procedure that Holmstedt and Rieders had performed.

In presenting the evidence against Genene Jones, the prosecution had called forty-four witnesses and introduced sixty-four exhibits. The nurse's attorneys were betting heavily on their efforts to discredit the state testimony. After summoning only seven witnesses, they rested their case.

Ron Sutton was disappointed not to have a crack at Genene Jones but pleased to discover that the defense had no other surprises to offer. Sutton felt confident that he had already countered the arguments the defense witnesses had made. The DA also believed he had triumphed in the battle of experts: The prosecution witnesses had been more numerous, more eminent, and more persuasive. And they had yielded little ground under challenge. Sutton and Rothe decided to devote rebuttal to eliminating any doubts that lingered about the succinylcholine test. First, the prosecutors read to the jury testimony that had been given earlier outside its presence by Dr. Holmstedt and Dr. Rieders. The testimony revealed that after Rieders had finished the testing on Chelsea's tissue and departed from Stockholm, Holmstedt had confirmed the results by running the tests again on his own. Next, the prosecutors called their only new witness: Dr. James Garriott, the chief toxicologist in the Bexar County medical examiner's office. Garriott affirmed to the jurors that the tests by Holmstedt and Rieders represented "conclusive" evidence that there was succinylcholine in the body of Chelsea McClellan.

Tuesday, February 14, was Valentine's Day and the birthday of Petti McClellan. But there was to be no celebration, for it was also the twenty-first day of Genene Jones's murder trial. Late that afternoon, testimony at last came to an end. Before sending the jurors home, Judge Carter advised them to bring an overnight bag and toothbrush to court the next morning. After hearing final arguments, the jurors would begin deliberations immediately and remain sequestered until they reached a verdict.

With testimony over, the rule that barred witnesses from sitting in on the trial was no longer in effect. The judge had at last moved the trial into a much larger courtroom, across from his own. Among the more than two hundred people who jammed it on the morning of February 15 were the mothers of three children Genene Jones was accused of harming. Reid McClellan, barred until the final day by order of Ron Sutton, was there too, sitting beside his wife, Petti. The defendant arrived at the courthouse wearing a choice item from her new wardrobe, a brown striped dress. Genene appeared relaxed and confident; it had not taken her long to recover from the shock of Kathy Holland's testimony.

Under Texas law, the state went first in closing arguments, the defense followed, and the state had the final word. By agreement, each side would have two hours. Ron Sutton decided to let his young part-time assistant, Scott Monroe, briefly introduce the prosecution argument; Monroe had been griping about his limited role in the trial. Then Nick Rothe would summarize the testimony the jurors had heard over the previous five weeks. Sutton would speak last, after the defense had taken its turn.

Nick Rothe rose from his seat at 9:30 A.M. The canny San Antonio lawyer had the task of reviewing the testimony, and there was much ground to cover. But he knew it was the entire puzzle, not a single piece, that would send Genene Jones to prison. The defense could nit-pick at an individual witness, perhaps even raise doubts about the cause of any one child's sudden arrest. But it would be hard for jurors to dismiss the big picture, the pattern of emergencies—or the emotional power of a helpless baby's death. To put the nurse behind bars, they had to keep that fresh before the jury, to make sure the weeks of numbing testimony did not obscure the point of this ordeal.

"What we need to do is to get back to what this is all about," Rothe told the jury. "It is about a dead little girl, this one, little Chelsea McClellan." Rothe held the child's portrait before the jurors' eyes. "It is about somebody else too," he said, turning toward the defendant with evident disgust—"a nurse, a self-proclaimed 'pediatric clinician.'" Rothe recounted Chelsea's first visit to Kathy Holland's office on August 24, the day after the clinic opened. "She had the misfortune to meet the nurse when she had the sniffles. That child, that baby, is alone with the nurse, and what is the next thing that happens?

"Down she goes!" shouted Rothe. "With what? *Seizure!*" The prosecutor paused, shifting to a tone of foreboding. "I have heard that word an awful lot. Like an epidemic of seizures running through the Hill Country of Texas in Kerrville—strangely enough, located only in the immediate vicinity of the nurse." Rothe left the defendant's name unspoken, keeping her a vague, evil presence. "That was the first one. And that was to be a portent of something horrible happening in Kerr County—because it didn't stop."

As Rothe began to speak of the events of September 17, his voice quavered with emotion. Rothe had never worked harder on a case; now he was close to exhaustion, and he didn't mind the jurors feeling his outrage. "Immunization shots," he mused. "At this point the sheer, audacious bravado of this nurse becomes very clear." The prosecutor held aloft an empty hypodermic needle, reenacting the chilling scene after the nurse gave Chelsea, sitting in Petti's lap, the first injection. "The child starts to tremble and shake, okay? And the mother said, 'There is something wrong with her!' And what does the nurse say? 'Oh, she is just mad. She is just a mad kid.'

"She gets a second needle. *Wham!* Then what happens?" Chelsea was limp as a rag doll, he said. Rothe turned to the poster-sized calendars with each arrest marked in red. *Look at the big picture; look at the pattern.* "There are rag dolls all *over* those calendars because they are all the *same*," he declared. With one exception: the week Genene was in the hospital. "No rag dolls that week because the nurse wasn't there."

And on the day the nurse returned to work?

"Chelsea McClellan! Down she goes! *Dead!*"

Rothe reviewed the other arrests, punctuating each with the cry.: Down she goes! "The whole thing is frightening. It is bizarre. It is terrible that some human being would do that to a baby, but worse, to babies—not one, but one after the other after the other." Rothe turned, pointed his finger at the defense table, and invoked the name of the accused for the first time. "The nurse is right *there!* The nurse that *killed* that baby is right there, and her name is *Genene Jones!*"

Speaking softly now, Rothe said he always struggled to find the right words to offer a jury. "Sometimes you just can't find the words, so you look other places and see that somebody else one time maybe said something that fits here. And I did that." The prosecutor looked down at his notes, scribbled late the night before from a borrowed Bible, and read from the Book of Matthew: *"But whoso shall offend one of these little ones which believe in me, it were better for him that a millstone were hanged about his neck and that he were drowned in the depth of the sea.*

"Ladies and gentlemen of the jury," said Rothe, "what I would suggest to you, after you review the evidence and read the charge and measure the proof, is that justice is what we are here for. And justice is ofttimes harsh. This baby being dead is awfully harsh and irrevocable." Rothe faced the defendant, stared into her eyes, and preached. "But I would ask you by your verdict to tie a millstone, if you will, of justice around this woman's neck and say by your verdict: guilty of the offense of murder of Chelsea McClellan."

Final argument was normally Burt Carnes's favorite part of trial. On this morning, however, ridden with fever and fatigue, the defense attorney felt lousy. A few days earlier, he had almost passed out in court while questioning a witness. Now he had two hours to speak, and he entertained doubts that he could stand up that long. Carnes knew that most in this courtroom mob wouldn't mind a bit if he fell flat on his face.

In natural contrast to the state, the defense wanted the jurors to pay attention to detail, to scrutinize not only *every* piece of the puzzle but the cracks that lay between them. Carnes praised the jurors for their attentiveness and frankly admitted that the defense was counting on just that. But he was already worried. An experienced trial lawyer could read jurors like a newspaper. The panel had absorbed Rothe's oration; its attention to Carnes's first words seemed merely cursory and polite. Anxious to capture the jurors' minds, Carnes swarmed into an attack on the prosecution. Composed as much of rhetoric as of fact, it was to be an argument that echoed the paranoid reasoning of the defendant.

The state had no interest in the truth about Chelsea McClellan, Carnes declared. "Obsessed" and "desperate," the prosecutors were throwing up a smoke screen with their testimony about the other children. "They are trying to stampede you," warned Carnes. The defendant was a scapegoat, victimized because she was aggressive and bossy and stepped on people's toes. "If they have proven anything about Genene Jones, it may be that she practiced a little medicine without a license." But that didn't make her a murderer.

From the beginning, the defense's first line of argument was that Chelsea McClellan had died from natural causes, not succinylcholine. Its secondary pitch was that *if* something had gone on, Genene had not done it. Although the arguments were mutually exclusive, Carnes argued both, in the desperate hope that the jurors would respond to one. The notion that someone else was responsible required an alternative culprit. Carnes offered them Kathy Holland, sitting that very day in the courtroom. Suddenly the doctor recalled all the children going limp, noted Carnes. Why had she not used that word in her medical records back in August and September of 1982? Why had she instead consistently described seizures—impossible, he insisted, with the administration of succinylcholine.

Carnes knew he had to address the gleaming red ink on the prosecution's giant calendars, reflecting the string of arrests. He told the jurors he was unsure what had happened but had some ideas. "I think there is a high possibility that we are dealing with a young doctor who is in her first clinic situation, just out of residency, a residency served in a hospital, where you are used to seeing very serious children in serious trouble, and who had a tendency to push the panic button and maybe over-reacted—and possibly overtreated. . . .

"Maybe it is total incompetence on Dr. Holland's part." The lawyer's voice reeked with insinuation as he offered a more sinister possibility. "Maybe *she* was doing something that was just flat wrong that *caused* the problems." As for the prosecution's explanation of the defendant's motive, it was "absurd," declared Carnes. "You are going to go out and harm these children to guarantee that they are going to get a pediatric ICU unit?" But Holland, on the other hand . . . Carnes's speculation became specific. After Chelsea's death, "Dr. Holland had to have been feeling the heat. To me it is a possibility that at that point Dr. Holland made the decision it was time to cover herself. It is a possibility that third vial of Anectine was Dr. Holland's vial, and she punctured it, she withdrew the succinylcholine, she filled it back up with saline, she planted it, and waited for Genene to do her next weekly inventory and all of a sudden find it."

Now Carnes backtracked, again taking up the claim that Chelsea had not died of succinylcholine in the first place. Even assuming the child had received the drug on September 17 in Holland's clinic, she had not been loaded into the ambulance for transfer to San Antonio until almost two hours later. The drug's effects would have worn off; the shots in the office *couldn't* have killed the baby. As for the testimony of DeAnna Armour—who said she had seen Genene inject Chelsea in the thigh just before the child was loaded into the ambulance—"that didn't happen," Carnes declared. "You *know* it didn't happen."

With only thirty minutes of his two hours remaining, Carnes shifted to a sympathetic tone for the first time. "Ladies and gentlemen, it is a sad fact that a pretty fifteen-month-old child passed away on September 17, 1982. And it is a shame. But there is not a thing in the world that you, or I, or anybody else can do to bring that child back. And it doesn't justify trying to railroad somebody on the kind of evidence the state has brought to you today or in the past four weeks."

For the next half hour, the exhausted defense attorney

wandered through an attack on the state's experts. Only when the judge advised that he had but a single minute remaining did Carnes return to his central theme. Consider motives, he pleaded. "If anybody has a motive for misrepresenting the truth, it is Dr. Kathy Holland. I think it is clear to you she is trying to cover her tracks. She is hanging Genene Jones out there to dry and letting her try to face the heat because of Dr. Holland's own incompetence or possible intentional wrongdoing."

Carnes raced toward the finish line, in a jumble of mixed metaphors. "We talked about the presumption of innocence. Mr. Sutton promised you he was going to chip away at that presumption of innocence until there wasn't anything left and you reached the inescapable conclusion that Genene Jones is guilty. I am going to tell you they spent four and a half weeks trying to cover it up. They have thrown blankets at it. They have put up smoke screens all around it. They have done everything in their power to direct your attention away from the facts of this case surrounding the death of Chelsea McClellan, under all that red lettering on the calendar, in an attempt to hide the truth from you, and confuse you, and panic you, and bully you into returning a verdict of guilty. Ladies and gentlemen, that presumption of innocence remains inviolate. It is still there. They have not dented it."

"Time," the judge announced.

Thrown off balance by the interruption, Carnes asked for a few extra moments and stumbled toward conclusion. "Ladies and gentlemen, I simply ask that you take the time, don't be totally infuenced by emotion. Take your time, reasonably sit down, and go through the evidence brought before you. Think about the testimony brought before you, and you will see the presumption of innocence remains. They have not met their burden of proof. They have not come *close* to meeting their burden of proof. And the law requires a verdict of not guilty."

This last day of arguments was the first day in which the judge had not adjourned court promptly as lunchtime loomed. Carter wanted to wrap up arguments first, so Ron Sutton stood to speak at 12:58 P.M., with many stomachs in the chamber rumbling. The DA's nerves lingered as this final hour loomed. The case had consumed him for more than sixteen months. Remarried during the opening days of the investigation, Sutton was divorced from his second wife on the Friday before jury selection began. The prosecutor blamed the breakup on the long hours he had dedicated to putting Jones behind bars. Obsessed, Carnes had called him, and obsessed Sutton was. With the exception of the defendant, her children, and the family of Chelsea McClellan, no one had more at stake in the trial's outcome. Victory meant glory, revenge, vindication, ambition. Defeat meant humiliation, shame, and political devastation.

Sutton had listened angrily to Carnes's personal attacks. Shaking with emotion, he told the jurors they had witnessed a typical defense attorney's ploy: putting everyone on trial except the defendant. "He seems to imply to you that either myself or Mr. Rothe, or the combination of the two of us, have enough prestige and power that we can go out and bring in some forty-some-odd witnesses from across Texas, the United States, and even go over to Sweden . . . and, in some form of conspiracy, have them commit a series of aggravated perjuries." Sutton waxed indignant. "I have been district attorney since 1977, and I don't think that if I had that reputation I would ever have survived this long as an elected official in the state of Texas." The prosecutor noted wryly the assortment of alternative theories the defense had argued. "The only thing that they have not suggested to you as to Chelsea's death is that she committed *suicide*."

Sutton's blunt speech lacked Rothe's seamless eloquence. But the DA from Junction was not trying to weave a narrative. Instead, he was taking advantage of having the last word, methodically taking up, then bludgeoning, each of Carnes's charges. Sutton reminded the jury that children who had received succinylcholine could look as if they were having seizures—either as the drug wore off or because they had received a small dose. "These extraneous offenses are certainly not to panic anyone," said Sutton, but to lay out the scheme that revealed Jones's "madness." If Carnes considered Jones's purported motive ridiculous, it was not the state's fault. "We didn't develop this motive. The defendant did." In defense of

Holland, Sutton said the doctor had relied "in good faith" on her nurse. "As with these kids, the faith was misplaced."

It was all familiar ground, and Sutton went through it one final time: the inquiries of the Sid Peterson hospital board, Holland's discovery of the tainted bottle, the confrontation with Genene, and the summons to the Texas Ranger that had led to sixteen months of investigation— and ultimately to this trial. Now, "it becomes your responsibility," Sutton told the jurors.

"You know, since I have been here in Georgetown, I have been very impressed with the beautiful lady that adorns the top of your courthouse. The statue of Justice is such a beautiful sight. . . . What more fitting symbol can you have on top of the courthouse, standing there with a sword, which represents justice being *swift* and *quick?*" Sutton paused to set up his point. "And *that* is what I think this case deserves, ladies and gentlemen."

Sutton's voice rose, as he brandished an empty hypodermic needle. "If Genene Jones should be allowed to walk out of this courtroom, acquitted on the basis of the testimony and the evidence you have before you, I would suggest that we go up here on the top of this courthouse and remove that sword from the statue of Justice and insert a *syringe!*" Now Sutton's voice grew soft as he stood next to the defendant and wagged his finger in her face. "Ladies and gentlemen, as we are here today in this most respected of rooms in any community, the hall of justice, I think if we will be real quiet for just a minute that we can hear the echo of the gates of *hell* slamming on Genene Jones's condemned soul for what she did to Chelsea McClellan." The nurse began to weep. "And I am sure," said the prosecutor, "that after due deliberations, you will reach the same conclusion."

The jury was out.

Thirty-One

"YOU MIGHT AS well just settle down and get a good book to read," Judge Carter told his court reporter after the jury filed out at 1:50 P.M. "We're going to be here for a while." Carter had never participated in a trial involving so much complex scientific evidence. He figured it would take the jury two or three days just to sort through it.

As the judge kicked back in his chambers, he soon heard the odd sound of chants outside his window. Carter went to check, and he discovered—to his astonishment—four or five women marching in a circle, picketing on the courthouse grounds. The women claimed that they were San Antonio mothers whose children Genene Jones had murdered. They carried signs demanding a conviction: HOW MANY MORE BABIES MUST DIE? and HOW MANY BABIES HAVE YOU KILLED, NURSE JONES? A crowd of TV cameras and the curious had already gathered to take in the sight. But it was their shouts that worried the judge. "We want justice!" they cried. "Justice for the people! Justice for the babies!" If the jurors heard the chants or saw the demonstration, it could offer grounds for a mistrial. Carter ordered the jury moved to a room on the opposite side of the courthouse. He dispatched sheriff's deputies to bar the women from coming inside and to ask them to chant quietly.

After grabbing a bite to eat, Ron Sutton killed time around the courthouse, chatting with spectators and giving interviews. Rothe and the rest of the prosecution

entourage returned to their command post at the Georgetown Inn, where reporters, court clerks, witnesses, and
assorted relatives of Chelsea McClellan drifted in and
out. Sam Millsap was there too, having driven up from
San Antonio for closing arguments. Bo Holmstedt had
already departed for Sweden, after a guided tour of the
Texas Ranger Museum in Waco. He left with a pair of
gifts: a white Stetson cowboy hat and a Texas-shaped belt
buckle that read "Dr. Bubba." A few people in the
prosecution conference room dipped into an ice chest for
a beer. But most had resolved to hold off until there was
something to celebrate.

The defendant awaited the verdict in a holding room at
the Williamson County jail. Despite her tears during
Sutton's summation, Genene had seemed buoyant lately,
grinning often as she chatted with her lawyers during
breaks. Jones's legal team had retired to Brookshire's
office in a far less sanguine mood. Aware that final
arguments had not gone well, the three weary lawyers
traded snippets of the macabre humor the trial had inspired. One joke suggested that the Texas prison system
had a good use for Genene's talents: giving the lethal
injection used to kill death row inmates. Another,
prompted by the extensive testimony about forms of seizures, proposed a new alcoholic beverage: the gin and
tonic-clonic. The defense lawyers favored whiskey themselves. They passed the time by sipping Jack Daniel's and
playing cards.

A little after 4:30 P.M., everyone in Brookshire's office
jumped with the jangle of the phone. Judge Carter was
calling for Carnes. The jury had been out less than three
hours. Surely it couldn't be . . .

It was not. Carter explained that the jurors had sent
out a note through the court bailiff. It seemed an item of
evidence was missing: Dr. Holland's medical record for
Chelsea's final visit on September 17. The jurors had last
seen it in Carnes's possession, when he read from the
document during final argument. The defense lawyer was
offended by the implication. Why, he knew better than
to take trial evidence out of the courtroom! But Carnes
checked anyway, and discovered to his chagrin that he
had accidentally placed the document among his court

papers, instead of returning it to the pile of trial exhibits.
After a brief conference in the judge's chambers, the
record was submitted to the jury at 5:15 P.M.

Forty-five minutes later, Brookshire's assistant fielded
a second call from the judge's chambers. Another note,
the lawyers figured. This time, they were wrong. The
jury had reached a verdict.

Jurors in a major trial must surrender themselves to
passivity and isolation. Twelve strangers must sit together
and listen silently in a courtroom for weeks, often barred
even from taking notes. The world is absorbed with what
they are witnessing, but they are barred from scanning
newspaper or television reports about the proceedings.
Until deliberations begin, they may not talk to anyone
about the case, even one another. Their daily comings
and goings, like the period of their servitude, are entirely
in the hands of others. It is an experience, particularly if
the trial is lengthy—and Genene Jones's case was now in
its fifth week—that tests the patience of even the saintly.
The attorneys for the defense had tried to select jurors
who, in the confines of such an environment, would tear
at each other's throats. A glimpse within Judge Carter's
jury room would have left them sorely disappointed.

From the very first day, the seven women and five men
sitting in judgment of Genene Jones got along as cozily
as a country church choir. Locked together for hours as
the attorneys battled over points of law outside their
presence, the jurors sipped coffee and tea and happily
engaged in small talk. The ladies brought in homemade
cookies and cakes. They chatted about their gardens and
joked about Ron Sutton's perpetually sagging suit pants.
One of the men solicited advice on flooring his barn.
Another arrived on Valentine's Day with a giant heart-
shaped box of candy for everyone to share. The smokers
within the group took pains not to annoy the others. And
everyone talked about children. Eleven were already parents, and the twelfth had quit her job because she planned
to have a baby.

After retiring for deliberations, the jurors elected Edwin Edwards, a fifty-four-year-old electrical engineer, as
foreman. Lawyers for both sides had considered him an
enigma. An even-tempered man who taught Bible classes

at his Baptist church on Sundays, Edwards wore a poker
face in the courtroom that made his sentiments inscrutable. But the engineer had made up his mind early. Familiar with the pain criminal acts could inflict—his first wife
had been killed by a drunk driver—Edwards had shed
any glimmer of doubt about Genene Jones's guilt.

After electing their foreman, the jurors broke for lunch
at the L&M Café in downtown Georgetown, in the pro-
tective custody of a bailiff. They returned to the jury
room about 3 P.M. and set about their task. Despite his
personal judgment, the newly elected jury foreman was
not the sort to browbeat others. From his seat at the
head of the table, Edwards began by passing around the
records and medical paraphernalia introduced as evidence.
One juror managed to impale his finger on an empty
syringe. Almost an hour was consumed in the quest for
the missing record in Carnes's possession. When the document arrived, Edwards went clockwise around the jury
table, asking each person to voice his sentiments.

One juror was convinced by Dr. Holmstedt's test. Another, the wife of a former serviceman who had been
wounded in Korea, made up her mind after hearing from
the army paramedics who had transported Jimmy Pearson. Just as the defense had feared, several jurors were
infuenced by Genene Jones's manner throughout the trial.
They had noticed her flippant air and the way she had
tried to stare down unfriendly witnesses. "She'd give
them the evil eye," remarked one juror. "She didn't have
the reactions an innocent person would have." As the
prosecution had hoped, most simply found the pattern of
emergencies overwhelming. It quickly became clear that
a solid majority favored conviction.

Two older women sat uncomfortably on the fence,
struggling with the notion that any mother could kill a
child. Ruth Armstrong, a sweet, grandmotherly lady of
sixty-six, was surprised to discover that so many others
had their minds made up already; she felt a bit overwhelmed by all the evidence that she had heard. Edwards
gently asked her to talk about her reservations. The
other jurors pitched in, explaining why they felt Jones
was guilty. The peer pressure worked its magic. "I guess
I began to think, 'What's the matter with me?' " Arm-

strong recalled later. "Everybody else thinks she's guilty beyond a reasonable doubt. I began to think, 'I guess *I* believe she's guilty.' " That left only Lillie Kipp, a fifty-three-year-old Wal-Mart store manager, who wrote on her jury form that the Bible was the last book she had read. Edwards led Kipp through every alternative explanation for Chelsea's death, dismissing each until they came to murder. "Lillie," he asked, "can you see any other possibility?" Pained by the task, Lillie Kipp was in tears. "I guess there's *no* other possibility," she said sadly.

Suddenly they were unanimous. They had been engaged in actual debate over guilt or innocence for less than an hour.

Edwards advised his flock that the defense might ask the jurors to state their verdict individually in the courtroom. They should rehearse that now, he said. "If you've never said it out loud, it might be too difficult for you." But first, he asked everyone to bow his or her head in silent prayer, advising, "You've got to make peace with yourself." Then, around the table, all twelve jurors, in the presence of their peers, pronounced Genene Jones guilty of murder.

"We have received a communication from the jury that they have reached a unanimous decision," Judge Carter announced from the bench when everyone had returned to the courtroom. Privately, the judge was shocked at the speed of the verdict. He figured emotion had carried the day.

"Before I bring in the jury, I want to inform everyone that there will be no demonstration upon receiving the verdict," declared Carter, intent on maintaining order until the end. "Sit quietly in your seats. There will be no bolting for the door. You will remain until you are dismissed, and there will be no demonstration from any person in the courtroom." Carter looked around to make sure his message was understood.

"All right, bring them in."

The jurors took their seats in the jury box at 6:10 P.M., four hours and twenty minutes after they had left. All twelve appeared somber. Ruth Armstrong and Lillie Kipp, the two brief holdouts, were crying.

"Mr. Foreman, has the jury reached a decision?"

Edwards rose. "Yes, we have, Your Honor."

"Hand it to the bailiff and pass it to me, please. Would the defendant please rise?"

Genene rose to her feet beside her attorneys.

Carter took the slip of paper from his bailiff and read: "The state of Texas versus Genene Jones in the 277th District Court of Williamson County, Texas. We, the jury, find the defendant, Genene Jones, *guilty* of murder. Signed, Edwin D. Edwards, foreman."

Genene slumped into her chair, began sobbing, and covered her face with a yellow handkerchief. After a few moments, Genene looked up through her tears at the jurors and glared at each of them. *The evil eye.*

Brookshire asked for a poll of the jurors. The clerk called the jurors by name—"Is this your verdict?" he asked—and each of them affirmed it was, just as each had done in the jury room.

Standing on either side of their client, Jim Brookshire and Burt Carnes supported Genene as she stumbled down the courthouse steps. A sheriff's car waited on the street to whisk Jones back to jail, but a heaving mob of press and onlookers blocked the way. As the lawyers elbowed through, the crowd encircled Jones and taunted her, screaming, *"Baby-killer!"* and *"You deserved it!"*

Inside the courthouse, the family of Chelsea McClellan stood at the center of a celebration. When the verdict was announced, Petti and Reid had embraced one another and wept. After court was adjourned, Sam Millsap shook hands with each member of the prosecution team and announced to the press: "Justice is done."

Under the rules of the Texas legal system, the jury would weigh punishment the next day, after hearing more evidence and arguments. Ron Sutton informed reporters that he would ask the jury to sentence Genene Jones to ninety-nine years in prison, the maximum possible under the law. But Reid McClellan told a newspaperman that he envisioned a more fitting punishment for the woman who had murdered his daughter: "I want her to have succinylcholine like Chelsea."

* * *

Those who would assess punishment spent the night in a Georgetown motel. Judge Carter had decided to sequester the jurors until they had agreed upon a sentence. Edwin Edwards, suddenly troubled about his role of imposing judgment on another human, rose from bed at midnight and went into the bathroom to avoid disturbing the court bailiff who was his roommate. There, perched on the lip of the bathtub, the jury foreman searched the hotel room Bible for guidance. He found comfort in the Book of Exodus, where Moses heeded the advice of his father-in-law, Jethro:

> . . . *provide out of all the people able men, such as fear God, men of truth, hating covetousness;*
> *And place such over them, to be rulers of thousands, and rulers of hundreds, rulers of fifties, and rulers of tens:*
> *And let them judge the people at all seasons. . . .*
> *If thou shalt do this thing, and God command thee so, then thou shalt be able to endure, and all this people shall also go to their place in peace.*

After three hours of reading and meditation in the bathroom, Edwards went to bed and slept soundly.

Intending to ask for probation, Genene's attorneys needed to prove her eligible by offering testimony that she had never been convicted of a felony. A relative usually performed that task, but members of Genene's family had been conspicuously absent throughout her trial. Gladys Jones had made only one brief appearance in the courtroom. Although she continued to care for Crystal, Gladys had virtually terminated communication with Genene by the time the trial ended. Angry about calls to her unlisted home number from members of the Christian group ministering to Genene, Gladys, on the day of her daughter's conviction, had sent Genene a curt postcard, absent salutation or signature. It read, in full:

> Maybe I didn't make myself clear about my telephone # so I'll write it down. I do not want this # given to anyone, church member or not and if I have

more calls, I'll have it changed again and will not give
it to anyone. This is a private, unpublished restricted
+ I intend to keep it that way.

The absence of a suitable character witness forced the
defense to put Genene on the stand to testify that her
record was clean. After the judge granted a defense
motion severely limiting cross-examination, the defendant
was summoned. Genene came forward stiffly, appearing
numb with shock from the verdict. She wore a blue dress
with white pinstripes. Her eyes, covered with blue-green
makeup, were visibly puffy from crying. A gold cross
hung from a chain around her neck. In a voice barely
above a whisper, Genene answered four routine questions from Brookshire. Sutton declined to ask anything,
and the defendant sat down after less than a minute.
There were no other witnesses.

In his closing argument, Carnes issued a plea for mercy.
He told the jurors that Genene had "no true intention to
kill Chelsea McClellan." The child's death was an accident, he suggested, caused by her unusual susceptibility
to succinylcholine. Once again, the defense asked the
jurors to consider allocating a share of the blame to
Kathy Holland, "who is practicing medicine today," he
noted, "and will go home and practice medicine tomorrow." Carnes begged the jury to display compassion, not
vengeance. "It is easy sometimes to forget that you are
dealing with a human being," he said softly. "I have
learned on this side of the bar that everybody is truly
human. I don't want you to go back and think of Genene
Jones as some object. I want you to think of her as a
person, a mother, a daughter. She has feelings. She feels
sorrow. She feels joy, just like all of us."

"Where was the mercy for Chelsea McClellan?" thun-
dered Sutton, when his turn before the jury came. "This
was no accident," he said, but a calculated murder, carried out for self-gratification. He asked the jurors to
"provide society with a paid-up policy of insurance to
prevent this defendant from committing these types of
atrocious acts in the future." Only the harshest possible
sentence would end succinylcholine's reputation as the
perfect murder weapon, declared the prosecutor. Only

the harshest sentence would deter others. Only the harshest sentence would be just.

"Let's compare Chelsea's fate to the defendant's," suggested Sutton. "The defendant sits here alive today. Mr. Carnes said a while ago that this defendant has feelings. This defendant suffers sorrow and joy. What about this little girl?" Sutton held aloft the photograph of Chelsea. The jurors looked away; several pulled out handkerchiefs. "You think today she has any feelings—any joy, any sorrow? No, not poor Chelsea. Today Chelsea is confined to a small little crypt—a dark, cold, lonesome crypt." Sutton paused to let the jurors conjure up the image. "For how long? For *eternity!* For eternity, ladies and gentlemen—not five years, not twenty years, not fifty years, not seventy-five years, or ninety-nine. But for *eternity.*"

Sutton pointed his finger at the defendant. "She shed no tears for Chelsea, but only for herself. *We* should shed a tear for Chelsea—and tell those others around the world that no longer, because of what happened today in Georgetown, Texas, will anyone pick up a syringe and attack little children."

At 11:30 A.M. on February 16, seven women and five men gathered for their final duty in a jury room at the Williamson County courthouse. "We've all found she's guilty," Edwards noted. "Now we have to decide: What should happen to someone who murders a baby?" With the stage set thus, there was little opening to argue for mercy. But there was little inclination to do so anyway. Almost all the jurors had noticed how Jones had glared at them after the verdict.

William McCauley, a six-foot-four-inch, 220-pound former marine, broke into tears as he argued for the maximum sentence of ninety-nine years. Ruth Armstrong and Lillie Kipp, once again, were hesitant. "Doesn't that seem like an awful lot?" one of them asked. "Yes," responded another juror. "But it's not as much as a thousand." The jury foreman, among the majority who could not imagine too harsh a punishment, pitched in. "Do you want her to walk on the sidewalk with your daughter?'' Edwards asked. The two women quickly came around.

The jury returned to the courtroom at 12:40 P.M.—only seventy minutes after departing for deliberations. In contrast to the day before, the defendant appeared composed as Judge Carter announced the sentence. Her lawyers had advised her the night before that she was likely to get the maximum. But as she sat down in her chair, Genene Jones began shaking.

In accordance with the judge's suggestion, the jurors met briefly in the jury room with attorneys for both sides before returning to the outside world. Jim Brookshire and Burt Carnes had hoped these twelve people would heed their pleas to blame Kathy Holland—the doctor in charge—for what had happened and thus excuse their client. Now, chatting with the jurors, the defense attorneys wondered if any among the twelve had taken what they'd said to heart. Finally, the members of the panel were free to go. As the jurors walked out of the room, Petti and Reid McClellan embraced each and offered thanks. The microbiologist, Ann Bradley, was the last to step outside. She hugged Chelsea's mother, then told her: "There wasn't any doubt. She won't be able to do it again."

At the Georgetown Inn, a party was in full swing. Between glasses of Scotch, Sutton and Rothe took turns telling war stories about the past five weeks of combat. Sam Millsap slapped everyone on the back. Sutton's legal assistant enlisted visitors to snap happy pictures of the winning team. They took photos of the DA's staff, the investigators, the witnesses, and the lawmen. Even the regulars among the reporters were invited to pose. Petti and Reid were there, along with Petti's sister and Reid's parents.

After an hour, liquor and fatigue had mellowed the mood to one of quiet satisfaction. A Kerr County sheriff's deputy, who had spent the trial ferrying witnesses back and forth, pulled out his guitar and began crooning a ballad he and Sutton had written about Genene Jones, titled "The IV Blues," which they sang to the music of an

old country-and-western song by Jimmie Rodgers called
"In the Jailhouse Now."

> *Well, I knew a nurse named Genene;*
> *She was bad, ugly, and mean.*
> *She had the fastest IV in town.*
> *She took it out each day,*
> *Just so she could play.*
> *She liked to knock those little babies down.*
>
> *She's in the jailhouse now.*
> *She's in the jailhouse now.*
> *She'll never do it again;*
> *Sutton's sent her off to the pen.*
> *She's in the jailhouse now.*

Thirty-Two

ONE WEEK AFTER a jury pronounced Genene Jones a murderer, B. H. Corum, whose San Antonio hospital had employed and sheltered her, tendered his resignation. Everyone involved insisted that Corum's departure had nothing to do with the continuing investigation of the pediatric ICU at Medical Center Hospital. But the event that toppled the executive director of the Bexar County Hospital District was so trivial that few could doubt the baby-deaths scandal was truly his undoing.

The incident was an example of Corum's tendency to regard the hospital as his personal fiefdom and its employees as his vassals. It began when his wife asked him to obtain a refill of her prescription for Phenergan, a non-narcotic drug used to combat nausea. Like all the institution's employees, Corum was allowed to have his personal prescriptions filled at the hospital pharmacy. But instead of presenting his wife's prescription to anyone, Corum phoned the director of hospital supplies and arranged for two bottles of Phenergan to be brought to him directly from the drug stockroom. For months after the incident, nothing happened. Then a stockroom employee, bitter about his harsh treatment by the supplies director, tipped off a superior.

Shortly after being hired, Corum had issued a memo reminding subordinates of hospital regulations on theft. Theft of "any monies or drugs" worth more than $20, it noted, constituted a "Group A" offense, punishable by dismissal. Corum's misdeed put him $12 over the limit; the two bottles of Phenergan were worth $32. In an emergency session, the hospital board decided to suspend the administrator for three days, pending further investigation. Three days later, Corum resigned his post. Those who wondered why the combative retired colonel would leave without a fight could look to the generous terms of his departure. Although his employment contract contained a clause that voided severance compensation for conduct deemed "malfeasance or misfeasance," Corum, after submitting his resignation, was awarded a full 120 days separation pay—twenty-five thousand dollars.

That did not stop hospital board chairman Thornton from declaring the episode an example of the institution's refusal to brook misconduct. "We hold most sacred the policy that states there will be no violations regarding medications tolerated," Thornton told the press. Bexar County DA Sam Millsap was amused to see the institution that had tolerated Genene Jones sounding so sanctimonious about a minor offense. He considered it a convenient excuse to get rid of Corum. "Thornton is a politician," Millsap said later. "He understands there are times when you have to do things to change appearances. If you've got somebody real beat up, you need to replace him with somebody who's not beat up."

Corum's unbattered replacement—appointed on an interim basis—was associate executive director John Andrew Guest. Only thirty-five, Guest already had worked at the county hospital for a decade. He had begun as an administrative resident, setting prices for the hospital cafeteria, and climbed steadily through the ranks. Guest advanced on his dedication, loyalty, and methodical attention to detail. A bearded, solidly built man from the Gulf Coast town of Galveston, Guest was a slice of American white bread—honest, earnest, and likable. But he also possessed the faults of a career bureaucrat; superiors found him unimaginative and slow to make decisions.

Since the first sign of trouble, Corum had punted to Guest the ugly chore of monitoring the pediatric ICU. While Corum occasionally had cut him out of meetings, Guest was intimately familiar with the allegations about

Genene Jones. Characteristically, he had taken no independent action to deal with the problem, even though his duties included day-to-day management of Medical Center Hospital. Guest also had served on Dr. McFee's Pediatric ICU Committee, the group that established the strategy of "judicious silence." When the criminal investigation in San Antonio began, Corum handed Guest the task of dealing with members of the DA's staff as well. He handled their endless requests for information without rancor or delay. Millsap and Nick Rothe had quickly come to dislike the abrasive Corum. Guest also knew plenty about what had happened, but his subordinate position and cordial manner made the prosecutors view him far less critically.

Nonetheless, suspicions remained high between the district attorney and his prey. With the Kerrville case closed (Sutton had announced plans to drop the remaining charges), attention once again focused on whether Millsap would seek new indictments—against Jones, the hospital and the medical school, or the individuals who ran them. Culpability was a theme of the report on the case by the ABC newsmagazine *20/20*, filmed weeks before Jones's trial in Georgetown but broadcast after the verdict. The piece traced the suspicions that had surrounded Jones at Medical Center Hospital, and included film of a Kerrville doctor blaming his counterparts in San Antonio for failing to warn anyone about her. Following the filmed report, host Hugh Downs pronounced the story perhaps "the most sinister situation we've ever reported on."

Hostilities flared in March, when DA's investigator Art Brogley discovered that Medical Center Hospital had recently ordered more than four tons of pharmacy records shredded. Claiming that the destroyed documents related to his investigation, Millsap said he was "shocked and angry" and threatened criminal charges. Overexcited by the controversy, one San Antonio paper even published a front-page profile of the junkmen who had shredded the records. But hospital officials insisted that nothing sinister had taken place—that they retained duplicates of everything important and that disposal of the papers was a routine bit of housecleaning. Still in the flush of suspi-

cion, Millsap then fielded a tip that the medical school
had sent twenty-five tons of records for shredding. After
obtaining a court order to bar their destruction, Millsap
dispatched investigators to impound the papers at a San
Antonio recycling center. A TV reporter who arrived
first decided to help himself to several documents; confronted later by Brogley, he sheepishly coughed them up.
After sifting through the records for days, Millsap's staff
discovered that nothing of significance had been lost—
except their time.

After more than a year on the case, Sam Millsap was
losing his fervor for waging war on the hospital district
and the medical school. Although appeals courts had yet
to rule on whether it was legal under Texas statutes to
charge such institutions with a crime, Nick Rothe had
been telling his boss for months that he couldn't make
indictments stick. Besides, is wasn't the *institutions* that
were evil, just some of the people that ran them. The
DA decided to limit his targets. Millsap contacted the
U.S. Attorney's office and provided its agents with a
briefing and documentation on the case. He would leave
it to the feds—with their power to cut grants, impose
fines, and investigate civil rights violations—to take on
the institutions. Millsap would set his own sights on individuals—on Genene Jones, in hope of producing an indictment for murder, and on those who supervised her,
for tolerating her misdeeds and covering them up.

Jones's trial on the one Bexar County charge that was
pending—for injury to a child in the heparin-induced
bleeding of Rolando Santos—would not begin until fall.
In late March, Nick Rothe resigned his post as deputy
DA and returned to private practice. Rothe, however,
retained responsibility for the investigation and trial
through a part-time appointment as special prosecutor.
His departure left one attorney and two investigators,
including Art Brogley, working full time on the case.

Charging Jones with murder was virtually a prerequi-
site to seeking indictments in the cover-up. If the nurse
hadn't obviously killed a child, how could they hope to
prosecute anyone for failing to stop her? For the next six
months, the investigators concentrated on the best pros-

pects they had, a handful of Jones's patients who had died unexpectedly in the ICU. Several had undergone autopsies; where the pathologist had removed and preserved body organs, the investigators sent tissue to toxicologists to test for the presence of improper drugs. The investigators were hoping for the sort of evidence that had convicted Genene Jones once—evidence that would provide more than a purely circumstantial case. But their task in San Antonio was far more complex. The kids at Medical Center Hospital had developed a baffling array of problems: seizures, bleeding, limpness, sudden urine output, breathing trouble, and irregular heartbeat. This meant the toxicologists had to test for an assortment of different drugs: Dilantin, Valium, potassium, heparin, and succinylcholine were just some of the suspects.

July brought a potential breakthrough, when Dr. Holmstedt's collaborator, Fredric Rieders, reported finding signs of succinylcholine in the brain tissue of two children. The problem was that the evidence was tentative, too weak to stand up in court. To confirm the results, the toxicologist would need tissue from the internal organs of the children. Millsap decided to order exhumation of the bodies, buried two and a half years earlier.

The early-morning gathering on August 7 represented a macabre reunion. Among the group were Nick Rothe, Art Brogley, Fredric Rieders, and Vincent DiMaio—all participants in the exhumation of Chelsea McClellan fifteen months earlier. But this setting was different: San Fernando Cemetery Number Two, the final resting ground for the families of San Antonio's Catholic West Side barrio. All around were the graves of dirt-poor Mexican-Americans who had died young—victims of stabbings, or tuberculosis, or childhood diseases for which they had never received inoculations. And this time, the bodies that were dug up bore no resemblance to china dolls. Each had rotted down to the skeleton; the flesh had turned to dust. Rieders returned to his lab in Pennsylvania empty-handed.

Unwilling to rely on the criminal-justice system, some parents of children who had died in the pediatric ICU were seeking their own form of redress. On August 16, survivors of thirteen children filed wrongful-death suits against Medical Center Hospital. All were represented by the brothers William and Tom Stolhandske.

Tom was a former All-American end for the University of Texas. He had been the most valuable player in the 1953 Hula Bowl, and went on to play four years of professional football. During more than two decades in San Antonio, both Stolhandskes had become actively involved in Democratic courthouse politics. Tom had recently left his elected post as a Bexar County commissioner. After learning early about the investigation, the Stolhandskes fed tidbits to eager reporters, shrewdly positioning themselves publicly as the lawyers for parents to call. All told, the Stolhandskes eventually would file eighteen lawsuits against Medical Center Hospital, each alleging that a child had died wrongfully in the pediatric ICU. Most of the babies were among those whom investigators suspected Genene Jones had harmed—including Chris Hogeda, whose parents had finally turned on the nurse. But the child of one set of plaintiffs had never been treated by Jones; another had never entered the ICU at all.

Some parents raised questions about whether it was merely publicity that had attracted so many Jones-related clients to the Stolhandskes. On August 20, 1984, Art Brogley interviewed Esperanza Zavala, the mother of Patrick, at her home. Following the conversation, Brogley detailed part of the conversation in his investigative log, a running diary he had kept since being assigned to the case:

On Wednesday, August 15, '84, a representative of the Stolhandske law firm contacted Mrs. Zavala at her residence and brought her and the Villarreals to the firm's office by vehicle. . . . [Lauro and Juanita Villarreal were the parents of three-month-old Paul, who had died in the ICU in September 1981 after elective surgery on his skull.]

Stolhandske [the log did not state which one] and [another attorney with the firm] conducted joint interview with Mrs. Zavala and the Villarreals.

Mrs. Zavala learned the firm had tried to contact

her earlier, on Tuesday, August 14, through her mother and at her residence.

Mrs. Zavala did not initiate contact with [the] Stolhandske firm or any other law firm regarding possible civil suit.

Mrs. Zavala and the Villarreals were told that the firm was in possession of their sons' medical records. Further, that the records revealed both children had been administered large doses of medications. Mrs. Zavala interpreted this remark to suggest the children may have died as a result of physicians' malpractice.

The parents were told the firm was "looking at 21 cases."

The parents were also told that the law firm would bring suit first against the UTHSC [the medical school]. The monetary recovery, according to Stolhandske and [the other attorney] would be a "total split" among all the families named as plaintiffs. The attorneys stated "each might receive 30–35 thousand dollars." They indicated the suit against the UTHSC should be resolved in about six months.

Afterwards, the law firm would bring suit against the MCH [Medical Center Hospital]. . . .

Mrs. Zavala agreed to sign "some papers" presented to her by the law firm. She was aware only that she agreed to become one of the firm's plaintiffs in the suits against the UTHSC and the MCH. Mr. Villarreal also signed an agreement . . .

In fact, things would go almost exactly as Mrs. Zavala was told. In exchange for a quick—and relatively cheap—out-of-court settlement, the Stolhandskes excluded the UT medical school from almost all their litigation. The suits against the hospital would linger for more than three years without ever coming to trial. In fact, there was little sign that the Stolhandskes ever planned to try the cases. They initiated few deposition or discovery requests, and at one point, most of the suits were slated for dismissal for lack of activity. But the number of cases allowed the Stolhandskes to bargain wholesale with the hospital. In early 1988, they reached an out-of-court settlement covering all the remaining lawsuits. The Stolhandskes apportioned the settlement money themselves among their clients (a practice that would make many plaintiff's atorneys uncomfortable), pocketed 50 percent plus expenses (an unusually high percentage for a case that never went to trial), and dismissed the litigation.

Bill Stolhandske said the 50 percent take for his firm was not unusual for such a complicated matter. And he denied any suggestion that his firm had improperly solicited business. He said no one representing his firm had approached any prospective client without invitation. In several cases, Stolhandske said, the firm received calls from relatives—aunts, uncles, and cousins—of children who had died in the ICU; those relatives, he explained, invited the lawyers to contact the parents of the deceased children.

A set of parents who retained another San Antonio attorney struggled to make it even to the courthouse. The parents of Terry Lynn Garcia, who had died in August 1981 after bleeding on the 3—11 shift in the pediatric ICU, gave their attorney a release so he could obtain a copy of their daughter's medical records. When several weeks passed without any action, the parents fired the lawyer. A citizen later called the DA's office to report finding Terry Lynn Garcia's medical records in a garbage bin. The parents subsequently decided to retain the Stolhandskes.

With the much-publicized failure of the exhumations, the San Antonio papers were openly wondering whether the DA would ever produce results to match his rhetoric. Assigning its political reporter to weigh the scales, the *Light* reported that the baby-deaths investigation had taken "a heavy toll on San Antonio—emotionally, financially, and in the delicate balance of public trust." Parents of children who died were suffering "the agony of uncertainty," while the public hospital was forced to operate "under the cloud of the most loathsome suspicions." After nineteen months, the paper concluded, "the toll the case has taken on the community far exceeds the legal actions that have been chalked up by District Attorney Sam Millsap and his staff."

But the quest for new indictments remained frustrating. In a half dozen cases, the DA's staff was agonizingly close to meeting the burden for a charge of murder. Each case seemed just one piece of evidence short: Lab results documenting an apparent overdose had disappeared; Jones was signed out to lunch at the time a child had died suspiciously; the memory of an important witness failed.

Irksome, too, was the knowledge that those who had tolerated Jones's actions—even defended and protected her—had gone unpunished. In February, Millsap and Rothe had briefed hospital board chairman Thornton and Guest on the evidence concerning Rolando Santos's heparin overdoses that nursing supervisors had virtually ignored. Thornton promised an internal investigation, and, indeed, one had begun. But when summer arrived, the internal hospital probe—like so many before it—was dragging on, with no result in sight.

One night, Nick Rothe went out for a beer with John Guest, a man he had come to like and trust. Rothe told the administrator there was no doubt that Genene Jones had murdered babies in his hospital. But Jones wasn't the only one who bore a measure of the responsibility. Rothe talked about the failure of the nursing hierarchy, from ICU head nurse Pat Belko to pediatrics supervisor Judy Harris to hospital nursing administrator Virginia Mousseau. "There is a possibility for this to happen again," declared Rothe, "because certain individuals remain in *positions* where this could happen again."

Guest looked puzzled. What did Rothe expect from him?

"John," said the lawyer, "there comes a time in a man's life when a man's gotta do what a man's gotta do."

In mid-August, Rothe flew to the Mexican resort of Cozumel for a long-overdue vacation. When he arrived at El Presidente Hotel on the balmy island, he discovered an urgent telephone message waiting for him in his room. It was from Millsap. After several unsuccessful attempts, Rothe finally reached the district attorney back in San Antonio.

"Nick, I don't know what this means," said Millsap, over the crackly long-distance line, "but Mousseau, Belko, and Harris resigned for personal reasons today." Rothe broke into a smile. "And there's a message for you from John Guest. It says: " 'A man's gotta do what a man's gotta do.' "

One month before Genene Jones's San Antonio trial was to begin, hospital board chairman Thornton gave the DA a call. After a year of painful public head-butting, Thornton had begun working to win Millsap's favor, consulting with the DA before making any major move at the hospital. Now Thornton asked about John Guest. Had the DA uncovered anything to suggest he was unfit for permanent appointment? Pleased with the recent purge of the nursing administrators, Millsap informed the board chairman that John Guest, the lone survivor at the top of the hospital hierarchy, had his blessing. On September 25, the board named Guest executive director of the Bexar County Hospital District, at a salary of $85,000 a year.

The second trial of Genene Jones, on a charge of injecting a baby with the blood-thinning drug heparin, began on October 15 and was to last but ten days. The defendant, believing that an emotional jury had convicted her in Georgetown, decided to let a judge decide her fate this time. Presiding was Bexar County district judge Pat Priest, respected widely for his fairness. Two court-appointed San Antonio lawyers, Royal Griffin and David Weiner, represented Genene Jones. Nick Rothe and assistant DA Raymond Fuchs served the state.

For reporters who had covered the proceedings in Georgetown, this trial seemed anticlimactic. But the citizens of San Antonio felt differently. After two years of headlines, the spectacle of the killer nurse—in the flesh! —drew overflow crowds. Afraid that someone would seek simpler justice, the judge ordered extra guards and insisted that spectators pass through a metal detector before entering the courtroom.

To those who had known Genene Jones at Medical Center Hospital, the evidence was familiar. Doctors and nurses testified that babies got sick when Genene was on duty, recovered when she was away, and got worse when she came back. Nurse Suzanna Maldonado described her diary of death, showing how many children had expired on the shift the LVN had worked. Maldonado recalled the death threat she had received after her complaint to Belko. Larry Hooghuis, the former pediatrics resident, testified that his patients went downhill when he was getting along badly with Genene. Hooghuis recounted the incident in which he had caught Jones about to inject Albert Garza with 333 times the proper amount of heparin; he testified that he had demonstrated the proper dosage to Jones by drawing the calculation on a bed sheet.

But the most damning piece of background testimony—for both the defendant and Medical Center Hospital—came from Dr. Gregory Istre, the Centers for Disease Control epidemiologist who had studied the pediatric ICU at Millsap's request. Introduced over defense objections, Istre's report validated every suspicion that Genene's critics in the ICU had reported to their superiors; it also refuted every excuse Jones's allies had offered in her defense. From 1980 to 1981, Istre testified, the pediatric ICU's death rate soared 178 percent. But the expert focused on what he labeled the "epidemic period"—the fifteen months from April 1981 through June 1982. During that period, forty-two children had died in the ICU. Thirty-four—81 percent—died between 3 P.M. and 11 P.M.

In studying the association between individuals and medical disaster, Istre identified nurses by numbers to avoid bias. The epidemiologist spoke dryly of statistics and probabilities, but the pattern he detailed was chilling. The strongest link, he testified, involved nurse no. 32. During the epidemic period in the ICU, nurse 32 had direct care of half the children who had died. On a shift nurse 32 worked, the doctor testified, a child was *ten* times more likely to die. During the same period, the link between the nurse and the growing number of sudden emergencies was even more dramatic. On a shift nurse 32 worked, a child was *twenty-five* times as likely to suffer an arrest.

What of the argument that the ICU was experiencing

more deaths and emergencies because it simply was getting sicker patients? Not true, said Istre. Study of medical charts showed that the children admitted during the "epidemic period" were no sicker than those treated in previous months. Genene Jones once claimed it was well known that patients died in the greatest numbers on the 3–11 shift. In studying other ICUs at the hospital—and the pediatric ICU before the "epidemic period" began— the epidemiologist found no such pattern. Istre also rejected the notion that more children died on nurse 32 because she cared for the sickest patients. Forty-three percent of her patients who died had a fair or good prognosis on admission. Other nurses lost only 19 percent of children admitted with such prospects.

"Would you tell the court who nurse 32 is?" asked prosecutor Ray Fuchs, at the end of Istre's second day on the witness stand.

The epidemiologist studied a sheet of paper, as though he wasn't sure, then looked up. "Genene Jones," he said.

The pattern had been repeated in Rolando Santos's brush with death during January 1982. Nurses testified that the four-month-old baby, admitted for pneumonia, was stable and improving before Jones came on duty. On four different days after Genene arrived, Rolando suffered emergencies, going twice into cardiac arrest. Kenneth Copeland, the attending UT pediatrician, vividly described the baby's uncontrollable bleeding. Dr. Copeland recalled discontinuing Rolando's heparin entirely after the lab reported that the baby had received an overdose. Yet during the 3–11 shift three days later, Rolando began pouring out blood again. Copeland told the judge that the baby was about to die when he injected him with protamine, the heparin antidote, and the bleeding suddenly stopped. A prosecution medical expert testified that a therapeutic dose of heparin for such a baby would be about 125 units. The expert estimated that Rolando, who was supposed to be getting *no* heparin, had received a minimum of 15,886 units.

Like Ron Sutton, Nick Rothe believed in ending his case with a surprise. His final witness was Kathy Ann Engelke, a twenty-year-old woman who held jobs at a

local supermarket and at a Dairy Queen. Earlier that
month, Engelke had spent a night in the Bexar County
jail, after being arrested for drunk driving. The following
morning, a woman she later learned was Genene Jones
was brought by the holding cell where Engelke was
confined.

"While you were in that cell," asked prosecutor Ray
Fuchs, "did you have a conversation with the defendant,
Genene Jones?"

"Yes, sir," said Engelke.

"How did that conversation begin?"

"She asked me what I was doing in there and I said,
'DWI.' And I asked her what she was in there for, and
she said, 'I'm Genene Jones, the nurse that killed the
babies.'"

Once again, Genene Jones declined to take the stand
in her own defense. In fact, the defense did not call a
single witness before resting its case on October 24. In a
passionate final argument, Nick Rothe noted that the
CDC epidemiologist had spoken of the "epidemic" in the
pediatric ICU, as though the deaths were caused by a
single disease. "There *is* a disease, and that disease is
sitting right there!" shouted Rothe, pointing at the defendant. "Genene Jones! Nurse no. 32!"

Judge Priest did not waste a moment before pronounc-
ing the nurse guilty. He immediately sentenced Genene
Jones to sixty years in prison.

Like their predecessors in Georgetown, Genene's San
Antonio attorneys announced their intention to file an
appeal.

In the week after the first conviction of Genene Jones,
B. H. Corum had resigned. In the week after the nurse's
second conviction, it was Marvin Dunn's turn. The dean
announced that he was leaving not only the UT medical
school but academic medicine and Texas as well. Dunn
was moving to California to become an executive with a
large hospital chain based in Beverly Hills.

On November 9, over lunch at an elegant downtown
club, Sam Millsap informed William Thornton and John
Guest that he would resolve whether to seek more indictments before New Year's Day. Aware that the time for

final judgment was at hand, assistant district attorney Joe Galenski, who had labored on the baby-deaths task force from the start, resolved to leave no doubt about his sentiments. On December 17, Galenski sent a memo to his superiors, Sam Millsap and Nick Rothe.

Based upon the Grand Jury investigation and the documents received during the two year investigation of Genene Jones and the Bexar County Hospital, I make these recommendations:

A. The following high managerial agents of the Bexar County Hospital be indicted under 7.23(b) Texas Penal Code for the omission of their duty to prevent the injury of a child namely: Rolando Santos while he was a patient in the PICU.

1. B. H. Corum
2. John Guest
3. Virginia Mousseau
4. Judy Harris
5. Pat Belko

B. I recommend that the following individuals be indicted as parties to the above offense.

1. Marvin Dunn
2. Robert Franks

C. I also recommend that the Bexar County Hospital as a corporation/association be indicted under 7.22(b)(2) for the actions of the following high managerial agents recklessly tolerating the injury of a child namely: Rolando Santos while he was a patient in the PICU.

1. B. H. Corum
2. John Guest
3. Virginia Mousseau
4. Judy Harris
5. Pat Belko

But Millsap already had made up his mind. He had accepted Rothe's advice that an indictment against the hospital, while certain to damage an important institution, offered little promise of reward. As for charges against individual administrators, they also would be difficult to sustain in court. Besides, Millsap reasoned, those he considered the worst culprits in the cover-up were already gone. At least partly because of his probe, B. H. Corum, Marvin Dunn, Pat Belko, Judy Harris, and Virginia Mousseau had all resigned.

On December 21, 1984, Millsap summoned the press to announce that the most expensive medical investigation in Texas history was over, after almost two years of work and one criminal indictment. Reading from a prepared statement, Millsap said he had worked from the start to resolve two major issues. First, had children in the pediatric ICU been intentionally harmed? Second, what had hospital and medical school officials known— and what had they done about it?

Genene Jones's San Antonio trial had answered the first question. Because of her conviction in Georgetown, Millsap said, "no useful purpose would be served by prosecuting additional charges against her." Results in the second area were less concrete. "Although objectionable for moral, ethical, and professional reasons, the behavior of hospital district and medical school officials violated no state penal statute. Accordingly, there will be no additional state prosecutions."

But this did not end the matter, insisted Millsap, anxious to avoid the impression that his much-publicized investigation of the cover-up had come to naught. The DA revealed that he had turned over evidence to the U.S. Attorney's office for contemplation of federal criminal charges. He announced that he would also file formal complaints with state licensing authorities against five people—Dunn, Corum, Belko, Harris, and Mousseau— for their inaction in the face of Jones's criminal behavior. Said Millsap: "We will vigorously argue before the appropriate licensing agencies that each of these individuals should be denied the right to practice their professions in the future." The DA added a word of praise for eight others: Suzanna Maldonado, Pat Alberti, and Eva Diaz, three nurses who had challenged Jones's actions; Kent Trinkle and Howard Radwin, the surgeons whose angry complaints had forced the Conn investigation; Dr. Ken Copeland, who had saved Rolando Santos; and former pediatric residents Cheryl Cipriani and Marisol Montes, who had volunteered information to the DA early.

"This investigation has been long, hard, and very productive," concluded Millsap. "The focus now shifts for final resolution to other forums, specifically the Justice Department and state licensing agencies. We pledge our full cooperation toward the final goal of producing full and complete justice for all concerned."

Art Brogley, the gumshoe who had spent the past two years tracking the misdeeds of Genene Jones and those who employed her, was bitter about the decision to bring the investigation to an end. Brogley had been unimpressed with the departure of Belko, Harris, and Mousseau. He figured the hospital was cutting its losses; he suspected his bosses had cut a deal. But what angered Brogley most of all was the failure to charge Genene Jones with murder for what she had done in the pediatric ICU.

Brogley's efforts had ultimately narrowed to two potential cases for indictment. The first concerned Joshua Sawyer, the smoke-inhalation victim who had displayed signs of improvement, then arrested twice and died in the presence of Genene Jones. Lab reports Brogley had discovered showed his blood contained a toxic level of Dilantin. The second was Patrick Zavala, whose postoperative death had set off the complaints of the surgeons.

Brogley had heard Nick Rothe explain over and over that they lacked enough evidence in either case—that they might win a conviction on emotion, but it would never stand on appeal. He had heard the arguments that even two more murder convictions would not affect how long Jones remained in prison. But to Brogley, that didn't matter. The investigator had spent months immersed in the brief lives of these children—and more than a dozen like them. Born to the indigent and powerless, the poor dumb slobs that gnawed at Brogley's bleeding heart, these kids were truly victims.

As Millsap's decision to pull the plug loomed, one afternoon Brogley had stormed into Rothe's office in a rage. If they didn't have enough evidence, the investigator preached, they should keep at it until they did. If it had been the mayor's daughter, perhaps a police captain's son—someone who could bring pressure—wouldn't they pursue it to the bitter end? It was all politics, railed

Brogley. They had no right to give up; Genene Jones had *murdered* these kids.

Nick Rothe nodded his head. "You and I know she murdered these kids," he said quietly. "But there's nothing anybody can do about it now."

Thirty-Three

EVEN AFTER RECEIVING judgment, Genene Jones reveled in the spotlight. In the days following her trial in Georgetown, she chatted happily to reporters for hours about the very events that she had been unwilling to discuss in court. A succession of media visitors found her in fine spirits; just days after collapsing in tears upon her conviction, she was mugging for photographers. "I'm not afraid of jail, because I'm innocent," Genene declared. "If I had to spend ninety-nine years in solitary, I could live with myself because I didn't do anything." Speaking from her jail cell, Genene griped that the Georgetown jury had fallen for a "snow job." Chelsea was a very sick baby, she explained. "You have to ask the Lord why she died." Genene professed her affection for the child she had been convicted of murdering. When Chelsea died, Genene said, "I cried for over a week." In one interview, the nurse even attacked Petti McClellan, calling her tearful court testimony "so obvious an act that it was an insult to Chelsea."

Always eager to surprise, Genene announced that she was engaged. She said she would marry Ronnie Rudd, the convicted auto thief with whom she had developed a romance in the Williamson County jail. But in a shrieking front-page headline—MASS KILLER CLAIMS "KILLER NURSE" LOVE—the San Antonio *News* suggested a different paramour: Henry Lee Lucas, the one-eyed drifter who professed to have raped and murdered more than one hundred women. The story attributed its mind-boggling report to an unidentified "lawman," who claimed Lucas had fallen in love with Jones and "wanted" her—"just like he wanted the others." Genene had already vented her unhappiness about even sharing the jail with Henry Lee. "There is one great difference between the two of us," she complained. "One, I am innocent. Two, he is guilty. I don't like being classified with the man. It's like good and evil."

Genene had spent much of her time behind bars working on a book about her ordeal, even preparing a list of prospective publishers in New York City. She abandoned the project after her conviction, having learned that Texas law barred convicted felons from reaping profit from books or films about their misdeeds.

But Genene continued writing her own account of her story in a revealing series of letters to Keith Martin, her friend from her years as a beautician. The two had resumed contact after Genene's indictment for Chelsea's murder, despite her deposition statements that Martin was the father of her daughter—and that he had later died in an automobile accident. Genene blamed her declaration that Martin was dead on a simple misunderstanding. The question of Crystal's paternity became a major subject of their correspondence.

In Kerrville, Genene had told Kathy Holland that her first husband, Jim DeLany, had fathered Crystal during a brief reconciliation after their divorce. She said she had named Martin as the father because her mother hated DeLany. Nonetheless, Genene sought, in these new letters, to persuade her gay friend that he was Crystal's father. Anticipating Martin's logical response—that he knew of no occasion when they had had sex—Genene offered an extravagantly creative explanation. She recalled a time during their earlier friendship when she had nursed him back to health from a severe fever. Genene informed Martin that he had engaged in sexual intercourse with her then, but that he didn't recall it because he was delirious.

Genene first offered this claim in a letter postmarked February 15, 1984, and presumably written as her defense attorneys were presenting their case in Georgetown. The back of the envelope carried the notation: SIT DOWN AND OPEN WITH EXTREME CAUTION. Inside was a snapshot of Crystal.

Dear Keith,

I must discuss an urgent matter with you prior to taking the stand. If I don't do it now, I'm afraid you will be hurt. I'm not sure there is anyway for you not to be hurt. Please believe me when I say there are no alterior motives for my telling you now. I just feel you have the right to know prior to the publications that will take place during the trial.

Do you remember the night of your illness when I was nursing you through. What I guess I mean is do you really remember that night.

From your reaction the day you met Crystal I felt you had some doubt about what happened.

Something did happen that night Keith. She being the end product.

"Please don't faint," Genene wrote. She said Crystal knew nothing about Keith being her father. And she declared that she didn't wish her revelation to cause him any problems. "We both know your lifestyle and it is one you have chosen. . . ." The letter was signed, "Love Genene."

In a brief note dated February 17—the day after her sentencing—Jones implored Martin to visit her in jail. She instructed him in a postscript to "Tell them your my brother—Keith Jones." Martin did not visit Genene. Instead, in an angry letter, he challenged her account of Crystal's conception. A few days later, Genene responded.

Dear Keith,

Please calm down. I thought I made it plain in that letter that the only reason I was even telling you was that at the time that letter was written I was going to take the stand. I was only concerned for your well being. I believe I also made it clear that I expected nothing from you. I only felt you had the right to know prior to any testimony.

As for initiating the sexual act? Wrong. During that night in your delirium I honestly thought it was me you wanted + that you realized you were making love to me, until you called me a mans name. It was then I realized you were delirious. And it was then, that I felt such great pain. . . .

Crystal is your daughter. . . .

. . . But please try to go on with your life as if this knowledge had never reached you. I am sorry now that I even told you. . . .

Genene said she had not taken the stand because it would have served no purpose. The jury was biased, she declared; it had reached its verdict during the first week of the trial. Jones also asked Martin to forgive her penmanship, explaining, "I have taken to the shakes for some reason. God bless my friend," she concluded.

In late February, Genene was transferred to the Bexar County Jail for a pretrial hearing in San Antonio. On February 28, she wrote Martin to denounce the report on her case on *20/20*, which had prompted him to ask questions. The complaint about the ABC broadcast—for which Genene had flown to New York to tape an interview—illustrated her love-hate relationship with the press. While blaming the media for her conviction and assailing their failure to embrace her perspective—that she was the innocent victim of a conspiracy—she continued to accept countless requests for interviews.

Dearest,

. . . 20/20 is no different than the local rags that are printed. . . . I think you know me well enough to know I could never hurt another human being. What + who I hurt was prestige + big money. And I'll tell you now, that if I had it to do over again, knowing what I know now, I would do it again. I would fight God for those kids, if I had to.

Before being transferred to San Antonio, Genene wrote,

she had met with Judge Carter, who "apologized for not making the paramount decisions that were needed. He feels I am innocent + assure[s] me the appeal will go through." But Genene said she knew she would have to spend many months in prison. She intended to use that time, she wrote, to better herself and grow. Her jailers were "extremely nice," but the prisoners were "filled with hatred." She was being kept in isolation in the hospital area "for my own safety."

Genene complained to the director of the Bexar County Jail, but it wasn't about her safety. Instead, she expressed unhappiness that her television, confiscated because of a malfunction, had not been replaced. "She probably liked things a lot better in Williamson County," the jail director told a local reporter. "She's probably not happy here, because we cannot give her the personal attention she was used to getting."

In a letter to Martin dated March 7, Genene declared that she now understood why she was in prison. She also elaborated on the fiction that Judge Carter considered her innocent and had offered an apology.

Sweet Man,
. . . Keith, this situation is so complex. I am just now understandiag, although vaguely, what's going on. Let me see if I can capsulize it.
I was responsible for the investigation at the hospital. . . . Myself and two other nurses. Because of that report the hospital district lost mega bucks. Administrators were fired, grants lost + all hell broke loose. After a press conference last year that I had the public became aware that the hospital was to blame + lawsuits were then filed. . . .
In looking back now, I feel that Kerrville was a set-up. The fact that Holland knew the situation at the hospital + her total 360° turn in testifying proved that to me. The district + the county have got to find some way out of that situation. They have to try + put the blame on someone else besides themselves. . . .

Genene added that she had met with Judge Carter and that he was helping with her appeal. In the meantime, she said, she remained in isolation—a place that was dark and smelly and frequented by rodents. "Write again soon my friend," she concluded. "I love your essence."

On March 26, Genene was rushed to the emergency room at Medical Center Hospital with a complaint of difficulty breathing. She was admitted for a short stay on the hospital's ninth floor, where she remained under guard; a few nurses from the pediatric ICU came to visit. The medical director of the jail said Genene suffered from chronic asthma attacks and a stomach ulcer. With her second trial postponed until October, Genene was transferred to her long-term home—the Texas Department of Corrections prison for women in Gatesville, called the Mountain View Unit.

In August, a TDC official, noting Genene's nursing background, wrote to the Bexar County Hospital District to ask if there was any problem with inmate Jones's being assigned to work in the prison hospital's dispensary. The letter leaked into the San Antonio press, forcing an embarrassed prison spokesman to offer a public assurance that they would find Genene a task that had nothing to do with medicine. In a September 14 letter to Martin, Genene sounded euphoric about the duties she had been assigned: making Cabbage-Patch-type dolls for sale to Texas law-enforcement officials. "They are adorable, + I love the work," she enthused. She reported that she had been transferred from a previous assignment in the kitchen "after quite a few threats with knifes and boiling water." The hostility toward her was on a "grand scale," wrote Genene. "I don't go anywhere without bodyguards."

Back at the Bexar County Jail one month later, Genene explained that she had waived a jury for her San Antonio trial because "there are not 12 people in the State of Texas who are not biased. . . . I certainly have no control over anything at this point, which is difficult for me . . ." Genene suggested to Martin that she had received a fresh round of abuse in the county jail. She added: "I'm not a physical fighter, I'm a lover as you well know, but it's coming down to push or shove + I have been pushed all I'm going to be. . . ."

Genene's reaction to her conviction came in a letter dated December 9. By then she had been returned to

Gatesville. Martin, who was developing growing doubts about the wisdom of the correspondence, was writing infrequently.

Opening her letter "Hello Stranger," Genene said she wished she could help Martin "deal with all of this." But that was impossible for the moment, Genene wrote suggestively, "because prisons tend to have eyes + ears that love money + because many will pay that money for any information they can give."

On December 15, 1984, Genene sent Martin a Christmas card, scribbling the notation: "Take care + remember my thoughts + prayers are with you always. Love Genene." On January 28, in response to Martin's continued denial that he had fathered Crystal, Genene wrote her final letter in their correspondence. There was no gushy term of endearment in this missive's salutation. Gone, too, was the tone of the benevolent born-again Christian, the "lover" who signed off with the assurance that her prayers were with him.

Keith,

Listen + listen well. There will be no, NO further discussions between you + I. . . .

I, of all people, should have known better than to be honest with you. You never knew what the word meant.

As for you "having a child"? You don't. You are *dead* as far as she is concerned and as far as I'm concerned.

You are right about one thing, Keith, you will burn in the pits of hell. In fact, you will occupy the deepest pit.

Take your friends + shove them where the sun don't shine.

As for my time. Obviously I'm doing it in here, much better than what you are doing yours in that prison you live in.

May your life reap everything + I mean everything you sow.

Genene

A few days later, Keith Martin received another letter from Gatesville. But this one was not from Genene Jones. It carried the name and handwriting of another inmate, who in vulgar and vivid prose claimed Genene as her sexual "territory" and warned Martin to steer clear. *"Stay in your own element (as small as it is) & leave my 'Queen' to me,"* the letter advised. It was signed: "Sincerely Yours, A Fuckers Nightmare."

Thirty-Four

I WENT TO visit Genene Jones on a dank, drizzly fall day, more than four years after we had first met in a trailer in San Angelo. A bleak agricultural community, Gatesville sat in the Central Texas plains, three hours northeast of San Antonio. Named for Fort Gates, a frontier army outpost that dated back to 1848, it was home to 7,100 people and three state prisons. The Mountain View Unit for women had been converted during the 1970s from an old home for delinquent boys. In a cluster of one-story buildings of cinder block and red brick, the prison had a capacity for 653 inmates, including some under maximum security. Ringing the property were two walls of chain-link fence, topped with ugly webs of razor wire.

The visiting room was in the most secure building on the property, occupied by the women on death row. A second fence surrounded the structure, and an armed guard in a tower kept watch over the grounds. After a quick pat-down, I was buzzed through an electronic gate to a fence-bordered path that led inside. The long, cement-floored chamber echoed like an empty locker room. A barrier—with Plexiglas at eye level, and wire mesh to the ceiling—ran the length of the room, separating inmates from visitors. There was no one on the other side. A single guard waiting at the end of the room informed me that Genene would be brought in shortly. I peered out a window, into a small, muddy courtyard. It was filled with

fat cantaloupes, an incongruous sight. "The girls on death
row grow them," the guard explained.

Chattering small talk to her escort, Genene arrived. It
was apparent instantly that she was different. She looked
lean and hard, having lost forty pounds since our last
face-to-face meeting. She wore white prison pajamas with
the word JONES and her inmate number—380650—on a
little orange tag on her chest. Blue makeup colored her
eyelids. Her speech, once cocky and insistent, had slowed
and softened into a Southern ghetto drawl. Her words
had softened too.

Absent were the four-letter epithets that once salted
her conversation. Genene sounded placid and relaxed,
even gentle. She had greeted me a bit warily, but warmed
quickly through the day. I had been told that she was
furious about the lengthy magazine article I had written
about her case. By the time I departed the prison, however, she acted as though I were a friend. "I'm less
angry," she explained, when I returned for a second visit.
"I had a lot of hatred for a lot of people. The hatred
came out of confusion because of the obvious question:
'Why? Why is this all centered around me?' But you have
to quit asking that after a while. You have to let that go,
just take a day at a time. If you hang on to hatred, it
destroys you."

It was religion that had made the difference. "I've
been given the time to sit down and understand the Lord.
I couldn't have made it without His peace and strength."
Genene had rediscovered the Lord but not yet determined His denomination. I asked about the Star of David
she wore on a chain around her neck; it had replaced the
cross she wore in Georgetown. "I'm leaning toward the
Jewish religion," she explained.

Within the prison's chain-link boundaries, most of the
inmates enjoyed a modicum of freedom. Rather than
individual cells, the women lived in communal dormito-
ries, forty-six prisoners to a room. They worked or attended classes during the day, had access to recreational
facilities for four hours, and until at least 10:30 every
night could come and go freely from a central dayroom
equipped with a television. Genene, however, was living

in voluntary isolation. Serious attacks upon inmates in the Mountain View Unit were virtually unknown. And despite her dramatic written remarks to Keith Martin, Genene acknowledged to me that no one in prison had raised a hand against her. Nonetheless, she had spent the last three months in solitary confinement—emerging only for showers and an hour of daily recreation—after telling the warden it was necessary to ensure her safety. Genene had spent much time before that on light-duty "medical assignment" for an assortment of ailments. Her health complaints permitted her to pull the relatively easy job of making the dolls about which she had written to Martin; in the prison system, they were called "Parole Pals." Even as we talked, Genene coughed frequently. She said she was suffering from the flu.

I asked the obvious question she had raised: If you are innocent, *why* you?

Genene shook her head. "I've never answered that. I figure sooner or later the question will answer itself." She was a good American, Genene declared. She always believed in the American way, in Truth and the System. Until the jury verdict in Georgetown. Now, she explained, she knew "the power of big money."

"The story of my conviction is about big money. When the state has unlimited funds to do anything they want to do and get anyone they desire—to fly to Sweden, to put on the drama of the century—and the *defendant,* who is indigent, has nothing, absolutely nothing but the truth to throw up there, and yet it's such a huge performance and staged so dramatically, the truth is just *buried.*"

Did she still believe she bore no personal responsibility for her fate—no blame for what had happened?

Genene's jaw set and her voice cooled. I was seeing a flash of the nurse of old. "That's not a belief," she stated. "That's a definite *fact.* I know I am responsible in a way for bringing it to the public viewpoint, but as far as being responsible for any death—no, I am not."

I was searching for a stray remark, a contemplative pause, an instant of hesitation—anything—to suggest that, five years after the events, a shred of doubt, even remorse, had infected her conviction. Did she think she could be the victim of some disease of the mind, a psychosis that led her to harm children without her conscious knowledge?

"No, I don't," she replied immediately. "Not at all. I've had a lot of time to sit and think. I don't have any doubts in my innocence. . . .

"I know what the facts are and what the truth is," said Genene. "Whether another human being alive knows is not important to me. That may sound cold, but I'm the one doing this time. I can look myself in the mirror. I believe in the Lord; I can look Him in the eye too. That's all that's important." What an odd speech, I thought, from a woman who had gone to such extremes to proclaim her innocence to the world.

We talked for hours during my two trips to Gatesville—about Genene's family and childhood, about her marriage and early career, and about the events that had put her behind bars. She informed me that except for normal teenage rebellion, she had gotten along splendidly with her mother. She said she had never felt any jealousy toward her older sister, Lisa. And she told me she had breezed cheerfully through Marshall High School, in a quiet and content adolescence. "I have nothing but beautiful memories of my childhood," she insisted.

We moved on. Genene told me she rarely attended parties in high school and was never present at a single one where alcohol was consumed. She had not pressured her mother for permission to wed Jim DeLany just days after her father's death. She said infidelity was not an issue in their marriage. It was untrue that she had boasted of shooting her brother-in-law in the groin. Keith Martin was not gay; he *was* the father of her child, and Genene had never told Kathy Holland anything to the contrary.

Although I had seen a copy, Genene insisted that she had never written a note to Pat Belko warning that she wouldn't leave Medical Center Hospital "without a bang." She denied ever owning a novel about a cult of murderous nurses called *The Sisterhood*, even though Dr. Marisol Montes had found a copy in the ICU with Genene's name inside the cover. Genene acknowledged that after her arrest, she had consented to an examination by San

Antonio psychiatrist Franklin Redmond. But she claimed
she had done so at the request of the prosecution—not
her own attorneys. She told me she had never sent a
Christmas card to William Thornton with the message:
"You and I know the truth." Although it was reported in
the press and her lawyers recalled is vividly, Genene
denied claiming to anyone that she was pregnant while in
jail. And she insisted that there had been no estrange-
ment with her mother; Gladys Jones, said Genene, had
visited her regularly in the Williamson County Jail.

By the end of our conversations, Genene had completed an account of her life that was astonishingly different from what I had gathered from dozens of those who
had known her. It clashed with reality not merely on the
basic issue of her guilt—of which I now felt certain—but
on a thousand details, small and unimportant, except as
they loomed in Genene's image of herself. Genene was
contradicting not only the sure recollections of others and
a voluminous written record, but facts she had told me
herself four years earlier. It was a measure of her sickness. She was rewriting the story of her life as if it were a
work of fiction.

After my final visit with Genene, I returned to San
Antonio and spoke to her sister. Lisa had recently had
her own conversation with Genene. The talk had filled
her with a similar sense of wonder. Genene had spoken
idyllically about their family, about the perfect relationship she had enjoyed with Lisa and Gladys. Genene
talked about how she had enlisted her mother to help
plot her legal defense, how they had battled valiantly
together to see that justice won out. "She had it like they
worked hand in hand," said Lisa. "This was not so. Both
Mother and I, we would read the paper to find out what
was going on. I don't know why she was telling me these
things. She was painting a picture of total harmony. It
wasn't that way."

Genene was reinventing their family history, as if speaking to someone who did not know better. "I don't know
what has happened in her mind," said Lisa. "She went
into it so extensively. She's changed everything all around."
Lisa had become accustomed to hearing Genene tell tall

tales. Often they involved her career, about which Lisa knew nothing. But this was clearly different. Said Genene Jones's sister: "She's trying to make it a dream world."

In 1951, a doctor in London published a brief article in *The Lancet,* England's most prestigious medical journal, about a phenomenon he called "Munchausen's Syndrome." He named the condition for an eighteenth-century German baron named Karl Friedrich Hieronymus von Munchausen, who captivated dinner guests with fanciful tales of his heroic deeds. "Like the famous Baron von Munchausen," wrote Dr. Richard Asher, "the persons affected have always traveled widely; and their stories, like those attributed to him, are both dramatic and untruthful."

Asher explained: "The patient showing the syndrome is admitted to hospital with apparent acute illness supported by a plausible and dramatic history. Usually his story is largely made up of falsehoods; he is found to have attended, and deceived, an astounding number of other hospitals; and he nearly always discharges himself against advice, after quarreling violently with both doctors and nurses.

" . . . Usually the patient seems seriously ill and is admitted unless someone who has seen him before is there to expose his past." Such patients demonstrate "an immediate history which is always acute and harrowing yet not entirely convincing—overwhelmingly severe abdominal pain of uncertain type, cataclysmic blood-loss unsupported by corresponding pallor, dramatic loss of consciousness and so forth."

Asher identified three characteristic features: "the acute abdominal type . . . Some of these patients have been operated on so often that the development of genuine intestinal obstruction from adhesions may confuse the picture"; the "hemorrhagic type, who specialise in bleeding from lungs or stomach, or other blood-loss"; and "the neurological type, presenting with paroxysmal headache, loss of consciousness, or peculiar fits.

"The most remarkable feature of the syndrome is the

apparent senselessness of it. Unlike the malingerer, who may gain a definite end, these patients often seem to gain nothing except the discomfiture of unnecessary investigations or operations. Their initial tolerance to the more brutish hospital measures is remarkable yet they commonly discharge themselves after a few days with operation wounds scarcely healed, or intravenous drips still running.

"Another feature is their intense desire to deceive everybody as much as possible. Many of their falsehoods seem to have little point. They lie for the sake of lying. They give false addresses, false names, and false occupations merely from a love of falsehood. Their effrontery is sometimes formidable, and they may appear many times at the same hospital, hoping to meet a new doctor upon whom to practise their deception."

Among the possible motives, Asher cited:

"A desire to be the centre of interest and attention. They may be suffering in fact from the Walter Mitty syndrome, but instead of playing the dramatic part of the surgeon, they submit to the equally dramatic role of the patient.

"A grudge against doctors and hospitals, which is satisfied by frustrating or deceiving them."

In addition, Asher concluded, "there probably exists some strange twist of personality."

Twenty-six years later, another British physician, Dr. Roy Meadow, published an article in *The Lancet* on a variation of the phenomenon, which he labeled "Munchausen Syndrome by Proxy." Meadow described mothers who put their children through needless medical procedures, often by falsely describing their symptoms or even by tampering with urine samples to provide false results. In two cases Meadow described, the mothers "had a history of falsifying their own medical records and treatment. Both had at times been labeled as hysterical personalities who also tended to be depressed." Unlike parents who felt uncomfortable in a hospital with their child, these mothers "flourished there as if they belonged, and thrived on the attention that staff gave them."

In 1982, Dr. Meadow described seventeen more cases

of Munchausen by Proxy. These cases included mothers who deliberately caused their children to bleed or suffer seizures, often with critical results. The mothers invariably seemed to enjoy lingering in the hospital with their sick children and formed close relationships with junior doctors and other parents. Their methods, wrote Meadow, "combined cunning, dexterity, and, quite often, medical knowledge." All the women he had studied were medically sophisticated, and "often the mothers had had previous nursing training."

A 1985 article by Dr. Meadow warned physicians of the following signs of Munchausen by Proxy:

(1) Illness which is unexplained, prolonged, and so extraordinary that it prompts experienced colleagues to remark that they "have never seen anything like it before."

(2) Symptoms and signs that are inappropriate or incongruous, or are present only when the mother is present.

(3) Treatments which are ineffective or poorly tolerated.

(4) Children who are alleged to be allergic to a great variety of foods and drugs.

(5) Mothers who are not as worried by the child's illness as the nurses and doctors, mothers who are constantly with their ill child in hospital (not even leaving the ward for brief outings), and those who are happily at ease on the children's ward and form unusually close relationships with the staff.

(6) Families in which sudden unexplained infant deaths have occurred, and families containing many members alleged to have different serious medical disorders.

Another 1985 journal article, published by British doctors A. R. Nichol and M. Eccles in *Archives of Disease in Childhood,* discussed the case of a mother who had been diagnosed as an example of Munchausen Syndrome by Proxy. Asked why she had fabricated her child's illness, the woman summed up her reasons: "I liked the sympathy, I needed my daughter to be ill so that I was important. I felt I was *somebody* in the ward." The woman added that she enjoyed spending time with the doctors who treated her children, and took pleasure in having outwitted them for so long.

In recent years, experts have applied the diagnosis of Munchausen Syndrome by Proxy to individuals who fabricate and induce medical problems in children under their care. Genene Jones fits the profile with extraordinary precision. Her sickness is not the result of a sudden psychotic break. It is the product of an entire lifetime—of impulses planted in an unhappy youth, nurtured in a troubled early adulthood, and tragically unleashed in the world of medicine.

Since childhood, Genene had always regarded herself as neglected, by family and peers alike. As an unattractive teenager, she developed the habit of telling lies to win attention. Instead of disappearing in adulthood, Genene's "love of falsehood" ripened like a malignant tumor. With growing skill, she used lies to abet her pathologic need for attention—an impulse that became increasingly difficult to satisfy.

Genene seized on the device of exaggerating medical problems even before she entered medicine. In her hands, Keith Martin's routine allergies became cause for a forecast of calamity; her son became the potential victim of a rare disease that made children go blind. But it was her employment as a nurse that provided the deadly combination of impulse and opportunity.

Genene was low on the totem pole, only an LVN. But in medicine, she quickly learned, a single event made *everyone* pay attention: the calling of a code. Genene came to know the glory of receiving credit for helping save a child's life. She came to relish the excitement of a medical emergency. Those who saw Genene following codes found her sweaty and excited, in an almost sexual euphoria. "You tune people out," she had told me. "It's an incredible experience. Oh, shit, it's frightening."

At first, Genene merely insisted on being in the midst of codes that happened on their own—whether or not her patient was involved. An ICU nurse had described

Genene's determination to be in the center of the action: "If there was a crash in the unit, she'd climb over everyone to get there." Then Genene manipulated Pat Belko and the young RNs on her shift to assign her the patients most likely to experience emergencies. At shift changes, Genene dramatically predicted that her patients would go sour.

After a lifetime of failure, in the pediatric ICU Genene belonged. Other nurses called her out to the ward to start IVs. The rookie RNs sought her help. Supervisors gave her praise. Genene made the unit her entire life; it seemed she hated to leave. Neglecting her own children, she worked countless overtime shifts, arriving early and leaving late. On one occasion, she was reprimanded for refusing to leave a child's bedside at the end of a double shift. On another, she reappeared in the pediatric ICU drunk at 5 A.M. and began to tinker with a patient's medical equipment. Only *she* could give the children proper care; they could not live without her. By 1981, work had become the foundation of Genene's sense of worth—the single thing that fulfilled her need to be important.

But then residents began to ignore her; Genene was the nurse who cried wolf. And the new RNs started to assert themselves; they stopped taking orders from an LVN. So Genene began to take steps to *force* everyone to pay attention. Heparin and syringes disappeared from the pediatric ICU crash cart. She began to inject children with the blood-thinner and an assortment of other powerful drugs. Patients started to experience unexpected emergencies, incongruous problems that occurred only when she was present. Genene had launched the epidemic.

Had Genene stopped after leaving the pediatric ICU, she might never have been caught. Medical Center Hospital wasn't going to tell anyone; "judicious silence" might have worked. But Genene *couldn't*—stop—couldn't go back to being just an LVN in just another small-town clinic. A second epidemic hit Kerrville; this time, it was succinylcholine.

Like the women who harmed their own children, Genene appeared too devoted to her charges to harm them. When a baby died, her grief—the wailing, the singing, the cradling of the corpse—exceeded that of any mother. So devoted was Genene that she seemed to place herself above the parents. Of Chris Hogeda, Genene had said: "He was *my* baby." And she had condemned Petti McClellan's testimony as "an insult to Chelsea's memory," as though Genene were better suited to judge.

Genene's personal medical history fit the Munchausen pattern as well: the repeated hospitalizations and emergency room visits, the dramatic attacks of abdominal pain and breathing problems, the vague complaints of muscle weakness—"always acute and harrowing yet not entirely convincing." Genene subjected herself to "the more brutish hospital measures," but doctors usually could determine no cause of her problem. Several had labeled her a hysterical personality.

The quest for attention did not diminish after people began to wonder whether Genene was harming children. Instead of shrinking from suspicions—first at Medical Center Hospital, then in Kerrville, finally from criminal investigators and the press—Genene repeatedly tempted fate, daring her accusers to act, relishing the thrill of center stage. In the midst of the county hospital's internal inquiries, she approached doctors and asked: "Do you think I'm killing babies?" At the meeting announcing the removal of the LVNs, she stood up and declared: "It's *me* you're after." In Kerrville, after Kathy Holland had confronted her with the bottle of succinylcholine, Genene orchestrated a dramatic suicide attempt, with a drug dose she knew would do no harm—if indeed she had swallowed any at all. There was the matter of her suicide note, with its suggestive reference to "seven people, whose life I have altered." After Holland dismissed the nurse, Genene's lawyer had advised her to leave the state; Genene instead relocated to San Angelo, just three hours away. And when she made bond after her arrest, Genene moved *back* to Kerrville. Finally, there was her remark to Kathy Engelke, a stranger in the Bexar County Jail, who for some reason hadn't heard: "I'm Genene Jones, the nurse that killed the babies."

One child-abuse expert familiar with the case has likened Genene's behavior to that of a volunteer fireman who sets a blaze, then appears first on the scene in hope of becoming a hero by putting it out. In discussing the desire for a pediatric ICU at Sid Peterson Hospital, Ron Sutton suggested a motive that was but a manifestation of the syndrome. Still another theory is that Genene was playing, manipulating the health of children to satisfy a power complex, without intending to kill any of them.

In the case of this nurse who murdered babies, subtleties of motive are beside the point. Genene Jones's behavior defines her clearly as a psychopath. For her, the rules of society did not apply. For her, the lines between truth and fiction, between good and evil, between right and wrong, did not matter.

How many children did she kill? That is impossible to say with certainty. But a coauthor of Dr. Istre's CDC study estimates that as many as fifteen children may have been murdered in the pediatric ICU at Medical Center Hospital. Adding the single death with which she was charged, that of Chelsea Ann McClellan, makes sixteen dead children, enough to make Genene Jones quite important indeed—as one of the most prodigious serial murderers in the history of American crime.

And what of Kathy Holland? The pediatrician acknowledges that she was aware of the suspicions that surrounded Genene Jones at Medical Center Hospital, even that she received a direct—if vague—warning from Dr. Robotham. This makes it difficult to accept Holland's claim that she suspected nothing—despite eight crises in her office, including at least one incident where Genene treated a patient on her own—until the discovery of the tainted bottle of succinylcholine. At the other extreme, it is also implausible that Holland participated in a conspiracy, a dark collaboration to build her practice by inducing arrests.

In the wide swath between these possibilities, I believe, lies the truth. Kathy Holland is a woman whose stubbornness shrouds deep insecurities. Having hired the nurse for her practice, despite the advice of others, she was determined to hold her ground. As she had with previous superiors—notably Pat Belko—Genene curried Holland's favor, then used her trust to manipulate the doctor into covering for her misdeeds. In Genene, Holland saw a woman like herself—victimized by men, persecuted unjustly, battered by life, struggling to make a go of things. Genene made Kathy Holland feel important. Theirs was never the classic relationship of superior and subordinate. The nature of their association was cast during Holland's residency, when Kathy was the nervous intern, Genene the confident, experienced nurse who took charge. It was residency, too, that bred Holland's medical philosophy. She had embraced Jim Robotham's attitude: In every subtle sign, there was a lurking medical calamity. With her nurse providing distorted clinical reports, Holland lacked the perspective to recognize that the children arresting in her office were hardly ill. As the emergencies continued, she shut her eyes to what was going on.

When all the trials were over, Kathy Holland decided to remain in Kerrville, despite a residue of local hostility that showed no signs of abating. Holland sold the house on Nixon Lane and began seeing patients in a modest yellow cottage about a mile from downtown Kerrville. She supplemented her income by moonlighting at San Antonio hospitals. But she could not perform her trade at the much smaller local hospital that was so critical to the rebuilding of her crippled practice. Although Ron Sutton made a point of declaring publicly that Holland had done nothing wrong, the Kerrville medical community refused to restore her privileges at Sid Peterson. Unwilling to walk away from the tragedy that had crippled her career and altered her life, stubbornly unwilling—yet again—to give in, Kathy Holland retained an attorney and filed suit against the hospital.

In this tragedy of few heroes, many share blame with Genene Jones. Among them is Kathy Holland, who has never acknowledged that her failure transcended poor judgment and naïveté. But responsibility also rests with the doctors and administrators in San Antonio who had known so much about the troubled nurse before the clinic in Kerrville even opened. They were the ones who had evidence she was harming children. They were the ones who tolerated her blackmail. They were the ones who refused to fire her for fear of litigation and scandal. They were the ones who sent her out into the world without a word of warning—just a warm letter of recommendation. Ultimately, those at Medical Center Hospital and the UT medical school must share much of the blame for what happened to Chelsea McClellan—and to the untold number of other children whom Genene hurt and whom Genene killed. Those people should have known better. Unlike Genene Ann Jones, they lacked the excuse of madness.

Epilogue

Genene Jones appealed her two convictions without success. Although her prison sentences totaled one hundred and fifty-nine years, under Texas law she will be eligible for parole when she has received credit for twenty. With good time, Jones could be considered for release as early as March 28, 1990—after less than seven years of incarceration. She would be thirty-nine years old.

Gladys Jones died on August 6, 1985, at the age of seventy-four. She was buried on August 9 in the family plot at the Lockhill Cemetery in San Antonio, beside her husband and her two sons. Three weeks later, Genene wrote Gladys's attorney from prison that "mother's death has been quite a shock, and I haven't really accepted it." Genene went on to inquire about her inheritance. There was not to be any; Gladys Jones left her entire estate, valued at $113,471.73, to her daughter Lisa, excluding Genene even from mention in her will.

Genene's daughter, Crystal, lived with her grandmother until Gladys died. Lisa assumed legal conservatorship and arranged for Crystal, then eight, to live with a great-aunt. Genene's son, Edward, remained in the custody of the state, where he could receive psychiatric counseling in a group home for children. Lisa occasionally takes the two children to visit their mother in prison.

A year after winning the conviction of Genene Jones in Georgetown, Ron Sutton made national headlines again—as prosecutor of the "slave-ranch" case, in which a family of Kerrville ranchers imprisoned drifters and brutally tortured one of them to death with an electric cattle prod. In 1988, influenced by his own conservative views and Texas's emergence as a two-party state, Sutton switched parties and easily won reelection as a Republican. He still harbors dreams of running for Texas attorney general.

Sam Millsap rejected advice that he switch political parties, and his bid for reelection in 1986 ended with defeat in the Democratic primary. Resuming the practice of corporate law, he became a partner in a San Antonio firm.

Nick Rothe, burned out from years as a criminal-trial lawyer, decided in 1988 to join the local firm of Stolhandske & Stolhandske, which had filed most of the lawsuits against Medical Center Hospital. Rothe planned to develop a specialty in medical-malpractice claims.

Art Brogley was fired from the DA's office in January 1987 in a purge by Sam Millsap's successor. In January 1988, he found work as a client-abuse investigator at the San Antonio State School for the mentally retarded.

After Genene Jones was convicted, the Texas Board of Vocational Nurse Examiners scheduled a disciplinary hearing to consider the status of her nursing license. In a letter, Genene responded: "If you have, as you say, investigated my case, you are already aware of my innocense + so should any learned *nurse* of the board. As evidence showed there was no crime committed. I should not be punished because of a 'media' conviction.' " On January 21, 1986, the panel concluded that Jones represented "an imminent peril" to the public health and voted to suspend her license "until such time as she appears before the board."

The Texas Board of Medical Examiners, after a lengthy investigation, decided to take no action against Kathy Holland.

The complaints that Sam Millsap promised against B. H. Corum, Marvin Dunn, Pat Belko, Judy Harris, and Virginia Mousseau also produced no sanctions.

After leaving Medical Center Hospital in 1984, B. H.

Corum started his own medical-consulting company in San Antonio. He specialized in recruiting doctors for rural communities, helping physicians enter private practice, and offering management advice to hospitals. Less than four months after Corum's resignation, a San Antonio newspaper reporter found him prospering. The resulting story was headlined: "RESIGNATION FROM BCHD PAYS OFF FOR CORUM."

Corum continued to decline requests for interviews about the tragic events at Medical Center Hospital. He did offer his perspective, however, on July 31, 1986, during a sworn deposition taken for the McClellans' civil suit. During almost a full day of questioning, Corum was asked when he first became aware, "either by way of statistical basis, a specific event, or a specific report," that Genene Jones had caused the injury or death of any infant in the pediatric ICU. Corum responded: "Sir, I don't think I have ever received any information that says that Genene Jones caused the death of any patients in the pediatric intensive care unit." Corum said he knew only that Genene Jones was present when a number of deaths occurred.

After resigning her position at Medical Center Hospital, Virginia Mousseau returned to Minneapolis and became a nursing administrator for Group Health, Inc., a 240,000-member health maintenance organization. In September 1988, she resigned her position with the HMO.

Judy Harris took a position as an instructor at the UT nursing school in San Antonio.

Pat Belko left nursing, obtained a real estate license, and took a job selling homes in San Antonio. In October 1988, with the real estate market in a slump, Belko quit and began devoting full time to her home and family. She is bitter about her treatment by Medical Center Hospital—treatment that she says destroyed her professional reputation. She believes that she was never given enough information to fire Genene Jones. "I think I gave them an awful lot of my life," Belko remarked during a January 1989 interview. "And they told me I didn't *do* enough. . . . Sometimes I feel like I may as well have been incarcerated myself." As for those who worked for her who say they were certain that Genene was killing children: "It makes me so mad that some of these people are built into such heroes . . .if they knew she was doing something, why didn't *they* call the police?"

Belko now accepts the theory that Genene Jones, crushed over her ouster from the pediatric ICU at Medical Center Hospital, deliberately harmed patients in Kerrville to foster a need for a pediatric ICU there. But she remains "unconvinced" that Jones intentionally harmed a single child at Medical Center Hospital.

John Guest remains executive director of the Bexar County Hospital District, where he is presiding over a period of unprecedented prosperity. Under Guest's direction, Medical Center Hospital has attracted more private patients and won increased support from taxpayers. In 1988, Guest initiated a five-year, $45 million hospital expansion program, to be financed entirely with annual budget surpluses.

Guest sat for a lengthy interview in the fall of 1988, after the litigation against Medical Center Hospital was resolved. "I now believe that Genene Jones did harm to kids in our hospital," he said. "That was never a predominant possibility [in our minds] at the time all this stuff was going on. . . . All of us are guilty of having blinded ourselves to the most evil possibility of all: that Jones was a murderer. Given what I know now, we should have all behaved very differently. . . ." Guest saw lessons for others in his institution's experience. "I don't want healthcare people to lose sight of the fact that there are evil people in the world. Our inability to recognize that, I think, is in part responsible for all of this. I would never have been able to believe that a caregiver could do something like this. It's not unthinkable to me anymore."

John Guest's improvement program at Medical Center Hospital began with a $750,000 facelift on the pediatric floor. The pediatric ICU, renamed the Pediatric Special Care Unit, was expanded to sixteen beds, stocked with new equipment, and redecorated in bright, cheerful colors. Mortality in the redesigned unit is low; by all accounts, it is running well. The nursing staff in the ICU once again includes LVNs.

Marvin Dunn worked for California-based American Medical International, the nation's third largest hospital chain, for about three years before becoming a private consultant. He now offers advice to academic medical centers. He lives in the Los Angeles area.

James Robotham remains associate professor of anesthesiology at Johns Hopkins medical school in Baltimore.

Robert Franks continues to serve as professor of pediatrics at the UT medical school in San Antonio.

Kent Trinkle had part of a lung removed after developing cancer, and became an active anti-smoking spokesman. He subsequently performed San Antonio's first heart transplant.

Jim Brookshire and Burt Carnes both continue in private practice in Williamson County.

Laura Little handled the unsuccessful criminal appeals for both Genene Jones and Henry Lee Lucas. She is now enrolled in a Ph.D program in clinical psychology at the Universisy of New Mexico.

Kathy Holland continues to practice pediatrics in Kerrville while pursuing her lawsuit against Sid Peterson Hospital. She helps pay her bills by moonlighting at hospitals in San Antonio. In 1985, Holland was married for a third time, again to a man much her senior, a retired Kerrville radiologist.

During the seven months before Genene's trial in Georgetown, Debbie Sultenfuss worked at a nursing home in the remote South Texas city of Eagle Pass. She abruptly left the position in January 1984. Sultenfuss now holds another job and lives with her parents in Natalia, Texas, about thirty miles south of San Antonio. A January 1989 phone inquiry to speak with her about Genene Jones brought a terse response from one of her parents: "I'm sorry; the subject of that is closed."

Petti McClellan enrolled in nursing school in August 1984 and became an LVN. After working at the Kerrville

VA Hospital for three years, she went to work with her mother, doing consulting work for doctors. Reid remains employed at the Central Texas Electric Co-Op, where he is now a troubleshooter.

The McClellans named the UT medical school and Medical Center Hospital as additional defendants in their $7 million lawsuit against Genene Jones and Kathy Holland. After extensive pretrial discovery and deposition-taking, the suit was settled out of court for an undisclosed amount in early 1988. With the help of money from the settlement, Petti and Reid built themselves a new home closer to Kerrville. In 1988, with Nick Rothe representing them, the McClellans adopted a baby girl. They named her Kiley Nicole.

Petti McClellan continues to visit the Garden of Memories Cemetery in Kerrville. She always goes on June 16 and September 17, the dates of Chelsea's birth and Chelsea's death. During each visit, Petti has discovered a bouquet of cut flowers on her daughter's grave. She has asked friends and relatives whether they left the flowers; they have told her they did not. The bouquets bring back chilling memories of the time, just days after her daughter's death, when Petti discovered Genene Jones in this place, wailing and moaning and crying out Chelsea's name. Before stalking off, Genene had left behind a bouquet. Now, when she visits her daughter's grave, Petti snatches up the blooms she finds and tosses them away.